#2

GEOFFREY W. BROMILEY

CHURCH, WORD, AND SPIRIT

Historical and Theological Essays in Honor of
GEOFFREY W. BROMILEY

Edited by James E. Bradley and Richard A. Muller

WILLIAM B. EERDMANS PUBLISHING COMPANY
GRAND RAPIDS, MICHIGAN

Copyright © 1987 by Wm. B. Eerdmans Publishing Co.
255 Jefferson Ave. S.E., Grand Rapids, Mich. 49503

Library of Congress Cataloging-in-Publication Data

Church, word, and spirit.
Bibliography: p. 299.
1. Theology. 2. Church history. 3. Bromiley, Geoffrey William.
I. Bromiley, Geoffrey William. II. Bradley, James E. III. Muller, Richard A.
(Richard Alfred), 1948–
BR50.C564 1987   230′.09   87-24447

ISBN 0-8028-3643-7

Contents

III. ESSAYS ON MODERN CHURCH HISTORY AND THEOLOGY

Preface

The essays in this volume are presented to honor Geoffrey W. Bromiley upon his retirement from Fuller Theological Seminary. In his varied roles as seminary professor, mentor, scholar, and author, Geoffrey Bromiley has made an unparalleled contribution to the modern renaissance of evangelical scholarship. His numerous publications are aptly celebrated by the contributors to this book, but in these introductory comments we wish to draw attention to the guiding theological principles that have characterized all of his labors on behalf of the seminary and the church. Bromiley's vocation is grounded in his conviction that the discipline of study is at its very heart a form of the ministry of Christ. Some gifted teachers do instill in their students a love of learning for its own sake (though it happens too rarely), but Geoffrey Bromiley did this and more. He brought to Fuller Seminary, and to the larger evangelical world, a vision of the urgent need for rigorous, uncompromising, dedicated scholarship as ministry. He constantly reminded us, as his students and colleagues, that scholarly activity can never properly be a mere adjunct to Christian ministry and that it would be an even greater mistake to think that we have a choice between ministry and scholarship.

In the lecture hall and in chapel talks that are still vivid in the memory of those of us who heard them, Bromiley taught that since scholarship is part of the ministry of Christ, it does not serve itself. Scholarship for the Christian, if it is truly evangelical, must point not to itself but to the word of God and to Christ. This scholarship is in a sense transparent. It will, in the case of biblical studies, for example, seek only to clarify, expound, and apply the word of God. Christian scholarship thus requires humility and self-sacrifice—qualities that have characterized Bromiley's service in a preeminent degree. In this light he maintains that a seminary is properly a center of this kind of scholarship, and that it therefore has a distinctive calling that will always distinguish it from any other institution, whether Christian or secular. It is called to serve the church by preparing men and women for Christian ministry through disciplined study. This perspective gave stability to Fuller Seminary in an era of rapid and unsettling change, and it continues to give direction to the school to this day.

Bromiley called several generations of younger scholars not to concentrate on popular and ephemeral publications but rather to give themselves to the time-consuming and demanding task of serious research and long-term projects that hold the promise of making a lasting contribution to the church. Although he always insisted that scholarly endeavors ought to have a significant influence on the practical life and mission of the church, and although his own ministry continues to testify to the many ways in which the fruit of serious study does influence the church, he often reiterates that we must not be preoccupied with relevance and immediate results.

These principles are evident in the character of Bromiley's published work. The extensive bibliography that concludes this volume surveys a vast array of articles, books, and translations, spanning a period of nearly fifty years. Bromiley's name is associated, above all, with the translations of Gerhard Kittel and Karl Barth. He translated Kittel's massive dictionary in its entirety, with a now-legendary accuracy, into flawless English. He rendered the same service for the greater part of Barth's *Church Dogmatics*—first sharing the labor with a team of colleagues and then, finally, assuming the task himself with the fourth volume. Bromiley has also translated Barth's *Ethics* and his lectures on Schleiermacher, together with various lesser essays, and he promises several more translations of Barth's major works from the comprehensive German edition now in progress. To this impressive effort must be added the translations of Thielicke's *Evangelical Faith* and several volumes by Jacques Ellul. It is not widely known, since his name does not appear in the books, that he also supplied the basic translation of the first two volumes of Thielicke's *Theological Ethics*.

Beyond these more renowned efforts, Geoffrey Bromiley is recognized for his work as a historian, primarily of the Reformation era. His two-volume biographical and theological study of Cranmer (1956) and his volumes *Baptism and the Anglican Reformers* (1953), *Sacramental Teaching and Practice in the Reformation Churches* (1957), and *John Jewell, 1522-1572: The Apologist of the Church of England* (1960) form the core of an extended analysis of sixteenth-century Protestant thought. His analysis focuses on the church and the sacraments but also touches on the doctrines of justification and Scripture and on the history and contents of the Thirty-nine Articles and the Prayer Book of the Church of England. These latter interests appear as the subjects of numerous articles, scholarly and popular, noted in the bibliography at the end of this volume. To this list we must add Bromiley's translations of Zwingli and Bullinger (1953) and his several articles on Luther, Calvin, and Zwingli. Readers of the bibliography will also note the series of articles related to Bromiley's dissertation research into late eighteenth- and early nineteenth-century German philosophical and religious thought.

Geoffrey Bromiley's written labors bear witness to a strong commitment to the church and to theology. Here, the learning amassed both in the work of historical research and in the work of translation is brought to bear on a practical and pastoral front. Bromiley has written book-length essays entitled *Biblical Criticism* (1948), *Reasonable Service: A Study in Christian Conduct* (1948), *The Baptism of Infants* (1955), *The Unity and Disunity of the Church* (1958), *Christian Ministry* (1960), *Children of Promise: The Case for Baptizing Infants* (1979), and *God and Marriage* (1980). These essays are supplemented by numerous articles—some appearing in *Christianity Today*, others in *Baker's Dictionary of Theology* (1960; 1984) and still others in the *International Standard Bible Encyclopedia* (1979-).

Yet another series of related articles that can be discerned in the bibliography discusses and analyzes, often with some evangelical and Reformed critique, the theology of Karl Barth. This labor is capped by Bromiley's *Introduction to the Theology of Karl Barth* (1979). Taken as a whole, the books, translations, and articles of the Bromiley bibliography bear witness to his consistent and unified commitment to scholarship, to teaching, to the church, and to the Christian faith. Throughout a career of distinguished scholarship, and through a distinctively Christian approach to his vocation, Geoffrey Bromiley has shown himself a servant of the church and of the word through the power of the Spirit. He has thereby given to us a rich and exceedingly valuable heritage of concerned thought on the meaning of true Christian scholarship.

This volume includes essays by three groups of scholars: Bromiley's students, scholars in Europe who have enjoyed the advantage of his linguistic skills, and friends and colleagues who have labored with him, some in the work of editing and translating and others in the broader calling of Christian scholarship. When we first undertook the process of requesting essays in honor of Bromiley, the responses to our letters of inquiry were uniformly enthusiastic, a fact that has made our task as editors unusually easy and enjoyable. The names of the contributors reveal something of the high esteem in which Bromiley is held by a wide array of distinguished Christian scholars. In keeping with his interests and concerns, we have settled upon the title *Church, Word, and Spirit,* and the essays are arranged in a chronological sequence and divided into three parts representing a traditional periodization of church history.

We wish to thank David A. Hubbard, president of Fuller Seminary, and Robert P. Meye, dean of the faculty there, for the support they gave this project from its inception. We are also grateful for the industry of Julia Brann Wilmot in compiling the bibliography of Bromiley's writings. Sandy Underwood Bennett, David Sielaff, and Janet Gathright did an expert job of typing and editing the manuscripts. It may be slightly disappointing to Bromiley to find the essays by Eberhard Busch and Jacques Ellul already translated into English, but the value of the volume is clearly enhanced for those who do not read German and French. We are indebted to Gary Sattler for the translation of Busch's essay, and the translation of the essay by Jacques Ellul is by Richard Muller.

JAMES E. BRADLEY AND RICHARD A. MULLER

Contributors

David Allan Hubbard is President of Fuller Theological Seminary

F. F. Bruce is Professor Emeritus, University of Manchester

Colin Brown is Professor of Systematic Theology, Fuller Theological Seminary

David F. Wright is Senior Lecturer in Ecclesiastical History, New College, University of Edinburgh

Cecil M. Robeck, Jr., is Assistant Professor of Church History, Fuller Theological Seminary

Philip Edgecumbe Hughes is Professor Emeritus, Trinity Episcopal School for Ministry

Thomas F. Torrance is Professor Emeritus of Church Dogmatics, University of Edinburgh

Robert A. Kelley is Assistant Professor of Systematic Theology, Waterloo Lutheran Seminary, Waterloo, Ontario

T. H. L. Parker lives in Cambridge, England

W. Stanford Reid is Professor Emeritus of History, University of Guelph

The Reverend Peter Toon lives in Boxford, Suffolk, England

Eberhard Busch is Professor of Reformed Dogmatics, University of Göttingen

James E. Bradley is Associate Professor of Church History, Fuller Theological Seminary

J. K. S. Reid is Professor Emeritus of Systematic Theology, University of Aberdeen

Jacques Ellul is Professor Emeritus, University of Bordeaux

Bernard Ramm is Professor of Christian Theology, American Baptist Seminary of the West

Howard John Loewen is Associate Professor of Theology, Mennonite Brethren Biblical Seminary

Daniel A. Tappeiner lives in Fountain Valley, California

Paul King Jewett is Professor of Systematic Theology, Fuller Theological Seminary

Helmut Thielike is Professor Emeritus of Systematic Theology, University of Hamburg

Richard A. Muller is Associate Professor of Historical Theology, Fuller Theological Seminary

Gary R. Sattler is Assistant Professor of Christian Formation and Discipleship, Fuller Theological Seminary

Geoffrey W. Bromiley: An Appreciation

David Allan Hubbard

Geoffrey W. Bromiley is best known to scholars and ministers in the Christian church as a prolific and sensitive translator of major theological works. Barth, Ellul, Kittel, Thielicke, Zwingli—the volumes of these seminal servants of the church lie at hand in countless studies and libraries wherever English is read, thanks to Bromiley's labors. His disciplined habit of spending the first few hours of each workday at his ancient, battered typewriter has opened to the rest of us the hearts and minds of some of the monumental thinkers of our day and has saved us incalculable amounts of time along the way.

All students of the Bible honor Bromiley as the editor of significant reference works. He assisted Everett F. Harrison with *Baker's Dictionary of Theology* (1960), which broke fresh ground in evangelical publications of the post–World War II era. He compressed Kittel's *Theological Dictionary* into one convenient and affordable volume (1985). And for almost thirty years he has labored diligently toward a comprehensive revision of the four volume *International Standard Bible Encyclopedia*, of which he has served as general editor and to which he has contrubuted scores of articles. Three volumes have already appeared, and the final volume is in the proof-stage, slated to appear in 1987 to complete the project.

Church historians know Bromiley as the author of two books on Thomas Cranmer, one biographical, the other theological, and of a study entitled *Baptism and the Anglican Reformers* (1953). More recently, Bromiley has authored a text based on his lectures in the history of theology: *Historical Theology: An Introduction* (1978). His commitment to the covenant understanding of baptism has been forcefully articulated in *Children of the Promise: The Case for Baptizing Infants* (1979). Calvin and his English counterparts also have left their stamp on Bromiley's definition and interpretation of ecclesiology in works like *The Unity and Disunity of the Church* (1958).

Bromiley is admired by nearly three decades of students at Fuller for the clarity and forcefulness of his presentation, for his remarkable range of learnedness, and for his profound interest in pastoral ministry. So impressive was his influence on his better students that many of them—some of whom have contributed to this volume—have pursued graduate studies and are now college and seminary teachers themselves. Geoffrey also helped to inaugurate the graduate programs in theology at Fuller and served as its director during their formative years. The graduate students in the Ph.D. and Th.M. programs have long been in his debt.

The foundations of this substantial ministry were carefully laid, layer by layer, both by divine providence and by Geoffrey's obedient response to God's guidance. Born into a Christian home in Bromley Cross, Lancashire, England, he was raised in the faith, and at confirmation he entered personally into the meaning of his baptism. That commitment was nurtured by the Inter-Varsity Christian Union at Cambridge University (CICU), where in 1936 he received first-class honors in French and German from Emmanuel College—an undergraduate education that primed him for the service of translation in which he has so distinguished himself. Following his theological studies, which he completed at Tyndale Hall, Bristol, he was ordained in the Church of England in 1938 and served in the Anglican parishes of Haverigg, Carlisle, and Haile in Cumberland, as well as St. Thomas's, Edinburgh (1951-1958).

His academic interests took him back to scholarship—to the University of Edinburgh for a Ph.D. degree, granted in 1943 for a dissertation on German intellectual trends from Herder to Schleiermacher, a work not published due to the exigencies of World War II. His stay in Edinburgh also resulted in his marriage to Isobel Stirling Whitelaw, whom he met at an Inter-Varsity meeting. His relationship with the University of Edinburgh is reflected in his years of lecturing at New College (from 1956 to 1958), where he built on his earlier ministry as Lecturer and Vice-Principal of Tyndale Hall, the Anglican theological college at Bristol (from 1946 to 1951). The university honored Geoffrey with two further doctorates—a D.Litt. in 1948 for his work entitled *Baptism and the Anglican Reformers,* and a D.D. in 1961 for his overall ministry in theological teaching, translation, and scholarship. On the latter occasion Professor Norman Porteous commented on the extraordinary accomplishment of gaining three doctoral degrees from one university: "the first is accident; the second is coincidence; the third is habit!" Bromiley brought this background to Fuller Seminary as Professor of Church History and Historical Theology in 1958, and thus was the school's first Anglican faculty member. His loyalty to his ecclesial tradition has expressed itself in many years of lecturing each week at Bloy House, the theological college of the Episcopal Diocese of Los Angeles.

He is appreciated by his colleagues for all the reasons that have shaped his worldwide reputation and more. From his arrival he had a marked impact on Fuller's life. His participation in faculty and committee meetings was cogent and effective. On a faculty already well stocked with forceful persons with strong opinions on how the institution should be run, Bromiley quickly became a power to be reckoned with. When I was called to Fuller in 1963, I soon learned how much was to be gained from listening to his advice and seeking his aid on the significant decisions that our faculty faced. The historical and theological perspectives that he brought to administrative and curricular concerns were particularly helpful. That massive learning, gained through years in the parish and decades of poring over the best in theological and exegetical scholarship, was not left in the classroom. Geoffrey carried it, as part of his very person, into all the forums, whether large or intimate, where issues affecting Christian faith and life were at stake. He was as unsparing in his time and energy in faculty service when the issues were substantive—new faculty appointments, major curricular changes, threats to faculty authority, tendencies toward bureaucracy—as he was impatient when he deemed them trivial. No other faculty member ever wrote me a memo like his "Reflections on the Fiscal Crisis and a Realistic Budget," including a summary list of income and expenditures, reordered so as to properly limit the amounts set for administration and thereby increase the sums available for educational endeavors. That and scores of other helpful gestures have endeared Geoffrey to my own heart with a bond that has only strengthened through the years.

A love of God's creation is also characteristic of Bromiley. Through his early morning hikes (once a week while he was teaching; three times a week now) he has kept himself physically fit and encouraged dozens of his friends and students to do the same. He is as familiar with the nooks and crannies of the San Gabriel mountains that fringe Pasadena to the north as he is with the intricacies of German syntax or the intrigues of Calvin's Geneva and Cranmer's Canterbury.

His family is just as beloved and admired as he. I have probably spent more time in the Bromiley home than I have in that of any other faculty member. My wife, Ruth, and I have found many things in common with Geoffrey and Isobel, not the least of which are our affection for Scotland, Isobel's birthplace, and our fondness for good tea. During the forty-three years of their marriage, Isobel has contributed richly to Geoffrey's ministry not only as a loyal, loving wife and a thoughtful, patient mother of their children but also as a friend and partner in obedient commitment to Christ and his gospel. Words like "glorious" and "bliss" do not come lightly from the lips of one raised in the dour climes of northeast Scotland, but Isobel will use them freely to describe the marriage that she and Geoffrey have enjoyed together. Their two daughters, Katherine and Ruth, both successful career women in their own right, gladly testify to the ways in which Geoffrey has effectively pursued the multiple tasks of teaching, scholarship, and family life. Katherine describes her father in this way: "As a father, he has not only been an example of godliness and humility, but also of loving and caring." Ruth, quoting Prov. 23:15, adds a note on her parents' constant encouragement to keep her heart right with the Lord: "I always knew that what would be pleasing to them would be to follow the Lord's direction. I still know that." Conversation with the Bromileys these days readily turns to updates on the progress of their six grandchildren. Katherine and Jim DeVries have four sons, Peter, Stephen, Philip, and Nathan; and Ruth and Tim Patterson have a son, Geoffrey Scot, and a daughter, Rebecca Marie—all in California, where the grandparents can relish each fresh sign of growth in the new generation.

Bromiley's practice of keeping some part of each day sacrosanct for translation and composition, his refusal to squander energy on pursuits deemed secondary, his passionate concern that his students grasp and be grasped by biblical truth, his daily commitment to the life, welfare, and integrity of the church, his single-minded confidence in the power of the gospel—all of these have flowed from his deeply personal love for Jesus Christ as Lord and Master and from his ardent desire that all persons everywhere know and serve, through the power of the Spirit, the triune God whose grace and truth have been fully revealed in that Lord Jesus.

Abbreviations

AC	*Antike und Christentum*
ACW	Ancient Christian Writers
AE	American Edition of Luther's Works
ANET	J. B. Pritchard, ed., *Ancient Near Eastern Texts*
AS	*Augustinian Studies*
BFCT	Beiträge zur Förderung christlicher Theologie
BHST	*Transactions of the Baptist Historical Society*
Bib	*Biblica*
BibOr	Biblica et orientalia
BKAT	Biblischer Kommentar: Altes Testament
BZRGG	Beihefte zur Zeitschrift für Religions- und Geistesgeschichte
CH	*Church History*
CHST	*Transactions of the Congregational Historical Society*
CJH	*Canadian Journal of History*
CJT	*Canadian Journal of Theology*
CT	*Christianity Today*
CTS	Calvin Translation Society
D.V.	*Dei verbum:* The Dogmatic Constitution on Divine Revelation
DS	Denzinger-Schönmetzer, *Enchiridion symbolorum*
EA	Erlanger Ausgabe
EAJT	*East Asia Journal of Theology*
EH	Eusebius, *Ecclesiastical History*
EKL	*Evangelisches Kirchenlexikon*
ExpTim	*Expository Times*
Herm.	*Hermeneia*
HKNT	Handkommentar zum Neuen Testament
HNT	Handbuch zum Neuen Testament
Int	*Interpretation*
JBL	*Journal of Biblical Literature*
JAOS	*Journal of the American Oriental Society*
JRH	*Journal of Religious History*
JR	*Journal of Religion*
JSNT	*Journal for the Study of the New Testament*
JSOT	*Journal for the Study of the Old Testament*
JTC	*Journal for Theology and the Church*
JTS	*Journal of Theological Studies*
KD	*Kerygma und Dogma*
KlT	Kleine Texte
L.G.	*Lumen gentium:* The Dogmatic Constitution on the Church
LCC	Library of Christian Classics
LD	Lectio divina
LQ	*Lutheran Quarterly*
LXX	The Septuagint
McCQ	*McCormick Quarterly*
MScRel	*Mélanges de science religieuse*

MT	Masoretic Text
MTL	Marshall's Theological Library
NovT	*Novum Testamentum*
NovTSup	Novum Testamentum, Supplements
NRT	*La nouvelle revue théologique*
NTS	*New Testament Studies*
PG	J. Migne, *Patrologia graeca*
PL	J. Migne, *Patralogia latina*
PMS	Patristic Monograph Series
RGG	*Religion in Geschichte und Gegenwart*
RSV	Revised Standard Version
SBT	Studies in Biblical Theology
SC	Sources chrétiennes
SC	*The Second Century*
SCJ	Studies in Christianity and Judaism
SE	*Studia Evangelica*
SHR	*Scottish Historical Review*
SJT	*Scottish Journal of Theology*
SNT	Society for New Testament Studies
SNTSMS	Society for New Testament Studies Monograph Series
SPAW	Sitzungsberichte der preussischen Akademie der Wissenschaften
SP	*Studia Patristica*
Str-B	[H. Strack and] P. Billerbeck, *Kommentar zum Neuen Testament*
TDNT	G. Kittel and G. Friedrich, eds., *Theological Dictionary of the New Testament*
THKNT	Theologischer Handkommentar zum Neuen Testament
TLZ	*Theologische Literaturzeitung*
TSK	*Theologische Studien und Kritiken*
TS	*Theological Studies*
TToday	*Theology Today*
TU	Texte und Untersuchungen
TWNT	G. Kittel and G. Friedrich, eds., *Theologisches Wörterbuch zum Neuen Testament*
WA	Weimarer Ausgabe—Weimar edition of Luther's works
WBC	Word Biblical Commentary
WTJ	*Westminster Theological Journal*
WUNT	Wissenschaftliche Untersuchungen zum Neuen Testament
ZKT	*Zeitschrift fur katholische Theologie*
ZNW	*Zeitschrift für die neutestamentliche Wissenschaft*
ZST	*Zeitschrift für systematische Theologie*

The First Church Historian

F. F. Bruce

The first Christian historian was the writer whom we commonly refer to as Luke, who composed a two-volume work that we call the Gospel of Luke and the Acts of the Apostles (whoever was responsible for giving them these titles, it was not the author himself). The prologue with which the twofold work begins (Luke 1:1-4) shows clearly enough that Luke had a historical model in view as he wrote his work.[1] His intention to follow that model is shown by the chronological notes which he introduces at the beginning of his story—his dating of the birth of John the Baptist "in the days of Herod, king of Judea" (Luke 1:5), his dating of the birth of Jesus by reference to a census held "when Quirinius was governor of Syria" (Luke 2:2), and his dating of John's public ministry with an elaborate synchronistic note (Luke 3:1-2) comparable to that with which Thucydides begins his account of the Peloponnesian War proper.[2]

While the prologue is designed as an introduction to both parts of the work, some of it is more relevant to the second part than to the first: when Luke claims to have had personal knowledge of his story "for some time back," he is in fact referring to portions of the narrative of Acts. Indeed, Luke's first volume does not properly belong to the genre "historical work"; it belongs to the new Christian genre "Gospel," for which a precedent had already been set by Mark. After Mark's initiative, there was only one literary form in which the story of Jesus could be told, and Luke followed that form.

But when he came to write his second volume (dedicated, like its predecessor, to Theophilus), he was a pioneer: no one had composed a record of the rise and progress of the primitive church before Luke did so. The "many" who, according to the prologue, had set themselves "to compile a narrative of the things which have been accomplished among us" seem to have confined themselves to aspects of the story of Jesus (as Mark did); Luke evidently does not know of anyone who had anticipated him in recording the history of early Christianity after the death and resurrection of Jesus.

PIONEER IN CHRISTIAN HISTORIOGRAPHY

There was a well established genre for the kind of work to which Luke now set his hand in his second volume: it was history. Martin Dibelius has discerned

---

1. See Robert L. Wilken, *The Myth of Christian Beginnings* (London: SCM, 1979), 32f.; see also Loveday Alexander, "Luke's Preface in the Context of Greek Preface-Writing," *NovT* 28 (1986): 47-74.

2. Thucydides, *The History of the Peloponnesian War*, 2.1.

even in the Gospel some features which show that Luke wished to write history rather than just tell stories; but in spite of the "small corrections" he made in the Gospel "in the interests of history, he still cannot be said to have entered the field of 'great' literature. He does so, however, with the Acts of the Apostles."[3] Here Luke embarked on a new enterprise, and the new task dictated a new style. Here he is a historian because he combines into a continuous and coherent whole both the traditions which were preserved in the primitive Christian community and what he himself discovered by inquiry and personal participation as he endeavored to trace the course of events from the early days. In bringing together this diverse material he had to exercise his own judgment on the connection and progress of events; he had to conceive a plan for his whole work and relate the persons and incidents figuring in his narrative to the outworking of that plan. Yet that plan had to conform to the actual course of history, or else the work would be historical fiction and not true history. To be sure, Ernst Haenchen thinks that the book of Acts does show some of the features of historical fiction when judged by the more exacting standards of our own culture;[4] but we should assess Luke's work by the historiographical standards of his own day—and these, as we shall see, were quite stringent.

Robert Wilken says that it was Eusebius who wrote "the first genuine history of Christianity."[5] He cannot bring himself to speak of Acts in these terms, for he does not think that "Luke intended to write a history in the fashion of Thucydides."[6] Yet he admits that Luke—writing not as a dispassionate researcher but as a committed Christian concerned with bringing his readers to share his own estimate of Jesus and the Christian faith—nevertheless "makes Christianity conform to some, if not all, of the canons of history."[7] In this he approached the work of Thucydides, who is generally held to mark the nearest approach in antiquity to our ideal of the objective and "scientific" historian. Yet it is doubtful if Thucydides was as dispassionate as is commonly supposed.[8] Even when exiled from Athens he remained an Athenian at heart as well as in fact. While he does not conceal the Athenians' most glaring crimes, his work, incomplete as it is, leaves many readers feeling that the Peloponnesian War was a tragedy, with Athens as the tragic hero. In fact, some have said, with some reason, that he composed his work on a tragic model.[9]

Eduard Meyer, the greatest twentieth-century historian of classical antiquity, held in contrast to Wilken that Luke was the one great historian who joins Polybius to Eusebius—the last of the genuinely Greek historians to the greatest of Christian

---

3. Martin Dibelius, "The First Christian Historian," in *Studies in the Acts of the Apostles,* trans. Mary Ling (London: SCM, 1956), 124.

4. Ernst Haenchen, *The Acts of the Apostles,* trans. Bernard Noble, Gerald Shinn, et al. (Oxford: Basil Blackwell, 1971), 103-10.

5. Wilken, *The Myth of Christian Beginnings,* 37.

6. Ibid., 33.

7. Ibid., 32.

8. Some unfashionable reflections on the common estimate of Thucydides as a "scientific" historian are offered by Moses I. Finley, *Ancient History: Evidence and Models* (London: Chatto & Windus, 1985).

9. See Francis M. Cornford, *Thucydides Mythistoricus* (London: Edward Arnold, 1907).

historians. Luke's work, he reckoned, "in spite of its more restricted content, bears the same character as those of the great historians, of a Polybius, a Livy, and many others."[10]

In the eyes of many students, such a verdict from a master of ancient history might seem exceptionally impressive; in the eyes of some others, however, Meyer's expertise was a handicap to him when he approached Luke-Acts. According to Philip Vielhauer, for example, "Meyer, who approaches Acts with the presuppositions of a historian of antiquity and treats it with the greatest confidence, misunderstands the nature of its accounts and the way in which they are connected."[11] One might ask if Vielhauer's own presuppositions were any more valid in the approach to Acts. But Meyer will survive such criticisms: he knew a real historical work when he met one.

HOW TO WRITE HISTORY

Lucian, the second-century satirist of Samosata, wrote an essay entitled *How to Write History*, in which he shows himself a shrewd critic of historiographical fashions. But before I speak of this essay, let me turn aside for a moment to refer to Lucian's *True Story*, a parody of popular collections of travelers' tales, in which he describes a visit to the place of punishment after death. In it, he says, "the severest torments were reserved for those who in life had been liars and written false history; the class was numerous, and included Ctesias of Cnidus, and Herodotus."[12] Ctesias of Cnidus was physician to the Persian king Artaxerxes II (404–359 B.C.). He lived at the Persian court for seventeen years and wrote a large work on the history of Persia and another on the history of India—both now extant only in fragments. His brief dismissal by Lucian is justified by all that we know of him. Herodotus, on the other hand, has survived the censures of all his detractors— he is too great to have taken lasting damage from any of them. He was a knowledgeable citizen of the world of his day and a shrewd and observant traveler. He appreciated a good story when he heard one and saw no reason to exclude it from his history—though he himself might not vouch for its truth.

In his essay *How to Write History,* then, Lucian criticizes some so-called historians who are eulogists more than anything else, and others (like Theopompus) who write like public prosecutors. There are yet others, he says, who cannot distinguish between history and poetry, or between history and philosophy. A historian should get his facts right—in geography, for example (he is particularly scathing about one writer who places Lucian's native city of Samosata between the Euphrates and the Tigris). Still others, he goes on, have no sense of relevance or balance and fill up their work with descriptions of scenery or even of feasting.

10. Meyer, *Ursprung und Anfänge des Christentums* (Stuttgart and Berlin: J. G. Cotta, 1921), 1: 2f. See also Arnold Ehrhardt, "The Construction and Purpose of the Acts of the Apostles," in *The Framework of the New Testament Stories* (Manchester: Manchester University, 1964), 64-102.

11. Philipp Vielhauer, "On the 'Paulinism' of Acts," in Leander E. Keck and J. Louis Martyn, eds., *Studies in Luke-Acts: Essays . . . in Honor of Paul Schubert* (Nashville: Abingdon, 1966), 50n.37.

12. Lucian, *True Story* 2.31.

A historical work, says Lucian, should start with a preface, which leads by a natural transition into the narrative. The true historian will not tell everything that happened: he should select the important events and record them with due brevity. Thucydides is thus the *beau-ideal* of the history writers, producing a work not to provide momentary pleasure but, as he himself says, to be a possession forever.[13] The historian should write like Thucydides, according to Lucian, consorting with truth and not with flattery, looking to the future hope, not to the gratification of the flattered.[14] While Thucydides introduced speeches at appropriate junctures in his history, his inferior imitators introduce them at inappropriate junctures, not because they make any contribution to the work but in order to give the writer an opportunity of indulging in rhetorical exercise.

THE DOMINANT THEME IN ACTS

How does the author of Acts measure up to Lucian's exacting standards? There is one dominant theme in Acts: Luke aims to show how the gospel, beginning at Jerusalem, ultimately became established at Rome. There was no doubt much more that could have been said about the expansion of Christianity in various directions during the first three decades after the death and resurrection of Christ, but Luke confines himself to its progress along the road to Rome.

He develops his theme biographically: he records what might be called the "Acts of Stephen and Philip," the "Acts of Peter," and the "Acts of Paul." After a series of pictures of the primitive church of Jerusalem in the first five chapters, he introduces us to the Hellenists in the church—for it was predominately they who promoted the advance of the gospel through the Roman world. Two leaders of the Hellenists receive special mention: Stephen and Philip. Stephen's so-called defense is a manifesto of Hellenistic radicalism, calling on the people of God to cut loose from the ancient traditions that impeded the progress of the gospel. When Stephen is stoned for his impiety toward the temple, Philip translates the terms of the manifesto into action by preaching the gospel to the Samaritans and then to an Ethiopian. And there were still other Hellenists, unnamed, who carried the same gospel to the Greek-speaking pagans of Antioch on the Orontes in North Syria.

But even the non-Hellenists in the Jerusalem church (the "Hebrews," as Luke calls them), or at least the more liberal among them, find themselves committed to the evangelization of Gentiles. Peter, their leader, has the distinction of preaching the gospel to a Roman military household in Caesarea and directing that they should be baptized. Philip and other Hellenists might already have done this kind of thing, but they were free-lance evangelists. For Peter to act in this way now was to make Gentile evangelization part of the church's official policy. No wonder that Peter had to leave Jerusalem soon afterward: such fraternizing with the occupying forces could not be tolerated. Having broken the ice at Caesarea and spoken out on behalf of Gentile liberty at the Council of Jerusalem, Peter disappears from Luke's record. Paul then comes into the foreground and stays there until the end of the Acts.

13. Thucydides, *History of the Peloponnesian War*, 1.22.
14. Lucian, *How to Write History*, 63.

Luke, oddly, never calls Paul "the apostle" in the special sense in which Paul himself claims the designation.[15] For Luke an apostle in the special sense must have been a participant in Jesus' ministry as well as a witness to his resurrection. But Paul is the outstanding preacher to the Gentiles. Paul's was not the only Gentile mission, as is evident from his letters; but Luke concentrates on Paul, even if, for purposes of economy and literary tidiness, he brings features of other missionary work into his record of Paul's mission.[16]

Antioch, Corinth, and Ephesus are Paul's successive bases, and in Ephesus he decides that Rome must be his next goal.[17] Luke knows that the gospel had reached Rome before Paul's arrival there, and he has no thought of concealing this fact. He tells how, on Paul's approach to Rome, some Christians from the city walked thirty or forty miles south along the Appian Way to welcome him and escort him for the remainder of his journey.[18] But when Paul, the "chosen vessel," reaches Rome and proclaims the kingdom of God there, albeit under house arrest, Luke has reached his goal. "Paulus Romae, apex evangelii."[19]

LUKE'S SOURCES

The attempt to discover the sources of a literary work is hazardous when the sources have not survived independently; in their absence, the best that can be achieved is some disciplined guesswork. There is a major difference in this respect between the third Gospel and Acts. One of the most important sources of Luke's Gospel has survived independently in the Gospel of Mark. Luke's use of Mark can be traced the more easily because of his tendency to arrange his Markan and non-Markan material in alternate blocks. And even in Luke's non-Markan material it is possible to exercise some measure of source-critical analysis, for part of that material is paralleled (sometimes more closely, sometimes less closely) in the Gospel of Matthew. But no such help is available for the source criticism of Acts: we have to do our best with the internal evidence of the book itself.

One rather obvious source, or sources, may be discerned in the "we" sections of the book—those sections in which the story is told in the first person plural. There are three of these, and all three are devoted largely to journeys by sea: (1) a voyage from Troas, near the Dardanelles, to Neapolis, the seaport of Philippi, to which the narrator and his companions then make their way by road before he takes his leave (16:10-17); (2) a voyage from the port of Philippi to Caesarea in Palestine, from which the narrator and his companions make their way by road to Jerusalem, before he again takes his leave (20:5–21:18); (3) Paul's voyage from Caesarea to Italy, which involves a storm at sea and a shipwreck off Malta; from Malta, when winter is past, the voyage is resumed in another ship to Puteoli, from

15. In Acts 14:4, 14, Paul and Barnabas together are referred to as "the apostles"; otherwise Paul is not called an apostle in Acts.

16. See Charles Kingsley Barrett, "Acts and the Pauline Corpus," *ExpTim* 88 (1976-77): 2-5.

17. Acts 19:21.

18. Acts 28:15.

19. Johann Albrecht Bengel, *Gnomon Novi Testamenti*, 5th ed. (1742; London and Edinburgh: Williams & Norgate, 1862), 489.

which the narrator and his companions make their way by road to Rome, where he takes his leave for the last time (27:1–28:16).

The traditional explanation of the "we" sections is that the author of Acts is telling his readers unobtrusively that he was present at the particular scenes described, that he was a fellow traveler with Paul and others on the journeys thus recorded. This account of the matter is supported by the impossibility of finding any stylistic differences between those passages and the rest of the narrative. The author is providing extracts from his own travel diaries. It could indeed be argued that the author of Acts has thoroughly worked over someone else's travel diaries and accommodated their style to his own. But if that were the case why did he leave the pronoun "we" unchanged? He did not do so in order to lend an air of verisimilitude to an otherwise bald and unconvincing narrative, because neither the "we" sections nor the rest is an otherwise bald or unconvincing narrative. Nor is it any more satisfactory to be told that the use of "we" is designed to give the reader an impression of greater vividness and immediacy.[20]

The simplest explanation is the most probable. It is unacceptable, however, to those scholars whose comparative study of Acts and the Pauline letters make it impossible for them to think that the author of Acts could have known Paul or been a fellow traveler of his. I have never found it impossible to think this, but I am sometimes given occasion to wonder if my critical faculty is as well developed as it ought to be.

The author of Acts may have drawn on other travel documents, over and above the contents of the "we" sections: an Anatolian itinerary, for example, might have provided the skeleton for the account of Barnabas and Paul's mission in Acts 13:13–14:26.

The first five chapters of Acts relate the steady increase of the Jerusalem church from the first Christian Pentecost onward, a story not unmarked by trouble. Twice the church's leaders fall foul of the chief-priestly establishment, and the tragedy of Ananias and Sapphira unmasks the serpent that lurks at the heart of every utopia; yet the general picture is that of a growing community, united in heart and soul under the leadership of the apostles, who themselves enjoy a special measure of the Spirit's guidance.

It is not difficult to recognize the author's use of a new source at the beginning of Acts 6. This chapter opens abruptly with the statement that, while the community was growing, a dispute broke out within it between the Hebrews and Hellenists. Nothing that has been said thus far prepares us for this revelation of the existence of two groups in the community. Luke appears now to be following a source in which the chief interest is focused on the Hellenists. The dispute between the Hebrews and the Hellenists, which concerned the fair distribution of the daily allocation of charity from the common stock, is resolved by the appointment of seven men to supervise this distribution. But all seven appear to be Hellenists. Five of them are not mentioned again, but the other two, Stephen and Philip, play a prominent part in the sequel—no longer as almoners but as leaders of the Hellenistic mission.

20. See Ernst Haenchen, "'We' in Acts and the Itinerary," *JTC* 1 (1965): 65-99.

The transition from the appointment of the seven almoners to the special ministry of Stephen and Philip is marked by one of a succession of progress reports with which Luke punctuates the course of his narrative (Acts 6:7). The account of the ministry of Stephen and Philip (Acts 6:8–8:40) seems to come from a Hellenistic source. Luke then turns to the conversion of Saul of Tarsus (9:1-30), followed (after another progress report) by an excerpt from what may be called the "Acts of Peter" (9:32–11:18). In 11:19 a rubric is introduced similar to that which in 8:4 inaugurates the story of Philip's evangelistic activity. Then those who were scattered (in the persecution that followed Stephen's death) "went about preaching the word." Now "those who were scattered . . . traveled as far as Phoenicia and Cyprus and Antioch." Luke here reverts to his Hellenistic source and follows it to the end of chapter 11, telling how the gospel reached Antioch on the Orontes, where it was preached on a large scale to the Gentiles.

The "Acts of Peter" are resumed in 12:1, with an abrupt reference to "Herod the king" (the elder Herod Agrippa). Then, from chapter 13 on, the narrative is taken up mainly with Paul's missionary progress from Antioch to Rome (apart from chapter 15, drawn from a Jerusalem source, which describes the so-called Council of Jerusalem and the promulgation of the apostolic decree to regulate the coexistence of Jewish and Gentile Christians in mixed churches).

Discerning the sources for the second half of Acts is an even more precarious task than it was for the first half, and I will not undertake it here. A modern historian covering the same ground would certainly exploit the firsthand information accessible in Paul's letters. It is generally agreed that Luke did not use them and probably did not know them, but a few scholars have drawn a contrary inference from the data. Outstanding among these has been Morton Enslin, in whose judgment "the letters of Paul . . . appear to have been the principal source used by Luke in reconstructing the activities of the man who brought to reality the Gentile mission."[21] Luke's creative genius developed incidental factual information found here and there in the letters in accordance with his basic conviction that what *should* have been *must* have been, and in fact *was*. But arguments for Luke's indebtedness to Paul's letters, like arguments for his indebtedness to the writings of Josephus,[22] create more problems than they solve and are far outweighed by arguments to the contrary.

SPEECHES IN ACTS

Speeches delivered by the principal characters formed an important element in ancient historical writing. An appropriate speech in the right context could sum up a situation, draw lessons from the narrative just concluded, or set out the program for the next phase of action.

---

21. Morton Scott Enslin, *Reapproaching Paul* (Philadelphia: Westminster, 1962), 27; see also his "'Luke' and Paul," *JAOS* 58 (1938): 81-91; "Once Again: Luke and Paul," *ZNW* 61 (1970): 253-71; "Luke, the Literary Physician," in David E. Aune, ed., *Studies in New Testament and Early Christian Literature: Essays in Honor of Allen P. Wikgren*, NovTSup 33 (Leiden: Brill, 1972), 135-43.

22. See Max Krenkel, *Josephus und Lucas* (Leipzig: Haessel, 1894).

The exemplar in reporting such speeches, as in so many other aspects of ancient historiography, was Thucydides. Early in his *History of the Peloponnesian War* he states his policy. He disclaims anything in the nature of precise verbatum reproduction, but he aims to make each speech suitable to the character and style of the speaker, as well as to his own intention in reporting it. Above all, he says, "I have endeavored, as nearly as possible, to give the general purport of what was actually said."[23] Naturally, since Thucydides reported the various speeches in his own language, a general literary similarity can be traced throughout them all, but this similarity does not extend to the sentiments expressed: Pericles expresses Periclean sentiments, while Cleon says the kind of thing that Cleon would say.

The speeches in Acts may properly be called Thucydidean. They are not like the speeches freely composed as rhetorical exercises by lesser historians (like Josephus) and put into the mouths of *dramatis personae* with little regard for appropriateness to speaker or occasion. Neither does Luke introduce speeches as vehicles for his own reflections or interpretations. The critical appraisal of the Jerusalem temple in Stephen's speech, for example, is more radical than Luke's own. For Luke, the temple is a holy place. But he knows that the appraisal that finds expression in Acts 7 was characteristic of one school of thought among the Hellenists, a school for which Stephen here acts as spokesman. Again, Luke manifests a nice sense of fitness in making Paul the only speaker in Acts to call Jesus the Son of God or to mention justification by faith or redemption by the blood of Christ.

There is a difference between Luke's usage of such speeches in the Gospel and his usage in Acts. In the Gospel the "speeches" reported are the utterances of Jesus; they already had a sacrosanct quality which forbade any free and easy adaptation of them. When we compare the Gospel of Luke with its sources—for example, when we compare his version of the Olivet discourse with Mark's—what impresses us, in F. C. Burkitt's words, "is not that Luke has changed so much, but that he has invented so little."[24] The quality of reporting was different in Acts, for Peter and Paul were not on a level with their Lord. They were his witnesses, and their testimony should be to the same effect. Since he was writing with this purpose in mind, Luke would not have been greatly troubled by the charges of more recent times that he has made Peter's speeches too Pauline or Paul's too Petrine. It was, he would have said, the same gospel that they were preaching.

Indeed, when Paul speaks in Gal 2:7-9 of his being entrusted with "the gospel to the uncircumcised" whereas Peter and his colleagues had been entrusted with "the gospel to the circumcised," he does not imply any difference between the two as far as the basic content of the preaching was concerned (differences in presentation are what one might expect). The content of Paul's own testimony is that he and the Jerusalem leaders were at one: "Whether then it was I or they, so we preach and so you believed" (1 Cor 15:11).

It is especially in his synagogue address at Pisidian Antioch (Acts 13:16-41)

23. Thucydides, *History of the Peloponnesian War*, 1.22.1. See Finley's remarks on this statement in *Ancient History: Evidence and Models*, 13-15.

24. Francis Crawford Burkitt, "Luke's Use of Mark," in F. J. Foakes Jackson and Kirsopp Lake, eds., *The Beginnings of Christianity*, Part 1, 2 (London: Macmillan, 1922), 115.

that Paul has been held to be too Petrine. The Petrine affinities in this speech (the only one of Paul's speeches in Acts addressed to a Jewish audience) may owe more to Luke than to either Peter or Paul. Paul argues, with reference to appropriate Scriptures, that God's promises to David have been fulfilled in Jesus, the climax of the fulfilment being reached in the Resurrection, for which eyewitness testimony is cited: "For many days he appeared to those who came up with him from Galilee to Jerusalem, who are now his witnesses to the people" (Acts 13:31). This is neither Pauline nor Petrine, but Lukan: it is a summary of Acts 1:3-8. We may be sure that Paul would have said, and in fact did say, "Last of all he appeared also to me" (as in 1 Cor 15:8).

Paul's speeches in Acts are samples: the synagogue address in Pisidian Antioch is a sample of his presentation of the gospel to Jews and God-fearing Gentiles who were familiar with the Old Testament story. His address to the Areopagus court in Athens (17:22-31) is a sample of his presentation to pagans. His address to the elders of the Ephesian church at Miletus (20:18-35) is a sample of his parenetic ministry to Christians (it is moreover his farewell to Christians in the Aegean world). And his speeches at Jerusalem and Caesarea (22:3-21; 24:10-21; 26:2-23) are apologetic in character, defending particularly the claim of Christianity to be the true fulfillment of the law and the prophets.

Of all these speeches, the one which has most consistently been denied as an expression of Paul's thought is his speech before the Areopagus. The author of the first three chapters of Romans could never have spoken like that, some have maintained. Let me suggest, on the contrary, that if the author of those three chapters were taken to Athens and invited to expound the first principles of his gospel to an audience of intelligent pagans, it is difficult to see how he could have argued much differently. Pagans have to be introduced to the living and true God before being told about his Son, whom he raised from the dead (1 Thess 1:9-10). The introduction to the living and true God in the Areopagus speech leads on directly to the resurrection of Christ and his coming to judge the world in righteousness.

The themes of the Pauline speeches are themes which Luke himself wishes to emphasize in his work, but he does not do violence to Paul by putting them into his mouth.

ACTS AND WORLD HISTORY

Luke, unlike the other evangelists, sets the story of Jesus in the context of world history, referring, for example, to the Emperors Augustus and Tiberius by name (Luke 2:1; 3:1). He does this in much greater measure in Acts, especially when the gospel leaves the confines of its Palestinian homeland and moves into the wider world of the Roman Empire. Even in Palestine we meet members of the influential Herod family—Antipas, tetrarch of Galilee and Peraea; the elder Agrippa, king of the Jews from A.D. 41 to 44, who "laid violent hands upon some who belonged to the church" (Acts 12:1); his daughters Drusilla (third wife of the procurator Felix) and Bernice; and his son, the younger Agrippa, who helped the procurator Festus draft the report on Paul which had to be sent to Rome when Paul appealed to Caesar.

Governors of other provinces appear from time to time in Luke's record. He gets their variable titles right for the period in question—Sergius Paullus, proconsul of Cyprus, for example, and Gallion, proconsul of Achaia. He knows that the province of Asia is administered by a proconsul, though there was an interregnum in the proconsulship at the time of the riot in the Ephesian theater, which explains the town clerk's generalizing plural: "there are such persons as proconsuls" (Acts 19:38, NEB). The whole account of the riot is full of local color. The town clerk, who succeeded at last in quieting the demonstrators, plays a part appropriate to the liaison officer between the municipal government and the Roman administration of the province. The Asiarchs who, on the same occasion, sent Paul friendly advice to keep out of the theater (Acts 19:31), were representatives of the leading cities of proconsular Asia. They played an influential part in the life of the province. The city of Ephesus itself is given its honorary title *neokoros* (temple warden) of Artemis (19:35). Today, only the fragments of the great temple of Artemis survive: "she whom all Asia and the world worship" has indeed been "deposed from her magnificence," in realization of the worst fears of Demetrius the silversmith (19:27). But the theater of Ephesus, where the riotous assembly met, still stands where it did, cut out of the western slope of Mount Pion.

The magistrates of Philippi, a Roman colony, are called "praetors" in Acts 16:20. Like the chief magistrates of Rome, they are attended by lictors, who used their rods, their official equipment, to inflict corporal punishment on Paul and Silas. At Thessalonica the chief magistrates are called "politarchs" (Acts 17:6, 8); this is the first occurrence of the term in literature, although politarchs are mentioned in many inscriptions as the chief magistrates of Macedonian cities.

The court of the Areopagus, which figures in the narrative of Paul's visit to Athens (Acts 17:19, 22), was the most venerable institution of that city. While it lost most of its ancient power in the democratic reforms of the fifth century B.C., it retained authority in the sphere of religion and morals. It was natural, then, that Paul—whom the Athenians took to be "a preacher of foreign divinities" (17:18) because of his talk of Jesus and the Resurrection—should be invited to expound his teaching to this body.

In the account of how Paul and his companions wintered in Malta after their shipwreck, Luke mentions a man named Publius, "the first man of the island" (Acts 28:7). This title is attested in both Greek and Latin inscriptions as the proper designation of the chief citizen of Malta.

It was not so easy to attain such accuracy in detail in Luke's day as it is today, when works of reference are conveniently accessible. But Luke's accuracy in detail is matched by his skill in conveying the authentic atmosphere of one place after another. Jerusalem, with its intolerant populace, forms a marked contrast to the cosmopolitan city of Antioch on the Orontes, where people of different creeds and races rubbed shoulders and had their rough corners worn away. It is thus not surprising to find Gentile evangelization flourishing in Antioch, with Jews and Gentiles meeting in brotherly concord in the church. Then there is Philippi, a Roman colony, with its self-important magistrates and its citizens so very proud of being Romans. There is also Athens, with its endless disputations in the Agora and its unquenchable thirst to hear about the latest novelty—in religion, philosophy, or anything else. And also Ephesus, with so many of its people depending for their living on the cult of Artemis. The cult had a reputation for the practice of magic, a reputation so widespread in the ancient world that a common term for written charms or spells was *Ephesia grammata*—"Ephesian writings." Converted magicians publically burned scrolls containing such formulae as Paul proclaimed a faith that liberated men and women from superstitious fears (Acts 19:19).

The practical upshot of all this is that Acts itself can safely be accepted as an authority in areas where its trustworthiness cannot be so easily gauged by external checks. Especially where Asia Minor is concerned, its record of the journeys of Paul and his companions provides the best evidence we have for the ease of travel and the actual lines of communication in parts of that peninsula during the first century.[25] A comparable claim can be made for its record of journeys by sea. In particular, the narrative of Paul's voyage to Italy and shipwreck off Malta has long been recognized as "one of the most instructive documents for the knowledge of ancient seamanship."[26] In another field, the references to Roman citizenship in Acts and the procedure of appealing to Caesar suit the conditions obtaining in the middle years of the first century and may confidently be used to fill in the knowledge available from other sources. Whatever the date of the final publication of Acts, its contents are true to their "dramatic" date—that is, the date at which the events recorded are represented as having taking place.[27]

ACTS AND THE LETTERS OF PAUL

There is one limited field, but a very important one, which provides a further set of checks on Luke's record of events. The letters of Paul written before his Roman imprisonment (in particular, 1 Thessalonians, Galatians, 1 and 2 Corinthians, and Romans), supply firsthand evidence for the most active years of Paul's Gentile mission—the years covered in the first half of Acts.

Paul's letters are occasional documents and give nothing like a connected account of his life and work during those years. Yet in them he refers to past phases of his career and mentions his plans for the future, so that they supply evidence stretching beyond the place and time of their composition. And, in spite of the many gaps they leave in the record, they mention several incidents in his career on which Luke is silent. For example, in 2 Cor 11:23-25 Paul refers to his frequent imprisonments (though Luke had recorded only one up to that point). He also refers to five occasions, unrecorded in Acts, when he was sentenced by synagogue authorities to thirty-nine lashes (a punishment which he could have avoided had he forsworn his Jewish identity), to three occasions when he was beaten with rods (of which Luke mentions only one), and to three experiences of shipwreck (at a point in his career when Luke has recorded none).

25. See T. R. S. Broughton, "Three Notes on St. Paul's Journeys in Asia Minor," in Robert P. Casey et al., eds., *Quantulacumque: Studies presented to Kirsopp Lake* (London: Christophers, 1937), 138.

26. Heinrich Julius Holtzmann, *Die Apostelgeschichte*, HKNT, 1, 2 (Freiburg im Breisgau: J. C. B. Mohr [Paul Siebeck], 1889), 421.

27. See Adrian N. Sherwin-White, *Roman Society and Roman Law in the New Testament* (Oxford: Clarendon, n.d.), 188f. and passim.

Luke is selective in his account of Paul's life and ministry, as he is in other matters. But he agrees with Paul in recording his upbringing as a zealous Pharisee, his persecution of the church, his coming to faith in Christ in the vicinity of Damascus through the appearance of the risen Lord, his escape from arrest at Damascus by being let down in a basket through a window in the city wall, his first postconversion visit to Jerusalem from Damascus, and his trip from Jerusalem to Syria and Cilicia (to Tarsus in the first instance, says Luke). In due course both sources bring him to Antioch as the colleague of Barnabas. From Antioch he pays his second postconversion visit to Jerusalem, this time in Barnabas's company (Gal 2:1; cf. Acts 11:30 and 15:2).

While Luke attaches great importance to the apostolic decree of Acts 15:29, which sets out the terms on which Jewish and Gentile believers might enjoy fellowship together, Paul has nothing to say about it. When Paul discusses in his letters the issues also discussed by the decree, he appeals not to it but to the first principles of the gospel. But the indirect influence of the decree can be traced in situations with which he deals in his letters. Moreover, he provides a probable occasion for the formulation of the decree when he tells in Gal 2:11-14 of the attempt at Antioch of the messengers from James to institute separate tables for Jewish and Gentile Christians. When Luke reports the parting of the ways between Paul and Barnabas at Antioch (Acts 15:36-40), we can understand the cleavage better when we remember that, in addition to the personal conflict between the two which Luke mentions, there was also Paul's loss of confidence in Barnabas after the latter went along with the charade of separate tables.

Luke's omission of controversies like that at Antioch inevitably affects his portrait of Paul, but it does not appear to spring from any desire to depict Paul as other than he actually was. Instead, he omitted such controversies for reasons associated with the aim of his work, which did not include unnecessarily rehashing old battles.

Paul's companions after his parting with Barnabas—Silvas (Silvanus) and Timothy—figure both in Acts and in Paul's letters. With them Paul evangelized some of the cities of Macedonia and then the city of Corinth. Their movements as recorded in the Thessalonian and Corinthian correspondence can be correlated with the narrative in Acts. The general sequence of Paul's movements in Acts 16:6–20:3 (Philippi—Thessalonica—Athens—Ephesus—Macedonia and Achaia—Judaea) is confirmed by numerous references in the epistles (1 Thess 2:2; 3:1; 1 Cor 2:1; 16:5-9; 2 Cor 12:14; Rom 15:25; 16:1, 23). Detailed correlation is difficult because Paul's account of his movements is not systematic but occasional and allusive; and Luke's account on the other hand is not as complete as we might imagine if we could not check it by references in Paul. For example, Luke omits all mention of Paul's second, "painful," visit to Corinth (2 Cor 2:1; 13:2). But in spite of all these limitations, we can construct a remarkably coherent outline of Paul's movements.

Paul's personal note in Rom 15:25-32, written as he was about to set out on his last journey to Jerusalem, provides a further control on the narrative of Acts. He tells the Roman Christians that before he can pay them his long-planned visit (see Acts 19:21), he must go to Jerusalem and complete the delivery of the relief fund for the mother church which he has organized in the churches of his Gentile mission field. He expresses misgivings about the reception awaiting him at Jerusalem; how well founded these misgivings were is amply illustrated from the narrative of Acts 21:17–26:32. His greeting to the Roman Christians from "all the churches of Christ" (Rom 16:16) chimes in with Luke's statement that on this voyage to Judaea Paul was accompanied by several members of churches that he had planted. Paul's letters indicate that these others, who came together at Corinth on the eve of embarkation (Acts 20:4), were delegates from the contributing churches bringing their churches' gifts to Jerusalem.

But why is Luke so reticent about this relief fund, which played so dominant a part in Paul's policy at this time? He says nothing about it, apart from the quite general statement which Paul makes in his defense before Felix: "After many years I came to bring my nation alms and offerings" (Acts 24:17). Various reasons for this reticence have been suggested. One probable suggestion is that the relief fund was misrepresented so as to form a plank in the indictment of Paul before Caesar, and that it was thus politic for Luke, or for his source, to say as little about it as possible. Paul himself regarded the fund not only as a gift for the church of Jerusalem but also (as Luke may imply) as a witness to the whole Jewish nation at the center of its life.

A man's unconscious self-portrait, visible in his letters to his friends, will naturally differ from his portrait through the eyes of someone else, even if that other person is an occasional collaborator and fellow traveler. When this is borne in mind, the difference between the two portraits of Paul offered to us in the New Testament will not seem too great.

LUKE'S PURPOSE IN WRITING

Luke writes with a moral and religious purpose, but he does not in this regard fall below the standard expected of ancient historians. History writing in antiquity had a didactic quality and aim. Even the "scientific" Thucydides wrote so that future generations might learn what results could be expected to spring from a particular pattern of events: one person is not very different from another, he said, and what has happened once is likely to happen again.

Luke writes in order that Theophilus (together, no doubt, with other readers of the same outlook) might know that the information he had received about the Christian beginnings was reliable. That this knowledge was not intended to be merely cerebral is suggested by the inclusion in the narrative of sermons and similar speeches, and by the emphasis on the guidance of the Holy Spirit in the records both of the preachers' movements and of the deliberations and decisions of the church. Luke writes, in fact, not only to defend Christianity but to commend it as an acceptable faith for intelligent, open-minded subjects of the Roman Empire. And he undertakes to do so by showing that the historical basis on which that faith rests is well attested.

***

Throughout his distinguished and productive career as an exponent and defender of the Christian faith, Geoffrey Bromiley has consistently remained mindful of its historical basis. It has been his ambition that, through his writings, others should share his assurance regarding the secure foundation of Christianity rightly so called. It seems appropriate, then, to present him with these reflections on an early believer who was both historian and historical theologian—the theologian of salvation history, as he has been called. May my thoughts here be a tribute of admiring gratitude for many services rendered to the cause of Christian learning and a token of forty-five years' friendship. *Ad multos annos!*

The Gates of Hell and the Church

Colin Brown

Geoffrey Bromiley has made a unique contribution to the theology of our time. Through his research, teaching, writing, and translating, the church has been immeasurably enriched. His interests embrace a wide span; yet common to them all is a concern for the fundamental theme of theology—the interpretation of the Word of God in Scripture in the light of the wisdom of the ages. I offer this study as a modest contribution to that endeavor. In it I seek to combine historical and systematic theology with biblical exegesis in an attempt to elucidate part of a verse in Matthew's Gospel. My study is divided into two parts. In the first part I shall take note of different interpretations that have been put forward in the course of the church's history, and in the second part I shall offer an alternative interpretation, drawing on insights noted in the course of the review.

I. INTERPRETATIONS OF MATT 16:18c

In reviewing interpretations of "the gates of hell" we shall look first at Protestant and Catholic theology and then at critical exegesis.

A. Protestant and Catholic Theology

1. The Protestant Tradition

The 1611 Authorized Version of the Bible gives the following translation of Matt 16:18: "And I say also unto thee, That thou art Peter, and upon this rock I will build my church; and the gates of hell shall not prevail against it." In giving this rendering King James's translators were following in the footsteps of William Tyndale whose 1534 version of the New Testament reads: "And the gates of hell shall not prevayle ageynst it"—a promise which gave hope, solace, and encouragement to many in the anxious days of the sixteenth century.

The Protestant Reformers saw in the verse a promise that the church would survive the attacks of its enemies both human and superhuman. In his sermon "Of the Holy Catholic Church" Heinrich Bullinger called it "a saying which is indeed a great comfort to the faithful in so many and so great persecutions intended to the utter destruction and overthrow of the Church."[1] Luther appealed to the text on numerous occasions. Typical of his treatment are his comments in his treatise *On the Councils and the Church* (1539). Christ, he declared, will find ways to

---

1. This sermon was the first of the fifth of Bullinger's *Decades* (1551). The translation is that of Geoffrey Bromiley in his edition of *Zwingli and Bullinger: Selected Translations* (LCC 24; London/Philadelphia: SCM and Westminster, 1953) 294. Bullinger goes on to warn against the assaults of Satan and of those in his power.

preserve the church against emperors, kings, and the raging of "a whole world of devils."[2]

But if the church is to perish, then Christ, upon whom it is built as upon a rock against the gates of hell [Matt 16:18], must perish first. If Christ is to perish, then God himself, who has established this rock and foundation, must perish first. Who would have suspected these lords to have such great power that the church, together with Christ and God himself, should perish so easily before their threats? They must be far, far mightier than the gates of hell and all devils, against whom the church has prevailed and must prevail.[3]

Calvin's treatment was less rhetorical, but it followed the same basic line. In his *Harmonia Evangelica* (1555), he took the passage to mean that "the church will stand victorious against all the weapons of the underworld *[omnes inferorum machinas]*." He pondered the question whether the word *it* in the phrase "shall not prevail against it" referred to faith or the church, eventually concluding in favor of the latter.

Against all the power of Satan the strength of the church will stand unvanquished: that is because the truth of God, on which its faith stands, will remain for ever unshaken. And to this thought corresponds that of John: "This is the victory which conquers the world, your faith" (1 John 5:4). This promise is especially worthy of note, that whoever are united to Christ and recognize him as Christ and mediator will remain to the end secure from all harm. For what is said of the body of the church applies to its individual members, insofar as they are one in Christ. However, we are warned by this that, as long as the church shall continue as a pilgrim on earth, it will know very little quiet but will be exposed to many assaults. The reason why it is denied that Satan will be victorious is that Christ will continually be opposed to him. Therefore, relying on this word of Christ, we securely exult against Satan and already by faith triumph over all his forces. Thus let us know that, as if summoned by the trumpet signal, we should always be ready and prepared for battle. The word *gates* no doubt denotes any kind of power and fortification.[4]

---

2. *Luther's Works* (ed. E. W. Gritsch; Philadelphia: Fortress, 1966) 41.10. See also Luther's *Evangelien-Auslegung* (ed. Erwin Mühlhaupt, 3d ed.; Göttingen: Vandenhoeck & Ruprecht, n.d.) 2.535, where Luther includes the papacy in the powers of the gates of hell.

3. *Luther's Works*, 41.12. In his treatise *The Keys* (1530) Luther declared that "the pope's church" was "an uncertain, vacillating and tottering church. Indeed, it is a deceitful, lying church, doubting and unbelieving, without God's Word." Therefore, it could not be the church to whom the promise of Matt 16:18 was made. See *Luther's Works* (ed. C. Bergendoff; Philadelphia: Muhlenberg, 1958) 40.348. In his *Instructions for the Visitors of Parish Pastors in Electoral Saxony* (1528) Luther declared that "There is no point of Christian doctrine which can make or bring greater joy to sincere souls than this by which we know that God wishes to rule over and protect us, as Christ has promised in Matt. 16[:18]: 'The gates of hell shall not prevail against it.'" See ibid., 304.

4. Author's translation from *Ioannis Calvini Opera Quae Supersunt Omnia* (ed. J. W. Baum, E. Cunitz, and E. Reuss; Brunswick: Schwetschke, 1891) 45.474.

In more recent days Karl Barth's interpretation echoes the Reformed tradition of understanding this passage, though without the reference to Satan.

Neither the wise and powerful of this world, nor the weak forms of Christianity itself, will succeed in setting a term to the community before its time is up and it has attained its goal. In spite of every opposing force it will always still be there, or be there again; and in some hidden way it will always be as young as in the first days, mounting up with wings as eagles. The gates of the underworld (Matt 16:18) will open up powerfully against it, but will not in fact swallow it up.[5]

These remarks occur in the course of a discussion on the Holy Spirit and the upbuilding of the Christian community. In typical fashion, Barth warns that it is not the community that will save itself through reliance upon its customs and traditions. It is because Christ is present in his community, not only as letter but as Spirit and Life, that "the gates of hell cannot swallow it up." "He, as the *totus Christus,* cannot die. That is why the community of His harassed and anxious saints also cannot die."[6]

2. The Catholic Tradition

If we compare the Reformed tradition of understanding this text with that of the early church and the Roman Catholic Church certain similarities and certain differences quickly emerge. Origen argued that the promises which initially applied to Peter in this passage could also be extended to others.

Anyone who is a Peter sees this; for Peter was capable of having the Church built upon him by the Logos and attained such ability that no gate of hell could prevail against him; the Logos lifted him from the gates of death that he might proclaim all the praises of God in the gates of the daughter of Zion.[7]

Alongside patristic expressions of confidence in the ultimate triumph of the church may be heard allusions to the institutional church. To Cyprian the words of Matt 16:18-19 conclusively established the indivisible unity of the Catholic church and at the same time presented a warning against the dangers of schism. The extant text of his *De ecclesiae catholicae unitate* (251) presents two versions of his teaching. In the so-called "Primacy Text" Cyprian declared that "a primacy is given to Peter, and it is (thus) made clear that there is but one Church and one Chair." He went on to ask if anyone deserts the Chair of Peter, "Has he still confidence that he is in the Church?" In the second version, in which he downplayed the importance of the papacy, Cyprian stressed the "equal dignity and power" of the apostles and proceeded to ask, "If a man does not hold fast to this

---

5. Barth, *Church Dogmatics* (tr. G. W. Bromiley; Edinburgh: T. & T. Clark, 1958) 4/2, 673.
6. Ibid., 4/2, 675.
7. Origen, *Contra Celsum* (tr. Henry Chadwick; Cambridge: Cambridge University Press, 1953) 6.77, 391; see also *Comm. in Matt.* 12, 32.

oneness of the Church, does he imagine that he still holds the faith?"[8] This led to the dire warning:

> Whoever breaks with the Church and enters on an adulterous union, cuts himself off from the promises made to the Church; and he who has turned his back on the church of Christ shall not come to the rewards of Christ; he is an alien, a worldling, an enemy. You cannot have God for your Father if you do not have the Church for your mother.[9]

In short, as Cyprian expressed it elsewhere, *salus extra ecclesiam non est.*[10]

But schism was not the only danger which confronted the early church. There was also the peril of succumbing to heresy. Commenting on the Latin text *Et portae inferi non praeualebunt aduersus eam,* Jerome observed:

> I myself judge the gates of hell *[portas inferi]* to be vices and sins or at least the doctrines of heretics by which men are enticed and drawn to the infernal regions *[tartarum].* Therefore let no one think that this is said of death, and that the apostles were not subject to death, whose martyrdom shines forth in splendor.[11]

In his comments on the passage, Hilary developed the theme of Peter as the celestial gatekeeper to whom judgment on earth had been committed. As the rock, Peter was the chosen foundation of the church which

> will break the laws of hell and the gates of Tartarus and all the confines of death. O blessed gatekeeper of heaven, to whose judgment are given the keys of access to eternity, whose judgment on earth will be the already decided authority in heaven, so that what on earth is bound or loosed will obtain also in heaven the condition of the same statute.[12]

The patristic comments designed to illuminate the understanding of the Gospels which Thomas Aquinas assembled in his *Catena aurea* (1262–1267) amplify the themes of temptation, oppression, and eventual triumph.[13] But a passage which Thomas attributed to Cyril further developed the twin themes of the gates as heretical error and Peter and his successors as the spotless guardians of the church.

8. Cyprian, *De ecclesiae catholicae unitate* 4, cited from *The Lapsed and The Unity of the Catholic Church* (tr. Maurice Bevenot, ACW 25; Westminster, Md./London: Newman and Longmans, Green, 1957) 46-47.

9. Cyprian, *De ecclesiae* 6, ACW 25.48-49.

10. Cyprian, *Ep.* 73, 21; cf. Augustine, *De baptismo contra Donatistas* 4, 17, 24.

11. Jerome, *Commentariorum in Evangelium Matthaei Liber* 3; tr. from *Commentaire sur S. Matthieu, Texte Latin* (ed. Emile Bonnard, SC 259; Paris: Éditions du Cerf, n.d.) 2.16. The pagan Porphyrius (d. ca. 304) appears to have taken the text as a promise that Peter would not die (cf. J. Jeremias, *TDNT* 6. 926n.52).

12. Hilary, *Commentarius in Evangelium Matthaei* 16,7; cited from Hilaire de Poitiers, *Sur Matthieu, Texte Critique* (ed. Jean Digon, SC 258; Paris: Éditions du Cerf, 1979) 2. 54.

13. Thomas Aquinas, Eng. tr. *Catena Aurea: Commentary on the Four Gospels, Collected out of the Works of the Fathers* (Oxford/London: John Henry Parker and J. G. F. and J. Rivington, 1841) 1/2. 585-86. Thomas cited Hilary, Jerome, Origen, Rabanus Maurus and a writer whom he mistakenly thought to be Cyril of Alexandria.

According to this promise of the Lord, the Apostolic Church of Peter remains pure and spotless from all leading into error, or heretical fraud, above all Heads and Bishops and Primates of Churches and people, with its own Pontiffs, with most abundant faith, and the authority of Peter. And while other Churches have to blush for the error of some of their members, this reigns alone immoveably established, enforcing silence, and stopping the mouths of all heretics; and we, not drunken with the wine of pride, confess together with it the type of truth, and of the holy apostolic tradition.[14]

For our present purposes, this pronouncement's lack of authenticity is of less significance than the fact that Thomas and his contemporaries believed that it represented a valid, patristic interpretation.[15] Already in a letter addressed to Michael Cerularius, Pope Leo IX had assured the patriarch that, since the holy church had been built upon the rock of Christ and Peter, it would never be overcome "by the gates of Hell, that is, by the disputations of heretics which lead the vain to destruction."[16] In the sixteenth century, the Council of Trent appealed to the promise "that the gates of Hell will never prevail" in its endorsement of the Niceno-Constantinopolitan Creed.[17] In the nineteenth century the First Vatican Council drew on the passage as it laid the foundations for the definition of the dogma of papal primacy and infallibility. Citing Matt 16:16-19 and John 1:21 and 21:15 and 17, the Council declared that "according to the testimonies of the Gospel the primacy of jurisdiction over the entire Church was promised and was conferred immediately and directly upon the blessed Apostle Peter by Christ the Lord."[18] From there the Council proceeded to amplify its teaching concerning the continuation of Peter's primacy in the Roman pontiffs, the power and nature of that primacy, and the infallible teaching authority of the Roman pontiff.

3. Common Factors in the Protestant and Catholic Traditions

If we pause for a moment to reflect on the interpretations that we have noted so far, it is apparent that they display both a diversity and a unity. The Reformed tradition sees in the text an assurance of the eventual triumph of the church over

14. Ibid.

15. It is now recognized that the *Liber Thesaurorum* is a forgery. Unfortunately Thomas drew heavily on it, not only in the *Catena aurea* but also in his *Contra Errores Graecorum* and *Summa Theologiae*. Cf. H. Burn-murdoch, *The Development of the Papacy* (London: Faber & Faber, 1954) 345-47, cf. 363; Hans Küng, *Infallible? An Inquiry* (London: Collins, 1971) 95-98; James A. Weisheipl, *Friar Thomas D'Aquino: His Life, Thought and Works* (2d ed.; Washington, D.C.: Catholic University of America, 1983) 168-73. Thomas's use of the work had far-reaching influence in the development of papal claims.

16. Leo IX, *In terra pax hominibus* 7 (1053); cf. *The Sources of Catholic Dogma* (tr. R. J. Deferrari from the 30th ed. of Denzinger's *Enchiridion Symbolorum;* St. Louis/London: B. Herder, 1957) nos. 351, 142. It is questionable whether the letter was actually delivered. It is omitted from Adolfus Schönmetzer's edition of Denzinger's *Enchiridion Symbolorum Definitionum et Declarationum de Rebus Fidei et Morum* (Barcelona/Rome/London: Freiburg i.B. and Herder, 1963).

17. Council of Trent, Session 3, Feb. 4, 1546. See Deferrari, *Sources,* no. 782; DS no. 1500.

18. *Constitutio dogmatica I de Ecclesia Christi,* Session 4, July 18, 1870, cap. 1. See Deferrari, *Sources,* no. 1822; DS no. 3053.

its enemies. The opposition may be human or superhuman. It may even include oppression of Protestants by Catholics. But the ultimate triumph of the true church is assured. The Catholic tradition likewise sees in the text a warning of tribulation and the promise of final victory to the Catholic Church. The opponents of the church may be supernatural, but they may also take the form of schismatics and heretics who seek to lead the faithful astray. On the face of it the two traditions of interpretation stand in diametrical opposition. Nevertheless, they share a common method, for both traditions approach the text by means of *a hermeneutic without exegesis*. None of the interpretations that we have noted so far have paused to ask what "the gates of hell" might mean in the linguistic, cultural, and religious context of their setting. The various interpreters have assumed that the mention of hell in the text somehow implies dire attacks on the church. The actual nature of the attacks and the identity of the attackers were determined not by exegesis of the text but by a hermeneutic which reflected on the nature of the opposition which the church happened to find itself threatened by at any given time in its history. Thus, "the gates of hell" could represent persecution in a time of persecution, schism at a time when the organic unity of the church was threatened, and heresy when the faith of the church was being undermined by heterodox teaching. Such interpretations represent extended applications of the text, but they do not carry us very far in determining the meaning of the text in the context of Matthew's Gospel.

B. Critical Exegesis

Critical exegesis in the last hundred years has endeavored to make good the shortcomings of the dogmatic interpretations of the text by determining its meaning in the light of the beliefs of the ancient world, the contextual background of Judaism, and the critical analysis of Matthew's Gospel. The conflicting interpretations both call in question and confirm the broad positions that have already been noted. In attempting to evaluate these interpretations I shall look first at certain general background considerations, then at various rival proposals, and finally at the question of authenticity.

1. General Background Considerations

The starting point for any exact determination of the meaning of Matt 16:18c must be the Greek text: *kai pylai hadou ou katischysousin autēs*. The RSV gives an interpretative rendering: "and the powers of death shall not prevail against it." However, as a footnote in the RSV indicates, a more literal translation of *pylai hadou* is "gates of Hades." But this raises rather than settles the question as to what precisely is meant by the "gates of Hades."

In the LXX the Greek word *hadēs* (Hades) occurs more than one hundred times, in most instances to translate the Hebrew *š^{e'}ôl* (Sheol), the underworld which receives the dead. Numerous scholars have drawn attention to the fact that the expression *pylai hadou* is to be found in earlier Jewish writings.[19] It occurs in the OT where King Hezekiah looks back on an apparently mortal sickness.

19. See Str-B, 1. 736; 4/2.1087-90 for rabbinic views; Adolf Schlatter, *Der Evangelist Matthäus. Seine Sprache, sein Ziel, seine Selbstständigkeit* (6th ed.; Stuttgart: Calwer Verlag, 1963) 509; Joachim Jeremias, *hadēs*, in *TDNT* 1 (1964) 146-49 (see esp. 148); idem, *pylē, pylōn, TDNT* 6 (1968) 921-28 (see esp. 924-25).

I said, In the noontide of my days
I must depart;
I am consigned to the gates of Sheol
[MT $b^e\check{s}a^{'a}r\hat{e}\ \check{s}^{e'}\hat{o}l$; LXX *en pylais hadou*]
for the rest of my years. (Isa 38:10)

In the Wisdom of Solomon the Lord is acknowledged as the one who is the healer of all things. He has "power over life and death"; he leads down "to the gates of Hades *[eis pylas hadou]*" and leads up again (Wis 16:13). But once the soul is in Hades, there is no release. 3 Maccabees tells of an impending massacre of Jews, and it describes the prayers of the assembled Jews who were standing "at the gates of Hades *[pros pylais hadou]*" (3 Macc 5:51). Similarly the author of the Psalms of Solomon recalls that for a moment his soul was poured out to death; he was "near the gates of Hades *[synengys pylōn hadou]* with the sinner" (*Pss. Sol.* 16:2). In each of these instances the expression is anarthrous, just as it is in Matt 16:18. Joachim Jeremias is doubtless correct in ascribing the absence of the definite article to the construct state of the underlying Hebrew $\check{s}a^{'a}r\hat{e}\ \check{s}^{e'}\hat{o}l$, and thus in seeing the term as a Semitism.[20] Hence "the gates of hell" are more accurately to be thought of as "the gates of Hades," and more strictly still as "the gates of Sheol." If the usage in Matt 16:18 corresponds to that in the above instances, then the expression denotes a way of speaking about death and dying.

In the intertestamental literature that we have just noted the term "gates of Hades" appears to be preferred to the older OT term "gates of death" (see Pss 9:13; 107:18; Job 38:17, where it also stands in parallel with "the gates of deep darkness"). Job 17:16 sets in parallel the expressions "go down to the bars of Sheol" and "descend . . . to the dust." If there is any substantial difference in the terminology it would appear to lie in the imagery evoked by its mention of Hades or Sheol.[21]

The OT allusions to "the gates of Sheol" and "the gates of death" suggest that Sheol was thought of (metaphorically at least) as a building or a city.[22] It also had the aspect of a pit or prison from which there was no escape (Pss 88:3-12; 107:10, 16; 142:7; Lam 3:6-9).[23] To be saved from this prison was to be saved from death. In the passages that we have noted so far, with the possible exception of Job 38:17,[24] the expression "gates of Hades/Sheol/death" denotes the one-

20. J. Jeremias, *TDNT* 6 (1968) 926.

21. Among those who see no material difference between the terms are Theodor Zahn, *Das Evangelium des Matthäus* (3d ed.; Leipzig: A. Deichert, 1910) 547, and Joachim Jeremias, *TDNT* 6 (1968) 924.

22. Nicholas J. Tromp, *Primitive Conceptions of Death and the Nether World in the Old Testament* (BibOr 21; Rome: Pontifical Biblical Institute, 1969) 152-54.

23. Ibid., 154-56.

24. Job 38:17 may be an instance of metonymy in which "gates of death" stands for death. However, a different interpretation to which David Allan Hubbard drew my attention appears to be much more likely. The context strongly suggests a parallel between "gates of death" and "gates of darkness." The overall context of the passage challenges Job on the mysteries of light and darkness. The picture probably has to do with the daily rising and setting of the sun under the world. There may well also be oblique references to pagan deities, like Mot and Tiamat, and a reminder of the inscrutability of the underworld in the light of Job's earlier comments on Sheol (Job 3:16-19; 10:21-22; 14:13-15; 17:11-16).

way entrance to the realm of the dead from which there is no return. Thus to be near these gates is to be dying. Or to put it in a modern idiom, to be at these gates is to be "at death's door." It is only when we look beyond the thought-world of OT imagery to later Judaism and more broadly at the thought-world of antiquity that we encounter more elaborate ideas.

Before we look at them, however, it is worthwhile to note certain other OT passages which may prove relevant to a better understanding of Matt 16:18. The psalm in the book of Jonah depicts the prophet crying "out of the belly of Sheol" (Jonah 2:2).[25]

> Then I said, "I am cast out
>   from thy presence;
> how shall I again look
>   upon thy holy temple?"
> The waters closed in over me,
>   the deep was round about me;
> weeds were wrapped about my head
>   at the roots of the mountains.
> I went down to the land
>   whose bars closed upon me for ever
> yet thou didst bring up my life from the Pit,
>   O LORD my God.
> When my soul fainted within me,
>   I remembered the LORD;
> and my prayer came to thee,
>   into thy holy temple. (Jonah 2:4-7)

Also relevant, in view of the significance of the "rock" in Matt 16:18, are those OT passages which speak of God as the rock who redeems, saves, and gives life (Deut 32:31, 37; Pss 18:2ff.; 62:2; 71:3f., 20; 78:35; 95:1).[26] Ps 27:4f. and perhaps Ps 61:2 contain an allusion to the temple rock on which the temple was built. Either implicitly or explicitly there hovers in the background the threat of death.

Ancient literature provides contrasting descriptions of the underworld. In Greek mythology Orpheus descended into the underworld in order to rescue his wife Eurydice.[27] In one form of the story the lord of the underworld grants permission for her return on condition that Orpheus not turn around to see if she was following before reaching the upper world. But in general there is no return for those who pass through the gates. Virgil describes the columns of adamant of the gates of the underworld.[28] A series of gates are found in the Mesopotamian account of the descent of Istar into the nether world which is a gloomy "Land of no Return."[29]

25. On the psalm see Duane L. Christensen, "The Song of Jonah: A Metrical Analysis," *JBL* 104 (1985) 217-31.

26. See N. J. Tromp, *Primitive Conceptions,* 205-7.

27. See W. K. C. Guthrie, *Orpheus and Greek Religion: A Study of the Orphic Movement* (2d ed.; London: Methuen, 1952) 29ff.

28. *Aeneid* 6.551; see also Homer, *Iliad* 5.646; 9.312; *Odyssey* 14.156; Aeschylus, *Agamemnon* 1291.

29. *ANET,* 106-9.

Egyptian writings also describe numerous gates through which the dead pass.[30] Here, however, it is not the gates which pose a threat but the gatekeepers, who are usually demoniacal beings who desire to hurt or kill those who pass through. By using the right powerful charm, however, one may pass through. The texts which deal with the gates provide the necessary knowledge in order to reach one's final destiny with Re in the heavens or in the realm of Osiris.

Slavonic Enoch 42:1A describes how Enoch saw "the guardians of the keys of hell, standing by the very large doors, their faces like those of very large snakes, their eyes like extinguished lamps, and their teeth naked down to their breasts." Slavonic Enoch 42:1J calls them "the guards of the gates of hell." References to more than one gate in Jewish writings raise the question of a distinction between intermediate and final states. In rabbinic literature the expression "gates of Sheol" occurs only in the *Targum of Isaiah* 38:10. This may well be due to the fact that from the middle of the first century A.D. Sheol came to be replaced by Gehenna in rabbinic thought, and the rabbis speak of the entrance(s) or gates of Gehenna.[31]

In the NT Gehenna is depicted as a fiery abyss (Matt 5:22; Mark 9:43-48). It is a place of judgment prepared *for* the devil and his angels to which the accursed are sent (Matt 25:41). It is a place of destruction, where God destroys both body and soul of the condemned (Matt 10:28). The hypocritical scribes and Pharisees are said to be sons of Gehenna (Matt 23:15). They will be sentenced to Gehenna for shedding the blood of the prophets (Matt 23:33). The allusions to *hadēs* in Matt 11:23, Luke 10:15, and Luke 16:23 suggest that *hadēs* has here also assumed the aspect of the place of judgment and perdition.

It would take us too far afield to examine the concept of the foundation-stone in rabbinic thought.[32] R. J. McKelvey contends that "the foundation-stone of Isa 28:16 was developed into an all-embracing tradition. The stone in Zion is foundation not only of the temple but of the universe. It is as much a psychological and theological as a geographical phenomenon. From this stone creation grows and draws its life. Here the destinies of the living and the dead are fixed. Here too the new world will emerge."[33] Although we cannot explore this idea, attention may be drawn to the thought of Jerusalem as the site of one of the entrances of Gehenna. In this regard, note the Babylonian Talmud tractate 'Erubin, which deals with sabbath regulations. In the course of a discussion of rebels and transgressors the following observation is made:

> R. Jeremiah b. Eleazar further stated: Gehenna has three gates; one in the wilderness, one in the sea and one in Jerusalem. "In the wilderness", since it is written in Scripture, *So they, and all that appertaineth to them, went down alive to the pit.* "In the sea", since it is written in Scripture, *Out of the belly of the nether world cried I, and Thou heardest my voice.* "In Jerusalem", since it is

---

30. Jan Zandee, *Death as an Enemy according to Egyptian Conceptions* (Studies in the History of Religions [Supplements to Numen] 5; Leiden: E. J. Brill, 1960) 114-25.

31. J. Jeremias, *TDNT* 6 (1968) 925.

32. For a brief survey see R. J. McKelvey, *The New Temple: The Church in the New Testament* (Oxford: Oxford University Press, 1969) 189-92.

33. Ibid., 192.

written in Scripture, *Saith the Lord, whose fire is in Zion, and his furnace in Jerusalem,* and the school of R. Ishmael taught: *"Whose fire is in Zion"* refers to Gehenna, *"And His furnace in Jerusalem"* refers to the gate of Gehenna.[34]

The first of the three OT allusions made here is to Num 16:33, which describes the fate of those who followed the rebellious Korah. The second of the allusions occurs in Jonah 2:2 in the verse immediately preceding the passage cited above from the psalm in Jonah. The third allusion is to Isa 31:9, which in the RSV reads:

> "His rock shall pass away in terror,
>   and his officers desert the standard in panic,"
> says the LORD, whose fire is in Zion,
>   and whose furnace is in Jerusalem.

There appears to be no consensus among contemporary OT scholars as to the precise meaning of this passage in Isaiah. It has been linked with the cult[35] and also with apocalyptic ideas.[36] In general it appears to be associated with the idea of the Holy One as a fire which consumes all evil and who dwells in Jerusalem (Gen 15:17; Isa 6:6-7; 10:12, 16-17; Zech 2:5; Mal 4:1). But in particular, it may refer to the association of Gehenna with Ge Hinnom, the valley south of Jerusalem, which came to be associated with eschatological judgment.[37]

2. Rival Interpretations

In the light of these somewhat diffuse general background considerations it is not surprising that conflicting interpretations of Matt 16:18 have been put forward. I shall now try to identify different types of interpretation and comment on them as I go along.

(1) *Christ's Descent into Hell as a Rescue Mission.* The eminent history of religions scholar, Wilhelm Bousset, saw Matt 16:18 as one of a number of NT passages which indicated "even if only in fragments, the strong popular and mythological conceptions of the struggle of Christ with the powers of the underworld, conceptions of which the theologoumenon of the preaching in Hades is only a feeble reminiscence."[38] Bousset took the text to mean that the gates of Hades will not be able to restrain those who lie on the other side of them. "The company

---

34. 'Erubin 19a, cited from I. Epstein, ed., *The Babylonian Talmud: Seder Mo'ed* (London: Soncino, 1938) 3. 130.

35. Georg Fohrer, *Das Buch Jesaja,* Zürcher Bibelkommentare (Zürich-Stuttgart: Zwingli-Verlag, 1962) 2. 118.

36. Otto Kaiser, *Isaiah 13–39* (The Old Testament Library; Philadelphia: Westminster, 1974) 318.

37. Hans Bietenard, *gehenna,* in C. Brown, ed., *The New International Dictionary of New Testament Theology* (Grand Rapids: Zondervan, 1976) 2.208. Cf. *Eth. Enoch* 27:1ff.; 54:1ff.; 56:3f.; 90:26f.; 2 Esd 7:36; *Syr. Bar.* 59:10; 85:13; *Sib. Or.* 1:103.

38. Wilhelm Bousset, *Kyrios Christos: A History of the Belief in Christ from the Beginnings of Christianity to Irenaeus* (tr. John E. Steely; Nashville/New York: Abingdon, 1970) 65. Bousset found further support for his view in the allusion to the keys of Death and Hades in Rev 1:18, the use of Ps 68:18 in Eph 4:9, and the mention of the appearance of the awakened dead in Matt 27:52-53.

of the righteous who have fallen asleep also belongs to the ecclesia triumphans. The gates of Hades are opened and they no longer hinder passage to freedom."[39] However, Bousset went on to say that "It really can no longer be doubted that these popular conceptions of Christ's journey into hell and of his struggle with the demons of the underworld contain a myth which originally had nothing to do with the person of Jesus but only later has been adapted to him."[40]

Despite his admiration for Bousset, Rudolf Bultmann found this interpretation untenable on the grounds that,

> apart from the fact that the descent into Hades is nowhere hinted at in the text, it is not possible to see any connection between the bursting of the gates of Hades by Christ's descent into hell and the phrase *ou katischysousin:* the Church has not been imprisoned in Hades! Indeed it is not so much as on the way there (*oikodomēsō* fut.)![41]

Bultmann went on to grant the feasibility of Schlatter's view (which we shall note under the third interpretation below). Members of the church are not promised deathlessness but resurrection. Nevertheless, Bultmann too was skeptical about the authenticity of the passage. Despite the Semitic character of the saying and thus its feasibility as an utterance of Jesus, Bultmann believed that it was an utterance of the Palestinian church which expressed "its eschatological consciousness of being the eschatological community of the Just."[42]

I shall comment on the question of authenticity later on. For the present it must simply be said that Bultmann is correct in noting that Matthew's Gospel contains no hint of a descent into hell of the kind envisaged by Bousset. The idea of such a rescue mission appears to belong to a later age.[43] Bousset's argument requires

39. Ibid.

40. Ibid., 66.

41. Rudolf Bultmann, *The History of the Synoptic Tradition* (rev. ed., tr. John Marsh; Oxford: Basil Blackwell, 1972) 139.

42. Ibid., 139f.

43. It is far from certain that such a mission is the intended meaning of 1 Pet 3:19, and there is nothing in the context of Matthew which warrants reading this interpretation into our text. The explicit idea of a rescue mission was not developed until a much later date. In an allusion to Ps 107:16 Tertullian declares that Christ has "broken the adamantine gates of death and the brazen bars of the underworld" (*De Resurrectione Mortuorum* 44). The language is evocative of Virgil's description of the columns of adamant of the gates of the underworld (*Aeneid* 6.551; cf. also Athanasius, *De Virginitate* 16). But in context Tertullian is speaking of Christ's resurrection. For accounts of Christ's activity in the underworld we have to turn to pseudepigraphal and apocryphal literature. The Odes of Solomon 42 puts into the mouth of Christ an account of how the dead ran to Christ imploring him to open the door for them (see also Odes 17 and 22; J. H. Charlesworth, ed., *Pseudepigrapha* [Garden City, N.Y.: Doubleday, 1985] 2.750f., 754f., 770f.). The Gospel of Nicodemus gives a vivid account of the trembling of the warders, the dismay of Hades and Satan, and Hades's vain attempt to have the demons make fast "the gates of brass and bars of iron." In response to a thunderous voice which cites Ps 24:7 (23:7 LXX), the gates are broken and the king of glory enters (5.25); E. Hennecke and W. Schneemelcher, eds., *New Testament Apocrypha* (London: Lutterworth, 1963) 1.743f. For further discussion of Christ's descent into hell see J. A. MacCulloch, *The Harrowing of Hell: A Comparative Study of an Early Christian Doctrine* (Edinburgh: T. & T. Clark, 1930) 217-26; Paul Althaus, "Niedergefahren zur Hölle," *ZST* 19 (1942) 365-84; Aloys Grillmeier, "Der Gottessohn im Totenreich," *ZKT* 71 (1949) 1-53, 184-203; Joachim Jeremias, "Zwischen Karfreitag und Ostern: Descensus

us to read into the text a mythological interpretation derived from extraneous sources and then to deny that Jesus himself could have entertained such views.

(2) *Exemption from Death.* In view of the saying in Matt 16:28 that "there are some standing here who will not taste death before they see the Son of man coming in his kingdom," Matt 16:18 has been taken as a promise that Peter personally is promised resurrection or exemption from death before the parousia.[44] However, the latter suggestion involves an emendation of the text.[45] Moreover, the imagery of the passage suggests that the gates are something which the church will pass through. The mention of Jesus' own violent death in Matt 16:21, the call to take up one's cross (16:24), and the saying about willingness to lose one's life (16:25) all suggest that the church is not promised exemption from death in the passage as it stands in the Gospel.[46] Rather, death is a reality that the church will encounter and triumph over.

(3) *Triumph over Death.* A number of scholars ha•e stressed that Sheol is not the same as "hell" in later Christian thought. In the passages noted above it is clear that Sheol is the abode of the dead. It is not the same as Gehenna, though in later thought Gehenna became a section of Sheol and in rabbinic tradition Gehenna eventually supplanted Sheol. None of the passages that we have noted give the impression that Sheol/Hades is the habitat of Satan and the powers of evil. Consequently, the basic thought of the passage is the promise of triumph over death. In his article on *hadēs* in *TDNT* Joachim Jeremias suggested that the passage is to be understood

> in terms of the ancient oriental and biblical cosmology according to which the underworld, located in the hollow earth, is enclosed by sacred cliffs. . . . In virtue of the promise of Jesus His community knows that it is secure from the powers of Hades . . . because by faith in Him it has access to the kingdom of

und Ascensus in der Karfreitagstheologie des Neuen Testaments," *ZNW* 42 (1949) 194-201; J. N. D. Kelly, *Early Christian Creeds* (3d ed.; London: Longman, 1972) 378-83; G. B. Caird, "The Descent of Christ in Ephesians 4,7-11," in F. L. Cross, ed., *SE* 2, TU 87 (1964) 535-45; E. G. Selwyn, *The First Epistle of Saint Peter* (2d ed.; London: Macmillan, 1947) 314-62; Werner Bieder, *Die Vorstellung von der Höllenfahrt Jesu Christi: Beitrag zur Entstehungsgeschichte der Vorstellung vom sog. Descensu ad infernos* (*Abhandlungen zur Theologie des Alten und Neuen Testaments* 19; Zürich: Zwingli-Verlag, 1949) esp. 43-48.

44. See Adolf von Harnack, "Der Spruch über Petrus als den Felsen der Kirche, Matt. XVI, 17f.," SPAW 32 (1918) 637-54; cf. also F. Kattenbusch, "Der Spruch über Petrus und die Kirche bei Matthäus," *TSK* 94 (1922) 97f. See also the literature noted by J. Jeremias in *TDNT* 6 (1968) 926. Some early interpreters took the view that it was a promise that Peter would not die before the parousia.

45. On Harnack's view the passage was a personal promise to Peter which in effect was: "You are Peter, and death will not conquer you." The reading of *sou* instead of *autēs* was traced to Tatian's *Diatessaron*. For literature discussing this question see Oscar Cullmann, *Peter—Disciple, Apostle, Martyr: A Historical and Theological Study* (2d ed.; London: SCM, 1962) 171.

46. Support for this interpretation is claimed from the fact that the gates of death/Hades in Isa 38:10; Pss 9:13; 107:18; Sir 51:9; *Pss. Sol.* 16:2; 3 Macc 5:51 all refer to being preserved from death. But these passages speak of being brought near to the gates, whereas in Matt the imagery seems to imply passing through them.

God. . . . In particular it knows that its dead are not in Hades, but in the presence of Christ.[47]

Adolf Schlatter observed that the thought in Matt 16:18 is hardly that of Hades sweeping people along like a stream through its open gates. The notion of a stream does not easily fit with the notion of gates. Nor is it likely that the promise is one of the exemption from having to pass through the gates of Hades. "The thought is more likely to be that even the disciples and those gathered by them to be the community of Jesus are destined to die and go through the gates; they are indeed 'the bearers of crosses'."[48] But this gives rise to the question, whether when Christ appears and calls his own the gates will be strong enough to contain those who were obedient to him unto death. The community is not promised immunity from death or immortality but resurrection. This, argues Schlatter, fits the context of the following verses, where Jesus not only predicts his own impending death and resurrection, but also warns would-be followers of their need to be willing to lose their lives for his sake (Matt 16:21-28). Similar interpretations have been put forward by other commentators on Matthew, including Erich Klostermann,[49] David Hill,[50] Robert H. Gundry,[51] and Rudolf Schnackenburg.[52] This line of interpretation seems to me to point in the right direction. My own proposal seeks to develop it still further. However, it should be noted that this view has not gone unchallenged.

(4) *Triumph over the Powers of Evil.* A number of modern scholars have restated in different ways the traditional view that the "gates of Hades" represents assaults upon the church by diverse powers of evil. The Catholic scholar, Ceslaus Spicq writes:

> One could understand that death (Hades) will not overtake the city of God, and that Christ guarantees to Peter the immortality of his church. But gates being symbolism for military and civil force, it is more normal to understand "the gates of hell" in the sense of infernal power vainly struggling against the kingdom of God on earth. That is to say, before being the sojourn of the damned, hell is the city of evil, the kingdom of Satan, the enemy of Christ and the prince of this world. Hell, according to the Gospel, is the place of demons to whom will be added perverse men excluded from paradise.[53]

The weakness of this interpretation is indicated by the fact the sole text cited in support is Matt 25:41, which does not depict hell as the city of evil, the infernal

47. Jeremias, *TDNT* 1 (1964) 148f.

48. Schlatter, *Der Evangelist Matthäus*, 509.

49. Klostermann, *Das Matthäusevangelium* (HNT 4, 4th ed.; Tübingen: J. C. B. Mohr [Paul Siebeck], 1971) 140.

50. Hill, *The Gospel of Matthew* (New Century Bible; London: Oliphants, 1972) 261-62.

51. Gundry, *Matthew: A Commentary on his Literary and Theological Art* (Grand Rapids: Eerdmans, 1982) 335. In view of the prominence given to martyrdom in Matt and 1QH 6:24-29, Gundry thinks that "'the gates of Hades' particularly represent death by martyrdom."

52. Schnackenburg, *Matthäusevangelium 1,1–16,20* (Die Neue Echter Bibel Neues Testament 1; Würzburg: Echter Verlag, 1985) 152. Schnackenburg likewise notes 1QH 6:24-26.

53. Quoted from Michel Carrouges, C. Spicq, G. Bardy, Ch.-V. Héris, Bernard Dorival, J. Guitton, *L'Enfer* (Paris: Editions de la Revue des Jeunes, 1950) 118.

headquarters of the powers of Satan. The "eternal fire" which the passage speaks of is prepared for the cursed, together with the devil and his angels. It is not a stronghold from which the latter make sorties in order to attack the church militant. This conception belongs to later tradition but not to Matthew's Gospel.

A more circumspect view is offered by Walter Grundmann, who maintains that

> The connection of the picture of the storming gates of Hades with that of the church built on the rock consists in that the rock of Hades shuts up and towers to heaven. At the same time in the application of the rock to Abraham a further allusion is given, for it is said of Abraham that he sits at the entrance to Gehenna and lets no circumcised man descend there. What was said of Abraham is applied to Peter: the people of God built on him will not become prey to the power of death.[54]

Grundmann was unspecific about the nature of the attack, but was confident that "the attack comes from Hades and breaks forth from its gates."[55] Similarly Bultmann envisaged the assault issuing from the gates but identified it with the woes that were to come in the end-time.[56] The idea that "the gates" indicate the attacking force has been argued by Theodor Zahn and M.-J. Lagrange. Zahn believed that the words *ou katischysousin autēs* meant that it was the gates that took the initiative in launching the assault on the church.[57] Lagrange pictured two strongholds in conflict.

> It is thus the struggle of one edifice which is the empire of evil against the Church which is the household of Christ. Satan is not named or designated more directly, nor even the infernal powers. But the gates are active; it is they which represent the city. This usage was well established in Hebrew; cf. Deut. 16:5, and especially Deut. 17:2; 1 Kings 8:37, where "gates" in Hebrew is translated by towns, and the city presupposes the king.[58]

In response to Zahn and Lagrange it must be said that their arguments fail to carry conviction. The verb *katischyō,* when followed by a genitive (as it is in Matt 16:18) means to *win a victory over, prevail over.* But the verb itself leaves open the question whether it is the attacker or the defender who wins the victory. Lagrange's argument reads into the text a train of thought that is not demanded by the text. The use of "gate" for "town" or "city" may be exemplified in NT writings by Acts 16:13 and Heb 13:12, though in neither passage could the literal sense be excluded. Moreover, in neither case does the notion of "gate" imply anything about the ruling powers in the city or suggest that the intended meaning of Mat-

---

54. *Das Evangelium nach Matthäus* (THKNT 1; Berlin: Evangelische Verlagsanstalt, 1968) 390-91, citing Str-B 1.119.

55. Ibid., 390.

56. Bultmann, *Theology of the New Testament* (tr. K. Grobel; London: SCM, 1952) 1.37; cf. H.-D. Wendland, *Die Eschatologie des Reiches Gottes bei Jesus: Eine Studie über den Zusammenhang von Eschatologie, Ethik und Kirchenproblem* (Gütersloh: C. Bertelsmann, 1931) 174-75.

57. Zahn, *Das Evangelium des Matthäus,* 548.

58. Lagrange, *Évangile selon Saint Matthieu* (8th ed.; Paris: J. Gabalda, 1948) 326.

thew is the powers of evil which exit through the gates in order to attack those on the outside.

The difficulty of wanting to identify the gates of Hades with the aggressive powers of evil was well recognized long ago by Alfred Plummer when he observed: "If aggressiveness were the prominent idea, we should hardly have the metaphor of a building with gates. Gates keep people in and keep people out, and are necessary for the strength of a citadel, but they do not fight."[59] But despite this warning, a succession of scholars have still wished to treat the passage as a prophecy of supernatural evil attacking the church.[60] To obviate the difficulty J. H. Bernard suggested that the present Greek text of Matthew represented a mistranslation.[61] He believed that the underlying imagery was that of the floods of evil beating against the rock (Ps 18; Matt 7:24; Luke 6:48; cf. Gen 7:11). He suggested that the Semitic original underlying *pylai* was not the Hebrew word for "gate" (*ša'ar*) but *ša'ar* ("storm"; cf. Isa 28:2). The difference between the two words is simply one of pointing, and the confusion is attested in Hebrew texts of Isa 28:2. Thus Bernard reconstructed the meaning of the verse as: "Upon this Rock I will build my Church and the storms of hell shall not prevail against it." In this way Bernard brought together the metaphors of the rock and the storm. But he was able to do so only at the expense of separating the gate from the keys. Moreover, his interpretation required the assumptions of a series of misunderstandings of the underlying Semitic words and also that Hades signified not the place of the dead but the bastion of the powers of evil.

More recently Robert Eppel has proposed a different emendation.[62] He suggested that the underlying Hebrew was not *ša^{a}rê* ("gates") but *šo^{a}rê* ("gatekeepers"). Thus *pylai hadou* should read *pyloroi hadou* ("gatekeepers of Hades"). Eppel further noted that this reading is found in the LXX version of Job 38:17, that *katischyō* is found in an active, aggressive sense, and that terrifying guardians of Hades are mentioned in Slavonic Enoch 42:1. Eppel concluded that Matt 16:18 contained a prophecy that "the church, which is the assembly of Christians, will be subjected to the vain assault of the demonic powers symbolised by the guardians of hell. . . . The image of the gatekeepers of hell corresponds to that of the power of the keys, conferred on Peter, gatekeeper of the realm of the heavens, and thus better illuminates the perfect unity of the logion: *Tu es*

59. Plummer, *An Exegetical Commentary on the Gospel according to S. Matthew* (London: Elliot Stock, 1909) 230.

60. Others who take this view include R. Bohren, *Das Problem der Kirchenzucht im Neuen Testament* (Zollikon-Zürich: Evangelischer Verlag, 1952) 63f.; Wilhelm Vischer, *Die evangelische Gemeindeordnung: Matthäus 16,13–20,28* (Zollikon-Zürich: Evangelischer Verlag, 1946) 20-22; Max Meinertz, *Theologie des Neuen Testaments* (Bonn: Peter Hanstein Verlag, 1950) 1.75. Vischer combines this view with that of Schlatter, and Meinertz sees the hellish underworld symbolized in the picture of death. Other views are noted by Bieder, *Der Höllenfahrt Jesu Christi*, 43-48, who, however, refuses to read into the text a reference to supernatural forces and insists that the passages refer to Jesus' own experience of death.

61. Bernard, "The Gates of Hades," *The Expositor*, 8th Ser. 11 (1916) 401-9; revised version in *Studia Sacra* (London, Hodder & Stoughton, 1917) 76-89.

62. Eppel, "L'interprétation de Matthieu 16,18b," in *Aux Sources de la Tradition Chrétienne: Mélanges offerts à M. Maurice Goguel* (Neuchatel/Paris: Delachaux & Niestlé, 1950) 71-73.

Petrus. . . ."[63] Eppel's reconstruction is ingenious, but is not without difficulties. Apart from the required emendation of the text, the interpretation presupposes that Hades is the abode of the evil powers. It also requires the "gatekeepers" to relinquish their appointed posts of guardians and assume the role of assault troops.

Alternative approaches have been proposed by Syriac experts who draw attention to the Syriac fathers and the Syriac tradition of Matt 16:18c, which reads *mûklê*—"bars" instead of "gates." One interpretation would therefore be an invasion of the realm of the dead by Christ and the church which the bars of Hades proved unable to withstand.[64] An alternative view is that *mûklê* might be a loanword from the Greek *mochlos,* meaning a "lever" or "crowbar," and that the underlying image is that of Hades, personified as a giant vainly trying to pry loose the firm rock on which the church is to be built.[65] However attractive these interpretations might be, they face the twin difficulties of showing that either of them was the original intended meaning and also of explaining how the Greek text of Matthew succeeded in obscuring the sense by introducing the idea of "gates."

In his *TDNT* article on *pylē, pylōn* Joachim Jeremias shifted somewhat from the interpretation given in his earlier article on *hadēs* (noted above in the discussion on the third interpretation). Jeremias now argued that

> The saying uses the symbol of the cosmic rock . . . which is the top of the hollow world-mountain and which has a double function, first, to support the sanctuary, and secondly, to close the underworld which is inside the mountain, which embraces the realm of the dead and the prison of the spirits, and from which the primal floods stream forth. . . .
>
> Within this concept *pylai hadou* is a *pars-pro-toto* term . . . for the ungodly powers of the underworld which assail the rock. This interpretation is supported by the linguistic consideration that *katischyein* then followed by a genitive is always active ("to vanquish") in Jewish Greek. Hence the *pylai hadou* are the aggressors. Since the two futures in Mt. 16:18 *(oikodomēsō, ou katischysousin)* are also meant eschatologically the reference is to the final attack of the powers of the underworld along the lines of the descriptions in Rev. (6:8; 9:1ff.; 20:3, 7f. . . .) and the Qumran psalm 1QH 5:20ff. Even the last and most terrible assault of the forces of the underworld will not be able to overcome the rock and the *ekklēsia* erected upon it.[66]

We need not dwell on the anachronisms contained in this account, nor on the non sequiturs in arguing that to vanquish implies that the victor must be the aggressor, nor on the view that the future tense of the two verbs implies an exclusive es-

63. Ibid., 73.

64. See Robert Murray, *Symbols of Church and Kingdom: A Study in Early Syriac Tradition* (Cambridge: Cambridge University Press, 1975) 228-36; and R. Köbert, "Zwei Fassungen von Mt 16,18 bei den Syrern," *Bib* 40 (1959) 1018-20.

65. See Stephen Gero, "The Gates or Bars of Hades? A Note on Matthew 16.18," *NTS* 27 (1980-81) 411-14.

66. Jeremias, *TDNT* 6 (1968) 927. I have omitted Jeremias's cross-references and references to scholarly literature, but see also his *Golgotha* (Leipzig: Verlag Eduard Pfeiffer, 1926) 55-77; and *Jesus als Weltvollender* (BFCT 33, 4; Gütersloh: "Der Rufer" Evangelischer Verlag, 1929) 62f.

chatological reference. We may simply say that Jeremias's earlier discussion of *hadēs* fit the text of Matt 16:18 much better than his later one. However, his allusion to the Hodayot or psalms of Qumran introduces a new point, which draws on the earlier work of Otto Betz.[67] Betz noted certain parallels between the Hodayot and Matthew 16. In particular, he saw 1QH 6:26f. as a free exposition of Isa 28:16f. and identified the allusion to the gates of death in the psalm with the power of chaos. Perhaps the most relevant portions of the psalm are the following (which I give in Vermes's translation):

> A counsel of Satan is in their heart
>   [and in accordance with] their wicked design
>   they wallow in sin.
>
> [I am] as a sailor in a ship
>   amid furious seas;
> their waves and all their billows
>   roar against me.
> [There is no] calm in the whirlwind
>   that I may restore my soul,
> no path that I may straighten my way
>   on the face of the waters.
> The deeps resound to my groaning
>   and [my soul has journeyed] to the gates of death.
>
> But I shall be as one who enters a fortified city,
>   as one who seeks refuge behind a high wall
>   until deliverance (comes);
> I will [lean on] Thy truth, O my God.
> For Thou wilt set the foundation on rock
>   and the framework by the measuring-cord of justice;
>   and the tried stones [Thou wilt lay]
>   by the plumb-line [of truth],
> to [build] a mighty [wall] which shall not sway;
>   and no man entering there shall stagger.[68]

Granting that the parallels are impressive, one may question what might be the connection between Hodayot and Matthew, and whether the constructions that Betz placed on the text are altogether warranted. Betz saw Jesus' nature miracles

---

More recently Jeremias has been followed by Bernard P. Robinson, "Peter and his Successors: Tradition and Redaction in Matthew 16.17-19," *JSNT* 21 (1984) 85-104. Robinson sees allusions to 2 Sam 7, Isa 28 and the book of Jonah. He takes the "bars of Sheol" (Jonah 2:6) to refer to the "watery abyss." He concludes: "Simon Peter will in some sense enjoy protection against the destructive forces of Sheol, for, as the son of Jonah, he will, like Jesus his master, prevail over death" (91).

67. See Betz, "Felsenmann und Felsengemeinde (Eine Parallele zu Mt 16.17-19 in den Qumranpsalmen)," *ZNW* 48 (1957) 49-77.

68. 1QH 6:21-27 cited from G. Vermes, *The Dead Sea Scrolls in English* (Harmondsworth: Pelican, 1962) 170-71.

as a victory over the power of chaos and thus as a kind of fulfillment of the psalm. Yet it must be pointed out that the psalm does not fit Jesus who, unlike the psalmist, did not escape death. The allusions to Belial in the Qumran writings are not necessarily identical with the "gates of death." Rather, it seems more natural to take the phrase in the same sense that it has in the OT and to see the reference as an allusion to being brought to the point of death.

In a recent article Richard H. Hiers has also appealed to the Hodayot and intertestamental literature in arguing that the command to bind and loose was originally an authorization to Peter and the Twelve to exorcise demons, though later it was understood to include plenary authorization for church leaders to resolve whatever problems might arise.[69] Broadly speaking, Hiers's argument has considerable force. However, the attempt to identify "the gates of Hades" with Satan does not stand up to close scrutiny, despite his appeals to Günther Bornkamm and William Manson.[70] As Hiers himself recognizes, in some NT writings at least the sphere of Satan is in the air or the heavens (Luke 10:18; Eph 2:2; 6:11-12; Rev 12:7-9). It is Satan's fate to be cast into the pit, where he is bound (Rev 20; cf. Jude 6-7). My point is not to deny that there is a connection between Satan or Beliar and Hades. Satan may be instrumental in bringing evil-doers to Hades (Heb 2:14; cf. *T.Reub.* 12:7; *T.Levi* 18:10-12 [cf. Luke 10:19]; *T.Sim.* 6:5-6; *T.Zeb.* 9:8; *Eth. Enoch* 10:4-10; 54:1–56:8; 1QH 3:29, 32; 6:22-24 generally). But we cannot speak of "Satan-Hades" as a single entity. In the OT Sheol is sometimes depicted as a devouring, monstrous beast, but this beast as such is not identified with Satan (Prov 1:12; Isa 5:14; Hab 2:5). In 1QH 3:17-18 it is both an enemy stronghold and a place of doom.

> [Hell and Abaddon] shall open
> [and all] the flying arrows of the Pit
> shall send out their voice to the Abyss.

> And the gates [of Hell] shall open
> [on all] the works of Vanity;
> and the doors of the Pit shall close
> on the conceivers of wickedness;
> and the everlasting bars shall be bolted
> on all the spirits of Naught.[71]

In short, Sheol symbolizes death, doom, and perdition.

---

69. Hiers, "'Binding' and 'Loosing': The Matthaean Authorizations," *JBL* 104 (1985) 233-50.

70. Ibid., 242. Bornkamm identified the gates with "the powers of the underworld," which could "achieve nothing" against the community of the end-time (see *Jesus of Nazareth* [tr. I. McKuskey and R. McKuskey with James M. Robinson; New York: Harper & Row, 1960] 187). Manson saw the saying against the broad background of Jesus' exorcisms and the Beelzebul charge in Matthew 12. He suggested that the one who is able to destroy both soul and body in Gehenna (Matt 10:28) might be Satan. He also noted Jesus' temptations and the petition in the Lord's Prayer to be delivered from the evil (*Jesus and the Christian* [Grand Rapids: Eerdmans, 1967] 83). However, he did not attempt a more precise exegesis of the gates.

71. Cited from G. Vermes, *The Dead Sea Scrolls*, 158.

3. The Question of Authenticity

We have already noted the reluctance of Bousset and Bultmann to attribute to Jesus the pronouncements of Matt 16:18. In fact, the whole question of the authenticity of Matthew's account of Peter's confession has received much attention in contemporary scholarship. The words attributed to Jesus in Matt 16:17-20 have no parallel in the other two accounts of Peter's confession of Jesus as the Christ (Mark 8:27-30; Luke 9:18-21). Nor is there explicit mention of the "church" *(ekklēsia)* in any of the four Gospels apart from Matt 16:18 and 18:17. But, as Günther Bornkamm points out, "the authenticity of the passage in Matthew xvi is mentioned chiefly because it is not easily compatible with Jesus' proclamation of the imminent coming of the kingdom of God."[72] Bornkamm therefore concludes that the words of Matt 16:18-19 form "a testimony to the founding of the Church on the resurrection of Jesus, and to the consciousness of the early Christians that they were the community of the end of time, against whom the powers of the underworld can achieve nothing."[73]

Against this type of skepticism Oscar Cullmann has shown that the absence of the term *ekklēsia* from the parallel accounts and from the Gospels in general is not a decisive argument.[74] The term itself is not a Christian creation but belongs to the Jewish sphere as the LXX translation of the Hebrew *qāhāl* denoting the people of God. Moreover, the notion of a messiah without a messianic community is unthinkable. Thus the promise to the church in Matt 16:18-19 is a promise of the Christ/Messiah concerning the messianic community.[75] It is understandable that those who reject Jesus' messianic consciousness should also reject the authenticity of Jesus' saying concerning the church. But Cullmann cautions those who think otherwise against premature rejection of the genuineness of the saying. He believed that the image of building a community was fully intelligible from a Jewish standpoint, especially in view of OT language about the *house* of Israel.[76] He concluded that Jesus had chosen Peter to play a special part in the founding of the messianic community[77] and that the gates of the realm of the dead lose their previously unconquerable power and must yield to the attack of the church.[78]

Despite his defense of the underlying authenticity of the passage, Cullmann was inclined to detach it from the occasion of Peter's confession and place it in the context of the Last Supper, when Jesus' death was imminent.[79] Nevertheless, he

---

72. Bornkamm, *Jesus of Nazareth*, 187.

73. Ibid.; see also Bornkamm, "The Authority to 'Bind' and 'Loose' in the Church in Matthew's Gospel: The Problem of Sources in Matthew's Gospel," reprinted in Graham Stanton, ed., *The Interpretation of Matthew* (Issues in Religion and Theology 3; Philadelphia/London: Fortress and SPCK, 1983) 85-97. Bornkamm treats the account in Matt 16 as "an 'ideal' sense containing traces of the beginning of a special Christian halakah in which we see the founding of the Church on Peter as the guarantor and authorized interpreter of Jesus' teachings" (94).

74. Cullmann, *Peter—Disciple, Apostle, Martyr*, 192- 99.

75. Ibid., 176-91.

76. Ibid., 199; see Num 12:7; Ruth 4:11; Amos 9:11.

77. Ibid., 242.

78. Ibid., 208.

79. Ibid., 191.

was anxious to stress that his general interpretation did not stand or fall with his theory about the setting. His view of the setting has not found widespread acceptance, and a cross-section of scholars, both Protestant and Catholic, locate the saying in a postresurrection setting.[80] Thus, whether it be regarded as an utterance of the risen Christ or a product of the Matthaean community, the saying is not regarded by these scholars as the words of the historical Jesus.

II. AN ALTERNATIVE INTERPRETATION OF MATT 16:18c

In putting forward an alternative interpretation I am conscious of flying in the face of a great deal of modern scholarship, not least in arguing for the authenticity of the saying. I will begin by noting points of agreement with views that we have examined. I will then enumerate various factors which influence my proposal. Finally, I will outline my conclusions.

A. Points of Agreement

1. A Semitism

There is widespread agreement that *pylai hadou* reflects a Semitic term. The absence of the definite article points to a Semitic grammatical construction. Moreover, the expression is attested in Jewish writings in connection with impending death. On linguistic grounds, then, the saying is feasible as an utterance of Jesus.

2. Hades as Sheol, the Abode of the Dead

I find myself in agreement with those scholars like Adolf Schlatter who treat the saying as a promise of triumph over death. Specifically, it is a prophecy that, despite the death of Jesus, the church will survive. In my view it is anachronistic to treat Hades or Sheol in Matthew as the infernal stronghold of Satan and the demons from which they attack the church. Sheol is not the abode of Satan but the abode of the dead. As A. H. M'Neile puts it, apart from the "awkward metonymy" involved in identifying Hades with the organized powers of evil, "it is doubtful if Hades was ever thought of as the *abode* of the powers of evil, from which they emerge to injure men."[81] At any rate, this would seem to be true of the time of Jesus. The sphere of Satan and evil spirits is in the air, the atmosphere,[82] and the wilderness[83] rather than the underground. The pit is the prison-house of Satan, not his stronghold.

80. See, e.g., Reginald H. Fuller, "The 'Thou Art Peter' Pericope and the Easter Appearances," *McCQ* 20 (1966-67) 309-15; Raymond E. Brown, Karl P. Donfried, and John Reumann, eds., *Peter in the New Testament: A Collaborative Assessment by Protestant and Roman Catholic Scholars* (Minneapolis/London: Augsburg and Geoffrey Chapman, 1973) 83-101, 105-7; Robert H. Gundry, *Matthew,* 335; Bernard P. Robinson, "Peter and his Successors," n.66; Pierre Grelot, "L'Origine de Matthieu 16,16-19," in *À Cause de L'Évangile: Études sur les Synoptiques et les Actes Offertes au P. Jacques Dupont, O.S.B., à l'occasion de son 70e anniversaire* (LD 123; Paris: Éditions du Cerf, 1985) 91-105.

81. M'Neile, *The Gospel According to St. Matthew* (London: Macmillan, 1915) 242.

82. See W. Eichrodt, *Theology of the Old Testament* (tr. J. A. Baker; London: SCM, 1967) 2.205-9.

83. See Matt 4:1; 12:43. For a review of beliefs about evil spirits in the NT world see Graham H. Twelftree, *Christ Triumphant: Exorcism Then and Now* (London: Hodder and Stoughton, 1985) 20-54.

Nor is there anything specific in Matt 16:18 to indicate that the gates signify the primal flood of evil which might also figure in the allusion to the houses built on rock and sand (Matt 7:24-27) and the days of Noah (Matt 24:36-39). In both these latter passages the emphasis falls on divine judgment and not upon the unleashing of the chaotic forces of evil. Elsewhere in the NT *hadēs* is the sphere of the dead, with overtones of corruption, destruction, and judgment (Acts 2:25-28, 31 [cf. Ps 16:8-11]; Matt 11:23 and par. Luke 10:15; Luke 16:23; Rev 1:18; 6:8; 20:13). I do not think that there are any substantial reasons for reading a radically different meaning into Matt 16:18.

3. Gates

Gates are means of entry and exit and also means of preventing entry and exit. In view of the widespread imagery of journeys into the underworld[84] and the existence of the set phrases "gates of death" and "gates of Hades/Sheol," it makes good sense to see the underlying imagery of Matt 16:18 as involving someone approaching and passing through the gates of Hades/Sheol. However, the gates will not prevail in the sense that they will not be able to keep the one who passes through them or put an end to his mission and cause. On the other hand, it would seem anachronistic to read into the text an implied crusade to liberate the dead in Hades.

4. Messianic Consciousness

It is not without significance that a number of scholars who reject the authenticity of the saying likewise reject Jesus' messianic consciousness. On the other hand, the pronouncement is consonant with messianic self-consciousness. Indeed, it can only make real sense on the lips of one who had received acknowledgment of his messiahship at a time when his own life was increasingly threatened.

B. Decisive Factors

1. Conflict with the Authorities

In ch. 12 Matthew has already given his account of how "the Pharisees went out and took counsel against him, how to destroy him" (Matt 12:14). The immediate occasion for this was Jesus' healing of the man with the withered hand on the sabbath, an episode recounted in all three Synoptic Gospels (Matt 12:2-14; Mark 3:1-6: Luke 6:6-11). J. D. M. Derrett sees in the account allusions to the biblical language of the outstretched arm in redemption.[85] By contrast the opponents of Jesus are in danger of stretching out their hands against the Lord's anointed. Why should the Pharisees be so hostile to Jesus? The answer, I believe, lies in the fact that they saw him as the kind of prophet described in Deuteronomy 13 who performs signs and wonders in order to lead the people astray.[86] Not only are the people

---

84. See Gertrude Himmelfarb, *Tours of Hell: An Apocalyptic Form in Jewish and Christian Literature* (Philadelphia: University of Pennsylvania Press, 1983).

85. Derrett, *The Making of Mark* (Shipston-on-Stour: P. Drinkwater, 1985) 1. 77-82.

86. See Colin Brown, *Miracles and the Critical Mind* (Grand Rapids: Eerdmans, 1984) 287-90, 300-25; idem, *That You May Believe: Miracles and Faith—Then and Now* (Grand Rapids: Eerdmans, 1985) 110-75; idem, "Synoptic Miracle Stories: A Jewish Religious and Social Set-

to pay no heed to such a prophet; they are, in fact, to kill him and so "purge the evil from the midst" of them (Deut 13:5).

The upshot is the charge that Jesus is casting out demons by Beelzebul or Satan (Matt 12:22-30; Mark 3:22-27; and Luke 11:14-15, 17-23; cf. Matt 9:32-34; John 7:20; 8:48, 52; 10:20). This charge is repudiated as patently self-contradictory. It is met by the claim that Jesus is acting under the power of the Spirit of God and by the solemn warning against blaspheming against the Holy Spirit (Matt 12:31-37; Mark 3:28-30; Luke 12:10). Thus, according to the Gospels, Jesus is already on a collision course with the religious leaders. The Pharisees have already taken counsel how to destroy him and have accused him of being Satanic but have not yet succeeded in making their charge stick. However, unless there was a fundamental change of heart and mind on their part, it would only be a matter of time before they succeeded in purging Jesus from the midst of the people of God.

2. The Sign of Jonah

Matthew 15 and 16 describe the smoldering hostility of Jesus' adversaries. Matthew 15 raises the question of who is really transgressing the commandments of God (Matt 15:2-3). Matthew 16 begins with a request from the Pharisees and Sadducees "to show them a sign from heaven." This leads to Jesus' pronouncement about "the sign of Jonah" (Matt 16:1-4 [cf. 12:38-39; Luke 11:16]; the pronouncement is omitted from the account of the request in Mark 8:11-13; Luke 11:16). The request for a sign is usually represented as a desire for conclusive demonstration of divine authentication. However, in view of the Pharisees' previous accusation of Jesus being in league with Satan, their decision to destroy him, and the reference to their tempting him, the request might have a more sinister motivation. Having failed to make the Beelzebul charge stick, there remained the possibility of getting Jesus to perform a sign which could then be construed as a piece of sorcery. What is more, the sign would have been performed before competent witnesses, that is, themselves, and the way would then be open to execute Jesus as a sorcerer (cf. Deut 18:9-22).

Jesus replies by referring to the sign of Jonah. Unlike other prophetic signs,[87] this was a sign that was done *to* the prophet. The book of Jonah tells how Jonah was commanded to go to Nineveh but instead took a ship to Tarshish. A storm came up, and the crew attributed it to the presence of an evildoer on board. When they threw Jonah overboard, the storm abated. However, Jonah was rescued by the fish, and he then proceeded on his mission to Gentile Nineveh.

Jesus refuses to perform a sign but says that a sign will be given to the evil and adulterous generation. It is a sign which they themselves will have a hand in per-

---

ting," *Foundations and Facets Forum* 2 (1986) 55-76. See the similar argument in August Strobel, *Die Stunde der Wahrheit: Untersuchungen zum Strafverfahren gegen Jesu* (WUNT 21; Tübingen: J. C. B. Mohr [Paul Siebeck], 1980).

87. See C. Brown, *Miracles and the Critical Mind*, 258f., 314f.; *That You May Believe*, 107ff., 136ff. For an account of the interpretations of the sign of Jonah see Hans F. Bayer, *Jesus' Predictions of Vindication and Resurrection: The Provenance, Meaning and Correlation of the Synoptic Predictions* (WUNT 2. Reihe 20; Tübingen: J. C. B. Mohr [Paul Siebeck], 1986) 110-45.

forming. In effect, Jesus is saying that the Jewish leaders will treat him like the crew of the ship treated Jonah. They see him as an evildoer who must be gotten rid of to save the ship of state. Like the crew, they believe that they are acting righteously. But God will come to Jesus' rescue, the decisive sign Jesus was pointing to.

A further ramification of the sign lies in the meaning of the name "Jonah." "Jonah" means "dove," recalling the descent of the Spirit "like a dove" after Jesus' baptism (Matt 3:16; Mark 1:10; Luke 3:22; John 1:32). The identification of Jesus in this way recalls his association with the Spirit which was the decisive manifestation of the kingdom (Matt 12:28). To his opponents, however, it was simply a manifestation of Beelzebul.

The identification of Jesus with Jonah may shed light on two further aspects of Matt 16:17-18. The first has to do with the name "Simon Bar-Jona" (i.e., Simon, son of Jonah). Simon had just identified Jesus as "the Christ, the Son of the living God" (Matt 16:16). Jesus reciprocates by saying of Simon: "Blessed are you, Simon Bar-Jona! For flesh and blood has not revealed this to you, but my Father who is in heaven." This does not mean that Simon's father was named Jonah. It means rather that Simon has now entered into a new relationship with Jesus. Through his confession of Jesus as the Christ, he is now in a relation of sonship to him.[88] Just as the OT speaks of the sons of the prophets, Matt 9:2 provides another instance of Jesus addressing someone as his son. Through his confession of Jesus, Simon is not only Peter the rock; he has also become the son of the new Jonah and must be ready to reckon with the fate of the new Jonah.

This last point brings us to the second aspect of Matt 16:17-18 enlightened by the identification of Jesus with Jonah. As we have already noted, the psalm in the book of Jonah speaks of Jonah's descent to Sheol (2:2)—"to the land whose bars closed upon me for ever," "the Pit" (2:6)—and also of his longing for God's "holy temple" (2:4, 7), which is identified with God's presence. In view of the allusions to Jonah in Matthew 12 and 16, it would not seem inappropriate to identify the bars of Sheol in Jonah with the gates of Hades in Matt 16:18. I shall comment on the significance of the temple presently.

3. Peter's Confession of Jesus as the Christ

Popular belief that Jesus was John the Baptist, Elijah, Jeremiah, or one of the prophets (Matt 16:14; cf. Mark 8:28; Luke 9:18) suggests that the Beelzebul charge had not found widespread acceptance among the people. But Jesus' question and Peter's reply mark a new stage in the intensification of the conflict with the Pharisees and religious leaders. The juxtaposition in Peter's reply of "the Christ" with "the Son of the living God" (Matt 16:16) is doubtless a Hebrew parallelism, for "Christ" and "Son of God" are messianic titles. The title Christ poses not only the question of the identity of its owner but also of the meaning of the title. The Greek *christos* and Hebrew *māšîaḥ* both mean "anointed." But this in turn

88. Other scholars who discuss the name Simon Bar-Jona in a similar way, though they treat it as secondary or redactional, include M. D. Goulder, *Midrash and Lection in Matthew* (London: SPCK, 1974) 387; and Bernard P. Robinson, "Peter and His Successors," 90.

raises the question, anointed by what or by whom? The answer given by the evangelists is that Jesus was anointed by the Holy Spirit at his baptism. The answer given by Jesus' enemies is that he was possessed by Beelzebul or Satan. If Satan was thought of as the prince of the power of the air, it could be that the opponents construed the accounts of the descent of the Spirit as the descent of Satan upon Jesus, which promptly caused him to go into the wilderness.

At any rate Peter's confession inaugurates a new phase in Jesus' activity and an intensification of the conflict with the religious leaders. All three synoptic evangelists proceed to relate Jesus' prediction of rejection, death, and resurrection. Matthew stresses the chronological link between the confession and the passion prediction and explicitly mentions the need to go up to Jerusalem.

"From that time Jesus began to show his disciples that he must go to Jerusalem and suffer many things from the elders and chief priests and scribes, and be killed, and on the third day be raised" (Matt 16:21). Peter's well intentioned hope that this might be avoided is rebuked as a Satanic hindrance (Matt 16:23).

4. Gates, Jerusalem, and the Temple

In addition to the various references to gates of Hades, Sheol, and death that we have already noted, we should note as well that gates were places where justice was enacted (see Ruth 4:1). If a couple had "a stubborn and rebellious son" who was deemed "a glutton and a drunkard," they were to deliver him to the elders of the city at the gate. There he would be stoned to death by all the men of the city "so that you shall purge all the evil from your midst; and all Israel shall hear, and fear" (Deut 21:18-21; cf. Matt 11:19; Luke 7:34). The Pharisees had such a purging in mind when Jesus was led out of the city and put to death at Golgotha, the place of the skull (Matt 27:33; Mark 15:22; John 19:17; cf. Luke 23:26; Heb 13:12).

Not only did the city walls of Jerusalem have gates; so did the temple. Indeed, the real significance of Jerusalem was that it housed the temple. In this context note Psalm 24, which asks "Who shall ascend the hill of the LORD?" and gives an answer that is echoed by Matt 5:8 (Ps 24:4). The Psalm goes on to proclaim:

> Lift up your heads, O gates!
> and be lifted up, O ancient doors!
> that the King of glory may come in. (Ps 24:7)

It may be that Jesus' entry into Jerusalem and the temple are to be seen as an implicit enactment of this psalm. Jesus is represented in Matt 12:6 as "something greater than the temple." If so, the allusion remains on the level of the implicit. On the other hand, Matthew contains explicit references to Psalm 118 in the context of Matthew's account of Jesus' entry into Jerusalem and the cleansing of the temple. Moreover, in this psalm the gates of the temple play an important part.

In Psalm 118 the Psalmist approaches the sanctuary in order to thank Yahweh for deliverance from his enemies and from death.

> I shall not die, but I shall live,
> and recount the deeds of the LORD.
> The LORD has chastened me sorely,
> but he has not given me over to death.

Open to me the gates of righteousness,
that I may enter through them
and give thanks to the LORD.

This is the gate of the LORD;
the righteous shall enter through it. (Ps 118:17-20)

H.-J. Kraus observes that the gates are called "gates of righteousness" on account of the scrutiny to which worshipers were subjected.[89] Only the righteous could enter (v. 20; cf. Psalms 15 and 24; Isa 26:2). To enter was indeed a sign of righteousness. Psalm 118 is particularly relevant for the understanding of Matthew for several reasons. The passage just quoted is followed almost immediately by the passage about the stone rejected by the builders which later became the chief cornerstone (Ps 118:22-23; cf. Matt 21:42; Mark 12:10-11; Luke 20:17; Acts 4:11; 1 Pet 2:7). Kraus sees the passage as meaning that "The one cast into the sphere of death resembled a stone which the builders threw away as unusable. Yet this stone has come to honor as the 'cornerstone'."[90] In Matt 21:42 the passage figures in a pronouncement at the conclusion of a *Streitgespräch* which results from Jesus' cleansing of the temple. It follows immediately the parable of the wicked husbandmen, in which the tenants of the vineyard mistreat and kill the owner's servants and then cast out the son and kill him as well. The Lord will take the vineyard away from the tenants, put them to death, and give the vineyard to other tenants. The point of the parable is plainly spelled out: "Therefore I tell you, the kingdom of God will be taken away from you and given to a nation producing the fruits of it" (Matt 21:44). After this pronouncement, the attempt to arrest Jesus is thwarted by fear of the multitudes who hold Jesus to be a prophet.

This, however, is not the only fulfillment of the psalm. Kraus sees verse 26 as a liturgical blessing pronounced by the priests from the sanctuary upon the one who enters (cf. Ps 24:5; Num 6:23).[91]

Blessed be he who enters in the name of the LORD!
We bless you from the house of the LORD. (Ps 118:26)

Sacrifice and thanksgiving then follow (Ps 118:27-29). The first part of this verse finds two echoes in Matthew. First, it is found on the lips of the crowds as Jesus enters Jerusalem (Matt 21:9; cf. Mark 11:9-10; Luke 19:38; John 12:13). Significantly it is the crowds and not the priests who welcome Jesus in this way. Equally significant is the omission of the second part of the verse, since the priests did not bless Jesus from the house of the Lord. The second echo is heard from the lips of Jesus himself as he concludes his lament over Jerusalem. "For I tell you, you will not see me again, until you say, 'Blessed is he who comes in the name of the Lord'" (Matt 23:39; cf. Luke 13:35). Jesus' action in entering Jerusalem and cleansing the temple was an enacted sign by which he was staking his claims

---

89. Kraus, *Psalmen* (BKAT 15/2, 5th ed.; Neukirchen-Vluyn: Neukirchener Verlag, 1978) 982f. Kraus draws attention to an Akkadian tablet which also describes a gate ceremony in the Esagila, the principle temple of Marduk. The text celebrates the restoration of one who went "down to the grave" (text in *ANET*, 600).

90. Kraus, *Psalmen*, 983.

91. Ibid., 984.

and reforming the whole structure of OT religion.[92] It was both abortive and decisive—abortive in the sense that it did not produce a reformation of Judaism but led to Jesus' own death; yet decisive in the sense that it led to the emergence of the church as a separate entity. In all this, Jerusalem retains an ambivalent status. It is "the city of the great King," and therefore one must not swear by Jerusalem (Matt 5:35; cf. 23:16-21). It played a climactic part in Jesus' ministry (Matt 16:21; 20:17-19; 21:1-17). Yet it was also the city of the evil king Herod, the city that was troubled by the tidings of the Magi (Matt 2:3). It was also the place from which Pharisees and scribes came to denounce Jesus (Matt 15:1). Above all, it is the city which kills the prophets and those who are sent to it.

O Jerusalem, Jerusalem, killing the prophets and stoning those who are sent to you! How often would I have gathered your children together as a hen gathers her brood under her wings, and you would not! Behold, your house is forsaken and desolate. For I tell you, you will not see me again, until you say, "Blessed is he who comes in the name of the Lord" (Matt 23:37-39).

According to Matthew's account, Jesus then left the temple for good and prophesied its destruction (Matt 24:1-2).

5. Irony

In all this there is a deep and pervasive irony. While it is impossible here to explore the subject of irony in the teaching of Jesus,[93] the interpretation of Matt 16:18c which I do wish to put forward could be described as an example of the deep irony that is to be found in the sayings of Jesus.

C. Conclusions

1. A Passion Prediction

Werner Bieder has observed that "It requires no untoward psychologizing if we reckon with the conjecture that even without explicit reference Jesus *thought of his own death*."[94] I wish to suggest that in Matt 16:18c we have precisely such an explicit reference. The Gospels describe Jesus' intention of going up to Jerusalem. His purpose was to cleanse the temple and to bring about a new order. To do this he would have to enter the gates of Jerusalem and the gates of the temple. His

---

92. For discussion of the so-called cleansing of the temple see C. Brown, *That You May Believe*, 127-29; Georges Barrois, *Jesus Christ and the Temple* (Crestwood, New York: St. Vladimir's Seminary Press, 1980); Bertil Gärtner, *The Temple and the Community in Qumran and the New Testament* (SNTSMS 1; Cambridge: Cambridge University Press, 1965) 105-22; David R. Catchpole, "The 'Triumphal' Entry," in Ernst Bammel and C. F. D. Moule, eds., *Jesus and the Politics of His Day* (Cambridge: Cambridge University Press, 1984) 319-34; William R. Telford, *The Barren Temple and Withered Tree* (JSNT Supplement Series 1; Sheffield: JSOT Press, 1980); E. P. Sanders, *Jesus and Judaism* (Philadelphia: Fortress, 1985) 61-90 (this volume includes reviews of recent interpretations). Jesus' action effectively put a stop to the offering of sacrifice on the eve of the Passover. In my view his action was a "baptism" intended to inaugurate a new era in which the previous functions of the temple would be superseded.

93. On irony see Jakob Jónsson, *Humor and Irony in the New Testament, Illuminated by Parallels in Talmud and Midrash* (BZRGG 28; Leiden: 1985).

94. Bieder, *Der Höllenfahrt Jesu Christi*, 46.

action would be an enacted fulfillment of Ps 118:19-26. Moreover, if this psalm is a royal psalm and the speaker is the king who enters the temple in thanksgiving, as Leslie C. Allen and others have suggested,[95] the imagery is particularly appropriate for one who has just been acknowledged the messianic king. In view of Peter's confession of Jesus as "the Christ, the Son of the living God,"[96] there would be a divine necessity upon Jesus to go to Jerusalem. The proper place to give thanks would be the temple. In order to enter the temple Jesus would have to pass through the gates of Jerusalem and the gates of the temple itself. But these gates would prove to be for Jesus the gates of Hades.

Although the crowds along the way welcomed Jesus in the language of Ps 118:26, the priests and religious leaders did not do so. They did not receive him as a righteous member of the covenant.[97] In fact, the minds of the religious leaders had already been made up: Jesus was a rebellious evildoer in league with Satan who performed signs and wonders in order to lead others astray. He must therefore be purged from the midst of the people.

Thus the prophecy that "the gates of Hades shall not prevail" against the church is a prediction of the passion and the ultimate triumph of Jesus' messianic mission. It expresses concretely and cryptically what Matthew elsewhere says in general terms: "From that time Jesus began to show his disciples that he must go to Jerusalem and suffer many things from the elders and chief priests and scribes, and be killed, and on the third day be raised" (Matt 16:21). Instead of the holy city welcoming its messianic king, Jerusalem will judge him and put him to death. But this action will not be the end of Jesus and his messianic community. At the same time Matt 16:18c contains a warning to the disciples that is spelled out more fully in the sayings of verses 26-27 about cross-bearing, losing and gaining life, and judgment. In my opinion the prophecy may well preserve the original form of the passion prediction which is elsewhere stated by Matthew and the other evangelists in general terms.

2. An Instance of Irony

We noted earlier a rabbinic idea that one of the entrances to Sheol was at Jerusalem. Indeed, Gehenna was named after a valley outside Jerusalem. The authorities at Jerusalem acted in the name of Yahweh, and, as in the case of Jesus, they exercised their authority in condemning some to death. In view of the way Jerusalem had treated the prophets and those who were sent, it is the city of death in an ironic sense. It is not the holy city but the unholy city which slays the righteous. The scribes and Pharisees "are like whitewashed tombs which outwardly appear beautiful, but within they are full of hypocrisy and iniquity" (Matt 23:27-28). The climactic act of Jerusalem's iniquity will be the slaying of the Lord's anointed. In this way, ironically, the holy city has become the gateway to Sheol.

95. Allen, *Psalms 101–150* (WBC 21; Waco: Word Books, 1983) 122-25.

96. Matthew's version of Peter's confession appears to be a parallelism in which Jesus is confessed as the Lord's anointed, the messianic king. See Brown, *That You May Believe,* 98-101, 134.

97. See Allen, *Psalms 101-150,* 121, on the covenant implications of righteousness in the psalm.

By going through the gates of Jerusalem Jesus was thus entering the city of Sheol. In my opinion, therefore, "the gates of Hades" is used as ironic designation for Jerusalem in its hostility to Jesus.[98]

3. A Reinterpretation of OT Themes

The question of the method of interpretation underlying the use of OT Scriptures in this context requires a separate study.[99] Clearly Psalm 118 belonged to a body of texts which figured in early Christian apologetics. The various OT allusions in Matt 16:13-28 may have been influenced by the Jewish lectionary.[100] If Jesus himself did not use Psalm 118 to interpret himself, we have to explain how it came to play such a decisive role in the early church. On the other hand, if Jesus did accept his identification as the messianic king, it would be appropriate for him to seek enactment of the psalm. I find attractive Bruce D. Chilton's suggestion that the account of the confession provides an illustration of Targumic interpretation in which the interpreter introduced his own understanding of the text that he was translating.[101] Although Chilton is cautious about the premature attribution of the passage to an actual dialogue between Jesus and the disciples, he finds the experiential approach to Scripture compatible with other instances of Jesus' usage of Targumic interpretation.

The course of events described by Matthew does not exactly fit the course of events described by the psalmist. The king in the psalm has been saved from death. He was like the rejected stone, but is now accepted as the chief cornerstone. He is welcomed into the temple and offers the sacrifice of thanksgiving. According to Matthew's account, however, Jesus has already been rejected and accused of being in league with Beelzebul. He enters the temple, where he is rejected once again. He then identifies himself with the stone the builders rejected, and himself becomes the cornerstone of the new temple and the sacrifice.

It would seem therefore that we have here an experiential reinterpretation of the psalm which was dictated by the course of events. In view of Jesus' rejection which had already taken place in the events described in Matthew 12 and which was reaffirmed by the rapid course of events after he cleansed the temple, the only way he could fulfill the psalm would be by establishing a new temple with a new order of ministry and with himself as the sacrifice. This interpretation of the saying about the gates of Hades thus provides the background for the statements in v. 19 about authority in the church.[102]

98. See the comment of R. Isaac in *Genesis Rabbah* 39: "wicked people are called dead while they are yet alive" (*Genesis Rabbah*, tr. Jacob Neusner [Atlanta: Scholars Press, 1985] 2. 64).

99. On the question of interpretation see Barnabas Lindars, *New Testament Apologetic* (London: SCM, 1961) 169-77; R. H. Gundry, *The Use of the Old Testament in St. Matthew's Gospel* (NovTSup 18; Leiden: Brill, 1967); A. T. Hanson, *The Living Utterances of God: The New Testament Exegesis of the Old* (London: Darton, Longman and Todd, 1983).

100. See Goulder, *Midrash and Lection,* 383-93.

101. Chilton, *A Galilean Rabbi and his Bible: Jesus' Use of the Interpreted Scripture of His Time* (Good News Studies 8; Wilmington: Michael Glazier, 1984) 172ff.

102. Recent discussions include J. D. M. Derrett, "Binding and Loosing (Matt 16:19; 18:18; John 20:23)," *JBL* 102 (1983) 112-17; Herbert W. Basser, "Derrett's 'Binding' Reopened," *JBL* 104 (1985) 207-300; Richard H. Hiers, "'Binding' and 'Loosing': The Matthaean Authorization"; and Tord Forberg, "Peter—the High Priest of the New Covenant?" *EAJT* 4 (1986) 113-21.

In view of the allusions to Jonah in Matt 12:39-41 and 16:4 and the points in the book of Jonah that we have already noted, it would seem that there are echoes of the Jonah theme in our passage. As with Jonah, the bars of Sheol closed behind Jesus, but they proved insufficient to hold him. Again, as with Jonah, the Lord heard Jesus in his holy temple. Moreover, just as Jonah was restored and sent on a mission to the Gentile world, so the mission of the risen Christ and his church embraces the Gentile world. To Matthew's church the passage may also throw some light on Peter as the Son of Jonah. Like Jonah of old, Peter was given a mission to the Gentiles, but also like Jonah, he was not entirely comfortable in that vocation despite its success.

4. Matt 16:18c and Matthew's Church

What then did Matthew intend in recording this passage which none of the other evangelists report? My answer is that first of all he was giving a passion prediction in its most laconic and ironic form. It expresses the essence of the conflict between Jesus and the Jewish leaders of his day. In so doing Matthew locates the origin of the church in the messianic consciousness of Jesus himself and in the repudiation of the church by Judaism. The passage is above all a word of encouragement. Peter is to believe that the hostile, persecuting powers that put Jesus to death will not prevail against the messianic community. In the postresurrection situation Matthew's church could see that the cross led to the Resurrection. Matthew's church could draw encouragement from the fact that the organized hostility of Judaism had not overcome the church and would not overcome it. They could be encouraged in the knowledge that the Christian messianic community had, in its separation from Judaism, its separate orders of authority, its own interpretation of the Scriptures, and its large Gentile component, its own divinely sanctioned legitimacy. And if these things held good for the church of Matthew's day, they hold good for the church of successive ages.

How Controversial Was the Development of Infant Baptism in the Early Church? [1]

David F. Wright

Baptism remains one of the most sensitive points of disagreement among the churches. Although the level of theological and historical debate has subsided since the stir excited by Karl Barth's celebrated rejection of infant baptism[2] and by the exchanges between Joachim Jeremias and Kurt Aland,[3] baptism has come increasingly to the fore in ecumenical discussion, largely as a result of *Baptism, Eucharist and Ministry*.[4]

But if paedobaptism has been a major topic of inter-confessional controversy intermittently since the sixteenth century, how controversial a subject was it in the early centuries of the church? This question is different from the modern historical one whether babies were baptized in primitive Christianity, and also from that of the biblical and theological rationale for baptizing them today—to which Geoffrey Bromiley has made an invaluable contribution from the perspective of Reformed theology.[5] The precise question before us in this essay is the extent to which the baptizing of babies was attended by argument and debate within the early church itself. But although it does not set out to confront the fundamental historical and theological issues, it will scarcely be able to avoid touching upon them here and there.

Although Christian baptism was often surrounded by contention in the patristic centuries, especially in the western church, the period saw no significant disagreement about the acceptability of baptizing babies. There is no precedent in the era of the fathers for the baptismal divide of the sixteenth and subsequent centuries. The magisterial Reformation equated the error of the Anabaptists with that of the

---

1. This is a revised and expanded version of a paper contributed to a Joint Study Group between representatives of the Church of Scotland and the Baptist Union of Scotland. An earlier contribution, similarly revised, is to appear in the *SJT* as "The Origins of Infant Baptism—Child Believers' Baptism?"

2. Barth, *The Teaching of the Church Regarding Baptism* (tr. Ernest A. Payne; London: SCM, 1948); idem, *Church Dogmatics* (tr. G. W. Bromiley; Edinburgh: T. & T. Clark, 1969), 4/4, 164-94.

3. Jeremias, *Infant Baptism in the First Four Centuries* (tr. David Cairns; London: SCM, 1960); Aland, *Did the Early Church Baptize Infants?* (tr. G. R. Beasley-Murray; London: SCM, 1963); Jeremias, *The Origins of Infant Baptism* (tr. Dorothea M. Barton; London: SCM, 1963). For Aland's subsequent works, see my forthcoming article (cited n. 1 above), n. 4.

4. *Faith and Order Paper* No. 111 (Geneva: WCC, 1982). See my evaluation, *Baptism, Eucharist and Ministry (the "Lima Report"): An Evangelical Assessment* (Rutherford Forum Papers, 3; Edinburgh: Rutherford House, 1984).

5. Bromiley, *Children of Promise: the Case for Baptizing Infants* (Edinburgh: T. & T. Clark, 1979).

Donatists of Roman North Africa[6] (and Anabaptists were punished under the provisions of anti-Donatist legislation enacted by the emperors of Christian Rome), but the Donatists' baptismal dispute with the Catholic church had nothing to do with the propriety of baptizing infants.

Nevertheless, the development of infant baptism in the early church was far from uncontroversial. The fourth century witnessed the widespread deferment of baptism, and the evidence of the inscriptions strongly suggests that this had happened in the third century also, albeit for different reasons.[7] Furthermore, the Pelagian conflict raised in an acute form the question why babies were baptized, and discussion of baptismal issues often exposed uncertainties relating to infant baptism. Solely in the idiosyncratic person of Tertullian did it appear to challenge the practice altogether, although this is not the whole truth.

NEW TESTAMENT ECHOES OF A PRIMITIVE CONTROVERSY?

Do the Gospel accounts of Jesus' blessing of the children (Mark 10:13-16, par.) preserve traces of a debate within the primitive Christian communities on whether babies should be baptized? New Testament scholarship yields no agreed answer to this question (nor indeed to the related question, which is not our concern here, whether the pericope reflects the uncontroverted practice of baptizing babies). The case for a *Sitz im Leben* in which the question of infant baptism was a live issue has been made chiefly by Oscar Cullmann and Joachim Jeremias.[8] They lean in particular on the use of the Greek verb *kōluein,* whose occurrence in baptismal contexts in New Testament writings and other early Christian literature they take to reflect a standard inquiry in primitive Christian baptismal procedure whether any hindrance existed to a candidate's baptism. The inclusion of this technical term shows, in Cullmann's words, "that those who transmitted this story of the blessing of children wished to recall to the remembrance of Christians of their time an occurrence by which they might be led to a solution of the question of infant baptism."[9]

The *kōluein* hypothesis has not gone uncontested. A. W. Argyle, for example, has objected that a technical liturgical verb would be unlikely to show such variation in the objects it governs as *kōluein* does—the candidate (Mark 10:14, par.; Acts 8:36; Ps-Clementines); water (Acts 10:47); the baptizer (Matt 3:14; Epiphanius); and God (Acts 11:17).[10] Other considerations must incline us toward

6. L. Verduin, *The Reformers and Their Stepchildren* (Exeter: Paternoster Press, 1964) ch. 1.

7. See E. Ferguson's suggestive study, "Inscriptions and the Origin of Infant Baptism," *JTS* N.S. 30 (1979) 36-46, which is discussed in my article (cited n. 1 above).

8. Cullmann, *Baptism in the New Testament* (tr. J. K. S. Reid; SBT 1; London: SCM, 1950) 71-80; Jeremias, *Infant Baptism in the First Four Centuries,* 48-55.

9. Cullmann, *Baptism in the New Testament,* 78. Neither Cullmann nor Jeremias notes that Cyprian uses *prohibere* thrice and *inpedire* four times in discussing the baptism of the newborn in *Ep.* 64:5-6 (discussed below).

10. A. W. Argyle, "O. Cullmann's Theory concerning *kōluein,*" *ExpTim* 67 (1955-56) 17. Cf. the guarded reserve of G. R. Beasley-Murray, *Baptism in the New Testament* (London: Macmillan, 1962) 324-25. The English translator of Cullman has not helped his case by using four different English verbs to translate *kōluein.* Cullmann's German and French each use only one— *hindern* and *empecher* respectively.

a verdict of uncertainty on the special role of *kōluein*. Although the claims that the synoptic narrative must be read against a context in which the baptizing of infants was disputed is not wholly dependent upon the *kōluein* hypothesis, the claim itself enjoys no more than some degree of plausibility. The conclusion must be that, if there are grounds for holding that the baptizing of babies began or was extended around the time Mark's Gospel was compiled,[11] we can do no more than conjecture that this development ran into controversy which the incident of the blessing of the children was invoked to resolve. It may be speculated that, if the practice of paedobaptism was hotly contested in these early decades, the dispute would have been expected to leave early discernible traces in early Christian writings, within or without the New Testament. Apart from the debatable *kōluein*, nobody claims that it has.

TERTULLIAN'S CONTROVERSY

Tertullian's well-known objections to baptizing infants, spelled out in his homily on *Baptism* (c. 200), should be interpreted not as opposition to a novel practice (his failure to state his objection in these terms being undoubtedly significant) but as a corollary of his broader approach to baptism. Although he expresses this in a highly characteristic fashion, it is not far removed from a remarkably common patristic understanding of baptism which should perhaps be regarded as the single most serious weakness of early baptismal thought. Tertullian's plea for delayed baptism therefore merits more extended treatment than his idiosyncratic presentations might suggest.

Tertullian is concerned with the profitability of baptismal reception. Deferment is advocated because it is "more profitable" *(utilior)*, in accordance with the candidate's character, attitude, and age *(Baptism* 18:4). Therefore, postponement is particularly appropriate in the case of young children. Tertullian gives no suggestion that he views baby baptism as invalid, as not true baptism at all, as though the person baptized as a baby could subsequently receive a proper (second) baptism. His quarrel with the baptizing of babies is not that of a latter-day credobaptist but seems to be twofold: it is needless, and it is attended with very great risk. On both counts it is unprofitable, or at least highly likely to prove so.

First, it is needless because baptism imparts the remission of sins and infancy is the age of innocence *(innocens aetas; Baptism* 18:5). The implication is clear: because of their innocence babies have nothing or little to gain from baptism. Tertullian does not unpack for his readers the implications of *innocens* in this celebrated phrase, but its primary reference must be to a baby's lack of sins of his own commission. We should not deduce from it that Tertullian held no belief in original sin, nor is it altogether safe to assert that "he could hardly have taken this attitude [to infant baptism] unless he had held lightly to the doctrine of original sin."[12] Al-

11. As Jeremias believed, prior to the English version of his *Infant Baptism in the First Four Centuries*. See Aland, *Did the Early Church Baptize Infants?*, 33-36, and my article cited above, for his change of mind.

12. Ernest Evans, ed. and tr., *Tertullian's Homily on Baptism* (London: SPCK, 1964) 101. See the full discussion in E. Nagel, *Kindertaufe und Taufaufschub. Die Praxis vom 3.- 5. Jahrhundert in Nordafrika und ihre theologische Einordnung bei Tertullian, Cyprian und Augustinus (Europ. Hochschulschr.* 23:144; Frankfurt am Main/Berne/Cirencester: Peter D. Lang, 1980).

though his doctrine has occasioned considerable debate, he is not reticent in speaking about the effects upon all mankind of Adam's fall. In particular, "he is more explicit and outspoken about this sinful bias [of a vitiated nature] than previous theologians,"[13] and in this treatise on *The Soul*, in a difficult passage, he declares every soul to be impure *(immunda)* until it is reborn in Christ.[14] This impurity is more than the soul's "investment by pagan influences before and after birth,"[15] although Tertullian makes much of these; it also, or rather primarily, encompasses a transmitted natural infection by sin.

But if *innocens aetas* provides no pointers to Tertullian's view of original sin, its place in the argument seems to suggest either that no close connection had yet been forged by him or the church between original sin and infant baptism or that, in his thought about the benefits of baptism, the sins of responsible free will loomed much larger than the inheritance from Adam, in whatever terms this was defined. The latter is the more likely explanation, and brings us in fact to the second reason why Tertullian advocated the postponement of baptism. We will have cause, however, to return to the former possibility.

The second, and weightier, consideration that argues for the utmost circumspection in giving Christian baptism are the risks attendant upon its premature reception. In his homily on baptism, Tertullian has far more to say about these than his one brief, tantalizing mention of *innocens aetas*. For they are not limited to infant candidates:

> With no less reason ought the unmarried also to be delayed until they either marry or are firmly established in continence; until then, temptation lies in wait for them, for virgins because they are ripe for it, and for widows because of their wandering about. (*Baptism* 18:6)

Tertullian ends this chapter with a sentence that takes us to the heart of his concern: "All who understand what a burden *(pondus)* baptism is will have more fear of obtaining it than of its postponement" (*Baptism* 18:6). It is this awsome *pondus* that should deter *sponsores* from promoting infant candidates, since death may prevent them ensuring the fulfillment of the baptismal promises they take on their behalf, or "the subsequent development of an evil disposition" in the baptized youngster may frustrate their (the sponsors') purpose (18:4).

The fearful prospect that governs Tertullian's counsel is that of serious post-baptismal sin. Indeed, the very fact that he argues as he does about the risks of the premature baptism of infants shows conclusively that baby baptism, however unwise, was real baptism, after which there remained no subsequent (second) baptismal washing. What surfaces here in Tertullian, and much more starkly elsewhere in his corpus, especially in his later (Montanist) treatise *De Paenitentia*, is by no means confined to his convictions alone. It was a pervasive belief among the

---

13. J. N. D. Kelly, *Early Christian Doctrines* (5th ed.; London: A. & C. Black, 1977) 176.

14. Tertullian, *De Anima* 40:1. See the helpful analysis in the edition by J. H. Waszink (Amsterdam: J. M. Meulenhoff, 1947) 446.

15. Evans, *Tertullian's Homily on Baptism*, 102. Kelly is a sounder guide, and cf. Norman P. Williams, *The Ideas of the Fall and Original Sin* (London: Longmans, Green & Co., 1927) 231-45.

fathers that the washing of baptism covered only those sins committed up to this point in one's life. Providing for sins committed after baptism, especially for grave offences, was a major problem in the early centuries, and was eventually responsible for the development of a system of ecclesiastical penance. In the literature of the period, a clear parallelism obtains between baptism and any subsequent opportunity for remission of grave sins; the latter could be spoken of as a "second repentance (penance)," or even as a "second baptism." Considerable controversy surrounded the questions whether, for what offences, and whether more than once such post-baptismal remission could be granted. The Monantist Tertullian was of course a strident contributor to these arguments, which constitute the background to the wording of the clause in the Nicene Creed, "one baptism for the remission of sins."[16]

The baptizing of babies and infants was bound to appear fraught with the greatest peril so long as such profound anxiety contemplated the possibility of moral lapses after baptism. At the very least, baptism should be given only to the person who asks for it, which in the context of Tertullian's baptismal treatise, must mean the person who receives baptism in the full knowledge of, even in spite of, its forbidding *pondus*. It makes no sense to entrust *substantia divina* to one too young to be trusted with *substantia terrena*. What emerges clearly from the battery of arguments Tertullian discharges is that baptism is most wisely received by the person whose preparation for it has been so thorough that his or her maintenance of baptismal purity thereafter is as fully guaranteed as possible. While this assumes in practice the baptism only of believers, it goes far beyond this essential requirement of credobaptist teaching. At the end of this chapter of *De Baptismo* Tertullian declares that "a person whose faith is entire [*integra*], i.e., who has sufficient faith in God, can be sure [*secura*] that though he defers his baptism God will not let him die unbaptized."[17] We must remind ourselves that Tertullian's position did not entail his treating the baptism of babies or young children as other than Christian baptism. In fact, in cases of "necessity," he seems to have regarded it as the proper course of action. "Necessity" was constituted routinely, it must be assumed, by the likelihood of death, and occasionally by the threat of persecution. Martyrdom in turn was another form of second baptism, a blood baptism which covered all outstanding sin, and was the supreme baptism inasmuch as it cut off every possibility of subsequent sin.

Tertullian's controversy with infant baptism turns out to reflect a framework of reference unlikely to be shared by any of the participants in latter-day baptismal

16. A further study would be needed to show the evidence for this. Briefly, the absence of references to "one baptism" in western creeds shows that its inclusion is unrelated to the (largely western) controversies over baptism; the specified purpose "for the remission of sins" indicates the reason for insisting on "*one* baptism"; and the exposition given by Cyril of Jerusalem, one of the earliest witnesses to such a clause in a creed and the first to provide an explanation of it, makes clear that it excludes the possibility of setting things right a second time if a person fails once after baptism (*Procatech.* 7). Chrysostom's comment is very similar (*Bapt. Catech.* 3:23).

17. Evans's paraphrase in *Tertullian's Homily on Baptism*, 106, of *fides integra secura est de salute* (*Baptism* 18:6).

disputes, at least among Protestants. On the other hand, baptism (or its higher sur-
rogate, martyrdom) was essential for salvation (*Baptism* 12:1, quoting John 3:5),
and hence had to be administered in emergency even to infants. But on the other
hand, because baptism's capacity to deal with sin was limited to the burden of
sin already accumulated by the candidate,[18] it must be sought only with the utmost
caution and sense of responsibility, and hence would normally never be granted to,
because never requested by, infants. It is fair to say that neither of these two fundamental convictions would command much assent in baptismal debate today.
Baptizers on both sides of "the waters that divide" are likely to place much greater
weight on a belief which the calculating prudence of Tertullian's theology inevitably undervalued—namely, that the gift or strengthening of the Spirit associated with baptism is God's provision enabling the baptized to overcome the
temptations that continue to assail him or her to the end of life. This conviction led
the early church to baptize catechumens when persecution threatened, so that they
might be fortified to stand firm in the hour of trial.

A PRACTICE IN SEARCH OF A THEOLOGY?

In Tertullian, it seems, the reality of original sin had scarcely begun to influence
the practice of baptism—although it was presumably original sin that created, or
contributed to, the "necessity" of baptism for dying babies. (But only in *dying*
babies was the need constituted by original sin allowed by Tertullian to override
prudential considerations and necessitate baptism.) Precisely because most of the
early references to infant baptism are so brief and allusive, not to say debatable, it
is difficult to speak with any confidence of the reasons why baptism was felt to be
necessary for babies in the first two centuries or so of the church's history. Hippolytus is the first to report what might be called the routine inclusion of babies in
baptism in his *Apostolic Tradition*, written c. 215, but he provides no evidence
whatsoever about the rationale of baby baptism. Since the whole of the rest of Hippolytus's account of baptism, including its preparation and sequel, assumes responsible believers as its subjects, we are left to draw the conclusion that babies too
needed to be saved from what responsible believers were saved from in baptism.
But if the plight of those needing baptism was held to lie in the sins they had committed, what could one say about babies or very young children who had committed no such sins? Early Christian writers commonly ascribe to infants innocence
or sinlessness,[19] attributes which should be read not so much as denying original

18. No clearer illustration of this common early Christian conviction could be given than that
of Chrysostom: "The sins committed before baptism are all cancelled by the grace and kindness
of the strength of Christ crucified. The sins committed after baptism require great earnestness,
that they may again be cancelled. Since there is no second baptism, there is need of our tears,
repentance, confession, almsgiving, prayer, and every other kind of devotion" (*De s. Pentecoste
hom.* 1:6; *PG* 50, 463).

19. For the evidence see Aland, *Die Stellung der Kinder in den frühen Christlichen Gemein-
den und Ihre Taufe* (*Theol. Exist. Heute* 138; Munich: Chr. Kaiser Verlag, 1967) 17-21; B. Klaus,
"Die Erbsündenlehre als Motiv des Kirchlichen Handelns in der Taufe," *KD* 15 (1969) 50-70, at
54-58; J. C. Didier, "Un cas typique de développement du dogme à propos du baptême des enfants," *MScRel* 9 (1952) 191-213, esp 194-200.

sin as reflecting a stage prior to its conscious articulation as a teaching of the church. What they assert, of course, is that young children have yet to commit the culpable, willful sins of their elders.

In this context it is not surprising that the practice of infant baptism became a potent factor in the development of the doctrine of original sin. It is now commonplace to refer to confirmation as a rite in search of a theology, but one could apply the same description of infant baptism in the early church. In the west, if not so obviously in the east, it found the theological justification it needed in the dogma of original sin. If there is a persisting controversy about infant baptism in the patristic age, it concerns primarily the question "why?" rather than "whether?", although the absence of confident answers to the former must to some extent have diverted pressure onto the latter.

There is no doubt that the custom of infant baptism was the single most powerful catalyst of the formulation of doctrines of original sin, and that the direction of argument moved from the accepted practice of infant baptism to the truth of the doctrine, and not vice-versa.[20] We have here an unmistakable illustration of the axiom *lex orandi lex credendi*. The church baptizes babies who, it is agreed, have not sinned *in propria persona;* therefore, we must believe that they are baptized for the cleaning or remission of original sin. Original sin must be part of the faith of the church; why else does the church baptize babies?

Although the contours of this argument are clearly recognizable from the third century until the Pelagian controversy in the fifth, it is not always possible to discern the backcloth to discussions in ecclesiastical practice or dispute. That they took place in very varied contexts is obvious enough from the contribution of Cyprian.

HOW CLOSE A CORRESPONDENCE TO CIRCUMCISION?

In one of his letters written in the name of a council of African bishops that met in the spring of 253, Cyprian reports the council's unamimous response to a question raised by bishop Fidus (of an unknown see).[21] Fidus believed that the analogy with circumcision decreed that babies should be baptized on the eighth day after birth and not before it. The letter reveals little more than this about Fidus's position. We do not know whether others shared his view, but it is a reasonable inference that disagreement with actual practice, whether established or innovatory, provoked the voicing of his opinion. If we may judge from the terms of Cyprian's refutation, Fidus had made three points in support of his case.

First, and least clear of the three, Fidus may have claimed that a baby of only two or three days old was not yet capable of receiving the divine gift of baptism. We cannot be certain in inferring that Fidus argued along these lines, but Cyprian's first rejoinder is to stress that the newborn baby is a completed creature of God, lacking nothing as a human being, and that age makes no difference at all in the

20. Jaroslav Pelikan, *Development of Christian Doctrine: Some Historical Prolegomena* (New Haven/London: Yale University Press, 1969) ch. 3.

21. Cyprian, *Epistle* 64 (numbered 58 in the *Ante-Nicene Christian Library* translation).

equality of the divine grace (*Epistle* 64:2-3). "The mercy and grace of God is not to be refused to anyone born of man."

Second, Fidus had undoubtedly pleaded the impurity of an infant in the first days after its birth, which made people shudder to kiss it. Cyprian has no patience with this kind of almost physical distaste, and seems ready to kiss and baptize even the baby still wet and unwashed from the womb. In embracing the freshly made handiwork of God, we in some sense kiss "the still recent hands of God themselves" (64:4). Scripture declares all persons clean.

Third, "spiritual circumcision ought not to be hindered by carnal circumcision." Cyprian's response implies the acceptance of the parallel between shadow and substance, but lays its main emphasis on the dissolution of the former once the latter had come in Christ (64:4-5).

The greatest interest of the letter, however, is found in the way Cyprian combines both original sin and the child's freedom from sin of his or her own in arguing for the earliest administration of baptism. The bishop of Carthage recommends a course of action directly contrary to that advocated by his earlier fellow-citizen, but odly enough he shared with Tertullian the ingredients out of which the two concocted such totally different recipes. For Cyprian, the fact that the newborn has not sinned on his or her own account but, "being born after the flesh according to Adam, has contracted the contagion of the ancient death at his earliest birth" (with both of which counts Tertullian would agree) argues for, not against, his or her speedy baptism, even to the extent of not waiting until the eighth day after birth. When the sins to be remitted are not his own but another's, he comes "the more easily" to the forgiveness of baptism. Arguing *a maiori ad minus,* Cyprian reasons that, if an adult convert's erstwhile flagrant wickedness is no bar to his baptism, nothing can possibly stand in the way of the baptism of the newborn innocent. The contrast with Tertullian's viewpoint could hardly be more marked, and it is difficult not to discern in this part of the letter a response to Tertullian rather than to Fidus. Otherwise Cyprian must appear to be wielding a theological sledgehammer to crack a minor procedural nut. He gives no hint that Fidus needed persuading of the doctrine of original sin, whereas the force of Cyprian's theological reasoning seems specifically designed to counter Tertullian's appeal to *innocens aetas.* The difference between them is attributable in large measure to the conjunction Cyprian makes between infant baptism and original sin. Although the sins needing remission are not the baby's own, they necessitate his baptism. Cyprian fancifully interprets the crying of the newborn as his tearful entreaty for divine grace, which by its very helplessness lays the more powerful claim upon the succor of baptism (*Epistle* 64:5-6). As he repeats three times in the letter (64:2, 5, 6), since God is merciful toward all, the grace of baptism is to be denied to none.

It was Cyprian's paradoxical contribution, in a writing in which the weight of the reasoning falls on the innocence of babyhood, to have made original sin part of the framework of thought about infant baptism for the first time in the west. The vigor of his episcopate, the prestige of his subsequent martyrdom, and the fact that he wrote with conciliar authority all conspired to exalt his letter as the authentic voice of Catholic tradition. It would prove a priceless weapon in Augustine's armory against the Pelagians.

AN APOSTOLIC TRADITION: ORIGEN AND ORIGINAL SIN

Cyprian's older contemporary in the East, Origen of Alexandria and Caesarea, is also a clear witness to the church's baptism of infants. In three passages from the later Caesarean period of his life,[22] he followed through an explicit chain of reasoning which concluded that, since baptism was given for the remission of sins and was administered according to the church's practice to *parvuli* as well as older persons, there must be something in infants requiring the baptismal washing, for otherwise there would be no rationale for their baptism. Since they have at no time committed sin, the answer is found in the uncleanness of which Job 14:4 (LXX) speaks: "None is pure from uncleanness [*sorde*], not even if his life on earth is but one day old." This text (which was not unknown to Cyprian)[23] was backed up by Ps 51:5 (50:7, LXX): "In iniquities was I conceived, and in sins did my mother give me birth." In fact, Origen's conception of original sin was hardly mainstream, although it remains disputed whether it developed toward a more orthodox configuration.[24] His belief in the pre-cosmic fall of pre-existent souls required that the sinfulness attested by Job and the Psalmist was the legacy, not of solidarity with Adam's sin, but of each soul's previous transgression. In this knowledge that all human beings were born into this world in impurity, the apostles mandated the church to give baptism to infants also.[25]

Not only does Origen press the practice of infant baptism into the service of his own speculative theory of pre-cosmic sin, but he is also the first Christian writer to claim the apostolic origin of the church's custom. Kurt Aland alleges that all his statements

> stand on the defensive against the belief that infants do not need baptism, on the ground that as infants have not actually committed any sins, they do not require forgiveness of sins. . . . There must have been circles and that not small and uninfluential, whose members held a different opinion as to the necessity of infant baptism and who correspondingly maintained a different practice, in that they abstained from baptizing infants. Hence arises Origen's appeal to the "tradition of the Church received from the apostles" . . . , which was the strongest argument that he possessed.[26]

This interpretation of Origen is quite unconvincing, and Jeremias's rejoinder makes much better sense.[27] Origen's argument proceeds not from the fact of the sinfulness of newborn babies to the need for their prompt baptism but in the

---

22. Origen, *Homilies on Luke* 14 (on Luke 2:22); *Homilies on Leviticus* 8:3; *Comm. on Romans* 5:9. It has been argued that Origen's lack of explicit reference to infant baptism in his Alexandrian writings implies that it was not practiced in the Alexandrian church.

23. Cf. Cyprian, *Testimonies* 3:54, where with Ps 51:5 and 1 John 1:8 it proves that "No one is without uncleanness and without sin."

24. Cf. Kelly, *Early Christian Doctrines*, 180-82. A rather different account of Origen's thought is given by Williams, *Fall and Original Sin*, 223-30.

25. Origen, *Comm. on Romans* 5:9.

26. Aland, *Did the Early Church Baptize Infants?*, 47.

27. Jeremias, *The Origins of Infant Baptism*, 69-74. He brings out well the context and sequence of thought of Origen's references.

reverse direction. He does, however, report that "the brethren" frequently discussed the question how infants could be baptized for the remission of sins (the purpose of all Christian baptism) when they had committed no sin of their own.[28] The debates within the Christian community which Origen refers to concerned not whether but why babies should be baptized.

Again we have found the rite in search of an agreed meaning. That this should be the case towards the middle of the third century in Caesarea may suggest that the practice can scarcely have been regularly observed there for almost two hundred years. If it is true that "there is no clearer instance of the control exercised by liturgical or devotional practice over the growth of dogma than that provided by the study of the relations between the custom of Infant Baptism and the doctrine of Original Sin,"[29] it is an entirely proper question why in this instance the *lex oran-di* took such a long time to establish the *lex credendi*—if, that is, infant baptism was, at least in Caesarea, a tradition of apostolic origin. Origen's reference to frequent ecclesiastical discussion of the theoretical justification for baptizing infants may therefore imply not that the practice was a recent introduction, still resisted by some of the brethren, but that by the 230s and 240s it had not had a sufficiently long history in the church of Caesarea to have evoked a received theological basis in the tradition. Origen's expositions were still needed to provide one. But it remains unambiguously clear from Origen that the practice pre-existed his explanation of it.

THE EAST AFTER ORIGEN: CONSENSUS ELUSIVE

It is not the purpose of this paper to trace the history of infant baptism in the church of the fathers but to attempt to ascertain how far it remained a subject of controversy. In the eastern church there is little indication that Origen's biblical discussions had much influence on beliefs about why babies needed baptism. There is in fact not much evidence that churchmen were unduly concerned about infant baptism at all, and the considerable body of fourth-century Christian literature in the east yields remarkably few references to it. After Origen the first witness is the Arian Asterius the Sophist, whose homilies on Psalms 1–15 were delivered probably in the second quarter of the fourth century. Three of these homilies[30] assume the baptism of newborn babies as the norm but do not connect it with sin or original sin. But baptism of infants is presented as protection against demons, heresy, and premature death. Indeed, it is difficult to point to a single eastern father in the fourth century who links infant baptism with sin or original sin.[31] Chrysostom's enormous corpus yields less than a handful of references to infant baptism, one of

28. Origen, *Homilies on Luke* 14 (on Luke 2:22).

29. Williams, *Fall and Original Sin*, 223.

30. Cf. J. C. Didier, "Le Pédobaptisme au IVe siècle. Documents nouveaux," *MScRel* 6 (1949) 223-46. The original texts are also given in the two main collections of sources: H. Kraft, *Texte zur Geschichte der Taufe* (KlT 174; 2d ed.; Berlin: Verlag Walter de Gruyter & Co., 1969) 41- 43; and Didier, *Le Baptême des enfants dans la tradition de l'Englise* (*Monum. Christ. Selecta* 7; Tournai: Desclée & Cie, 1959) 28-30.

31. For references see Didier, *Le Baptême des enfants*, 233-35; and Didier, "Un cas typique de développement du dogme," 204-11.

which asserts that "we baptize little children, even though they have no sins," in order that they may receive gifts such as righteousness and adoption and become members of Christ and the abode of the Spirit.[32] The Cappadocians, like Chrysostom, plead with their congregations not to delay their baptism, but nearly always, it seems, with adult converts in view. Their pleas are hardly ever directed toward parental responsibility for their offspring in the matter of baptism. Several prominent fourth-century fathers, although of Christian parentage, were not baptized until adult years. In the east these included John Chrysostom, Basil the Great, and Gregory of Nazianzus.[33]

The sole writer to address the issue of the delay of infant baptism directly is Gregory of Nazianzus in his oration on baptism. His counsel is clear. Babies in danger of death must be baptized without delay, "for it is better that they should be unconsciously sanctified than depart this life unsealed and uninitiated." Circumcision is cited as the warrant for so doing. But for others Gregory advises a wait until they are about three years old,

> when they may be able to listen and to answer something about the sacrament, so that, even though they do not perfectly understand it, yet at any rate they know the outlines, and then to sanctify them in soul and body with the great sacrament of our consecration. . . . They begin to be responsible for their lives at the time when reason is matured and they may be instructed in the mystery (for of sins of ignorance owing to their tender years they have no account to give), and it is far more profitable on all accounts to be fortified by the font, because of the sudden assaults of danger that befall us.[34]

That this and similar questions on the timing of baptism were currently matters of discussion among Christian congregations may be implied by the way Gregory responds in his *Oration* to real or imagined objections and queries.

32. Chrysostom, *Baptismal Cetecheses* 3:6 (ed. A. Wegner, *Jean Chrysostome. Huit catéchèes baptismales inédites;* SC 50; Paris: Editions du Cerf, 1957) 153-54; P. W. Harkins, *St. John Chrysostom: Baptismal Instructions* (ACW 31; Westminster, Md./London: Newman Press and Longmans, Green & Co., 1963) 57. When Jeremias wrote *Infant Baptism in the First Four Centuries* (1958, 1960), he was aware of Chrysostom's cetechetical comment only in the form of Augustine's quotation in *Against Julian the Pelagian* 1:6:21-22 (cf. 94n.7). Julian had cited Chrysostom's text in a Latin form (*non coinquinatos . . . peccato,* "not defiled by sin"), which demonstrated to Julian that Chrysostom did not believe in original sin in infants. Augustine was able to correct him by producing Chrysostom's Greek.

33. Cf. Jeremias, *Infant Baptism in the First Four Centuries,* 88-89, for details. Basil's exhortation (*Homil.* 13:1, 5; *PG* 31, 424, 432) illustrates the pastor's dilemma. In urging young and old alike to be baptized without delay, he stresses that the whole of life is the right time *(kairos)* for baptism, which must have militated against an insistence on invariable paedobaptism.

34. Gregory of Nazianzus, *Oration* 40:28; 40:17 is presumably to be read in terms of this later passage, but the consistency is not obvious: "Do you have an infant child? Do not allow sin any opportunity. Let him be sanctified from babyhood, and consecrated by the Spirit from his tenderest days." He goes on to refer to Samuel, who was consecrated to God immediately after birth. Gregory's mention in sect. 23 of those who "because of infancy" have been unable to receive baptism indicates, not the existence of "some parts of the church where paedobaptism was unknown" (Williams, *Fall and Original Sin,* 290n.4), but simply infants' dependence on negligent parents.

We cannot, however, speak to controversy about infant baptism in this period in the east. Much remains obscure. Baptism is generally assumed to be necessary for salvation, but little clarity is forthcoming on what babies are to be saved from. More is said about the positive gifts imparted to them in baptism, which is also viewed as fortifying the baptized against the perils of life. A poem of Gregory of Nazianzus in speaking of baptism describes it as the seal of God—for infants only a seal, but for adults a remedy as well as a seal.[35] But overall the evidence is too scanty to allow us to delineate a consensus. Gregory of Nazianzus shows that there was scope for considerable variety of teaching, and all that seems agreed is an unwillingness to adopt the standpoint of Origen, the first articulate advocate of infant baptism in the eastern tradition. We must not forget however, that it was in circles strongly influenced by the Cappadocians (among whom Gregory of Nyssa appears to ignore infant baptism altogether)[36] that the phrase "one baptism for the remission of sins" found its way into the Nicene Creed. When this is set in the context of the teachings of the fourth-century Greek fathers about infants and baptism, it is difficult to regard it as having any intended reference to paedobaptism. It could be paraphrased in the following terms: insofar as baptism is given for the remission of sins (which, it is agreed, is not the case with the baptism of babies), a person may receive it only once.[37]

THE WEST AFTER CYPRIAN

It is easy to overlook the overwhelming extent to which the body of early Christian writing about infant baptism is dominated by Augustine's works, very largely against the Pelagians.[38] The critical issue raised early in the fifth century by Pelagius and, more acutely, his associate Caelestius was simple enough. Their denial of the transmission of original sin dismantled what Augustine depicted as the traditional theological rationale for the practice of baptizing infants—given that, as was agreed on all sides, infants had no sins of their own commission which required baptismal remission. Augustine and other African bishops not unnaturally feared that the airing of such questions would stiffen parental reluctance to bring their babies to the baptistry, at a time when churchmen in the west no less than

35. Gregory of Nazianzus, *Carmina Dogmatica* 9:91-2 (*PG* 37, 463-64, with note ad loc.). Cf. Williams, *Fall and Original Sin,* 289-90. Neither Kraft nor Didier includes this text.

36. Cf. Williams, *Fall and Original Sin,* 278-80. It is not at all clear from Gregory of Nyssa's treatise *On Infants Who Die Early* whether the problem it tackles arises from their not having received infant baptism or from their dying before reaching the appropriate later age for baptism. Since infant baptism is not mentioned, the latter seems more likely. Gregory's *Against Those Who Defer Baptism* likewise makes no allusion to infant baptism. His sermon *The Baptism of Christ* attributes to the newly baptized old person the innocence of the baby and the new-born infant's freedom from accusations and penalties (*PG* 46, 579).

37. On this issue, see Williams, *Fall and Original Sin,* 553-54, who also concludes that those who framed or included this clause could only have had believers' baptism in mind.

38. In Didier's collection (*La Baptême des enfants),* material from the first four centuries occupies 44 pages (including 10 pages of inscriptions), while Augustine is allotted 60.

in the east were striving to overcome the widespread delay of baptism. Augustine's *Confessions* did not hesitate to criticize even his own mother for refusing to have him baptized during a serious childhood illness, despite his pleas.[39]

But how firmly established in the western tradition was the doctrine of original sin as the strongest theological undergirding for baby baptism? The Pelagians appealed to earlier fathers, but invariably with reference to the transmission of sin from Adam and never explicitly on the grounds for baptizing infants.[40] In the ascetic circles to which they belonged, the related issue of the origin of the soul remained the subject of lively debate, fired in particular by continuing controversy over the teachings of Origen;[41] but, whereas this was a question to which, as even Augustine was only too aware, Scripture and tradition yielded no incontrovertible answer, could the same be claimed for the presence of original sin in infants as the reason why they had to be baptized if they were to be delivered from damnation? Augustine could with some justice lay claim to an identifiable current of western doctrinal reflection on this subject. After Cyprian, whose *Epistle* 64 was, of course, Augustine's star witness for the prosecution, there is a gap in the evidence comparable to that in the east. But toward the end of the fourth century, the convictions of western churchmen emerged into the light of day with a clarity that eludes us in the east. A decretal of Siricius, bishop of Rome, in the year 385 urges the prompt baptism of infants whose age prevents them speaking for themselves, lest, dying unbaptized, they should lose eternal life and the kingdom of heaven—thus neatly excluding in advance the distinction the Pelagians would make between the two.[42] In a letter of A.D. 400, Jerome, a westerner writing in the east, seems to imply that infants are baptized for "sin,"[43] but the most important catholic contributor prior to Augustine was Ambrose of Milan. He not only presents a well-developed doctrine of Adamic fall and its effects upon all humanity (described by N. P. Williams as "Augustinianism before Augustine"),[44] but he also

39. Augustine, *Confessions* 1:11:17-18.

40. Cf. especially Augustine, *Nature and Grace* 61:71– 67:81. Augustine also discusses earlier fathers' opinions in *Against Two Letters of the Pelagians* 4:8:20–12:34; and *The Grace of Christ and Original Sin* 1:42:46–50:55.

41. Cf. Robert F. Evans, *Pelagius: Inquiries and Reappraisals* (London: A. & C. Black, 1968) ch. 2.

42. Siricius, *Epistle* 1:3 (Kraft, *Texte zur Geschichte der taufe,* 67; Didier, *Le Baptême des enfants,* 36).

43. Jerome, *Ep.* 107:6. Jerome is inculcating parental responsibility for children. Until they reach years of discretion, both their *mala* and their *bona* are attributed to their parents—"unless you happen to suppose that the children of Christians, if they have not received baptism, are themselves liable for (their) sin [*reos . . . peccati*] and that guilt [*scelus*] is not ascribed to those who declined to give them baptism. . . ." Is Jerome implying that infants are baptized for their own "sin" but that, where baptism is withheld from them, their parents become laible for their sin? Yet *scelus* appears not to be synonymous with *peccati* but to designate the particular offence of parental neglect. In *Ep.* 85:2, 5, Jerome responds to an enquiry from Paulinus of Nola: "how the children of believing, that is, baptized parents are 'holy' [cf. 1 Cor 7:14], seeing that without the gift of grace afterwards received [in baptism] and kept they cannot be saved." Jerome's reply does not question Paulinus's assumptions.

44. Williams, *Fall and Original Sin,* 300.

makes no distinction between infants and adults in talking about sin as constituting the need for baptism. Yet even Ambrose falls far short of the decisive sharpness of Augustine's refutation of Pelagian teachings. The bishop of Milan disappoints us if we are looking for an umambiguous declaration that infants are baptized for the forgiveness of original *guilt,* although he certainly taught this doctrine.[45]

AUGUSTINE AND THE PELAGIAN CONTROVERSY

It was, therefore, the peculiar distinction of anti-Pelagian Augustine to make the bonds uniting infant baptism to original sin, in the sense of guilt as well as weakness, disease, or corruption, so firm as to remain virtually unbreakable for over a millennium in the western church. But although it has become commonplace to treat the Pelagian controversy as a western—and typically western—affair, the suggestion has well been made that "Probably the germ of the controversy was the now undisputed fact that differing explanations of infant baptism were held in the East and in the West."[46] The teaching of Caelestius, which first significantly disturbed catholic churchmen in Carthage in 411, maintained that infants were baptized not in order to be delivered from the condemnation attendant upon original sin, and hence not to exchange salvation and eternal life for perdition and death, but in order to secure entry to the kingdom of heaven.[47] Although Caelestius could not challenge the use of the formula "for the remission of sins," he was unable to salvage any real meaning for it in his baptism of infants; "it is fitting, indeed, to confess this lest we should seem to make different kinds of baptism."[48] Pelagius' position was virtually identical; if anything, he exacerbated its provocativeness by insisting that "We hold one baptism, which we affirm ought to be administered to infants in the same sacramental formula as to adults"[49]—which was handy grist to Augustine's mill, as we shall see.

The first of Augustine's anti-Pelagian treatises is entitled *The Merits and Remission of Sins and the Baptism of Infants* (411-412). Much of the first and third books are directed against the central Pelagian convictions about Adam's sin and infant baptism, but the precise target of book one is probably the *Liber de Fide* of one Rufinus the Syrian, an obscure figure who is nevertheless credited in one source with being the inspirer at Rome of the whole Pelagian heresy. His *Liber* certainly includes an attack on the transmission of sins and the damnation of infants and an assertion that infants are baptized for admission to the kingdom of God.[50] This Rufinian-Caelestian-Pelagian approach to paedobaptism is formally

45. Cf. Didier, "Un cas typique de développement du dogma," 202-4; Williams, *Fall and Original Sin,* 304-6.

46. Eugene TeSelle, *Augustine the Theologian* (New York: Herder and Herder, 1970) 280; "Rufinus the Syrian, Caelestius, Pelagius: Explorations in the Prehistory of the Pelagian Controversy," *AS* 3 (1972) 61-95, esp. 86-87.

47. Augustine, *Ep.* 157:22; *The Grace of Christ and Original Sin* 2:22–6:6.

48. Augustine, *The Grace of Christ and Original Sin* 2:6:6.

49. Ibid., 1:32:35, 2:1:1, 2:21:24.

50. TeSelle, *Augustine the Theologian,* 279; and his "Rufinus the Syrian"; see also Gerald Bonner, "Rufinus of Syria and African Pelagianism," *AS* 1 (1970) 31-47; and his *Augustine and Modern Research on Pelagianism* (Villanova: Villanova University Press, 1972) 9, 19-31.

similar to that of eastern churchmen, such as Gregory of Nazianzus[51] and John Chrysostom; and the eastern—in particular the Syrian or Antiochene—affinities of Pelagianism have been explored by scholars.[52] Pelagius and Caelestius found a more sympathetic hearing in the east than in the west, and although each side accused the other of innovation and heresy, the Pelagians in addition threatened their opponents with condemnation by the churches of the east.[53] There are, then, good grounds for discerning, as a significant contributory factor to the controversy, at least the absence of consensus, if not a clear disagreement, between east and west on the significance of infant baptism.

The dispute was not whether infants should be baptized but why.[54] When Caelestius complained to Innocent, bishop of Rome, that he was being defamed for refusing baptism to infants, whereas he had always maintained that they should be baptized, Augustine countered that Caelestius was misrepresenting the charge against him in order to dismiss it more readily.[55] For Augustine the answer to the question "why?" emerged with crystal clarity from a consideration of basic Christian beliefs.

(1) By ancient tradition of apostolic authority[56] the church baptizes infants who neither have committed sins of their own nor can answer for themselves in the baptismal ritual. Although the movement of Augustine's argument does not often proceed from the church's traditional practice to the doctrine of original sin as the sole indispensable basis for it, it does so on some occasions: "What necessity could there be for an infant to be conformed to the death of Christ by baptism, if he were not altogether poisoned by the bite of the serpent?"[57] When accused of Manichaeism for maintaining the transmission of sin, he responds that, long before the time of Mani, infant candidates for baptism were being exorcized with exsufflation, showing that they needed deliverance from the power of darkness.[58] It can, moreover, be plausibly claimed that the whole shape of his defense of original sin takes as its starting point the datum of ecclesiastical practice.

(2) The church knows only one baptism, and that "for the remission of sins."[59] Augustine resisted, and not only in this particular, the kind of distinction between the baptism of infants and the baptism of adult believers which had, as we have seen, found some currency among the Greek fathers, and which he regarded the Pelagians as advocating. His consistent principle was to insist at every turn on the application to infants of the church's understanding and practice of baptism.

(3) Newborn babies are included in the one humanity of which all sinned in

---

51. Cf. Williams, *Fall and Original Sin,* 345.

52. See the studies of Evans, TeSelle, and Bonner noted above, and the literature to which they refer.

53. Augustine, *The Proceedings of Pelagius* 11:25.

54. Augustine, *Sermon* 294:2.

55. Augustine, *The Grace of Christ and Original Sin* 2:4:3, 2:17:19, 2:18:20.

56. Augustine, *Baptism* 4:24:30.

57. Augustine, *Merits and Remission of Sins* 1:32:61, cf. 3:4:7.

58. Augustine, *Marriage and Concupiscence* 2:29:50.

59. Augustine, *Sermon* 293:11.

Adam and of which none is saved except in Christ. "That infants are born under the guilt of [Adam's] offence is believed by the whole Church."[60] If infants have nothing from which they need to be saved, then Jesus cannot be their savior, for only the sick need a doctor.[61]

(4) None, not excluding baby children, is saved in Christ except through baptism.[62] Punic-speaking Christians in Africa spoke about baptism as "salvation." Unless infants pass into the company of believers through the sacrament divinely instituted for this purpose, they will undoubtedly remain in the darkness of sin.[63]

(5) Infants are saved through baptism as believers, not as non-believers. Augustine recalls that by ancient custom the church calls baptized infants "believers" (fideles, pistoi),[64] as the inscriptions bear out. They believe in the hearts of others (parents or other sponsors) and they confess through the tongues of others, thus fulfilling the requirements of Rom 10:10.[65] Just as they were wounded by another's disobedience, so they are healed by another's confession of faith. It must be remembered here that, in baptismal practice at this time, the infant's parent or sponsor responded to the question, "Does he/she believe?" with the direct affirmative "He/she believes."[66]

(6) Infants who die unbaptized are lost and condemned, although their punishment will be "more tolerable" and "milder" than those who have sinned on their own account.[67] In Augustine's book there is no middle ground for infants dying unbaptized akin to the Pelagians' "eternal life" outside the kingdom of heaven. Catholic faith provides no warrant for believing that they may attain to forgiveness of their original sin.[68]

In addition to this tireless rehearsal of these basic teachings of the church which confound the errors of the Pealagians, Augustine also deploys some ad hominem arguments. Since they grant infants salvation and eternal life without baptism, how would they respond to someone who wanted to grant them the kingdom of heaven as well? They would appeal to John 3:5[69]—a text which since the second cen-

60. Augustine, *Epistle* 166:21. In this letter Augustine pleads with Jerome to demonstrate to him the consistency of the creationist view of the soul's origin (which holds that God creates a soul afresh for each person—Augustine's preferred option on this disputed question) with the fundamentals of the faith, such as those in para. (3) here. Cf. also *Ep.* 166:24-28, and 157:11, 18.

61. Augustine, *Sermon* 174:7-8.

62. Augustine, *Sermon* 174:9.

63. Augustine, *Merits and Remission* . . . 1:24:34-35.

64. Augustine, *Sermon* 294:14.

65. Augustine, *Sermon* 176:2; cf. *Epistle* 98:9-10 for a different approach, and 98:2 for a community of souls that avails to the child in baptism through the shared possession of the Spirit by parent and child alike.

66. Cf. Didier, "Une adaptation de la liturgie baptismale au baptême des enfants dans l'Église ancienne," *MScRel* 22 (1965) 79-90.

67. Augustine, *Epistle* 186:29; *Merits and Remission* . . . 1:16:21; *Enchiridion* 93; *Against Julian* 5:11:44.

68. Augustine, *The Soul and its Origin* 3:9:12. On this question see the chapter on "The Salvation of Infants" in Geoffrey Bromiley's *Children of Promise*, 91-104.

69. Augustine, *Sermon* 294:5-8.

tury had played a major role in shaping the church's baptismal beliefs. If it were not for this text, the Pelagians would not accept infant baptism at all![70]

More often, however, Augustine has to reply to Pelagian counter-arguments which appeal to the principles of transmission and solidarity that were so important in his own account of catholic doctrine. For example, if Adam harms those who have not themselves sinned, Christ should benefit those who have not believed.[71] We have already noted, in section (5) above, part of Augustine's rejoinder. He also turns the tables on the objectors by showing that it is they who accept that Christ benefits those who do not believe, for they cannot deny that in baptism Christ benefits infant non-believers.

An objection that Augustine dealt with in one form or another on many occasions claimed that, if sinful parents produced sinful offspring, parents cleansed of original sin through baptism should surely produce offspring no longer subject to original sin. His counter-attack is nothing if not versatile.[72] He contends that the claim is tantamount to assuming that baptized Christian parents should be expected to bear baptized Christian children, but male babies were not begotten already circumcised by circumcised fathers! If 1 Cor 7:14 is cited in this connection, then whatever *sanctified* might mean when applied to the unbelieving spouse or children of a Christian, it will prevent no more the child than the spouse from perishing unless they are subsequently baptized. Moreover, the parallelism does not always obtain; whereas all infants contract sin through their parents, some are presented for baptism by other persons.[73] In any case, parents generate, not regenerate their offspring. "Even renewed parents beget children not out of the first-fruits of their renewed condition, but carnally out of the remains of the old nature";[74] for concupiscence, which is one element of original sin, persists in the baptized. "The fault of our nature remains in our offspring so deeply impressed as to make it guilty, even when the guilt of the self-same fault has been washed away in the parent."[75] The true benefit of birth from Christian parents is to be brought by them without delay to the saving waters of baptism.

Augustine was also asked how it is that a child profits from its parents' faith at baptism but is not prejudiced by their later fall from faith when they seek the aid of pagan gods for the healing of the child. He argues that, by virtue of baptism, the child becomes "a soul having a separate life," so that Ezek 18:4 now governs its destiny. The bond of guilt contracted in natural birth, once cancelled in spiritual rebirth, cannot be reimposed by subsequent parental sin.[76]

It did not escape Augustine that to place such a weight on the necessity of baptism for infants provoked the most searching questions about the accidents of bap-

---

70. Augustine, *Merits and Remission* . . . 1:30:58.

71. Augustine, *Sermon* 294:17-18.

72. Augustine, *Merits and Remission* 2:9:11, 2:25:39–27:44, 3:8:16– 9:17; *Sermon* 294:16, 18.

73. Augustine, *Epistle* 98:6.

74. Augustine, *Merits and Remission* 2:27:44.

75. Augustine, *Grace of Christ* 2:39:44.

76. Augustine, *Epistle* 98:1-2.

tismal administration. "The baptized mother bewails her own little one who was not baptized [before death], while the chaste virgin gathers in for baptism the off-spring of outsiders, exposed by an unchaste mother."[77] Often when the parents are eager and the ministers prepared for giving baptism, it is still not given because death intervenes.[78] Since the Pelagians acknowledge that baptism confers some good value on babies, even they cannot evade the issue altogether. They refuse to ascribe such discrimination to fate or divine election, and must therefore base it on merit, but no such option is available for Augustine. Even the infants who are successfully brought to baptism come crying and kicking; "grace cleaves to them even in their resisiting struggles."[79] In this priority of grace, an inscrutable divine providence is at work. The diverse fortunes of infants afford the best il-lustration known to Augustine of the truth that grace is bestowed according to God's election. "Must we so attribute it to the negligence of parents that infants die without baptism that heavenly judgments have nothing to do with it?"[80] We must conclude that it was of God's choice that he did not keep this particular child in this life a little while longer in order that it might receive baptism.[81]

At this point we have reached the end of the road in more senses than one. If the tradition of baptizing infants acted as a powerful catalyst in the formulation of the western church's high doctrine of original sin, so too, it seems, the somewhat random reception of it by infants was a contributory factor in the formulation of its doctrine of divine election. This is not to claim that Augustine had no other grounds for developing his theology as he did than the implications of infant bap-tism and its haphazard administration. It is merely to recognize how his theologi-cal understanding took shape under the pressure of controversy and harsh ex-perience.

Few paedobaptists, however, will be able to follow Augustine all the way. The Pelagians were the heirs of the long and widespread uncertainty of earlier Christian generations about why newborn children needed to be baptized. Such lack of clarity bred discussion and even controversy. In a Tertullian and a Gregory of Nazianzus, and perhaps in those responsible for the later childhood baptisms at-tested by third-century inscriptions, as well as in the wider post-Constantinian deferment of baptism, this absence of consensus issued in the avoidance of in-fant baptism, in theory or in practice. It was Augustine who finally set the neces-sity of paedobaptism on an impregnable basis. But here lies the rub. For if at last the rite had found its theological rationale, it was one that today's practitioners of infant baptism will scarcely be able to endorse, except perhaps to a very minor extent. We are left in the somewhat uncomfortable position of receiving the traditional observance from the early church, while at the same time rejecting the main planks of the theology in which the church of the fathers found its con-clusive justification.

77. Augustine, *Against Two Letters of the Pelagians* 2:6:11.
78. Augustine, *Gift of Perseverance* 12:31. Cf. Williams, *Fall and Original Sin,* 377, for an illustration starkly depicting this division at the font.
79. Augustine, *Grace and Free Will* 22:44.
80. Augustine, *Gift of Perseverance* 12:31.
81. Cf. TeSelle, *Augustine the Theologian,* 323-24.

But there is one point on which the voice of Augustine deserves to be seriously heeded. It is a strength of his anti-Pelagian corpus that he endeavors to treat the baptism of infants on all fours with the baptism of adult candidates. We may judge the way he did this to be not very successful, although the rite he knew was obviously framed on the assumption that confessing believers were the normative subjects of baptism with only minimal adjustment made for those who could not answer for themselves. Nevertheless, the challenge to avoid setting up two kinds of baptism has rarely been far distant from the advocacy of infant baptism. Moreover, the subsequent separate development of rites of confirmation and their reformed substitutes has exposed paedobaptists to the associated temptation of treating infant baptism as something less than real and complete Christian baptism. Augustine's theology, however unacceptable as the definitive response to the persistently controversial question "why?" in the early history of infant baptism, at least counsels us both against distinguishing too sharply between infant and adult baptism and against denying full, unqualified integrity to the baptism given to babies.

Canon, Regulae Fidei, *and* Continuing Revelation in the Early Church

Cecil M. Robeck, Jr.

The subject of "continuing revelation" is often a volatile one in today's church. Supporters of such an idea see in it a testimony to the immanence of God, a God who has spoken in times past but who nevertheless continues to speak to people in ways which are peculiarly and particularly relevant to them in the present.[1] On the other side of the issue stand those who argue that any claim to continuing revelation violates Jesus Christ as the ultimate *Logos* of God (John 1:1-4, 14; Heb 1:1-4). They contend that such a concept detracts from genuine apostolic faith and undermines the authority of Scripture as a closed canon.[2]

In the case of the Church of Jesus Christ of the Latter Day Saints, belief in new and continuing revelation has led to an array of documents with some level of canonical status.[3] Doctrinal themes unique to Seventh-Day Adventism have been provided with added emphasis by a claimed linkage with the activity of the "prophetic" Spirit.[4] Many are the so-called "Christian" cults whose reliance

1. B. Yocum, *Prophecy: Exercising the Prophetic Gifts of the Spirit in the Church Today* (Ann Arbor: Word of Life, 1976) 11, 138; I. C. Stanton, *Has God Said? A Record of Prophetic Promptings to Our Generation* (Los Angeles: International Church of the Foursquare Gospel, 1980), foreword; A. Bittlinger, *Gifts and Graces: A Commentary on 1 Corinthians 12–14* (Grand Rapids: Eerdmans, 1968) 108; D. Gee, *Concerning Spiritual Gifts* (1949; Springfield, Mo.: Gospel Publishing House/Radiant Books, 1980) 60-61.

2. Typical of this position is the statement by F. E. Vokes, "The Opposition to Montanism from Church and State in the Christian Empire," *SP* 4 (1961) 526, which declares that "to replace the unique revelation of God in Christ with a later revelation, or to add another, will so alter the balance as to make the Faith no longer essentially Christian." Cf. W. J. Chantry, *Signs of the Apostle: Observations on Pentecostalism Old and New* (Edinburgh: Banner of Truth Trust, 1976) 27, who calls it a *"de facto* denial of the sufficiency of Scripture." Similarly see R. L. Raymond, *What About Continuing Revelations and Miracles in the Presbyterian Church Today? A Study of the Doctrine of the Sufficiency of the Scripture* (Philadelphia: Presbyterian and Reformed, 1977); T. R. Edgar, *Miraculous Gifts: Are They for Today?* (Neptune, N.J.: Loizeaux Brothers, 1983) 83-84; and B. B. Warfield, *Counterfeit Miracles* (1918; London: Banner of Truth Trust, 1972) 12-13.

3. *The Book of Mormon* and especially *The Pearl of Great Price* as well as *The Doctrine and Covenant of the Church of Jesus Christ of Latter Day Saints* are examples of revelatory claims offered by that tradition. D. S. Crowther's *Gifts of the Spirit* (Bountiful, Utah: Horizon, 1983) contains extended treatments of the subject of continuing revelation in the LDS tradition. See also G. B. Arbaugh, *Revelation in Mormonism: Its Character and Changing Form* (Chicago: University of Chicago Press, 1932).

4. A number of books have been written in the Adventist tradition which outline the function of the continuing gift of prophecy. Among them are A. G. Daniells, *The Abiding Light of Prophecy* (Mountain View, Ca.: Pacific Press Publishing Association, 1936); W. A. Spicer, *The Spirit of Prophecy in the Adventist Movement: A Gift that Builds Up* (Washington, D.C.:

upon untested prophetic claims have deceived or disappointed their followers even when those claims have been proven to be groundless.[5] The doctrine of papal infallibility and the high value placed upon the teaching of the magisterium and the role of tradition in Roman Catholic teaching may also be linked to the concept of continuing revelation. Such teachings are troubling to many Protestants who see them as challenging the ultimacy of scriptural authority.[6]

More recently the claims of Pentecostals as well as those of many within the wider charismatic renewal have raised similar questions. Their claims to manifest spontaneous prophetic utterances, words of wisdom or knowledge, the ability to speak in tongues and to receive a meaningful interpretation of the *lalia,* coupled with some of their more radical excesses, have provided ample grist for the mill to keep the debate interesting.[7] It may even be the case that the current charismatic practice of "prophesying" has contributed to the recent renewal of interest in this charism being shown by New Testament scholars worldwide.[8]

Review and Herald Publishing Association, 1937); C. B. Haynes, *The Gift of Prophecy* (1931; Nashville: Southern Publishing Association, 1946); and more recently *The Spirit of Prophecy: Treasure Chest* (Glendale, Ca: Prophetic Guidance School of the Voice of Prophecy, 1960).

5. See for example L. Festing, H. W. Riecken, and S. Schacter, *When Prophecy Fails: A Social and Psychological Study of a Modern Group that Predicted the Destruction of the World* (1956; New York: Harper Torchbooks, 1964).

6. See F. J. Paul, *Romanism and Evangelical Christianity: A Study of Origins and Development* (London: Hodder and Stoughton, 1940) 4-6; R. H. Fuller and R. P. C. Hanson, *The Church of Rome: A Dissuasive* (1948; London: SCM, 1960) 67, 92; F. V. Filson, *Which Books Belong in the Bible? A Study of the Canon* (Philadelphia: Westminster, 1957) 155-62; R. M. Brown and G. Weigel, *An American Dialogue: A Protestant Looks at Catholicism and a Catholic Looks at Protestantism* (Garden City, N.Y.: Doubleday, 1960) 84-92. The position affirmed by Roman Catholics at Vatican II is that the Church "has always regarded, and continues to regard the Scriptures, taken together with sacred Tradition, as the supreme rule of her faith." D.V. 21. Cf. A. Dulles, "The Bible in the Church: Some Debated Questions," in G. Martin, ed. *Scripture and the Charismatic Renewal* (Ann Arbor: Servant, 1979) 16-19. On the subject of papal infallibility see L.G. 25. References to the documents of Vatican II are to A. Flannery, ed. *Vatican Council II: The Conciliar and Post Conciliar Documents* (2 vols.; Collegeville, Mn.: Liturgical Press, 1975, 1984)

7. See D. P. Williams, *The Prophetical Ministry (Or the Voice Gifts) In the Church* (Penygroes, New Zealand: The Apostolic Church, Ga. Headquarters, no date); A. Labonte, *Exploring the Gift of Prophecy* (Pecos, N.M.: Dove Publications, 1974); M. T. Kelsey, *God, Dreams, and Revelation: A Christian Interpretation of Dreams* (Minneapolis: Augsburg, 1968); J. A. Sanford, *Dreams: God's Forgotten Language* (Philadelphia: Lippincott, 1968); D. Wilkerson, *The Vision* (Old Tappan, N.J.: Fleming H. Revell/Spire, 1974); R. B. Hall, *Anyone Can Prophesy* (New York: Seabury, 1977).

8. Among such studies have been D. E. Aune, *Prophecy in Early Christianity and the Ancient Mediterranean World* (Grand Rapids: Eerdmans, 1983); M. E. Boring, *Sayings of the Risen Christ: Christian Prophecy in the Synoptic Tradition* (SNTS 46; Cambridge: Cambridge University Press, 1982); T. M. Crone, *Early Christian Prophecy: A Study of its Origin and Function* (Baltimore: St. Mary's University, 1973); G. Dautzenberg, *Urchristlich Prophetie* (BWANT 4; Stuttgart: W. Kohlhammer, 1975); E. E. Ellis, *Prophecy and Hermeneutic in Early Christianity* (Grand Rapids: Eerdmans, 1980); W. A. Grudem, *The Gift of Prophecy in 1 Corinthians* (Washington, D.C.: University Press of America, 1982); D. Hill, *New Testament Prophecy* (MTL; London: Marshall, Morgan & Scott, 1979); U. B. Müller, *Prophetie und Predigt im*

I

Lest claims of personal revelation and discussions of the appropriate role of revelation be thought of as relatively recent additions to the ongoing theological discussion, it would pay to review the evidence. Scripture is replete with examples of such claims, from the dream of Jacob at Bethel with its divine promise (Gen 28:10-17) to the prophetic dreams of Joseph concerning his future role among his brothers (Gen 37:5-11). They extend from the prophetic ministry of such figures as Moses, Samuel, and Elijah to the confrontation between competing prophetic claims in Jeremiah's day (Jer 27:1–28:17).

One need not look far within the earliest Christian community to recognize that claims to personal revelation, whether through dreams, visions, prophetic oracles or other similar phenomena, were equally prevalent. Jesus warned his disciples that false prophets would come among them (Matt 7:15-23), indeed, that such prophets would often be successful (Matt 24:11, 24-25; cf. Mark 13:22-23). John set forth similar warnings to his readers (1 John 4:1-6) but made personal prophetic claims for himself (Rev 1:1-3, 9-19). Peter had a vision of a sheet full of "unclean animals" which he used to justify his initial evangelistic excursion among the Gentiles (Acts 10:9-20; 11:1-12). And Paul affirmed prophetic activity among the Corinthians (1 Corinthians 12–14) and the Thessalonians (1 Thess 5:19-22), while at the same time acknowledging that prophetic claims needed to be submitted to community review (1 Cor 14:29, 37-38; 1 Thess 5:21a).

Nor did prophetic claims cease with the close of the first century. Coming as it did at the turn of the century, the *Didache* made room for what was perceived to be a legitimate itinerant prophetic ministry.[9] It also allowed for the ongoing exercise of prophetic prerogatives by those who were regularly attached to specific communities.[10] Ignatius of Antioch wrote a short letter to the Philadelphian Christians sometime during the opening two decades of the second century in which he spoke of his own experience of prophecy. He recorded for his readers two oracles which he claimed he had delivered spontaneously to the congregation in a loud voice with the Spirit's complicity.[11]

Within a decade came another work, probably Roman in its origin, the product of a little known Christian named Hermas. *The Shepherd of Hermas* contained what were purported to be a series of visions, and it provided guidelines to distin-

---

Neuen Testament (SNT 10; Gütersloh: Gerd Mohn, 1975); J. Panagopoulos, *Prophetic Vocation in the New Testament and Today* (NovTSup 45; Leiden: E. J. Brill, 1977); J. Reiling, *Hermas and Christian Prophecy: A Study of the Eleventh Mandate* (NovTSup 37; Leiden: E. J. Brill, 1973); one should also also note the study by É. Cothenet, "Prophétisme dans Le Nouveau Testament," *Supplément au Dictionaire de la Bible* (Paris: Letouzey & Ane, 1971, 1972) fascicle 46-47, cols. 1222-1337.

9. *Did*. 10.7; 11.1-12.

10. *Did*. 13.1-7.

11. Ignatius, *Phld*. 7.1-2; W. R. Schoedel, *Ignatius of Antioch: A Commentary on the Letters of Ignatius of Antioch* ed. H. Koester (Herm.; Philadelphia: Fortress, 1985), 205-6; F. J. Dölger "*Theou Phōnē* Die 'Gottes-Stimme' bei Ignatius von Antiochien, Kelsos und Origenes," *AC* 5 (1936) 218-23.

guish between true and false prophets.[12] *The Shepherd* played a significant role in the devotional life of the early church. Irenaeus called it *hē graphē* or *scriptura*, although it is as yet unclear as to whether or not he meant to place it on the same level as the apostolic writings.[13] Clement of Alexandria cited it repeatedly in the *Stromata*,[14] and the visions of Perpetua appear to have been heavily influenced by it as well.[15] On the other hand, Tertullian found it to be offensive on the grounds that it was lenient to adulterers and the *lapsi*.[16]

In Gaul, Irenaeus debated pointedly with gnostic revelatory claims, among them those of the magician, Marcus, whose targets typically were the fortunes and virtues of older women.[17] Irenaeus was also aware of the claims of those whom he called "false prophets," most probably certain Alogi who repudiated John's Gospel.[18] According to Eusebius, Irenaeus also acted as an emissary for certain brethren in Gaul, for whom he carried a report to Bishop Eleutherus in Rome which outlined Montanist activities in the Rhone valley.[19] In spite of his awareness of and interaction with these other than orthodox claims to prophetic inspiration, Irenaeus contended that legitimate manifestations of this gift were nonetheless to be found among Christians,[20] and even more forcefully he contended that those who rejected the charism of prophecy out of hand were "of no use to God. . . ."[21]

Hippolytus, influential in both the east and west, wrote at the close of the second century and well into the third. Like his predecessor Irenaeus, he was alert to the antics and doctrines of various gnostic teachers. He attributed the teachings of Marcus to "visions,"[22] and he also noted that Apelles employed a "prophetess" named Philumene whose revelations *(phanerōseis)* he published and circulated.[23] His concerns with the activities of Montanism were related to the fact that the adherents to that movement were generally said to be unwilling to test the prophetic claims of their leaders. At times, then, they were "overrun with delusion."[24]

In spite of his criticisms of Gnosticism and Montanism, Hippolytus, like those who preceded him, argued for the continuation of the immediate authority of the Spirit as it was manifest in the dynamic expression of certain charismata. In-

12. See especially *Herm. Man.* 11.

13. Irenaeus, *Against Heresies,* 4.20.2. On Irenaeus's use of the term *scriptura* see B. Sesboué, "La prueve par les Ecritures chea S. Irénée; a propos d'un texte difficile du Livre III de l'*Adversus Haeresis,*" *NRT* 103 (1981) 872-87.

14. Clement of Alexandria, *Stromata,* 1.1.1; 1.85.4; 2.3.4; 4.74.4; 6.131.2; etc.

15. Compare, for instance, *The Passion of Perpetua and Felicitas* 4.6-7 with *Herm. Vis.* 4.1.4-8.

16. Tertullian, *On Modesty* 10:12.

17. Irenaeus, *Against Heresies,* 1.13.

18. Ibid., 3.11.9.

19. Eusebius, *EH* 5.3.4–5.4.3.

20. Irenaeus, *Against Heresies,* 5.6.1. On this passage see my article "Irenaeus and 'Prophetic Gifts,'" in P. Elbert, ed., *Essays on Apostolic Themes: Studies in Honor of Howard M. Ervin* (Peabody, Ma.: Hendrickson, 1985) 109-11.

21. Irenaeus, *The Demonstration of the Apostolic Preaching,* 99.

22. Hippolytus, *The Refutation of All Heresies,* 6.37.

23. Ibid., 7.26; 10.26.

24. Ibid., 8.12.

deed, revelatory gifts were apparently enlisted by Hippolytus as in some sense making a meaningful contribution to the safeguarding of the apostolic tradition.[25] Teachers who were "reminiscent of the New Testament prophets"[26] regularly exhorted the Christians of Hippolytus's day to faithful attendance at local congregational gatherings. Revelations were also allowed a legitimate role in recognizing certain individuals as possessing healing gifts within the church.[27]

About the same time, Origen, who taught first in Alexandria (A.D. 203-231) and later in Caesarea (A.D. 232-253), was sufficiently vexed by the claims on behalf of the Pythian oracle and Montanism, and by the arguments of Celsus on Christian prophets, to address himself to the subject. He argued forcefully against the claims of ecstasy *(ekstasin)*, frenzy *(maniken)* and loss of consciousness as signs of genuine prophetic activity.[28] He maintained, instead, that genuine Christian prophets manifested clear vision at the moment of revelation which enabled them to declare the profundities of Christian doctrine as revealed by the Spirit.[29] He chided the neoplatonic skeptic, Celsus, for failing to tell the truth about his observations of prophetic activity in Phoenecia and Palestine.[30]

None of these abuses, however, led Origen to deny the genuineness of prophetic claims in his day. While he believed that it was in the province of all Christians to prophesy if they sought the "higher gifts,"[31] he argued that it was not appropriate for women to do so in the church.[32] Men could prophesy, however, and their prophetic insights were often helpful in providing biblical understanding and spiritual growth.[33]

Montanism, or the New Prophecy, was at first only a local phenomenon limited to the regions of Phrygia in Asia Minor. About A.D. 172 its prime mover, Montanus, and two of his female disciples Pris[cill]a and Maximilla began to prophesy

25. Ibid., 1.5; 38.4; and possibly 16.25.

26. B. S. Eaton, ed. *The Apostolic Tradition of Hippolytus* (1934; Cambridge: Archon Books, 1962) 104; Hippolytus, *Apostolic Tradition*, 35.2-3.

27. The similarities between 1 Tim 4:14 (cf. also 1 Tim 1:18) and Hippolytus, *Apostolic Tradition* 15, are striking. In each passage there is either a recognition or discovery of another charism which is made known by a prophecy *(dia prophēteias)*, or revelation *(di' apokalypseōs)*, and there is mention of the laying on of hands. In the case of Hippolytus, the laying on of hands is unnecessary, since those laypersons whose ability to heal has been discerned by revelation are sufficiently tested by the fruit of their efforts at employing the charism.

28. Origen, *Contra Celsum*, 7.3. Cf. Plutarch, *Obsolescence of Oracles*, 438 A-B (51).

29. Origen, *Contra Celsum*, 7.3; idem, *On First Principles*, 6.17.

30. Origen, *Contra Celsum*, 7.8-12.

31. Origen, *Homily on Exodus* 4:5; C. Jenkins, "Documents: Origen on 1 Corinthians," *JBL* 10 (1909) 41, Fragment 73.

32. While Origen acknowledged that Miriam had led the women (Exod 15:20-21), Deborah had been a prophetess (Judg 4:4), and Philip had four virgin daughters who prophesied (Acts 21:9), he nonetheless argued that it was the men, Isaiah and Jeremiah, and not these women who were allowed to speak within the temple. For a woman to do so was both dishonoring and shameful. Jenkins, "Origen on 1 Corinthians," 41-42, Fragment 74.

33. Origen, *On First Principles*, 6.17. For further assessment of Origen's understanding of the gift of prophecy see my article "Origen's Treatment of the Charismata in 1 Corthinians 12:8-10," in C. M. Robeck, Jr., ed. *Charismatic Experience in History* (Peabody, Ma.: Hendrickson, 1986) 115-19.

within the Christian community. They attracted many[34] who then carried their message to the reaches of the empire.[35] While Montanism exhibited apocalyptic and ascetic tendencies, the most significant problem it posed in the early church was the question of how seriously its claims to prophetic authority were to be taken. In many places its claims to divine inspiration directly confronted the claims of certain long-standing traditions,[36] and established ecclesiastical leadership.[37] This ultimately led to its rejection as a heresy.

Tertullian represented the interests of the New Prophecy in third-century Carthage. He was a firm believer in continuing revelation, basing his convictions on a popular Montanist reading of John 16:12-13. Jesus had predicted the Paraclete's role as the *restitutor* rather than the *institutor* of discipline; nevertheless the Paraclete would reveal those things which were told Him.[38] While others might judge the Paraclete's rulings as "novel" and "burdensome," Tertullian argued that they were consistent with Jesus' teachings, and that they should be tested against the *regula fidei,* a fixed summary of apostolic faith. What one believed, he argued, inevitably affected what one did.[39]

It is noteworthy to see how Tertullian employed the oracles of the New Prophecy. While they were thought to provide spontaneous inbreakings of the mind of the Spirit within given situations, they were also understood as clarifying the truth he believed already to be present in the apostolic writings. He used them as *supplementary evidence* for what he perceived to be the teaching of Scripture on such subjects as Hades and the abode of the righteous dead, the role of suffering in discipleship, the need for strict Christian discipline, the suppression of the flesh, the resurrection of the body, the existence of the Trinity, the corporeal nature of the soul, the veiling of women in the church, the importance of monogamy, and the merits of fasting.[40]

While some would argue that *The Passion of Perpetua and Felicitas* is a product of Montanism,[41] it would seem rather that what has been interpreted as

34. Among those followers were Miltiades, Themiso, Proculus, Theodotus, and Alexander. See Eusebius, *EH* 5.14.1; 5.16.8.

35. To the west it reached as far as Gaul (Eusebius, *EH* 5.3.4–5.4.3) and Spain (Pacien of Barcelona *Epistle* 1.3). It found acceptance for a period of time in Rome (Tertullian, *Against Praxeas,* 1.5). It was prevalent throughout Asia Minor (Eusebius, *EH* 5.14.1; 5.16.4, 7, 17, 22; 5.18.1-2) and probably, according to the account given by Firmilian (Cyprian, *Epistle* 75.7, 10, 19), in Syria (Eusebius, *EH* 5.19.1-4), as well as in Phoenecia and Palestine, if Celsus bore witness to their activities (Origen, *Contra Celsum,* 7.9-10). Later their influence was felt strongly in North Africa, as is abundantly evidenced from the writings of Tertullian.

36. Jerome, *Epistle* 41.3; cf. Tertullian, *On Fasting* 2.1-4; 5.4; 10.8, 13; 13.6; 15.3-5.

37. Eusebius, *EH* 5.16.9-10.

38. Tertullian, *On Monogamy* 4.1; 2.2.

39. Ibid., 2.2-3: "*Adversarius enim spiritus ex diversitate praedicationis appareret primo regulam adulterans fidei. . . .*"

40. See Tertullian's references in the following: *A Treatise on the Soul* 55.2-5; *On Flight in Persecution* 9.4; *On Modesty* 21.7; *On Chastity* 10.5; *On the Resurrection of the Flesh* 11.2; *Against Praxeas* 8.5; *Treatise on the Soul* 9.4; *On the Veiling of Virgins* 1.1-7; 17.3; *On Monogamy* 14.3-4; On Fasting.

41. J. DeSoyres, *Montanism and the Primitive Church* (Cambridge: Deighton Bell, and Co., 1878) 44-45, 140; T. D. Barnes, *Tertullian: A Historical and Literary Study* (Oxford:

Montanist in character is just as easily explainable as typically present in a vibrant form of Christianity and is not unique to Montanism.[42] Yet the visionary or revelatory experiences of the martyrs and the literary framework in which the redactor set them caused them to become archetypal for "all later Acts of the Christian Martyrs."[43] To say that various manifestations of continuing revelation were prevalent among the martyrs is to underscore the obvious.

Cyprian's tenure as bishop of Carthage was pregnant with reports of visions, revelations, and prophecies which were enlisted to support and confirm certain ecclesiastical appointments,[44] provide comfort to Confessors,[45] exhort the Christian community toward unity,[46] and give personal direction to Cyprian during times of crisis.[47] It is true that Cyprian's own claims to revelation are open to question on the ground of personal motivation,[48] but if half of what Cyprian claims about the extent and the nature of visions among laypersons, confessors, children, bishops, priests, and martyrs is true, then their presence in the North African church was no less than spectacular. Other examples could be cited at length,[49] but this brief survey should be sufficient to demonstrate the vigor with which a variety of revelatory claims, orthodox, Gnostic, and Montanist, continued to be made, well into the middle of the third century. The original apostles had long since disappeared, yet there were claims by some as late as Cyprian, which would undoubtedly argue that they stood within the apostolic tradition, thereby assuring a judgment of "legitimate" on their revelatory claims.

What were the factors which made such claims possible? Why was it the case that some Christians were considered credible witnesses to revelatory experiences while others were not? Why could the visions of Saturus and Perpetua be upheld as orthodox to the extent that first Tertullian and later Augustine would use them to support doctrinal positions?[50] Why, on the other hand, were the revelatory claims of the Gnostics, Marcus and Apelles, as well as certain Montanists, dis-

---

Clarendon, 1971) 77; G. Bardy, *La Vie Spirituelle d' après Les Pères des Trois Premiers Siècles* (Tournai, Belgium: Desclée et Cie, 1968), 1.216.

42. P. de Labriolle, *La Crise Montaniste* (Paris: Ernest Leroux, 1913) 341-42; W. C. Weinrich, *Spirit and Martyrdom: A Study of the Work of the Holy Spirit in Contexts of Persecution and Martyrdom in the New Testament and Early Christian Literature* (Lanham, Md.: University Press of America, 1981) 225-36.

43. H. Musurillo, *The Acts of the Christian Martyrs* (Oxford: Clarendon, 1972) xxv.

44. Cyprian, *Epistles* 39.1, 4; 40; 48.4; 63.1; 66.5, 10; 70.3.

45. Ibid., 10.4; 58.1; 78.1-2; 6.1-3.

46. Ibid., 11.3-6, which includes four such visions.

47. Ibid., 16.4; 7.

48. So, A. von Harnack, "Cyprian als Enthusiast," *ZNW* 3 (1902) 177-91. There were contemporary skeptics in Carthage such as Florentius Pupianus who apparently nicknamed Cyprian "the dreamer." *Epistle* 66.10.

49. See, e.g., *The Martyrdom of Polycarp*, 5, 9, 12, 16; *Barnabas*, 16.9-10; Justin Martyr, *Dialog with Trypho*, 82; 87-88; *First Apology*, 36; as well as numerous gospels, apostolic pseudepigrapha, acts of apostles, and apocalypses.

50. Tertullian, *Treatise on the Soul* 54.1–55.5, esp. 55.4; Augustine, *On the Soul and Its Origin* 1.10; 2.10; 3.9.

missed almost out of hand as heretical?[51] And why would Irenaeus refer to *The Shepherd of Hermas* as *hē graphē* or *scriptura,* while Tertullian would look anxiously about, expressing relief that at least in North Africa it was not given such a lofty assessment?[52] It is to questions such as these that we now turn our attention.

II

That the manifestation of prophetic gifts was on the decline in the early church has long been observed. What has not always been clear is the reason for such a decline. Adolf von Harnack argued at the end of the nineteenth century that it was the formation of the New Testament canon which "put an end to a situation where it was possible for any Christian under the inspiration of the Spirit to give authoritative disclosures and instructions."[53]

Related to this position, but approaching it from a different angle, is the argument more recently promoted by David Hill and affirmed by David Aune. It involves the explanation that the decline of genuine prophetic claims was linked to the attendant rise of the more predictable teachers and theologians.[54] The suggestion made by Hans von Campenhausen parallels this explanation nicely, yet it is nuanced further by what he calls the ascendancy of "traditional apostolic truth." His suggestion is not so much that the decline came about through a struggle between two opposing schools, an official ecclesiastical one which rose up against a spontaneous "charismatic" one, since those in official positions possessed the Spirit, and those who might be described as "charismatic" received spiritual power to teach the "traditional apostolic truth." Rather, it was when the so-called "charismatics" became too closely identified with schism, sectarianism, and heresy that the official ecclesiarchs intensified their own authority with its accompanying safeguards.[55]

James Ash has built upon von Campenhausen's argument but has reached yet another conclusion. He contends that it is not canon, nor heresy, nor even concern with "traditional apostolic truth" per se which contributed to the decline of prophetic gifts, but that "the charisma of prophecy was captured by the monarchical episcopate, used in its defense, and left to die an unnoticed death when true episcopal stability rendered it a superfluous tool."[56]

Undoubtedly, each of these suggestions has something to contribute to our comprehension of what was taking place in the evolution of the church's self-understanding during that early period when the idea of a Christian canon was yet in

51. Irenaeus, *Against Heresies* 1.13; Hippolytus, *The Refutation of All Heresies* 6.37; 7.26; 10.26; 8.12; Epiphanius, *Panarion* 48.11; Didymus, *On the Trinity* 3.41.1; Cyril of Jerusalem, *Catechetical Lectures,* 16.8.

52. Irenaeus, *Against Heresies* 4.20.2; Tertullian, *On Modesty* 10.12.

53. Harnack, *History of Dogma* (tr. N. Buchanan, 1896; New York: Dover Publications, rpt. 1961) 2.53.

54. Hill, *New Testament Prophecy,* 191; Aune, *Prophecy in Early Christianity,* 338.

55. H. von Campenhausen, *Ecclesiastical Authority and Spiritual Power in the Church of the First Three Centuries* (tr. J. A. Baker; Stanford: Stanford University Press, 1969) 178.

56. J. L. Ash, "The Decline of Prophecy in the Early Church," *TS* 37 (1976) 252.

a fluid state. If continuing revelation through visions and prophetic oracles made a significant contribution to the lives of these Christians, so too did the development of such items as the teaching office, canons of truth or *regulae fidei,* and ultimately a fuller concept of Scripture. By way of contrast to the personal claims of divine inspiration, each of these developments tended to steer the Christian community in the direction of greater stability. It should come as no surprise, then, to realize that traditional studies of canon were undertaken with this in mind.

That to some extent this was the way the biblical canon came into its own should not be denied. In more recent days, however, James A. Sanders has worked extensively in the area of "canonical criticism," coming to the conclusion that the subject of canon was related not only to the question of *stability,* but also to *adaptability.*[57] The seeds to such a conclusion run deeply within the canonical literature itself. Such affirmations that would later be understood to be biblical confessions of faith concerning the oneness of God (Deut 6:4; Mark 12:32-33; Eph 4:6), the messianic nature (Matt 16:16; John 6:68), the divine sonship (John 1:49; Acts 8:37), and the lordship of Jesus (Rom 10:9; 1 Cor 12:3; Phil 2:11) as well as the importance of the Incarnation (1 Tim 3:16; 1 John 4:2; Phil 2:7) are readily apparent. The making of these confessions, some of the earliest if yet fragmentary Christian creeds,[58] guaranteed stability to the fledgling church, but they did so precisely because they were also adaptable to the challenges which were being met in ever new and changing environments.

If such a conclusion is warranted in the development of canon, it would seem that it could be a useful tool by which to assess the role of continuing revelation as it was experienced by Christians within the first three centuries. In a sense, the development of the various *regulae fidei* were steps along the way, each acting as a summary of those points of doctrine, which, according to Sanders's schema spoke to the majority of the community and communicated some power which they sought, a power which either affirmed or challenged the community's self-understanding.[59] To say that what distinguished true from false prophets and the acceptance or rejection of their revelations was their hermeneutic is certainly true. The texts themselves did not change radically but the interpretations sometimes did. In the long run, the issue of hermeneutics may prove to be the single most significant factor in enabling the community to discern the ultimate veracity of the "prophet's" oracle. Intrinsic to this approach is one of the oldest prophetic tests, the test of fulfillment.[60] It was a test invoked in the classic confrontation between

57. J. A. Sanders, "Adaptable for Life: The Nature and Function of Canon," in F. M. Cross et al., eds. *Magnalia Dei: The Mighty Works of God: Essays on the Bible and Archeology in Memory of G. Ernest Wright* (Garden City, N.Y.: Doubleday, 1976) 531; cf. J. A. Sanders "Text and Canon: Concepts and Methods," *JBL* 98 (1979) 5-29; and J. A. Sanders, *Canon and Community: A Guide to Canonical Criticism* (Guides to Biblical Scholarship 6; Philadelphia: Fortress, 1984).

58. J. N. D. Kelly, *Early Christian Creeds* (3d ed.; New York: David McKay, 1972) 13-23; Philip Schaff, ed. *The Creeds of Cristendom* (rev. David S. Schaff 1931, 6th ed.; Grand Rapids; Baker, 1985) 2.3-8.

59. Sanders, "Adaptable for Life," 538.

60. This was a test set forth in Deut 18:20-22, a test which was to be accompanied by the invocation of the death penalty, clear evidence of the seriousness of the challenge of false prophecy to the believing community. Cf. Deut 13:1-5.

the word of the Lord as spoken by Jeremiah and the word which Hananiah spoke (Jer 28:15-17). Israel was forced to live out the word of the Lord as spoken by Jeremiah, involving an extensive Babylonian captivity, in part because they followed too readily after the words of Hananiah.

There were other tests, too, especially within the earliest Christian community. They often involved the analysis of personal character and the fruit which derived from it (Matt 7:15-23), or they were related to questions of prophetic purpose and methodology (1 Cor 14:4, 29-33a, 37-38). That such tests were employed well into the post-apostolic era is also apparent from their inclusion in such works as the *Didache* and the *Shepherd of Hermas.*[61] Personal charismatic claims and self-reported tales of ecstatic experiences in themselves were a place to begin, but they were ultimately insufficient for distinguishing between the true and false in matters of continuing revelation.

Yet, the most significant test applied to the claims of continuing revelation was that of content. Its validation lay in its consistency with the apostolic tradition or in its fulfillment. It is true that certain Gnostics, especially the Marcusian Gnostics present in the Rhone valley[62] as well as the Montanists who lived throughout Asia Minor,[63] were criticized repeatedly both in matters of character and method; but more often than not, the ultimate test included some form of content assessment.[64]

At least two explanations make themselves readily apparent in this regard. First, it may have been thought that bizarre and disruptive behavior would work sufficiently well as its own best deterrent, so that even the new convert would question such activity. Second, and probably more to the point, the recording of new and continuing revelatory claims made them accessible to further analysis, indeed, their very writtenness turned these new "traditions" into "pasts" which invited, even demanded, such study.[65] Until such new and written revelatory claims had been adequately studied and discerned by the Christian community to have validity, they could be understood as challenges to community stability, or as literary agents of *instability*.

As the early church struggled with the issue of a developing canon it was confronted with numerous claims of divine inspiration from many quarters. The tension between the issues of stability and adaptability were real tensions. Ultimately they were settled in one of several ways.

A. *Some claims were accepted as having validity even by the larger Christian*

---

61. *Did.* 11.4-6, 8-10, 12; 12.1; *Herm. Man.* 11.5-14, 16.

62. Irenaeus, *Against Heresies* 1.13.3-4; 3.11.9.

63. Eusebius, *EH* 5.16.13; 5.18.3-4, 11; 5.16.7; 5.17.2; Epiphanius, *Panarion* 48.4-7.

64. Justin Martyr, *Dialog with Trypho* 37; 82; Irenaeus, *Against Heresies* Pref 1; 1.13.3; 1.14.1–1.15.3; Clement of Alexandria, *Stromata* 2.8; Epiphanius, *Panarion* 48.11; Eusebius, *EH* 5.16.9, 17-19; 5.18.2. In the case of Montanism, the content issues tended to focus upon pronouncements concerning praxis rather than those of doctrine (although the latter were not totally absent), since several of the movement's primary antagonists found its doctrinal affirmations to be sufficiently orthodox as to be acceptable; cf. Hippolytus, *The Refutation of All Heresies* 8.12; Ephiphanius, *Panarion* 48.1; Jerome, *Epistle* 41.3.

65. P. Perkins, *The Gnostic Dialogue: The Early Church and the Crisis of Gnosticism* (New York: Paulist, 1980) 8-9.

community, but with limited adaptability and applicability. In all likelihood these were the most numerous of all the revelatory claims with which the early church had to deal. Among these claims were two distinct types.

1. First were those which were narrowly focused. For the most part they included the more or less isolated claims that a certain individual had experienced some form of divine condescension, revelation, dream, or vision, or that this individual had received some specific word or prophetic oracle from the Lord. For the most part, *it was a word which was understood to speak to the actions that either a specific individual or a small group was to undertake at a given time.*

Examples of this type of revelation are present even in the New Testament. At least two of them appear in Luke's historical and theological treatment of the earliest Christian community. In one instance it is simply stated that the Holy Spirit made it clear to a small group of prophets and teachers that Barnabas and Saul were to be set apart to undertake a specific missionary activity (Acts 13:1-3). The context says nothing of what kind of testing was undertaken to determine the validity of this directive. It only indicates that in obedience the directive was followed.

Some years later, the prophet Agabus gave another revelation regarding Paul. "Thus says the Holy Spirit," he proclaimed. He went on to predict that Paul would be taken prisoner in Jerusalem and handed over to the Gentiles (Acts 21:10-14). Reaction to this predictive word, which apparently came as one among several along Paul's journey (cf. Acts 20:22-23), was mixed. On the one side was the majority opinion held by those who heard this prediction as a *directive* (cf. Acts 21:4, 12) indicating that Paul should not continue his planned itinerary. On the other side was Paul, who understood the continuation of his journey to be consistent with his own experience of being "bound in the Spirit" (Acts 20:22) to go to Jerusalem. He apparently understood the word not as a directive, but merely as *predictive.* Ultimately, Paul and the majority came to an understanding whereby the will of the Lord was invoked (Acts 21:14). The primary relevance of this oracle to the church was clearly limited at first, expanding only as it was contextualized within the larger account known as Luke-Acts, and understood according to a different hermeneutic. Its initial significance was fulfilled within a very limited time span in the life of Paul.

The experiences of other early Christians, even post-apostolic Christians, were similar. Polycarp received a vision from which he concluded that he would be burned alive. His biographer was careful to note that this prophetic word was fulfilled just as Polycarp had predicted it would be.[66] Similarly, Polycarp's biographer recorded the case that there were those who bore witness to the reality of a *bath qôl,* a heavenly voice, which gave a final word of encouragement to Polycarp as he entered the amphitheater.[67]

The diary of Perpetua gives three accounts of visions she claims to have experienced.[68] Shortly after her arrest as a Christian during the persecution authorized by

66. *Martyrdom of Polycarp* 5.2; 12.3; 16.2.
67. Ibid., 9.1.
68. *The Passion of Perpetua* 4.1-10; 7.1-10 and 8.1-4; 10.1-14.

Septimius Severus[69] about A.D. 202, Perpetua was encouraged by her brother to request a vision from the Lord. Its purpose would be to provide Perpetua and her immediate family with advance information regarding the outcome of her imminent trial. Would she undergo a *passio* or be released? Perpetua did as requested, received her vision, and from it she and her brother concluded that the *passio* was inevitable. Perpetua's later visions of her deceased brother Dinocrates enabled Perpetua to resolve a personal anxiety over his eternal state. Her vision of the Egyptian wrestler gave her confidence that she would overcome the power of the devil by sustaining a successful martyrdom. In each case, these visions brought a particularized word of clarity, strength, comfort, or direction to an individual in the midst of an otherwise intolerable state of affairs.

The writings of Cyprian indicate that such phenomena continued to occur in his day in the North African church. Cyprian's claim to personal revelation which led him to leave Carthage in the midst of the Decian persecution,[70] and his appeal to his own visions in matters of Christian unity while he was absent,[71] have raised legitimate questions as to what extent his own claims may be taken at face value.[72] Even so, others such as Celerinus[73] were said to have been helped through the reception of visions. Apparently many bishops of the North African church were appointed as a result of divine *dignatione*.[74] Furthermore, many were the confessors and martyrs who were encouraged, comforted, and strengthened by such things during their suffering.[75]

In each of these instances there appears to have been no competition either with the *regula fidei* as it was understood within the given historical context or with any form of canon. They were merely understood as personal words or instructions, which on their initial appearance were divinely given to specific people in a specific location for specific purposes. They might be understood as having limited relevance or adaptability beyond the immediate context. In the case of Acts 13:1-3 and Acts 21:10-14, the relevance of these oracles was expanded only insofar as they were placed within the larger context of Luke-Acts. A number of later oracles and visions would be said to be consistent in their purpose with the

---

69. On the evidence for a formal edict authorizing such a persecution see the discussion by W. H. C. Frend, "Open Questions Concerning the Christians and the Roman Empire in the Age of the Severi," *JTS* N.S. 25 (1974) 340-43; but see T. D. Barnes, *Tertullian: A Historical and Literary Study* (Oxford: Clarendon, 1971) 150-51.

70. Cyprian, *Epistles* 20.1; 16.4; 7. He had at least one devotee, his biographer Pontius, who believed and propagated Cyprian's claim. Pontius, *Passion of Cyprian* 7.

71. Cyprian, *Epistles* 11.3-6; 66.10.

72. Harnack, "Cyprian als Enthusiast," 179, 183-84, 190; P. Hinchliff, *Cyprian of Carthage and the Unity of the Christian Church* (London: Geoffrey Chapman, 1974) 26. By way of contrast, see M. M. Sage, *Cyprian* (PMS 1; Cambridge, Ma.: The Philadelphia Patristic Foundation, 1975) 204; and P. Brown, *The Making of Late Antiquity* (Cambridge: Harvard University Press, 1978) 79-80 and esp. 124n.99.

73. Cyprian, *Epistles* 39.1.

74. Ibid., 63.1.

75. Ibid., 10.4; 58.1; 78.1-2; 6.1-3. The words of Jesus in Matt 10:19-20 (Cf. Luke 12:11-12; 21:11-19; Mark 13:9-13) demonstrated to the North African Christians of this era a close relationship between a legitimate use of the gift of prophecy and martyrdom. Cf. *The Passion of Perpetua* 4.1-10; 10.1-13.

words of Jesus as recorded in Matt 10:19-20. Still others could be said to be consistent with Paul's understanding of the role of prophecy as outlined in 1 Cor 14:3. They contributed to the stability of the Christian community in a particular place at a particular time during particular circumstances, but they carried within themselves no ongoing normativity, no universal applicability, and no competition to already existing norms. As such, they held limited authority.

2. A second group of visions and oracles which received limited acceptance were *those which were directed to individuals or groups but with limited time spans in which they were said to be fulfilled,* or they were understood as having *local or sectarian rather than personal relevance.* It is conceivable that Agabus's prophecy before the believers at Antioch regarding the imminent famine over all the world would have been considered as fitting this model were it not for the fact that ultimately it found its way into the context of the canonical Acts 11:27-30. In its original *Sitz im Leben,* it became the impetus by which a collection was begun for the relief of fellow believers in Judea, and it was fulfilled, according to Luke, "in the days of Claudius." Hence, its initial relevance has been permanently lost to the worldwide church since it was apparently intended to encourage an offering, and the event it predicted was consummated two millenia ago. It does not fit this category, however, in that somewhere along the way it was given a new context, a context which enabled it to be repeated, a context which allowed it, in its entirety, to be adapted to the benefit of new people in new places in other times. Within this canonical context, the text remains unchanged, but the interpretation given it is new. It now depicts the concern of the Spirit of God for the needs of the people of God while demonstrating the ability of some Christians to meet the needs of other Christians. It may also teach something about the legitimacy of certain elements of prophetic content within the church. But twentieth century Christians need not be concerned to heed the warning of Agabus in the same way the church at Antioch once did. The hermeneutic has obviously changed.

The fact that *The Shepherd of Hermas* was described by Irenaeus as *hē graphē* or *scriptura,* that it was not considered as Scripture but as decent devotional literature by the framers of the Muratorian Canon,[76] and that it was decried by Tertullian would all tend to indicate that the relevance or adaptability of its relevatory claims was thought to be more regional and local than universal. Yet Tertullian, who would deny legitimacy to *The Shepherd,* himself championed a number of sectarian and regional oracles and visions or ones of limited value.

The redactor who was responsible for preserving Perpetua's visions, as well as a vision recorded by another martyr, Saturus, and for weaving them into the larger narrative framework of *The Passion of Perpetua and Felicitas,* saw in them a broader significance than is apparent even from an in-depth exegesis of the visions themselves and the events surrounding them. There were other writings of which the redactor was aware, ancient ones in which deeds of faith *(fidei ex-*

---

76. ". . . *ideo legi eum quidem opertet, se publicare vero in ecclesia populo, neque inter Prophetas, completo numero, neque inter Apostolos, in finem temporum potest."* The Latin text is from A. H. Charteris, *Canonicity: A Collection of Early Testimonies to the Canonical Books of the New Testament* (Edinburgh: William Blackwood and Sons, 1880) 8.

empla) were recorded, writings which evidenced the elements of both stability and adaptability. On the side of stability, these writings functioned to demonstrate God's grace *(Dei Gratiam)* to his people. On the side of adaptability, these writings simultaneously provided for the ongoing edification *(aedificationem)* of those who read them.[77] In short, the redactor was aware of a number of older works which functioned authoritatively for the Christians of North Africa, probably the writings of Scripture.

Yet, the redactor of *The Passion* understood Perpetua and her colleagues to be standing within the same stream of salvation history as those whose deeds of faith had been previously recorded. And the redactor saw in Perpetua's visions and martyrdom the same critical elements, a witness to God's grace, and a source of inspiration to other Christians. The primary difference, as the redactor explained it, was that they were more recent,[78] and the redactor believed that she or he had a Spirit-impelled mandate to share them with the current and coming generations.[79] To record these visions accomplished several purposes for the redactor. It was to bear witness to the fact that the Holy Spirit was still present and active in the church, giving gifts to the people of God.[80] It was to bear witness to the truthfulness of God's promise of an effusion of his Spirit in the last days, an effusion which the redactor said was taking place at the present time.[81] It was to encourage the weak and despairing by recounting the reality of selected manifestations of divine grace *(gratiam divinitatis)* in recent history.[82] And it was to bear witness to the fact that God always does what he promises, a fact which provided a substantial apologetic to the unbeliever but which also declared a stable relationship with and the continuing blessing of God to the faithful.[83]

Whether or not the redactor understood *The Passion* merely as an example of fine apologetic or devotional literature or as an authoritative work to be embraced by the entire Christian community is a question without a clear answer. That the redactor understood his or her own actions to be those of an obedient response to the will of the Holy Spirit is clear. The fact that Tertullian, just a few years later, would use portions of Saturus's vision to support a theological point[84] and the fact that Augustine would, over two centuries later, use Perpetua's vision of Dinocrates in a similar way and preach at least four sermons based upon this work[85] would tend to speak favorably of its widespread usage in North Africa. Augustine's denial of *The Passion* as having a place in "the canon of

---

77. *The Passion of Perpetua* 1.1.

78. Ibid., 1.2; 1.5.

79. Ibid., 16.1; 10.15.

80. Ibid., 1.3-6; 21.11.

81. Ibid., 1.4. The paraphrase is from Acts 2:17-18, and the use of the imperfect *effundam* to translate the future *echeō* is significant in contemporizing the promise of Joel 2.

82. Ibid., 1.5.

83. Ibid., 1.6; 21.11.

84. Tertullian, *A Treatise on the Soul* 55.4, and possibly 53.6 where the vocabulary of Saturus's vision is readily apparent, e.g., *caro, angelus, liberato, lux.*

85. Augustine, *On the Soul and Its Origin* 1.10; 2.10; 3.9; the sermons appear in translation in W. H. Shewring, *The Passion of S. S. Perpetua and Felicity MM. Together with the Sermons of S. Augustine on these Saints* (London: Sheed and Ward, 1931).

Holy Scripture" *(canone Scripturarum)* and the recognition by the redactor of *The Passion* of the temporal limitations on the value of such events,[86] tends to support the conclusion that neither Augustine nor the redactor saw the work as having a universal value in the same way that the writings of the apostles and prophets enjoyed it. Yet this work, including its revelations, did have value for the church of the third, fourth, and fifth centuries.

The Montanists were criticized for recording their prophecies in written form for wider circulation.[87] The fact that Tertullian quotes certain of the oracles which were given nearly half a century earlier in Asia Minor would tend to support this allegation.[88] So too would his use of the phrase *"sermone illo"* in his correspondence with Fabius, for it would appear that while this phrase should be translated "that oracle," its interpretation would seem to make reference to "the famous one" or "the oracle with which we are both familiar" or even "the oracle which has been circulated among us."[89]

In spite of this, however, Tertullian's use of such oracles seems always to be of a supplementary nature. He does not hold them to be samples of *regula fidei,* or of canon, but rather he argues that these oracles, as well as the visions which occur in his own church at Carthage, illustrate and affirm what Scripture teaches.[90] What Tertullian does appear to believe regarding continuing revelation is that it is a legitimate function of the Spirit-Paraclete which fulfills Jesus' promise recorded in John 16:12-13a.[91]

He is equally clear that within the Paraclete's portfolio lies the ability to act as the vicar of the Lord. By this means the Spirit is free (a) to provide direction to the discipline *(disciplina dirigitur)* of the church, (b) to reveal the Scriptures *(scripturae revelantur),* an idea which approximates the concept of illumination, and (c) to reform the intellect *(intellectus reformatur).*[92] Furthermore, it is anticipated that what was proclaimed must be consistent with *the* rule of faith *(regula fidei).*[93] For Tertullian, belief in the *regula fidei* is critical. It must be held in the highest regard, since an adulterated *regula fidei* inevitably leads to an adul-

---

86. Augustine, *On the Soul and Its Origin* 3.9; *The Passion of Perpetua* 1.2.

87. Eusebius, *EH* 5.18.5.

88. Tertullian, *On Exhortation to Chastity* 10.5; *On the Resurrection of the Flesh* 11.2; *Against Praxeas* 8.5.

89. Tertullian, *On Flight in Persecution* 9.4.

90. J. F. Jansen, "Tertullian and the New Testament," *SC* 2 (1982) 195, 199; A. F. Walls, "The Montanist 'Catholic Epistle' and Its New Testament Prototype," in F. L. Cross, ed. *SE* 3:2 (Berlin: Akademie-Verlag, 1964) 443; C. M. Robeck, Jr., "The Role and Function of Prophetic Gifts for the Church at Carthage, AD 202-258" (Ph.D. diss., Fuller Theological Seminary, 1985) 223, 225, 235-36, 265, 267.

91. Tertullian, *On Monogamy* 2.2-3; 4.1; *On the Veiling of Virgins* 1.4-5, 7.

92. Tertullian, *On the Veiling of Virgins* 1.4-5.

93. The rule of faith, and in this instance Tertullian is adamant that there is only "one, alone immoveable, and irreformable" rule, appears in the present passage *On the Veiling of Virgins* 1.4 and in slightly longer versions in at least two other works: *The Prescription Against Heretics* 13 and *Against Praxeas* 2. An insightful article which analyzes the *regula fidei* and Tertullian's understanding and use of it is L. W. Countryman, "Tertullian and the Regula Fidei," *SC* 2 (1982) 208-27.

terated form of preaching.[94] What a person believes affects what that person does, or, as Sanders puts it, "a community's *ethos* issues from its *muthos.*"[95] As far as Tertullian is concerned, the context of the *regula fidei* involves a repeatable constant which is applicable within *all* Christian communities, but further clarification is possible on issues not specifically addressed by the *regula fidei,* that is, on points of discipline and conversation.[96]

Tertullian's view of Scripture is equally strong. To be sure, by his day the concept of a New Testament canon, while not yet complete, was clearly well on its way. The books that he accepted were accepted largely because they had been written by apostles or by "apostolic" individuals.[97] Thus, they provided a stable norm, an apostolic tradition so to speak, by which the the faith and practice of the Christian community could be measured. Nothing was to be added to or deleted from these writings.[98] Coupled with this idea was Tertullian's other argument: "What Scripture does not note, it denies."[99] On the other hand, he accepted the writings of Scripture as involving the speech of the Holy Spirit.[100] Thus, while they pointed toward stability, the presence of the Spirit as interpreter left them open to new application. It made them adaptable to the needs of life. He did not expect contradiction or novelty to arise in any further revelation, but he did believe in the Spirit's role as revealer and illuminator.

Tertullian argued repeatedly that revelatory claims needed to be tested.[101] And he assured his readers that such claims were, indeed, examined on a regular basis in the church of North Africa. In the case of a certain "sister" who had a vision of the soul, Tertullian appears to have invoked judgments of person and character (she was a "sister" who was known to be gifted in this regard and whose consistent counsel had proven helpful to other Christians), judgments of method (there was no disruption of others when she received her visions, but rather a prime sample of the fulfillment of Paul's injunctions in 1 Cor 14:29-33 that revelations should be tested, controlled, and orderly), and judgments of content (Tertullian calls upon God and the apostle Paul to act as witnesses to the revelation's genuineness).[102] Tertullian then proceeded to argue that this vision was consistent with the teachings of Jesus in Luke 16:23-24 and with those of the apostle John in Rev 6:9-11.[103]

---

94. Tertullian, *On Monogamy* 2.3.
95. Sanders, "Adaptable for Life," 537.
96. Tertullian, *On the Veiling of Virgins* 1.4.
97. Tertullian accepts many New Testament writings but does not mention 2 Peter, 2 and 3 John, and James. He also may have questioned Hebrews. Cf. *Against Marcion* 4.2.1; 4.5.1; 5.1.5; 5.21.1, etc.
98. Tertullian, *Against Hermogenes* 22.5.
99. Tertullian, *On Monogamy* 4.4; *On Exhortation to Chastity* 4.2-3; *The Chaplet* 2.4. Ash, "The Decline of Ecstatic Prophecy," 243, points to this as evidence that Tertullian "was himself a champion of the emerging concept of canon."
100. Tertullian, *On Idolatry* 4.5.
101. Tertullian, *A Treatise on the Soul* 9.4; *On Monogamy* 2.3.
102. Tertullian, *A Treatise on the Soul* 9.3-4; for a contrary reading of these facts see H. J. Lawlor, "The Heresy of the Phrygians," *JTS* 9 (1908) 487.
103. Tertullian, *A Treatise on the Soul* 9.8.

In spite of Tertullian's care to explain, even repeatedly, the role which the Spirit played in matters of discipline—a role which was expected to be consistent with the *regula fidei* and the apostolic writings of a developing canon—it is equally clear that not all Christians agreed with his assessment. Even in Carthage there were those who left before this "sister" shared her revelation. Ultimately, various practices which the New Prophecy supported as being consistent with the *regula fidei*, and with Scripture, were criticized. Tertullian, for example, asserted that certain practices of fasting proclaimed by the New Prophecy were not inconsistent with the *regula fidei*.[104] He acknowledged that many judged them as *false* prophecies,[105] but he contended for their legitimacy, pointing toward the keeping of certain Jewish fasts, more frequent fasts, prolonged fasts, and certain dietary restrictions.[106] His detractors argued that these expectations were actually a reimplimentation of the Galatian heresy.[107] Later, Jerome would criticize the fact that while fasting was consistent with the apostolic tradition, the New Prophecy had moved the practice from a voluntary status to a mandatory one.[108] Thus the ultimate judgment of Jerome was not so much that the proponents of such practices were in doctrinal error as it was that whatever legitimacy they did have was local, temporal, and a matter of conscience, and that the church at large should not be condemned for believing this to be the case.

Cyprian's report to Cornelius, bishop of Rome, regarding a meeting of the bishops of the Synod of North Africa which was convened in Carthage in A.D. 256, makes clear that their decree on the lapsed was influenced by "many and manifest visions."[109] Cyprian's own view of Scripture, which in addition to the Old Testament included the "apostolic tradition" and the "evangelical authority" of the Gospels and the epistles written by the apostles, and which also understood these writings as revealed by the Holy Spirit and as constituting God's truth which demanded obedience, is important for this discussion as well.[110] So, too, is his understanding that Jesus' warning about false prophets arising in the church was a real possibility in his own day.[111]

Cyprian's description of a previous council held in A.D. 251 indicates that the discussion focused around arguments which were brought forward from Scripture.[112] It appears also to have been the case in A.D. 256. The bishops met to discuss the subject of discipline for the lapsed. Their discussion was governed by Scripture but informed or supplemented by arguments from the current political situation and from many visions.[113] While their revelations provided some

104. Tertullian, *On Fasting* 1.3.
105. Ibid., 1.5; 14.2, 4.
106. Ibid., 2.1, 3-4; 5.4; 10.8, 13; 13.6; 15.2-3, 5.
107. Ibid., 2.6; Gal 4:10.
108. Jerome, *Epistle* 41.3; cf. Origen, *On First Principles* 2.7.3.
109. Cyprian, *Epistle* 57.5 *"visiones multas et manifestas."*
110. Ibid., 73.13, 15, 17. Cyprian did not, however, make use of the books of Hebrews, James, Jude, 2 and 3 John, or 2 Peter.
111. Cyprian, *Epistle* 73.16; *Treatise* 1.14-15. Cf. *Epistle* 43.5; *Treatise* 1.11-12.
112. Cyprian, *Epistle* 55.6.
113. Ibid., 57.5; W. H. C. Frend, *The Donatist Church* (Oxford: Clarendon, 1952) 137-38 notes that each bishop shared a "Scriptural text, backed by argument." Augustine uses a

modicum of stability to the bishop's council and the North African scene during a period of persecution, these revelations were not understood—even by those who discussed them—as being equally applicable to the whole church. Thus while they enjoyed limited acceptance, it was an acceptance which was temporally and geographically confined, and they gained that acceptance only insofar as they were consistent with the apostolic writings. Primary authority went to those writings within the developing canon.

B. *Some claims were rejected as having no validity because they were judged to be inconsistent with the apostolic tradition and, therefore, were held to have no legitimate applicability.* Applicability and adaptability by themselves were not acceptable as norms for determining ultimate validity, ultimate usefulness, or ultimate truth. Jesus noted that false prophets would arise to lead many astray (Matt 24:11, 24) thereby indicating that certain revelatory claims would run counter to his own teachings. Paul spoke of the charism of distinguishing spirits (1 Cor 12:10), encouraging the Corinthians (1 Cor 14:29) and the Thessalonians (1 Thess 5:19-22) to test their revelations, thereby indicating that not all revelatory claims were valid (cf. 2 Thess 2:2). John wrote of false prophets who did not confess Jesus Christ as having come in the flesh (1 John 4:1-3). He contended that he and the other apostles were valid witnesses to Jesus as God incarnate. Thus to take a docetic position was to side with the spirit of error (1 John 4:6).While later theologians would qualify the claims of the didachist,[114] the author of the *Didache* understood that document as providing a summary of the Lord's teaching by the twelve apostles to a Gentile audience. In it were recommended several tests to enable the Christian community to distinguish between true and false prophets. Some of these tests focused upon specific issues of life-style such as whether an itinerant "prophet" stayed in one place longer than one or two days (*Did.* 11.5) or whether the "prophet" asked for a fee (*Did.* 11.6, 12). There are two tests which bear special mention. First, the teaching of the self-announced teacher or apostle or prophet was judged to be acceptable if it did not contradict the teaching of the *Didache*. If it did it was to be rejected.[115] Thus a form of what one might call the "apostolic tradition" was assumed as normative by the didachist, a form summarized in the *Didache* for certain Christian communities. Second, the genuine prophet could be discerned if it could be determined that the prophet held to the "ways of the Lord."[116] Once again there was a body of knowledge—in this case the teachings of Jesus in the Sermon on the Mount, a series of prescriptive teachings, and a number of valid activities—which were to be normative for those communities. A clearly articulated *regula fidei* or a formal canonical list was not mentioned, but the teachings of Moses, Jesus, and Paul as articulated by the didachist played a significant and normative role.

---

similar format in his argument against Vincentius Victor. He cites the vision of Perpetua, but he notes that it is not a canonical vision wherein ultimate authority must lie. Augustine, *On the Soul and Its Origin* 3.9.

114. Athanasius, *Ep. Fest.* 39; Eusebius, *EH* 3.25.

115. *Did.* 11.1-2.

116. Ibid., 11.8.

In *The Shepherd of Hermas* one was instructed to discern the true prophet by observing the prophet's life (*Mand.* 11.7). The false prophet spoke not at the initiative of the Spirit, but at the behest of seekers, in the fashion of pagan soothsayers (*Mand.* 11.2-6), and often for a fee (*Mand.* 11.12). Yet, like the writer of the *Didache*, the author of *The Shepherd* suggested that knowledge of the truth, and consistency with that truth, were important aspects to be observed in genuine prophets. False prophets "ruin the minds" of Christians (*Mand.* 11.1), mixing true and false words (*Mand.* 11.3). If the opposite may be said of the genuine prophet, then there must also have been a body of knowledge which was understood to be acceptably orthodox among the faithful. Again, we are not aware of any particular *regula fidei* or canonical listing, but the author's concern suggests that some normative standard was known to the community.

One of the most significant and persistent problems confronted by the leaders of the early church was what has come to be called Gnosticism. There was no single gnostic theology, no single gnostic movement, within or outside the church. It was, however, a genuine threat, even in the New Testament, to what was considered to be orthodox Christian teaching. Paul challenged an incipient form of Gnosticism in Corinth which apparently took pride in unrestrained glossolalic displays, unassessed prophetic phenomena, and uncontested visionary claims.[117] The docetic form of a proto-Gnosticism which the apostle John observed in Asia Minor was also related to claims of continuing revelation (1 John 4:1-6). Furthermore, second and third century Gnosticism tended to develop a significant body of literature, often working with the apocalyptic genre,[118] including what have been identified as "revelation dialogues."[119] Revelations, it would seem, formed the basis for many of the teachings espoused by a range of gnostic teachers.[120]

117. Paul's teaching on wisdom and knowledge in 1 Cor 1– 3, his use of irony in outlining what these "Gnostics" should have "known" (1 Cor 5:6; 6:3, 9, 19), his correctives on the relationship between "knowledge" and love (1 Cor 8:1-3, 7-13; 13:2-13), his acknowledgment of the legitimacy of bits of knowledge as charismata of the Holy Spirit (1 Cor 12:8), his guidelines on the appropriate use of tongues and prophecy (1 Corinthians 14), and even his disparaging remarks regarding his own visions, revelations, and *Himmelsreise* given in response to those who would question his apostolic authority (2 Cor 12:1-10) all point in this direction. Cf. W. Schmithals, *Gnosticism in Corinth: An Investigation of the Letters to the Corinthians* (tr. J. E. Steely; Nashville: Abingdon, 1971); and R. P. Spittler, "The Limits of Ecstasy: An Exegesis of 2 Corinthians 12:1-10," in G. F. Hawthorne, ed., *Current Issues in Biblical and Patristic Interpretation* (Grand Rapids: Eerdmans, 1975) 259-66.

118. Many of these writings appear in E. Hennecke, *New Testament Apocrypha* (2 vols., ed. W. Schneemelcher, tr. and ed. R. McL. Wilson; Philadephia: Westminster, 1964); and J. M. Robinson, ed. *The Nag Hammadi Library in English* (San Francisco: Harper & Row, 1981).

119. Perkins, *The Gnostic Dialogues,* 26.

120. See above, nn. 17, 23. Like Marcus and Apelles, Valentinus and Marcion allegedly received revelations. See Hippolytus, *The Refutation of All Heresies* 6.37; Tertullian, *Against Marcion* 1.18. Ultimately Irenaeus began, and Tertullian concluded, the enormous task of refuting Marcion's claims by working with his own canon and the *regula veritas* or *regula fidei* which was available to them. On this see W. R. Farmer, "Galatians and the Second-Century Development of the *Regula Fidei*," *SC* 4 (1984) 143-70, esp. 156-70. With respect to Marcion's "revelation," Tertullian also attempted to demonstrate its nature as false by appealing to the idea that "true" revelations occurred during the apostolic era while "false" revelations came later. See R. J.

It may well be the case that the question of what constituted the legitimate limits of authority, and the limits of apostolic authority in particular, formed the basis of most of the encounters between the gnostic and orthodox sectors of the early church.[121] For the orthodox, authority lay in the continuity between the apostles and bishops, and in an alleged singularity of doctrine. Tertullian tied both of these arguments together when he stated that God gave to Christ what Christ revealed to the apostles and the apostles preached to the churches. All contrary doctrine was ipso facto false doctrine. It had its source elsewhere.[122] These two ideas were, in the words of Elaine Pagels, "wholly interconnected: those whose faith relies solely upon the 'apostolic witness' themselves must look *only* 'to the churches' and their bishops . . . for guidance."[123]

By way of contrast, gnostic writers and teachers tended to stand over against the received tradition. To be sure, this was not always the case, for they did consider themselves to be Christians. Marcion accepted much of Paul though he rejected the Old Testament; and according to Hippolytus, Basilides cited 1 Cor 2:13 calling it "scripture" (*The Refutation of All Heresies* 7.14.3). Yet at times they did deny the tradition of Moses.[124] They also tended to deny the validity of the "apostolic tradition" and its ability to bear witness to Jesus by highlighting one or more of the disciples, or the visionary role of outsiders such as Mary or Philip, at the expense of the whole community of disciples.[125] In addition, they sometimes placed a premium on continuing revelation and claims to personal inspiration by such teachers as Valentinus, displaying them as though they had superceded the traditions of the imperfect apostles.[126] Such denials of the orthodox standard of apostolic tradition clearly put these gnostic teachers on a collision course with the orthodox.

The tendency of the Gnostics to accept the newer claims of revelation in lieu of the older traditional teachings of the apostles sometimes applied also to their own teachings. Zostrianus, for instance, wrote that he put away his (previous Gnostic?) tradition and "did not use it again,"[127] choosing instead to follow the revela-

---

Hoffmann, *Marcion: On the Restitution of Christianity: An Essay on the Development of Radical Paulinist Theology in the Second Century* (AARAS 46; Chico, Ca.: Scholars, 1984) 67. Obviously, Tertullian only had *certain* "revelations" in mind when he posited this thesis.

121. E. H. Pagels, "Visions, Appearances, and Apostolic Authority: Gnostic and Orthodox Traditions," in B. Aland et al., eds., *Gnosis: Festschrift für Hans Jonas* (Göttingen: Vandenhoeck & Ruprecht, 1978) 415-30; cf. D. R. MacDonald, *The Legend and the Apostle: The Battle for Paul in Story and Canon* (Philadelphia: Westminster, 1983).

122. Tertullian, *The Prescription Against Heretics* 21. Cf. Ireneaus, *Against Heresies* 1.10.1-2.

123. Pagels, "Visions," 428. Cf. Ireneaus, *Against Heresies* 3.4.1.

124. *Ap. John* (CG 2.1.13): "But I said, 'Lord, what does it mean. . . ?' And he smiled and said, 'Do not think it is, as Moses said. . . .'" Cf. Ireneaus, *Against Heresies* 3.12.13.

125. Cf. *Ap. Jas.* (CG 1.1.2) in which the writer claims that in a post-resurrection encounter with the disciples Jesus called James and Peter apart from the rest that he might "fill them," instructing the others to "occupy themselves with that which they *were about.*"

126. Ireneaus, *Against Heresies* 1.13.6; 1.25.2; 3.12.12; Tertullian, *The Prescription Against Heretics* 23.1.

127. *Zost* (CG 8.1.14); Cf other examples in Perkins, *The Gnostic Dialogue,* 81.

tions of *his* revealer. Yet it must be reiterated that there was such a thing as a developing gnostic tradition.

Irenaeus scoffed at such ideas in gnostic teaching because they undercut the stability of the apostolic teaching. He accused these gnostic teachers of following a *viva voce* which revealed to each in turn the latest formulation of "truth."[128] Tertullian was scandalized by the idea that the various gnostic sects did not hold their teachers in high regard, wryly observing that "their very unity . . . is schism."[129] Yet herein lies a significant difference between the orthodox and the gnostic, between the revelations which were judged to be valid for the larger Christian community, even though limited in their ability to be adapted to new situations, as over against those offered by various gnostic Christians as examples of "adaptable" teachings which found no such acceptance amid the whole church.

Irenaeus categorized his gnostic opponents as those who "falsify the oracles of God" and who, by means of philosophical arguments, snare the simple-minded to make inquiry. He went on to observe that whether by imagination run rampant or by claims to continuing revelation, they "dreamed" their Scripture-injuring system into existence,[130] a system which ran counter to the revealed truth.[131] Such acts made these Gnostics appear as though each was attempting to outdo the next. Imagination and originality in revelatory claims were acknowledged among gnostic Christians as marks of a dynamic spirituality.[132] "Adaptable" would have been the gnostic judgment of their own oracles, but they lacked the stability which the orthodox community valued because they were thought to replace or update the "apostolic tradition."

In short, then, the orthodox prized the stability which the community of faith enjoyed in light of the God-given, Christ-mediated, apostle-preached, bishop-protected revelation which the church as a whole had chosen to accept. The Gnostics prized ingenuity and adaptability in the form of creative visions and revelations that went beyond the more stable orthodox traditions. Such revelations were understood to convey a reality to a vibrant form of spirituality; they communicated and encouraged an independent spiritual life; and they witnessed to an immanence of God to those who accepted them.[133]

One may conclude that at least in this facet of revelatory assessment the subject of stability played a primary role in the rejection of many gnostic "revelations." The willingness of the Gnostics to move beyond even the apostles brought ill repute to their teachings. A lack of consistency with Irenaeus's canon of truth *(regula veritatis)* or Tertullian's rule of faith *(regula fidei)* led ultimately to the rejection of those teachings.[134] Furthermore, the experience of the church as a

128. Ireneaus, *Against Heresies* 3.2.1; 1.18.1.

129. Tertullian, *The Prescription Against Heretics* 43.

130. Ireneaus, *Against Heresies* Pref 2; 1.9.3.

131. G. Vallée, *A Study in Anti-Gnostic Polemics: Irenaeus, Hippolytus, and Epiphanius* (SCJ 1; Waterloo, Ont.: Canadian Corporation for Studies in Religion, 1981) 16-17.

132. Pagels, "Visions," 427.

133. Ibid., 442.

134. Farmer, "Galatians," 143, 159, suggests that Paul's term "truth of the gospel" *(hē alētheia tou evangeliou)* in Gal 2:5, 14 became the basis for Irenaeus's term "canon of truth"

Christian community which understood itself as teaching the same doctrine everywhere, a doctrine passed on to them from the apostles, was raised by the orthodox to counter the individual claims of special revelation which were ultimately judged as being invalid. To have accepted the gnostic claims as valid and adaptable within the church would have been a deathblow to the system of leadership and doctrine as the church knew it. Thus the overall threat which gnostic revelations posed to the identity of the entire Christian community was too great to allow their acceptance. Stability was essential. Adaptability alone could not carry these revelations to a place of acceptance in any normative fashion within the larger Christian community.

C. *Some claims were accepted as having universal validity and ongoing adaptability by the larger Christian community.* It is clearly to argue against the evidence to claim that it was obvious from the start which works would be progressively recognized by the church as being genuinely inspired, which would contribute to the universal stability of the Christian community while also allowing for ongoing adaptability, and which would play an ultimately authoritative role in the faith and conduct of the life of the whole church. Yet it does seem clear that the earliest Christians worked with the Old Testament Scriptures that they had inherited from synagogue life but now interpreted through Christian eyes, and that they maintained an oral tradition including portions of the life and teachings of Jesus. It is also the case that some communities had access to letters which they had received from Paul or others of the apostles or apostolic associates such as Luke or John Mark.

Summaries of crucial elements of the faith appeared in the earliest forms of the apostolic preaching[135] as well as in the form of creedal fragments found in certain of the epistles.[136] These elements became important in the ongoing articulation of the Christian faith, many of which ultimately found their way into the various formulations of *regula fidei*, and into the framework of early catechetical training.

Hans von Campenhausen has cogently argued that among the earliest Christians there was no New Testament document or set of documents whose stated purpose provided it with a special or normative position "alongside the existing Old Testament 'scripture.'" Nonetheless, the historical testimony to Jesus Christ, and the significance of his word and work "from the very first possess[ed] especial sanctity and special authority to control men's lives."[137] Indeed, it formed the basis of the Christian tradition which was passed on from one generation to the next.

(kanona tēs alētheias; regula veritatis), which in turn developed into Tertullian's "rule of faith" *(regula fidei)*. Irenaeus mentions this "canon of truth" or *regula veritatis* in *Against Heresies* 1.22.1; 3.2.1; 3.11.1.

135. C. H. Dodd, *The Apostolic Preaching* (rev. ed.; London: Hodder & Stoughton, 1944) 17, has isolated seven, while R. H. Mounce, *The Essential Nature of New Testament Preaching* (Grand Rapids: Eerdmans, 1960) 62-63, 83-84, would reduce them to three.

136. Kelly, *Creeds*, 16-18.

137. H. von Campenhausen, *The Formation of the Christian Bible* (tr. J. A. Baker; London: Adam & Charles Black, 1972) 103-4.

Yet it was a history which was understood to be deeply rooted in the history of Israel and in the literary works which uniquely governed the life of that community. As Samuel Terrien has observed, one can make much of Hellenistic influence on the writers of the New Testament, but ultimately one must recognize that these writers had "an extremely precise familiarity with the Hebrew Scripture" and that "only a Jewish pattern of religious thinking, immersed in the Hebraic theology of presence, could have enabled the early Christians to formulate" their interpretations of the historical Jesus.[138] Two writers whose works were ultimately judged to provide stability to the church's self-understanding, in part because of their appeal to continuity with the "tradition," were the apostle Paul and Luke. Yet their works were open to the future, themselves a reinterpretation of the past centered upon the person of Jesus the Christ.

Paul's comments to the Corinthians indicate that even though Christ had appeared to him in what might be called a visionary encounter,[139] he still stood within the apostolic tradition, passing on to his readers *(paredōka)* what he had himself received *(ho kai parelabon).* The content of the *paradosis* he had received, and with which the Corinthians were already familiar, included the statements that:

> Christ died for our sins *in accordance*
> *with the scriptures,* that
> he was buried, that
> he was raised on the third day *in*
> *accordance with the scriptures,*
> and that
> he appeared to Cephas, then to the twelve. Then
> he appeared to more than five hundred
> brethren at one time, most of
> whom [were] still alive, though
> some [had] fallen asleep. Then
> he appeared to James, then to all the apostles. (1 Cor 15:3-7)

In this brief review of the *paradosis,* Paul appeals to the writings of Israel to explain the work of Christ for the forgiveness of sin. Twice he argues that Christ's work, accomplished in the death, burial, and Resurrection, were, in fact, accomplished "in accordance with the scriptures" *(kata tas graphas),* surely a clear reference to those writings having authority within the Jewish religious community. Paul's second appeal to tradition comes not from certain writings but from living witnesses. His claim for the reality of the Resurrection lies with the prediction of *tas graphas* and the appearances of the risen Christ to such people as Peter, the twelve, some five hundred brethren at one time, James, and all the apostles. Only after building the context for the truthfulness of the *paradosis* does Paul enter his own experience which he seeks to show as merely one among the many, consistent with theirs, but no greater.

---

138. Samuel Terrien, *The Elusive Presence: Toward a New Biblical Theology* (New York: Harper & Row, 1978) 416.

139. Acts 9:1-9; 22:6-11; 26:12-18.

Hence to this *paradosis* Paul appended his own testimony that "last of all, as to one untimely born, he appeared also to me" (1 Cor 15:8). Thus while Paul mentioned his own revelatory experience he did not wish to communicate to his readers the idea that he himself or his teachings were in any way superior to, had superceded, or were inconsistent with the received tradition. While he admitted to the abundance of revelations he received from God, he refused to join with those who boasted in such private experiences, since they called attention to the recipient rather than to the Christ who gave them (2 Cor 12:1-10). Paul's genuine apostolicity was demonstrated not through "spiritual exploit" but in weakness, and within the context of a received tradition experienced by many others before him. He therefore sought to assure his readers of his commitment to an ongoing consistency with that tradition, which was passed on by those who had been closest to Christ, the disciples. He did not contest their leadership, nor did he stand over against their teaching.[140] Yet it would be foolish to believe that these few items he enumerated to the Corinthians formed the totality of the tradition that he and his readers had received. The tradition surely had other elements such as a reference to the second coming, but the total tradition had not in Paul's writings been settled in any fixed form. Even so, it is wise to observe, as Charles Gore did long ago, that Paul and the other apostles were "ministers of a 'tradition' to which they themselves [were] subject, a tradition 'once for all delivered.'"[141] As such, one sees the tradition expand as Paul reviews it in light of his own experience with the risen Christ.

Luke also drew heavily upon those who had preceded him in the faith. Interviews with contemporary "eyewitnesses and ministers of the word" (Luke 1:2) gave him much material with which to work and guaranteed his commitment to a historically based tradition. They helped him gain an appreciation for the facts. Yet he reached clear back to the prophet Joel with new insight to explain the place and mission of the church since the ascension. Indeed, the multiple strata discernible in the Joel passage as it appears in Acts 2 provide a significant illustration of adaptability and stability working together in those words of Luke which would ultimately be accepted as authoritative for the church.

The Joel prophecy (Acts 2:17-21; Joel 2:28-32 [MT 3:1-5]) is restated in the Petrine citation, which in turn forms the basis of a typical example of early Christian preaching.[142] The Petrine citation, as Luke recorded it, may well have been lifted from a later, liturgical "synagogue sermon"[143] in proem homily form.[144] Its ultimate application, however, is made clear by the apostolic associate, Luke.

Joel's word seems originally to have been occasioned by a massive locust in-

---

140. Von Campenhausen, *Formation*, 106; Kelly, *Creeds*, 17.

141. Charles Gore, "The Holy Spirit and Inspiration," in Charles Gore, ed., *Lux Mundi: A Series of Studies in the Religion of the Incarnation* (1889; London: John Murray, 1913) 248.

142. Dodd, *The Apostolic Preaching*, 17.

143. J. W. Bowker, "Speeches in Acts: A Study in Proem and Yelammedenu Form," *NTS* 14 (1967-68) 105.

144. E. Earle Ellis, "Midrashic Features in the Speeches of Acts," in A. Descamps and A. de Halleux, eds., *Mélanges bibliques en hommage au R. P. Béda Rigaux* (Genbloux: Duculot, 1970) 307-9. This article has also been published under the title "Midraschartige Züge in den Reden der Apostelgeschichte," *ZNW* 62 (1971) 94-104.

festation (Joel 1:4; 2:25), which brought desolation to a land also ravaged by drought and brush fires (Joel 1:19-20; 2:3). Joel understood it as judgment from the hand of Yahweh, a harbinger of the coming Day of the Lord. It would be a day of destruction, desolation, and calamity for the nations of the world (Joel 3:2-15, 19). Joel's appeal to Israel was for repentance, into which Israel entered (Joel 2:18) and which ultimately resulted in an abundant restoration of the land (Joel 2:19-27). Yet Joel's word had both immediate and eschatological ramifications. He saw this repentance and restoration as prophetic of how Yahweh would eschatologically vindicate Israel before the nations (Joel 2:27–3:21). The evidence of Israel's renewal and vindication would be the pouring out of Yahweh's Spirit "upon all flesh," enabling them to participate in ecstatic, prophetic activities such as dreams, visions, and prophecy itself (Joel 2:28-29). Yet Joel's perspective on the meaning of "all flesh" was clearly limited to the community of religious Israel.[145]

Peter's use of the Joel citation appears in what might be described as an authentic, yet skeletal, kerygmatic presentation. Peter chose the Joel passage to provide an adequate answer to a questioning crowd (Acts 2:12-13). It answered the question "What does this mean?" for the Jews who observed the multitude speaking in tongues. It supplied the logical and, to the Jewish audience, the understandable explanation of the miraculous manifestations depicted both literally and symbolically in the Pentecost event, namely, that God had once again intervened on the historical scene and fulfilled a long-standing eschatological promise—the pouring out of the Spirit.

The midrashic exposition of the Joel citation contains a variety of peshered elements which Ellis has forcefully argued is indicative of "a transitional pattern in the early Christian use of Scripture."[146] It provided an opportunity for the proclamation of the basic points of the kerygma, Jesus' death (Acts 2:22-23), resurrection (Acts 2:24-32), and exaltation (Acts 2:33-35). As a consequence of God's act in Jesus Christ, the house of Israel was called upon to recognize the lordship and messiahship of the Jesus they had crucified just days before (Acts 2:36).[147]

Luke's ultimate use of this Joel citation is broader still. His purpose is less kerygmatic, more didactic. He, too, must adapt the oracle to the new situation while providing continuity with the past and stability for the present and future. The reference to Joel appears to provide a direct link from Yahweh's promise to the people of God given through Joel to the life, ministry, and fulfillment of the promise made by Jesus (Luke 24:49; Acts 1:8) in the miraculous events of the day of Pentecost (Acts 2:1-4), and finally to the place and role of the church in the "last days." The new historical situation involved the mission of the church in light of a delayed parousia, a mission which implied that Joel's reference to "all flesh" included not only the house of Israel but also the Gentiles (Acts 1:8).

---

145. Leslie C. Allen, *The Books of Joel, Obadiah, Jonah and Micah* (NICOT; Grand Rapids: Eerdmans, 1976) 98; Arvid S. Kapelrud, *Joel Studies* (UUA 1948/4; Uppsala: Lundequistska Bokhandeln, 1948) 131; Hans Walter Wolff, *Joel and Amos* (Herm.: Philadelphia: Fortress, 1977) 67; J. Lindblom, *Prophecy in Ancient Israel* (Philadelphia: Fortress, 1973) 202.

146. Ellis, "Midrashic Features," 309.

147. Bowker, "Speeches in Acts," 96-111; Ellis, "Midrashic Features," 303-13.

In a sense, then, the Joel prophecy and its fulfillment on the day of Pentecost provided the occasion for Luke's own exposition of the ongoing pouring out of God's Spirit, first upon the believing Jew, then in ever expanding concentric circles through Samaria (Acts 8) to the most distant parts of the world (Acts 10ff.). The early church saw through Luke's eyes the reality of the elements of adaptability and stability which were inherent in the various strata of Luke's inclusion of Joel's prophecy. The church, too, saw these features in Luke-Acts, as Luke sought to tell Theophilus, and the church, what God was doing in the church and what God would have the church continue to do in the "last days." It was a message which was consistent with God's plan; and it was communicated through the prophets, Jesus himself, the apostle Peter, and the earliest Christian community. It was thus consistent with the apostolic tradition—indeed, it became part of what was considered to be the apostolic tradition.

III

In summary, then, I have attempted in this study to survey a variety of prophetic claims and early Christian writings from the first three centuries in light of some features of contemporary canon criticism. These writings and claims to prophetic inspiration came from many quarters within the church—orthodox, sectarian, and heretical. It was observed that they could be separated into several categories which enabled us to observe their relative value in the ongoing life of the church.

In the first category are those oracles or writings which spoke specifically to an individual or group from within the tradition at a given point in time. These claims contributed generally to the *stability* of that individual or group at that time. Indeed, they may have had local significance, but ultimately they lacked ongoing universal significance for the whole church. They could be affirmed as having value, though only of a limited nature for a portion of the church. Thus while they could often be judged as genuine expressions of God, conveyed through the Holy Spirit, they posed no genuine threat to those works which were ultimately understood as normative for the whole church.

In the second category are those oracles or writings which arose from outside the traditional framework, and which addressed an individual or group at a given point in time. At first hearing, they tended to appear to be adaptable for life, but their violation of the tradition from without put them in competition with the tradition itself. Thus they did not pose an ultimate threat to those works which were ultimately understood as normative for the whole church since they lacked an "orthodox" base which would contribute not only adaptability but stability to the life of the church.

In the third category are those oracles or writings which arose from within the tradition and as such contributed to the stability of the tradition. On the other hand, they proved to have a message which leaped boundaries of time, gender, culture and geography. That is, they proved also to be adaptable for life from that time and place forward. It was these writings which the church ultimately understood as having normative value for the entire people of God. They may not all have been accepted with equal rapidity, and they may not all have been equally evident as contributions to stability and adaptability, but they have been accepted nonetheless.

One might conclude from this survey that those claims to revelation which lack consistency with the canonical norm or the *regula fidei* as determined by the church should not be accepted; indeed, that they may be viewed as heretical by the church because they undermine the stability of the church. Those claims to revelation which do not undermine the church but instead challenge it to live a life which is consistent with its calling to exhibit an *ethos* consistent with its *mythos* need not be understood as competing with the canonical norm. It may be the case that they provide insight on or illumination of the norm for the community in a specific time, place, or situation.

Some Observations on the History of the Interpretation of Holy Scripture

Philip Edgcumbe Hughes

That the sense in which the text of the Bible is understood is a matter of first importance for the life of the church is hardly a matter of dispute, for from the earliest times the doctrine of Scripture has been acknowledged as the canon or standard by which Christian belief and practice should be governed. It is perhaps surprising that the allegorical method of interpretation should have had so powerful a fascination for many able minds. The fondness for allegorization was not a phenomenon merely of the medieval period; it was there in the subapostolic days and it persists still, quite luxuriantly, in certain Christian circles of our own day. The notion that a scriptural passage may be interpreted in more than one sense also has a long history. In particular, the opinion was for long widely approved that there are four senses inherent in the text—the literal or surface sense, the allegorical or deep sense hidden below the surface, the tropological or ethical sense for daily conduct or practice, and the anagogical sense which directs the thoughts up to heavenly and eternal realities. The earliest mention known to us of this fourfold sense of Scripture is found in John Cassian (c. 360–c. 430).[1] In chapter 8 of the First Conference of Abbot Nesteros, one of the 24 *Collationes Patrum* or conversations (doubtless imaginary) with well-known solitaries or hermits, we read:

> *Practical* knowledge is distributed among many subjects and interests, but *theoretical* is divided into two parts, namely, the historical interpretation and the spiritual sense. . . . But of spiritual knowledge there are three kinds, tropological, allegorical, anagogical, of which we read as follows in Proverbs: "But describe these things to yourself in three ways, according to the largeness of your heart."[2]

Jerusalem, Cassian explained by way of example, can be understood in four senses: "historically, as the city of the Jews; allegorically, as the church of Christ; anagogically, as the heavenly city of God, 'which is the mother of us all'; tropologically, as the soul of man, which is frequently subject to praise and blame under this title."[3] And he adduced 1 Cor 14:6 as a proof-text from the New

---

1. F. W. Farrar asserted that the first traces of the fourfold sense occur in the works of Eucherius, bishop of Lyons, who was the author of a volume on hermeneutics, *Formulae spiritualis intelligentiae* (*History of Interpretation* [1886, republished in Grand Rapids, 1979] 26); but Cassian's *Collationes patrum* was written some thirty years or more before the death of Eucherius in the middle of the fifth century.

2. John Cassian, *The Conferences* 2.14.8, citing Prov 22:20 (LXX). Cassian was evidently following, as Origen and Jerome had done before him, the questionable, and still cryptic, rendering of the LXX (cf. the Vg.).

3. Ibid., citing Gal 4:26.

Testament confirming the rightness of the fourfold method: "But now, brethren, if I come to you speaking with tongues what shall I profit you unless I speak to you either by revelation (= allegory) or by knowledge (= tropology) or by prophecy (= anagogy) or by doctrine (= history)?"[4]

Two centuries earlier, Origen (c. 185–c. 254) had propounded a *threefold* understanding of the sacred text. The indebtedness of Cassian to Origen, whether conscious or not, is suggested by the fact that Origen held that the interpretation of Scripture in three senses was justified and indeed enjoined by Prov 22:20 (LXX). Origen saw the three senses he distinguished as corresponding to the threefold constitution of man as flesh, soul, and spirit: the plain or historical sense, suitable for simple persons, answering to the "flesh" of Scripture; a more profound sense, suitable for those who have made some spiritual progress, answering to the "soul" of Scripture; and the most profound or esoteric sense, suitable for those who are perfect, answering to the "spirit" of Scripture. For this last sense Origen claimed the support of 1 Cor 2:6f.: "We speak wisdom among those who are perfect, but not the wisdom of this world or of the rulers of this world; but we speak the wisdom of God in a mystery, the hidden wisdom . . ."[5]—a conception that accords with the gnostic rather than the Pauline mind.

Although Origen is regarded as the most extravagant exponent of Christian allegorical interpretation, he was by no means the inventor of the allegorical method. There are some instances of its usage in the pages of the New Testament; and Philo of Alexandria, an older contemporary of the New Testament authors, was a dedicated allegorist who, as a Jew, attempted to marry Old Testament narratives with the rational and ethical conceptions of Greek philosophy. Moreover, the ancient legends of the wanderings of Ulysses, immortalized in the epics of Homer, had been subjected to allegorical interpretation well before the Christian era by thinkers among the Greeks themselves, and this practice was continued into the Christian era by Stoic writers such as Seneca and Plutarch. It is hardly surprising that there was a place for it, too, in the writings of the Gnostics. But it is also found in the works of a number of Christian authors. Especially attractive to the latter was the story of Ulysses and the Sirens. The alluring songs of the sirens were designed to distract mariners from their task of navigation so that their ships were smashed to pieces on the rocks. But Ulysses overcame this hazard by pouring wax into the ears of his men to deafen them to the singing of the Sirens and by having the crew bind him to the mast, thus rendering him incapable of responding to the music.

In this context, let us note the following admonition offered by Clement of Alexandria (c. 150–c. 215).

Let us then flee habit as we would a dangerous headland or the menace of Charybdis or the legendary Sirens. . . . "Urge your ship from that smoke and billow." Fellow mariners, let us flee this billow: it spews forth fire; it is an accursed island heaped with bones and corpses, and in it a bold courtesan, Pleasure, sings, delighting with popular music. . . . Sail past this song; it

4. Ibid.
5. Origen, *De principiis* 4.1.11.

leads to death. Just exert your will and you will conquer perdition. Bound to the wood, you will be delivered from destruction. You will have the Logos of God for your pilot, and the Holy Spirit will bring you to the heavenly harbor. Then you will contemplate my God and be initiated into the sacred mysteries; you will enjoy those things laid up in heaven for me, which "ear has not heard and have not entered into the heart of any man."[6]

In Clement's allegory, what was the wood of the mast for Ulysses becomes the wood of the cross for Christians. One should remember, however, that it was pagan Greeks whom Clement was addressing; consequently an allusion of this kind was intended to strike a sympathetic chord. Clement's apologetic works are in fact full of quotations from the poets and philosophers of the Greeks, and his attitude was one of contempt and sarcasm for their superstitions and the absurdities of the gods they believed in. Thus he had no compunction in holding up Ulysses to ridicule as "the old man of Ithaca" who "eagerly longed to see, not the truth, not the fatherland in heaven, not the true light, but smoke."[7] Edifying thoughts derived allegorically from the adventures of Ulysses turn up in other places than Alexandria and in other patristic writings—such as the treatise of *The Freedom of the Will* by Methodius, bishop of Olympus in Lycia (who died, fc. 311),[8] and the *Commentary on Luke* by Ambrose, bishop of Milan (339–397).[9] The allegorizing interpreter had a keen eye for any term or dimension that might seem to provide a peg on which to hang theological truths; for example, the mention of wood in whatever form or connection would almost automatically be seen as carrying a hidden reference to the cross,[10] and numbers would be regarded as pregnant with esoteric significance. But a practice which envinces little or no concern for the context and the natural meaning can hardly be treated seriously as authentic hermeneutics.

A very early example of allegorization is present in *The Epistle of Barnabas,* which was probably written during the last quarter of the first century by an Alexandrian Christian. The author refers to Abraham who, "looking forward in spirit to Jesus," introduced the rite of circumcision "after receiving the teaching of the three letters." The statement that "Abraham circumcised ten and eight and three hundred men" seems to be based on a faulty recollection of the Genesis narrative; for Genesis 17, where circumcision is prescribed and performed, does not

6. Clement of Alexandria, *Exhortation to the Heathen* 12.1ff. Citations are from the *Odyssey* 22.226 and 1 Cor 2:9.

7. Clement of Alexandria, *Exhortation to the Heathen* 9.86. The smoke mentioned was that of Ulysses' own hearth.

8. Methodius, *The Freedom of the Will*, ad init. The approach of Methodius was by way of contrast: "The singers (of Christian truth) are not the deadly Sirens of the Greeks, but a divine choir of prophets, with whom there is no need to stop the ears of one's companions, nor to load oneself with bonds. . . ."

9. Ambrose, *Commentary on Luke,* proem, where, in addition to various other references to *The Odyssey,* he observed that whereas "Ulysses had to be bound bodily with chains to the tree," to be a Christian "the soul has to be bound by bonds to the wood of the cross, lest it should be moved by lascivious enticements and the course of nature diverted into the peril of lustful desire."

10. See, e.g., Justin Martyr (c. 100–c. 165), *Dialogue with Trypho* 86.

mention the number who were circumcised. The figure 318 has been transported from chapter 14, where it is said that Abraham led forth a force of trained men, 318 in number, for the purpose of rescuing his nephew Lot from his captors. It is the number, however, that is seen as containing a significant communication of knowledge. The technique employed is that of *gematria* according to which each letter of the alphabet has a specific numerical equivalence. Thus 10 corresponds to the letter iota (I), 8 to the letter eta (H), and 300 to the letter tau (T); and the number 318 (10+8+300) is represented by the Greek letters IHT. But IH we recognize as the first two letters of the name ἸΗΣΘΥΣ, Jesus, and T stands here for the cross to which it is similar in shape. Accordingly, the number 318 reveals the cross of Jesus, whence flows the grace of our salvation. "Barnabas" assures his readers: "No one has been admitted by me to a more excellent piece of knowledge than this, but I know that you are worthy."[11] The same interpretation recurs more than a hundred years later in Clement of Alexandria who, relating the number 318 more accurately to its position in Gen 14:14, asserts that Abraham's servants, "having fled to the Sign and the Name," were in a state of salvation and became lords of the unbelieving nations.[12]

Because of his supposition that beneath the plain surface of the text there lies hidden truth of the most profound character the allegorist is predisposed to disinter esoteric meaning from virtually any detail of virtually any passage, and in doing so to find what in fact is not there and what, despite declarations to the contrary, was absent from the mind of the author. There is some justification for associating the allegorical method of biblical interpretation with the city of Alexandria, which in the days of the primitive church was a thriving center of Greek culture, the home of Philo, a breeding-ground of Gnosticism, and the habitat of what has been called Christian Platonism. There is also good reason for linking the more natural and straightforward method of the interpretation of Scripture according to its plain sense with the city of Antioch, whose school could claim to have trained such distinguished preachers and commentators as Diodore of Tarsus (d. c. 390), John Chrysostom (d. 407), Theodore of Mopsuestia (d. 428), and Theodoret (d. c. 458). But exponents of these methods were to be found in many different localities and were not necessarily connected with either of these cities. Even though the extreme allegorist might be orthodox in his theology, his handling of the biblical text was governed by a false presupposition that was damaging to his dignity and integrity and could be used no less ably by the heresiarch for his own purposes. If anything is evident from the history of ecclesiastical controversy, it is that heresy has always been based on the misinterpretation of the text of Scripture.

Thus Irenaeus (c. 130–c. 200) complained that the system of the Valentinians was one "which neither the prophets announced, nor the Lord taught, nor the apostles delivered, but of which they boast that beyond all others they have a perfect knowledge [gnosis]," and also that they attempt to give their system an ap-

---

11. *The Epistle of Barnabas* 9.

12. Clement of Alexandria, *Stromata* 6.11. There is much more in this place on the significance of numbers. See also, e.g., Origen's interpretation of the terms and dimensions given in the account of the construction of Noah's ark (Gen 6:14ff.), in his Second Homily on Genesis.

pearance of biblical respectability by "adapting with an air of probability to their own peculiar assertions the parables of the Lord and the sayings of the prophets and the words of the apostles." But in doing so "they disregard the order and connection of the Scriptures" and "dismember and destroy the truth."[13] Tertullian (c. 160–c. 220), in his *Scorpiace* (or "Antidote for the Scorpion's Sting"), insisted that the Scriptures were to be understood in their plain sense and not explained away by subtle arguments. He was referring particularly to heretical "scorpions" who, where one thing was expressed in the words, imposed their own different meaning by resorting to "allegories, parables, and riddles."[14]

Disturbed over the widespread misinterpretation of the Bible in his day, Augustine (354-430) attempted to bring the church back to an appreciation of the importance of the plain and natural sense of the text. "Anyone who takes a meaning out of Scripture other than the writer intended goes astray, but not through any falseness in Scripture," he warned in his book on *Christian Teaching,*[15] which is essentially a work on biblical hermeneutics. He admonished his readers that just because a passage was clear and easy to understand it was not on that account to be despised, for it was edifying in itself and it also cast a helpful light on passages that were difficult to understand. He explained, in a manner that would be echoed by the reformers of the sixteenth century, that "the Holy Spirit has, with admirable wisdom and care for our welfare, so arranged the Holy Scriptures as by the plainer passages to satisfy our hunger and by the more obscure to stimulate our appetite," adding that "nothing is dug out of those obscure passages which may not be found set forth in the plainest language elsewhere."[16] To comprehend the plain things was indeed absolutely essential, "for among the things that are plainly laid down in Scripture are to be found all matters that concern our faith and our manner of life."[17]

He also denied emphatically, in his work *The Spirit and the Letter,* that St. Paul's statement in 2 Cor 3:6, that "the letter kills but the spirit gives life," had anything to do with or gave sanction to the practice of allegorization which treated the literal sense as inferior and even harmful—as had been supposed by Origen and other allegorists,[18] and has continued to be supposed by many right up to the present time. Origen unhesitatingly numbered himself among "those who believe that the sacred books are not the composition of men, but that they were composed by inspiration of the Holy Spirit." He was, however, obsessed with the notion, which would prove so fascinating to the mystics and cabalists of a later period, that "the treasure of divine meaning is enclosed within the frail vessel of the com-

13. Irenaeus, *Adversus haereses* 1.8.
14. Tertullian, *Scorpiace* 11.
15. Augustine, *De doctrina christiana* 1.26.
16. Ibid., 2.6.
17. Ibid., 2.9.
18. Augustine, *De spiritu et littera* 6ff. Earlier, however, in *De doctrina christiana* 3.5, Augustine had related 2 Cor 3:6 to the interpretation of the text, warning against "taking a figurative expression literally" and against "blind adherence to the letter." Though such admonitions may be commendable in themselves, they are alien to the apostle's intention in this place; and Augustine is chargeable with inconsistency in his interpretation of 2 Cor 3:6.

mon letter." Consequently, he spoke disparagingly of "the worthlessness of the letter."[19]

Augustine had no wish to deny that there are figures and metaphors in the biblical writings. The proper sense of any particular passage was what was important, and that sense might be literal or figurative. He therefore advised his readers to "beware of taking a figurative expression literally," pointing out that "it is assuredly a miserable slavery of the soul to take signs for things and to be unable to lift the eye of the mind above what is corporeal and created, so that it may drink in eternal light."[20] But the opposite mistake was equally to be avoided: "In addition to the foregoing rule, which guards us from taking a metaphorical form of speech as if it were literal, we must also pay heed to that which tells us not to take a literal form of speech as if it were figurative." The application of these rules was a matter both of common sense and also of familiarity with the plain teaching of Scripture. And so Augustine formulated the following principle: "Whatever there is in the Word of God that cannot, when taken literally, be appropriately referred to purity of life or soundness of doctrine you should recognize as figurative."[21]

He illustrated this principle by reference to a number of different passages. In John 6:53, for instance, the saying of Christ, "Unless you eat the flesh of the Son of Man and drink his blood, you have no life in you," "seems to enjoin a crime or an outrage: therefore it is a figure." But the precept, "If your enemy is hungry, feed him, if he is thirsty, give him drink" (Rom 12:20; Prov 25:21f.), commands an act of kindness and is to be taken literally.[22] Moreover, the connotation of a figurative term may vary, according to the requirements of the context. Thus in the teaching of Christ the word "leaven" has both a bad sense (Matt 16:6, "Beware of the leaven of the Pharisees") and a good sense (Luke 13:21, "The kingdom of God is like leaven"). Elsewhere in the New Testament the simile of a lion is applied both to Christ (Rev 5:5) and to the devil (1 Pet 5:8). "What more liberal and more fruitful provision could God have made in regard to the divine Scriptures," Augustine asked, "than that the same words might be understood in different senses, which are sanctioned by the concurring testimony of other passages no less divine?"[23]

There were three rules proposed by Augustine for the student of the Bible to follow: (1) know the books of the Bible, committing them to memory as far as possible; (2) carefully search out and master what is plainly taught in them; and (3) in the light of what is plain investigate what is obscure.[24] These rules are far more sensible than the seven rules of Tyconius for the understanding of Scripture. Though Augustine also set them down approvingly, they are in the main a prescrip-

---

19. Origen, *De principiis* 4.1.11-28, where the subject is discussed at some length. Origen even maintained that interwoven in the biblical history were accounts of events that did not happen, or could not have happened, but which were there for us to penetrate below the surface to the hidden truth intended by God. He therefore urged that we should "search the Scriptures" in order "carefully to ascertain how far the literal meaning is true, and how far impossible."

20. Augustine, *De doctrina christiana* 3.5.
21. Ibid., 3.10.
22. Ibid., 3.16.
23. Ibid., 3.27.
24. Ibid., 2.9.

tion for figurative interpretation and in themselves are of little worth.[25] Augustine also appreciated the importance of a knowledge of the original languages of Scripture—though it is said that he himself had no Hebrew and was shaky in Greek! It must be remarked that Augustine did not studiously follow the excellent standards of interpretation he had himself propounded, but seemed much inclined to indulge in exegesis of an exceedingly fanciful and allegorical character—for example, when expounding the miracles of Christ in his lectures on the Gospel of John.

The hermeneutical principles of Augustine were reaffirmed in the ninth century by Rabanus Maurus (d. 856). Rabanus studied under Alcuin at Tours and then served successively as instructor and abbot in the monastery of Fulda before finally being appointed archbishop at Maintz. A self-confessed collector or accumulator of the opinions and expositions of others, his numerous works of exegesis were essentially catenas of patristic quotations. In this respect he was following a practice that had become widely accepted by scholars. Chrestomathy of this kind freed him from the suspicion of plagiarism, and his concern was to promote the study and the right understanding of Holy Scripture. His rules of interpretation, borrowed from Augustine, were set forth in the third book of his work *The Training of Clergy.*[26] In reference to Rabanus's judgment that "where the books of the divine Scriptures are concerned it is very rarely and with the greatest difficulty that ambiguity in the words themselves can be found which either the context of the passage where it occurs or the intention of the writers or a study of the commentators or an examination of the original language will not solve,"[27] Ceslaus Spicq has observed that "it is surprising that, fortified by such valuable hermeneutical rules learnt from St. Augustine, the Middle Ages made so little use of them."[28] The unhealthy influence of the allegorical method and its fantasies in the medieval period needs no elaboration here. Our purpose is to show that even in these centuries when sane and vital exegesis was in short supply there were still outstanding scholars who wished to see it restored to a governing position of the life of the church.

The light of a more sober kind of interpretation shone forth again in the twelfth century in the work of Hugh of St. Victor (d. 1141). Prior of the abbey of St. Victor in Paris, Hugh gained a reputation as Alter Augustinus, a "second Augustine." His *Didascalicon* or *Manual of Doctrine* was the equivalent in emphasis and content of Augustine's treatise *On Christian Doctrine,* and the principles of interpretation he enunciated afresh were applied in commentaries or "explanatory annotations" *(adnotationes elucidatoriae)* on various books of the Bible. The *Didascalicon* also served to supplement a work of introduction for Bible students entitled *Preliminary Notes on the Biblical Writings and Writers.* Hugh recognized three senses of Scripture: the historical, the allegorical, and the tropological. It was his contention that the literal meaning of a passage was not necessarily limited to the historical sense, but coincided with the intention of the inspired writer. If the

25. Ibid., 3.30-37. The work of Tyconius, *Liber regulatorum,* was written c. 380.
26. Rabanus Maurus, *De clericorum institutione* 3.6, *PL* 107.383ff.
27. Ibid., col. 388.
28. C. Spicq, *Esquisse d'une histoire de l'exégèse latine au moyen age* (Paris, 1944) 42.

author's intention was figurative (allegorical) or ethical (tropological), then that was the literal sense of the passage. Hugh did not eliminate the anagogical sense but treated it as an aspect of the allegorical sense. Where the sense intended by the writer was not clear, he required that any interpretation offered must accord with the "analogy of faith," that is, with the main doctrines of the faith plainly taught elsewhere in Scripture. He perceived that fanciful and exotic interpretations could only obscure the truth and mislead the seeker. Hugh's hermeneutical position is well summarized in the following paragraph from his prologue to the book of Ecclesiastes:

All Scripture, if expounded according to its own proper meaning, will gain in clarity and present itself to the reader's intelligence more easily. Many exegetes, who do not understand this virtue of Scripture, cloud over its seemly beauty by irrelevant comments. When they ought to disclose what is hidden, they obscure even that which is plain. I personally blame those who strive superstitiously to find a mystical sense and a deep allegory where none is, as much as those who obstinately deny it when it is there.[29]

For Hugh of St. Victor the literal sense was fundamental to a right comprehension of the teaching of the Bible. "Do not boast of your understanding of the Scriptures as long as you are ignorant of the letter," he wrote; "for to be ignorant of the letter is to be ignorant of what the letter signifies and of what is signified by the letter."[30]

In the same century the hermeneutical principles of Thomas Aquinas (d. 1174), the most notable of the medieval scholars, also had much in common with the position defined by Augustine. Aquinas recognized only two basic senses of Scripture, the historical or literal and the spiritual; but he treated the latter as susceptible of a threefold division comprising an allegorical sense according to which "the things of the Old Law signify the things of the New Law," a moral sense according to which "the things done in Christ or in those things that signify Christ are signs of the things we ought to do," and an anogogical sense according to which "the things in eternal glory are signified." He retained the prevalent terminology but not the prevalent priorities of the allegorists, for he stressed that the spiritual sense "is based on and presupposes the literal sense": the spiritual sense could not be treated as something independent of the literal sense, since words themselves necessarily have their own significance, and any further significance which constitutes the spiritual sense flows from that primary significance. Thus it was his contention that the spiritual sense, when present, was inherent in the purpose of a particular passage, and was serious and edifying rather than fanciful and clever.

The fantastic claims of the allegorists, moreover, had the effect of denying the competence of the ordinary people to interpret the meaning of the text, thereby taking the Bible out of their hands. But Aquinas reasserted the important truth that God's written word is addressed to every man and every woman. "It befits Holy Scripture, which is proposed to all without distinction of persons," he wrote,

29. Hugh of St. Victor, *De scripturis et scriptoribus praenotatiunculae, PL* 175.113.
30. Ibid., *PL* 175.14.

". . . that spiritual truths are propounded under the similitudes of corporeal things, so that even the uneducated who by themselves are unable to grasp intellectual things may understand it." In any case, "truths expressed under metaphors in one passage of Scripture are more clearly explained in other passages"; and, no less importantly, "nothing necessary for faith is contained under the spiritual sense that Scripture does not openly convey through the literal sense elsewhere."

The term *literal* was in fact used with two different connotations by Thomas Aquinas: (1) as denoting the plain significance, which as such may be a "historical" passage in the proper sense, or which may be shown by the context to carry a "spiritual" significance; and (2) as denoting the sense intended by the author, which then is identical with the spiritual sense. But, further, "the author of Holy Scripture is God," and therefore the true literal sense is the sense that God intended. On this understanding, the New Testament, which declares the fulfillment in Christ of the ancient types, promises, and prophecies, is at one and the same time the literal and the spiritual sense of the Old Testament. As his exegetical writings show, Aquinas, like Augustine and others, did not always succeed in resisting the temptation to resort to allegorization in a manner that is certainly questionable. His principles of interpretation, however, were clearly and soundly conceived, as we have indicated, and as the following passage confirms.

The parabolical sense is contained in the literal, for by words one thing is signified properly and another figuratively; nor is the figure of speech itself, but that which is figured, the literal sense. When, for example, Scripture speaks of God's arm, the literal sense is not that God has such a bodily member, but that he has what is signified by this member, namely, effective power. From this it is plain that nothing false can ever underlie the literal sense of Holy Scripture.[31]

Moving on the fourteenth century, there are two distinguished scholars, Nicholas of Lyra and John Wycliffe, whose contributions in the realm of hermeneutics merit our attention. The Frenchman Nicholas of Lyra (d. 1340) was a member of the Franciscan order who spent the major part of his life studying, writing, and teaching in Paris. He was also the author of a fifty-volume commentary on the whole Bible.[32] We should notice particularly his postulation of a twofold literal sense *(duplex sensus literalis)*. In effect, he was carrying further the principle of biblical interpretation from the point at which Thomas Aquinas had left it. While acknowledging, as did Aquinas, the four traditional senses of Scripture,[33] Nicholas, again like Aquinas, approved but two categories, the literal and the spiritual, assigning the allegorical, tropological, and anagogical senses to the latter, and maintaining that the literal sense was the basis of the spiritual.[34]

31. Thomas Aquinas, *Summa Theologiae* 1a,1,9f.
32. Nicholas of Lyra, *Postillae perpetuae in vetus et novum Testamentum.*
33. See Nicholas of Lyra, *De commendatione scripturae sacrae in generali,* prolog., *PL* 113.28. Nicholas defined the four senses in this couplet:
Littera gesta docet, quid credas allegoria,
Moralis quid agas, quo tendis anagogia.
34. Ibid., col. 29.

Obviously, it is important to have an accurate text if one is to determine the proper sense of a passage; and Nicholas, who was thoroughly trained in Hebrew and Greek, was concerned to restore as far as possible the original text where it had been corrupted by incompetent copyists and ignorant "correctors" or distorted by propagators of heterodoxy. He complained that his difficulty in establishing sound methods of exegesis was compounded by the practice of numerous commentators who, neglecting the literal sense, expended their energy on the fabrication of a multiplicity of mystical senses, often without regard to the requirements of grammar, syntax, or context.[35] "It should be known," he wrote, "that the literal sense has been practically obliterated because of the method of exegesis commonly passed on by others, who, even though they have said many good things, have paid too little attention to the literal sense and have proliferated mystical senses to such a degree that the literal sense is in danger of being stifled in the midst of so many mystical interpretations."[36] He also taught that the literal sense was not necessarily exhausted by the historical circumstances of a particular passage—far from it, for a passage might have a deeper significance that was more fully literal than the superficial historical sense. Hence the conviction of Nicholas of Lyra that the same passage may have "a historic and mystical sense," and that, while "the historical truth must be retained, yet it should be related to a spiritual understanding"; consequently, "the same passage sometimes has a double literal sense."[37]

Similar conclusions were reached and propounded in England by John Wycliffe (d. 1384), who was familiar with the expository writings of Nicholas of Lyra and referred approvingly to him as "a modern but prolific and talented commentator on Scripture according to the letter."[38] Wycliffe likewise emphasized the fundamental importance, indeed the indispensability, of the "letter" or literal sense. Without disputing the legitimacy of the four commonly accepted senses, he too contended that when all was said and done there were really no more than two senses, the literal and the spiritual, and that the spiritual sense of a passage was in a natural manner dependent on and derived from the literal sense—so much so that the spiritual sense was properly speaking itself literal, and the interpreter of biblical truth should expound the literal sense in two ways, first as a grammarian, and then as one instructed by the Holy Spirit regarding the spiritual understanding of the passage. Since Holy Scripture is the Word of God, with God, not man or even the church, as its primary author, "the Holy Spirit teaches us the sense of Scripture, just as Christ opened its sense to the apostles."[39] The sense intended by the Holy Spirit was the sense concerning which the interpreter must receive instruction from the Holy Spirit. In this way he would be preserved from the fanciful excesses of those who "rashly overturn the whole sense of Scripture by denying the literal sense and inventing a figurative sense at will."[40]

---

35. Ibid., col. 30.
36. *De intentione auctoris et modo procedendi,* prolog, secund. in ibid., col. 30.
37. Ibid., cols. 31f.
38. Wycliffe, *De veritate scripturae sacrae* 12.
39. Wycliffe, *De civili dominio* 3.26.
40. Wycliffe, *De veritate scripturae sacrae* 12.

Wycliffe held, moreover, that Scripture was a unity and that its wholeness should not be violated. When rightly handled, Scripture does not contradict Scripture; therefore a particular passage must be interpreted in a manner consistent with the whole sense of Scripture. This, again, was the analogy of faith. Tearing Scripture apart was the policy of heretics. Wycliffe accordingly affirmed that "all Holy Scripture is the one Word of God,"[41] that "the whole law of Christ is one perfect word proceeding from the mouth of God,"[42] that constant study of the Bible was necessary "because one part of Scripture often explains another" and familiarity with the parts leads to an appreciation of the whole,[43] and that "it is not permitted to tear Holy Scripture apart, but to expound it in its integrity according to the sense of the author."[44] The reinstitution of biblical authority was carried a stage further by Wycliffe in his recovery of the principle that the Bible was intended to be the book not just of priests and professors but of every man and woman: as the perfect truth addressed to mankind, God's word was something "which all men are bound to know, to defend, and to observe."[45] This meant that biblical truth, which is the seed of eternal life (Luke 8:11), must not only be faithfully preached, but must also be available to all in their own language, so that all may possess and be able to study the Scriptures for themselves. Hence the diligent labor which Wycliffe and his fellow workers devoted to the translation of the Bible into English.[46]

It is of interest to find another Engishman arguing, in a manner distinctly his own, that the text of Scripture has but a single sense, rather than a plurality of senses. This was John Colet (d. 1519), the reforming dean of St. Paul's Cathedral, who before the close of the fifteenth century had attracted large and enthusiastic audiences at Oxford to hear his expositions of the Epistles of St. Paul. Colet gave an explanation of his judgment regarding biblical interpretation in a letter he wrote to Erasmus in the year 1499, in which he expressed his dissent from Erasmus's view that "the Holy Scriptures are by their own native fecundity productive of numerous senses." It was not that he wished to deny "the exuberant fecundity and fulness" of the Scriptures, Colet said, but his own conviction was that "their fecundity consists in producing not many things, but one thing only, and that absolutely true." The issue, as Colet saw it, was inseparable from the unity of God and the unity of his truth. Thus he wrote:

The Holy Spirit, who is the parent of the Holy Scriptures, and who is fecundity itself, as in himself he produces in accordance with his own power one and the same truth, so by his veridic word he necessarily draws out one sense only for us, and that absolutely true. But if, either in the hearing or in the reading of that divine word, numerous and various senses should arise for numerous and various persons, I would not conclude that their multiplicity sprang from the

41. Wycliffe, *De civili dominio* 3.19.
42. Ibid., 3.12.
43. Ibid., 3.9.
44. Ibid., 3.4; cf. 3.6.
45. Wycliffe, *De veritate scripturae sacrae* 7.
46. Wycliffe, *De officio pastorali* 2.2a.

fecundity of Scripture, which is so great that it has but one sense, and that absolutely perfect, but much rather that it sprang from the sterility of human minds and from impotence to arrive at the place where the true and simple truth lies hidden.

It accorded with the majesty of the Spirit of God, Colet maintained, that his was "a certain proper kind of speaking which is his own and singular." Therefore he whom the Spirit has admitted into the inner sanctuary of Holy Scripture "will see nothing there except one and the same powerful, most true, and most perfect sense."

Colet observed, further, that "where there were many opinions either one alone must be true or none," that "nothing is more frugal and sparing of words than the mind, and that spirit, which is most fecund."[47] This, however, was a sentiment which echoed not so much the mind of Wycliffe, whom Colet had read,[48] as the Pythagorean notion of verbal economy extolled by Pico della Mirandola, whom he had met in Florence and admired. Colet's interest in the works of Pseudo-Dionysius had also been aroused by his friendship with Pico and others of the Florentine circle (who, of course, believed that these works were the authentic writings of St. Paul's Athenian convert).[49] In his treatise *The Ecclesiastical Heirarchy*, Colet again affirmed the uniqueness of the sense of the New Testament text:

> In the writings of the New Testament, saving when it pleased the Lord Jesus and his apostles to speak in parables, as Christ often does in the Gospels and St. John throughout the Revelation, all the rest of the discourse, in which either the Saviour teaches his disciples more plainly or the apostles instruct the churches, has the sense that appears on the surface; nor is one thing said and another meant, but the very thing is meant which is said, and the sense is wholly literal.

Colet's emphasis on the fundamental importance of the literal sense is also apparent in his assertion that "where the literal sense is, there the allegorical is not always along with it; but, on the other hand, where there is the allegorical sense, the literal sense is always underlying it."[50] This was very much in line with the perspective of Wycliffe and with the Augustinian hermeneutical principle.

Not only was Colet's exposition of Romans and 1 Corinthians in 1499 sound and strong, but it also displayed a firm grasp and formulation of what later came to be known as the Reformed doctrine of justification. It is impossible to doubt that both his theological perspicacity and his method of biblical interpretation influenced the minds of those earliest of the English reformers who, later on, used to meet to study the Scriptures together at the White Horse Inn in Cambridge.[51]

47. The Latin text of Colet's letter is given in *Erasmi Opera* (Lyon, 1704) 5.129ff.

48. See *The Colloquies of Erasmus* (tr. Craig R. Thompson; Chicago: University of Chicago Press, 1965) 305, where "Gratian Pullus" is a name used for John Colet.

49. See Acts 17:24.

50. Colet, *Two Treatises on the Hierarchies of Dionysius* (tr. J. H. Lupton; London, 1869) 106f.

51. Cf. John Foxe, *Acts and Monuments* (New York, 1965) 4.253. William Tyndale may, as a student, have listened to Colet's Oxford lectures and he and others may well have heard him later preaching in London when he was dean of St. Paul's.

Finally, in this selective survey, recognition must be given to the significant role played in the history of biblical interpretation by Jacques Lefèvre d'Etaples (d. 1536), whose career, intellectually and spiritually, enacted not only the departure from the wasteland of medieval scholasticism but also the transition from Renaissance to Reformation (though Lefèvre himself remained in the Church of Rome to his dying day). Revered by his contemporaries as the equal in scholarly preeminence of his friend Erasmus (who also died in 1536), Lefèvre gave notice of a crucial turning point in his life with the publication of his *Fivefold Psalter (Quincuplex Psalterium)* in July 1509—that is to say, the very month and year of the birth of John Calvin and eight years before Martin Luther burst upon the public consciousness. In the introductory epistle to this work he announced his discovery of the incomparable sweetness of the Scriptures and, bidding farewell to human philosophy ("all human learning seemed to me to be darkness in comparison"), declared his intention to devote his life thenceforth to the study of the sacred text.

Like Nicholas of Lyra, Lefèvre propounded a twofold literal sense:[52] on the one hand is "the improper sense of those who are blinded and fail to see, and who therefore understand divine things only in a carnal manner"; and, on the other is "the proper sense of those who see and are enlightened." Thus perceived, the true literal sense was that "which coincides with the Spirit," the first author of Scripture by whom our understanding must also be enlightened. To state it otherwise, "the literal sense and the spiritual sense coincide," since the true sense is "the sense which the Holy Spirit speaking through the prophet intends." That this was so was confirmed by the way in which the apostles in the New Testament, themselves inspired by the Holy Spirit, proclaimed the fulfillment in the person and work of Christ of the types and prophecies of the Old Testament. Lefèvre, indeed, asserted that Christ was "the beginning and the end of the whole psalmody," as of the other biblical writings. Consonant with his belief in "the harmony of the Scriptures" *(concordia scripturarum)*, his hermeneutical perspective had become strongly christological.

There can be no question of the formative influence of Lefèvre on hermeneutical studies from the moment of the publication of his *Fivefold Psalter*. In all essentials, the principles of interpretation he expounded were to become the principles of Reformed exegesis. The *Fivefold Psalter* was widely acclaimed and eagerly read by the scholars of Europe, and one of those who studied it diligently was a young and unknown monk named Martin Luther. We know this because a hundred years ago a copy of the first edition of the *Fivefold Psalter* was found in the library of Dresden with its margins profusely annotated in the handwriting of Luther. Luther's principles of biblical interpretation would come to coincide closely with those of Lefèvre, who in this connection may be called his master. The publication in December 1512 of Lefèvre's great *Commentary on the Epistles of St. Paul* bore testimony to the effectiveness with which he was applying his own principles to the

---

52. *Duplex sensus literalis*—the same expression that was used by Nicholas of Lyra. Guy Bedouelle, *Le Quincuplex Psalterium de Lefèvre d'Etaples* (Geneva, 1979) 94, 96f., may be right in suggesting that Lefèvre borrowed it from Nicholas, with whose writings he was familiar and to whom there are references in the *Quincuplex Psalterium*. The text of the introductory letter is given, in the original Latin, in Eugene F. Rice, Jr., *The Prefatory Epistles of Jacques Lefèvre d'Etaples and Related Texts* (New York/London, 1972) 192ff.

exposition of the sacred text. Those doctrines which subsequently would be central and distinctive in the theology of the Reformation are clearly stated in this impressive volume. The last period of Lefèvre's life was devoted singlemindedly to the translation of the Bible into French and the preparation of commentaries on the text of Scripture for the benefit of his fellow countrymen. It was the work of one who was a true pioneer, and it may justly be said to have been carried on to still richer fulfillment by John Calvin, who when a young man, in the spring of 1534, visited and consulted with the aged Lefèvre in Nérac.[53]

It has been my purpose to show that across the centuries there has been a line, or a recurrence, of scholarly commentators who have stressed the fundamental importance of the literal or natural sense of the biblical text and have deplored the practice, which was for so long dominant, of imposing on the language of Scripture unnatural meanings that a low estimate of the worth of the literal sense has encouraged. The principle at stake is well summed up in the admonitory words of Augustine: "If the historical foundation of Scripture is removed, you will find that you are building on air."[54]

53. On the work and influence of Lefèvre see my *Lefèvre: Pioneer of Ecclesiastical Renewal in France* (Grand Rapids: Eerdmans, 1984) esp., regarding the scope of this essay, 53ff.

54. Augustine, *Sermo 2, De tentatione Abrahae a Deo, PL* 38.30.

The Hermeneutics of John Reuchlin, 1455-1522

Thomas F. Torrance

John Reuchlin is generally acknowledged to be the father of Hebrew studies in the western church, for it was through his early work on Hebrew grammar and vocabulary, *De Rudimentis Hebraicis,*[1] that the learning of Hebrew really became possible for Christians, and through his zeal and persistence that interest in the Hebrew Scriptures increased rapidly in spite of opposition. Apart from his contributions to humanism, in Latin, Greek, and Hebrew letters, Reuchlin's great importance for the history of Christian thought lies in the new understanding of the Word for which he had struggled so hard in attempting to set it free from the sophisticated and syllogistic thinking of the Schoolmen. What helped him perhaps most of all was what he called the *veritas hebraica,*[2] the new way of looking at things that he had acquired from his knowledge of Hebrew and of the Hebrew Scriptures. His characteristic humanist fascination for language led him to reflect upon the nature of Hebrew and its distinctive idioms and peculiarities, but this coincided with something he had learned from Plato's *Cratylus*[3]—the relation of language to the realities it is employed to denote. Hence he drew a close connection between true knowledge *(vera apprehensio rei)* with the study of language *(ponderanda verborum vis est).*[4] In this way he made a discovery which gave him the leitmotif for all his future work: the contrast between the scholastic understanding of *Word* as essentially an intellectual occurrence, and the biblical understanding of *Word* as a wonderful and creative happening. That is the subject of his early and (for our concern) most important work, *De verbo mirifico,* which was first published in 1494 at Basel. This discovery lent greater fascination to his study of Hebrew and Hebrew writings, all of which was directed to elucidate the *miraculum* of God's Word communicated through the Scriptures.

By orientation and temperament Reuchlin belonged to the Augustinian tradition in the western church, with a more mystical slant.[5] Moreover, as an interpreter

---

1. Reuchlin, *De Rudimentis Hebraicis* (1506); idem, *Primi Graecae et sacrae Hebraicae linguae* (1537). For a complete bibliography of Reuchlin's works see Josef Benzing, *Bibliotheca Bibliographica* 18 (Bad Bocklet: W. Krieg, 1955).

2. Reuchlin, *De verbo mirifico* (1552) 2.11 (p. 144); idem, *De accentibus et orthographia linguae Hebraicae,* fol. aii, etc.

3. *De verbo mirifico* 2.7 (p. 129); 2.8 (p. 136f.); 2.9 (p. 196); 3.5 (p. 249); 3.12 (p. 283).

4. Ibid., 1.8 (pp. 54, 60); *Der Augenspiegel* 13, 14.

5. See *De arte cabalistica* (1612) 1 (p. 617), where Reuchlin speaks of man's soul as born from the mouth of God and breathed into his face by the divine Spirit as the illumination of his mind.

of the Scriptures Origen held a special place in his affection. The Platonic influence mediated to him through these sources was reinforced by Pythagorean and Neoplatonist elements acquired through his contact with the Italian leaders of Renaissance thought, Marsilio Ficino and Pico della Mirandola. But through the latter Reuchlin's interest in the *Jewish Cabbala,* with its strange mystical and linguistic lore,[6] was also reinforced; and that, together with the *veritas Hebraica* which he imbided more and more from his study of the Hebrew Scriptures, modified considerably his Platonic tendencies. That is apparent, for example, in the way in which he holds the distinction between the *mundus intelligibilis* (or the *mundus superior sive archetypus,* as he often prefers to call it), and the *mundus sensibilis,*[7] and in his rejection of the Orphic notion of man's participation through likeness or proportion in divine being.[8]

For Reuchlin God is essentially the creator who made the world out of nothing and is infinitely transcendent over it. As the Light of all light he created also the invisible and intelligible world, for there is no understanding and no light appart from his. He is *supersupremus* over both the *mundus sensibilis* and the *mundus intelligibilis.*[9] It is his creative Word alone that bridges the chasm between God and the creature and makes communication between them possible, giving rise to true human knowledge of God.[10] It is this *Verbum mirificum* that is the secret of all human life and knowledge, and indeed of all creation. It is the understanding of this *Verbum Dei* that Reuchlin seeks as he weighs the force of the Hebrew through which this knowledge has been mediated.

One might well describe this as a "mysticism of the Word," for what Reuchlin rejoices in is a mystical experience through hearing the ineffable rather than through vision.[11] He does not contrast these sharply, for vision, the seeing of the invisible, has its proper place.[12] But because it is only through the Word that emanates from the innermost being of God that he is known, it is in the experience of hearing the Word—*receptio ab auditu*[13]—that there takes place the transition or ascension of man into the divine mystery.[14] Like God's name, his Word is inexpressible by man; yet it is expressed through the speech of God and must therefore be heard in a wonderful way appropriate to its ineffable nature. That is what Reuchlin is struggling with in his curious reflections upon the Tetragrammaton (YHWH):[15] the communication to man in his "imbecility" of the transcendent self-

6. See Reuchlin's *De arte cabalistica* as well as the *De verbo mirifico* for these tendencies; also *Der Augenspiegel* 12f.

7. *De arte cabalistica* 1 (pp. 641f., 665ff., 719f.); *De verbo mirifico* 2.18 (p. 174); 2.21 (pp. 214, 220).

8. *De verbo mirifico* 1.2; see also 3.10-12.

9. *De arte cabalistica* 1 (pp. 642f.); 2 (pp. 665f., 689ff., 707); 3 (pp. 715ff.).

10. *De verbo mirifico* 3.2; *De arte cabalistica* 1 (p. 642). Reuchlin likens the Word to Jacob's ladder, *De arte cabalistica* 2 (p. 670); *De verbo mirifico* 2.9.

11. *De verbo mirifico* 3.10 (pp. 271ff.); 3.3 (p. 236).

12. Ibid., 1.9 (p. 61).

13. *De arte cabalistica* 1 (p. 623); 2 (pp. 657f.); see also *Der Augenspiegel* 17 and following.

14. *De verbo mirifico* 2.6 (pp. 122f.).

15. Ibid., 2.18 (pp. 191ff.); 3.13 (pp. 288ff.).

revelation of God. To justify this ultimate experience in hearing God's miraculous Word Reuchlin tends to appeal to Aristotle's notion that first principles are by their very nature beyond demonstration,[16] and to have recourse to Cabbalistic and Pythagorean mystical speculations, which he often mixes up in weird ways with his reflections upon the biblical narratives. There is much here that is inevitably quite strange to us and rather undisciplined; yet it does represent something extremely important: Reuchlin's rejection of any attempt to penetrate into knowledge of the divine being by processes of reasoning, and also of any attempt to reduce what we know of God to syllogistic argumentation or to corrupt it by "the sophisms of Aristotle."[17] He will have nothing to do with the mixing up of divine knowledge with natural things, nor with appeals to Gregory Nazianzus and Athanasius in support.[18] Knowledge of God is by faith alone *(sola fide)*—the proper faith *(recta fides)* that comes from hearing—and is rooted in revealed truth, in God's own pronunciation of his divine name. In *De arte cabalistica* this tends to be seriously obscured with naive and almost superstitious ideas, but in *De verbo mirifico,* written before Reuchlin became so steeped in Cabbalistic lore, there is a clear line of thought of great importance for our inquiry.

The latter book is constructed on the basis of a dialogue which Reuchlin (under the name Capnion) conducts with a representative of Greek philosophy (Sidon, a Pythagorean) and a representative of the wisdom of Judaism (Baruch). Over against the views of the Greeks, in which he has obviously steeped himself, Reuchlin maintains that the Word or *Logos* of God is *Verbum* as well as *Ratio.* And over against the view of the Jews he maintains that the Word or *Dabhar* of God is his *Hand* (that is, his Deed) as well as his Word. To both he insists that it is only through this creative and wonderful Word and the communication or conversation it sets up between God and man that man can acquire knowledge of God or read the sublime things that utterly transcend his feeble capacities.[19] This is the Word that became flesh in Jesus Christ. Therefore it is in and through him, and in accordance with the human form which the Word has taken in him, that men may attain to the knowledge they desire. Hence Reuchlin seeks to bring his Greek and Jewish interlocutors to faith in Jesus Christ as the Way, the Truth, and the Life leading to the Father.

After the opening discussion with Sidon and Baruch, the book moves on to the main theme in which Reuchlin, through the exposition of Capnion, sets out his doctrine of "the one Word." At the outset a distinction is drawn between the knowledge of inferior and mutable realities which is really *opinio* and the knowledge of superior and immutable realities which is *sapientia* or *scientia* in the proper sense. These sublime realities are beyond the capacity of man, for he is unable to penetrate into them through the power of his own reasoning *(cogitatio),* but

16. Ibid., 2.9 (pp. 183f.); *De arte cabalistica* 2 (p. 659).

17. This is all the more significant in view of the fact that Reuchlin had a thorough knowledge of the works of Aristotle, to the study of which, he says, Greek recalled him. Yet the complaint was that these studies alienated him from Roman piety. See his *De accentibus et orthographia linguae hebraicae,* fol. aiif.

18. *De arte cabalistica* 2 (pp. 659ff.).

19. Cf. Ibid., 1 (p. 651).

they may be discerned by him, by the eye of the mind *(acis mentis)*, although not apart from the shining of divine light and truth.[20] The mode of this perception or knowledge is *faith*. Just as through our senses we apprehend sensible things, and through the intelligence apprehend intelligible things, so through faith we know God in a way appropriate to him.[21] This takes place through a covenant relation *(pactum, unio, confoederatio)* which God sets up between man and himself, as he places man in the midst of the universe in which he shares alike in things below and things above, directing faith to what is above and reason to what is below.[22] While there is no proportion between God and man *(nulla hominis erga deum proportio)*, because God is infinite and man is finite, God nevertheless freely enters into relations with man *(libenter versari cum hominibus)*, establishing fellowship *(societas)* and communication *(communicatio)* between himself and man. It is faith that is the bond *(vinculum)* between the love of God for man and the hope of man for God—but faith answers to the miraculous act of God through his Word in which he gives us to participate through an indescribable union.[23] Here Reuchlin admits that we are up against something ultimate, like the presuppositions or first principles or axioms with which we work in mathematics and physics, something which we can only acknowledge in joyful obedience.[24] To this Capnion's companions readily assent, but they press him to fulfill his promise to speak about the Word by which we are placed in nature, but through which we may rise above nature, and by which miracles are wrought.[25]

Before resuming the argument Reuchlin pauses to note that here, where we are concerned with God who precedes all and who effects everything, the proper approach is one of wonder and reverence. It is through humility that we are made fit hearers of something so great, while faith, hope, and love all play their part in our understanding.[26] "Blessed be the God of Israel who only does wondrous things," he cites—God alone works miracles, and not man. Therefore when we know him it can only be through an "indescribable union" with him created by the miraculous power of his Word.[27] We acknowledge that our understanding of this wondrous operation can never be adequate to it, so that in our act of knowing we have to rely upon revelation from above and attribute everything to his glory.[28]

When Reuchlin attempts to offer an account of this relationship between man and God set up by the divine Word he is at a loss, for he has no adequate tools with which to set forth his understanding of it. He is determined, however, not to reduce it through syllogistic reasoning to the knowledge of clear-cut apprehensibility loved by the Schoolmen, for that would not be to respect its divine majesty. He

20. *"Nisi revelatione divina,"* De verbo mirifico 1.9 (p. 62); *"nisi lucente Deo"* 1.11 (p. 71). Cf. also 1.17 (p. 90): *"nulla ratione prompta coactus, nisi sola divinae revelationis auctoritate"*; and *De arte cabalistica* 2 (pp. 662f.).

21. *De verbo mirifico* 1.9 (pp. 60f.).

22. Ibid., 1.10.

23. Ibid., 1.11; 1.19 (p. 96).

24. Ibid., 1.15; cf. *De arte cabalistica* 2 (p. 658).

25. *De verbo mirifico* 1.17 (p. 92); 2.1 (p. 99).

26. Ibid., 2.2.

27. Ibid., 1.2 (p. 71); 2.5 (p. 116).

28. Ibid., 2.3; *De arte cabalistica* 2 (pp. 662f.).

keeps on saying that it is "indescribable" *(innarrabilis)* and that it can be apprehended only in a way appropriate to its mysterious character *(proprietate occulta)*.[29] He does try to feel his way forward through analogies taken from nature and from language which are not very helpful and often obscure his exposition, but the main line of his thought is fairly clear, even if at times it is somewhat fanciful.

Reuchlin points out that the relationship through the Word with which he is concerned is not something irrational but on the contrary arises in the divine employment of the human mind as his instrument through admitting it into a fellowship with the divine Mind. The conversation that results from this is grounded on a divine decree before the creation of the world and is rooted in the eternal Logos, for even from eternity God rejoiced to have fellowship with man.

> Accordingly the Lord of eternity rejoicing in our society and counting among his delights the sanctified mind of man as, so to speak, bordering on his own nature and deriving from him, when he sees it submitting to him in sedulous worship and constant devotion, continually strives as an exceedingly abundant nutritive power to transform it, as far as human weakness allows, not only by the warmth of his love but by a secret propriety to direct it toward himself; so that man may migrate into God and God may dwell in man.[30]

This migration into communion with God is established and fortified by covenant acts *(pacta)* on a confederation *(confoederatio)*[31] such as that into which God placed Israel when he drew it out of the workhouse of the Egyptians *(de ergastulo Aegyptorum)*, delivering it from servitude and redeeming it by his mighty arm and great judgments, taking it to be his people and giving himself to them as their God.[32] But at its heart this is an operation of God which is secret and hidden from us, like the vegitative and digestive activities in nature of which we stand in ignorance.

> Thus in this utterly divine movement unto God *[in hoc divinissimo in Deum transitu]* there are some words *[verba quaedem]* which we know and some which we do not know. But this *vinculum verborum* unites both parties, *Deus enim spiritus, verbum spiratio, homo spirans*. God is called *Logos*, named Word by the same term by which the human reason is expressed in a similar way of speaking. God is discerned by mind, and conceived by the Word, so that as he makes the mind his invisible abode, he takes up his audible dwelling in words—not all words, not any words that happen to be used, but those which God has first provided for us, and which human ingenuity has not thought up, For God knows the thoughts of men, that they are vain. But God's thoughts are redemptive and saving, permanent, invincible, and sure. As he thinks, so it will be; as he determines, so it will come to pass. The Lord commands the universe and who can hinder him? Therefore not all words carry the divine presence *[igitur non omnia verba numen possident]*.[33]

29. *De verbo mirifico* 2.3, 6(2).
30. Ibid., 2.6; cf. *De arte cabalistica* 2 (p. 670).
31. *De verbo mirifico* 2.18 (p. 193).
32. Ibid., 2.6; 2.18 (p. 192).
33. Ibid., 2.6 (pp. 122f.).

God himself, the great God of the world and of man, or his sharp-sighted angels, have composed, at his command and by his providence, the words that echo the music of eternity and, in accordance with his saving economy, convey to men divine things. Hence we have the literary form of God's revelation which has been handed down to us from ancient times.[34]

This raises a discussion about the nature of the Hebrew language which, according to Reuchlin, is the medium in which God converses with the angels—not that God speaks Hebrew with himself, for the Word in God is something utterly transcendent and ineffable, and which cannot be grasped by the human mind. That is the significance of the unpronounceable divine name, YHWH, which as he pronounces it to men is his divine self-revelation.[35] But Hebrew does have a peculiar and unique place in the divine economy; it was not only the original language of revelation but remains the language in relation to which even the New Testament is to be understood.[36] Most of the rest of the second book of *De verbo mirifico* is taken up with the question of inspired writings, and especially of the idioms and distinctive characteristics of the Hebrew Scriptures—the *veritas hebraica*.

The significance of this may be judged from a comparison with the view of Aquinas that God and the angels converse wordlessly.[37] However fanciful Reuchlin's notion may appear to us,[38] he is insisting that Word has an eternal place in the being of God. Because God is Word in himself, he converses with his creatures in words. It is from a source in God's creative speech that all man's ability to employ words is derived. But words as such have no divinity about them and tell us nothing about God. Just as no one knows what is in man's heart but his own spirit, so no one knows God or his Mind except his own Spirit and he to whom he grants revelation of himself through his Spirit and Word.[39] The Scriptures, however, are the written form of God's Word because they are the providentially formed and appointed medium through which he comes to converse with us by the power of his Spirit.[40] Reuchlin's view of the relation of this divine speech to angels is governed in part by Aristotle's idea that word is the *messenger* that announces to another what is in a person's mind—that is, a sort of *angel*.[41] It involves a creative act on the part of God's Word, but what he communicates is through creaturely media. Hence in the union set up between man and God by his words, there is a nonobjectifiable element and an objectifiable element—or, as Reuchlin expresses it, some of these words we know and some we do not know.

34. Ibid., 2.6 (p. 123); *De arte cabalistica* 3 (pp. 725ff.). It is the inner aural receiving and handing on of the divine word that is the theme of Reuchlin's cabbalistic musings.

35. *De verbo mirifico* 2.8, 15ff.

36. Ibid., 2.8 (p. 136); 2.11 (pp. 144ff.); 2.12 (pp. 154f.).

37. Thomas Aquinas, *Summa Theologiae* 1a, q.107, a.1.

38. Reuchlin reminds us that we have to speak of these sublime things *humano more, propter imbecillitatem nostram*. See *De verbo mirifico* 2.18 (p. 176).

39. Ibid., 2.13 (pp. 155ff.).

40. Ibid., 2.6 (p. 123); cf. *Der Augenspiegel* 15: *Die schrift ist ain zaichen der wort.*

41. *De verbo mirifico* 2.13 (pp. 155ff.); 3.3 (pp. 236f.). See also *De arte cabalistica* 2 (pp. 722f.), where Reuchlin relates it to Exod 23:20f. The influence of Philo is also apparent here in his assimilation of *logoi* with *angelos*. See *Opera Philonis*, ed. L. Cohn, 1.152, 463.

That is as it ought to be for at the heart of our conversation with God we are concerned with an intractable miraculous event.[42]

This helps us to understand another aspect of Reuchlin's teaching in which he
directs close attention to the *idiomata* of the Hebrew text, pointing out that they are
so distinctive that they cannot be adequately translated into another language,
and that unless we read the Scriptures in their original Hebrew we shall not understand them properly.[43] This does not mean that somehow the divine revelation is
to be discerned in the peculiar structure of the Hebrew language as such, but that
through study of the *idiomata* and *proprietates* of the Hebrew Scriptures we are
paying attention to the sign-language *(signa, symbola, signacula)* which they
employ to direct us beyond to the unique and ineffable speech of God.[44] That is
why Reuchlin never tires of insisting that we encounter *miracle* in the Bible. We
can get the Word of God no more through etymological or philological examination of the Hebrew than through the logical argumentations of the Schoolmen. But
we must allow ourselves to be guided by the nature of what is actually and literally written to *hear* God speaking—it is in that act of hearing, which is essentially a
miracle, that we really hear the Word of God. In other words, it is *by faith* that we
hear, and *through hearing* that we understand God's Word, that is, in a way appropriate to the wonderful nature of God's speaking.[45]

Another aspect of the Word of God that Reuchlin is concerned to emphasize is
the dynamic force. God's Word exercises the widest *imperium* and the fullest
power resides in it.[46] God's Word includes his act, so that when he utters it, it fulfills what he intends.[47] He remains faithful to it and supports it with his divine
being. Thus in the Old Testament the self-revelation of God through his Word and
the making bare of his mighty arm mean the same thing.[48] God's Word is his Hand
as well as his Word.[49] That is why it is not amenable to treatment in mere ideas or
logical connections, and why understanding of it can only begin after the action of
God upon us, in a reflection upon what he has both spoken and performed, and
through participation in his Spirit. The Word of God is a mighty, active, creative
thing, a life-giving emanation, as it were, of his own divine energy.[50]

That is the point at which Reuchlin begins his account of the Word in the third
book of *De verbo mirifico,* in which he seeks to carry his readers through to a
profounder understanding of the Word incarnate in Jesus Christ.[51] This is the *ver-*

42. *De verbo mirifico* 2.6 (pp. 122f.).

43. Ibid., 2.11; 2.12; 2.18.

44. This is what Reuchlin called *symbolica theologia* at *De arte cabalistica* 3 (p. 713). It is
partly for this reason that Reuchlin is so fascinated with the *Cabbala.*

45. Compared to that divine speaking, Reuchlin says, citing from Origen, that men must be
considered not only ineloquent but even mute. *De verbo mirifico* 2.15 (p. 163).

46. Ibid., 3.2 (p. 229); *Der Augenspiegel* 17f.

47. *De verbo mirifico* 1.15 (p. 81); 2.6 (p. 123); 2.11 (p. 150); 2.18 (pp. 192f.).

48. Ibid., 2.18 (p. 192).

49. Ibid., 3.3 (pp. 235f.); 3.11 (pp. 276ff.). See *De arte cabalistica* 3 (pp. 765f.).

50. Cf. *De arte cabalistica* 2 (pp. 660ff.); and *Johann Reuchlins Briefwechsel* (L. Geiger ed.;
Tübingen, 1875) 125, letter 117.

51. His biblical starting point is Heb 11:3; John 1:1ff.; Rev 19:16; 1 Cor 1:28. *De verbo
mirifico* 3 (pp. 228f.).

bum rationale or the *ratio verbalis*, the creator of the universe and the disposer of everything. Using the familiar analogy of the *verbum internum hominis* which proceeds from the mind, Reuchlin proceeds at once to speak of Christ as the Word who proceeds from the Father's Mind, the only begotten Son of God, whose name, according to Isaiah, is called Wonderful *(Mirificum),*[52] but to whom David and others also give the name of God's *Hand.*[53] Just as it is the office of the word to announce what goes on within the mind, to fetch out from the depths the secrets of thought, and to lay open the will of the speaker, so he is most aptly deemed to be the Son and Word of the Father, since no one has ever seen God, but the only begotten Son who is in the bosom of the Father has announced him to us. He is therefore the Angel or Messenger of the great Counsel who reveals to mortals the sublime purposes of God.[54] He is in fact the substantial and substantive Word of the Father, the wholly adequate Word and perfect Image of God, through whom we know him who previously was not known by us. He that hath seen me, said Jesus, has seen the Father. Thus the whole substance of God is revealed in one brief Word *(tota substantia brevi sermone aperta).* No one knows the Father except the Son and he to whom the Son reveals him. He is the *imago vivens et volens* of God.[55]

We need not follow Reuchlin's account in detail, but we must note the point of supreme importance he is intent on getting across: the *consubstantiality of the incarnate Word* with the eternal Father, for in Jesus the eternal hypostatic expression of the Father has been given human form. That is the astounding novelty *(novum)* that God has created in the earth; he now converses with men humanly as Immanuel, God with us. In Jesus the deity of the Word has assumed human nature and is united to it, so that he who was from the beginning, as John says, the Word of life, has been heard with human ears and seen with human eyes, and handled with hands. That is the Word that is announced in the gospel. That is, the ineffable Word, the unpronounceable name of God, can now be spoken by a human mouth.[56] Reuchlin goes on to expound the Chalcedonian Christology and the doctrine of the Holy Trinity and the traditional terminology, but he applies it with immense emphasis to the epistemological question that concerns us in this inquiry. In Jesus, God the Word is present hypostatically, in his own proper person, speaking to us face-to-face, humanly. What is in the stream is in its source, what is in Jesus is in the God of eternity. It is as such that Jesus is the Way, the Truth, and the Life, and he is that so exclusively that there is no way to God the Father but by him.[57] "Hence the Word, although he is the eternal Son of God, born of the substance of the Father before the ages, nevertheless was born of the substance of the Virgin in time, perfect God and perfect Man of a rational soul and

52. Isa 9:6; *De verbo mirifico* 3.3 (p. 234). This is of course what gives Reuchlin the title for his work.

53. Ps 74:11, etc.; *De verbo mirifico* 3.3 (p. 235).

54. *De verbo mirifico* 3.3 (p. 236).

55. Ibid. (p. 237). Reuchlin speaks of Christ as *mentis nostrae objectum supremum . . . per quem plane tandem in Deum transeanus in comprehensibilem.* See *De arte cabalistica* 1 (p. 649).

56. 1 John 1:1; *De verbo mirifico* 3.4 (pp. 240ff.).

57. *De verbo mirifico* 3.8; see esp. p. 263.

subsisting in human flesh."[58] It is in and through him that the indescribable communion between man and God through the miraculous operation of God's Word is consummated, that the sublime self-revelation of God to which nothing on earth is commensurate is made apprehensible to man, that the ineffable name of God can be taken on human lips. Thus in the divine *economy,* "the Word clothed himself with human flesh that we through his saving contact with us may more easily follow up our accommodation to him, when with these eyes and our several senses we embrace that very Word, no longer ineffable as before, within the compass of letters, but can even denote it with an utterable word and an understandable sound."[59]

There follows a discussion of the names *Christ* and *Jesus,* Messiah and Savior,[60] in the course of which Reuchlin sets out to show in his abstruse linguistic reflections how the miraculous and wonderful name of the Word comes to be uttered by a human voice. The Word himself descended into human flesh and spoke human words with a human voice in such a way that divine speech passed into human speech and letters; yet this happened in such a way that the human speech and letters retained the imprint and seal or character of the divine Word. What Reuchlin tries to do, admittedly not very clearly, is to apply the classical doctrine of the two natures of Christ in one person to the relation between divine utterance and human utterance in the incarnate Word. It is a miraculous relation that we have there, and therefore is only explicable from the side of the divine creative act. That is denoted by the saying that the Word is Arm or Hand of God as well as his Speech. As he became incarnate through the Spirit, as it is the Spirit who utters the Word of God in the Incarnation, so it is only through the power and unction of the same Spirit that we may hear and understand the Word.[61] Reuchlin notes the importance of rejecting the heresy of Nestorianism and affirming the teaching of the Council of Ephesus that in the person of the incarnate Word who came out from the eternal Father, divine and human natures cannot be separated.[62]

In the concluding sections of his book Reuchlin shows that it is in the name of Jesus and through his Word that God is still at work miraculously among men to reveal himself to them and save them. God manifested his name to Christ; and he has manifested it to the disciples, and through them to the world, so that it is in and through Christ and his cross that we are adopted into communion with God. There is no Christ without the cross—that in fact is the *ratio* of the incarnate Word and of our participation in the mystery of God.[63]

How are we to describe the application of this, then, to the actual interpretation of the Holy Scriptures? In seeking to answer that we must not forget that after writing *De verbo mirifico* Reuchlin went on to write his epoch-making work on

58. Ibid., 3.8 (p. 254); cf. 3.11 (pp. 276f.).

59. Ibid., 3.10 (p. 273). See also 3.11 (pp. 279f.); and 3.16 (pp. 302ff.).

60. According to Reuchlin *Jesus (yhshwh)* is the revelation of *Yahweh (yhwh),* the addition of the *shin* to the Tetragrammaton standing for the Name *(shem)* of the Messiah. *De verbo mirifico* 3.12 (pp. 280f.); *De arte cabalistica* 3 (p. 770).

61. *De verbo mirifico* 3.11-13.

62. Ibid., 3.14 (p. 296). See also *Der Augenspiegel* 12.

63. *De verbo mirifico* 3.16-20.

Hebrew grammar and vocabulary, *De rudimentis Hebraicis* (1506), followed by a short textbook for reading Hebrew, *In septem psalmos poenitentiales hebraicos interpretatio de verbo ad verbum* (1512), and then his second book on the Hebrew language, *De accentibus et orthographia linguae Hebraicae* (1518). The mysticism of the Word had its counterpart in a severely linguistic and grammatical treatment of the Scriptures. And then on top of that again we have to take into account *De arte cabalistica,* published in 1517, in which he developed his symbolic philosophy of Hebrew mysteries.

(1) First of all we must emphasize that Reuchlin was a humanist of a special kind: he was a lawyer with a religious passion for truth, the truth of letters, the truth of equivalence in statement, the truth at the bottom of things, in the original sources. His first insistence therefore was upon reading exactly what stood in the text, every jot and tittle of it. Hence of his book on Hebrew rudiments he once wrote: *In hoc enim rudimentorum libro saltem hoc unum te docebo, ut scripta legas, non ut legenda scribas.*[64] At this stage he keeps theology out of things, and so he wrote in the same work that he was not concerned to write as a theologian about statements but as a grammarian about words.[65] Grammatical knowledge when carefully undertaken, he maintained, did not yield superficial results, but served to reveal the true and genuine sense of Scripture through bringing to our attention the distinctive properties of the words used.[66] Hence when he produced his edition of the penitential Psalms he offered a word-for-word *(de verbo ad verbum)* interpretation in order to help the student discern the inherent characteristics and distinctive properties of the language.[67] This involves the conviction that the Scriptures cannot be properly understood or interpreted except on the basis of the original languages in which they were written, for in interpreting one language into another it is not possible to carry through into it these distinctive characteristics or all its original power.[68]

It is interesting to note how Reuchlin's training and profession as a lawyer and judge influenced his method here: it must be specified and defined *(descripta definitaque methodus).*[69] Two examples of that may be given. In his Hebrew dictionary, which he assembled with great labor and sweat and persistence,[70] he determines the meaning of each word by noting definite cases. He then builds up their meaning, not primarily on etymological grounds (there is very little of that in Reuchlin), but on the grounds of specific instances of employment. The importance of this emerges as he keeps on pointing out how much the old Latin translation has mistaken the meaning of the Hebrew.

A different example of his method is to be seen in the little work *De arte*

---

64. Cited from Ludwig Geiger, *Johann Reuchlin. Sein Leben und seine Werke* (Leipzig, 1871) 127.

65. *De rudimentis hebraicis* 123.

66. *De accentibus et orthographia linguae hebraicae*, a iii.

67. See *Johann Reuchlins Briefwechsel*, 189, letter 163.

68. *De verbo mirifico* 2.12 (p. 155).

69. *De accentibus et orthographia*, xix a iv.

70. *Johann Reuchlins Briefwechsel*, 175, letter 151.

praedicandi which he wrote for the preachers of Denkendorf Abbey in thanks for their kindness to him. While the little handbook does have something to say about how to compose and deliver the sermon, it is mostly concerned with arid grammatical distinctions and connections, precisely the sort of thing that a juristic hermeneutics would require in order to determine in the most matter-of-fact way the plain sense of the statements and no more than that. On the other hand, when it comes to the application of the exposition to the lives of people, Reuchlin falls back upon the familiar threefold sense of Scripture (i.e., in addition to the literal sense determined by grammar alone): the tropological which is its "moral" application to the man himself, the allegorical which is the "civil" application to his relations with his fellow Christians, and the analogical which concerns men's relations with divine things.[71] Along with the literal sense, and the grammatical exegesis appropriate to it, it is the anagogical sense that is most important, for here the sacred Scriptures must be handled in such a way that they fulfill their purpose in *raising man up* to communion with God and so to a spiritual understanding that excedes nature *(naturam excedit)*. This carries us to the second thing that has to be emphasized.

(2) The Scriptures must be read and interpreted in a new way in which we let God himself speak to us through them directly. This was the significance that Reuchlin attached to his study of Hebrew and his interpretation of the Hebrew Scriptures. After trying various versions, he says, nothing he learned out of all the languages joined him to God more *(plus me deo conjungit)* than his occupation with the Scriptures in Hebrew.[72] They have the divine seal or character inwardly imprinted upon them, a majesty that points back to God the divine speaker.[73] This was greatly reinforced by his conviction (which we have already noted) that in the Hebrew Scriptures we have the language of the original revelation. "In reading Hebrew," he says, "I seem to see God himself speaking, when I consider that it is by means of this language that God and the angels have passed through their communications to men in a divine manner. Thus I am shaken with dread and fear, yet not without a certain unspeakable joy following wonder or rather amazement, which I will call wisdom, about which the divine Word says, 'The fear of the Lord is the beginning of wisdom.'"[74]

This represents a very basic shift in the conception of the Word, which was bound to affect exegesis and interpretation. It came about through the turning away from the Latin text to the Hebrew and through the fresh understanding of the biblical teaching which that opened up. We learn in it that "the great God wills to be signified not by any likeness or representation or image, but by the voice alone" *(maximum Deum nulla similitudine, nulla effigie, nulla imagine, nisi sola voce sig-*

---

71. *De arte praedicandi,* fol. aii. See also *De arte cabalistica* 3 (p. 716), where Reuchlin mentions, in addition to the literal and allegorical senses, a great variety of other ways in which to interpret the Scriptures. Here he has in mind the "fifty gates" through which cabbalistic art reaches the mysteries of the sacred writings.

72. *Johann Reuchlins Briefwechsel,* 123, letter 115.

73. Ibid., 16.

74. Ibid., 123, letter 115.

nificari velle).[75] It is the voice that mediates between God and man,[76] the voice which we hear in the Scriptures, but God's voice is his Spirit *(Vox Spiritus est)*. Reuchlin cites from John 3:8: "His Spirit blows where he wills, and you hear his voice but do not know where he comes from and where he goes."[77] This means that while we know God through reception of his Word by hearing *(ab auditu)*, it is not everyone who hears, for the hearing is a wonderful and miraculous happening corresponding to the miraculous activity of the Spirit.[78] That is the kind of hearing to which we have to learn to lay ourselves open in the reading and interpreting of the Sacred Scripture, giving attention to "the new and original kind of speaking in the divine Scripture, which is called the mouth of God" *(novum et nativum in divina Scriptura dicendi genus, quale os Dei locutum est).*[79]

As Reuchlin makes clear in *De verbo mirifico*, this leads straight to Jesus Christ, for he is the wonderful Word of God who has penetrated into human existence and into human speech. It is his Word that is articulated in the letters of the Scripture, for in him the ineffable is spoken to man, and the unutterable is pronounced and may be pronounced. Moreover, what happened in Christ Reuchlin considered to have a backward reference to the Old Testament writings. What is written in the Old Testament as well as in the New Testament all relates to him and his work, for all else that happened before the time of Christ was ordained to point forward to him.[80] In the human nature and form of Christ we have the Word that proceeds from the Father and has come down from the heavens. In him the Lord has thrust out his hand from above, and God is seen on earth in conversation with man.[81] That is the Word which we encounter and hear in the Holy Scriptures, the potent, living, energetic Word of God which heals and saves, and which is identical with the name of Jesus Christ.[82]

When Reuchlin writes in this vein it is difficult not to think of him as a forerunner of the Reformation, and certainly he had not a little influence upon Melanchthon, his nephew, and upon Luther himself. But we must note another side to Reuchlin which affected his approach to interpretation: his application of the anagogical method to the disclosure of abstruse mysteries.

75. *De verbo mirifico* 3.12 (p. 283). Cf. *De arte cabalistica* 1 (p. 651): *id est Spiritus, Verbum, Vox.*

76. *Johann Reuchlins Briefwechsel*, 105, letter 102: *Vox enim fuit mediatrix Dei et hominum, ut in Pentateucho legimus, at non quaelibet vox, sed tantum Hebraica, per quam Deus voluit arcana sua mortalibus innotescere.*

77. *De verbo mirifico* 3.12 (pp. 283f.).

78. *De arte cabalistica* 1 (p. 623).

79. *Primi Graecae et Sacrae Hebraicae Linguae* a2. While Reuchlin speaks realistically like this of *audire sermonem ab ore Dei*, he insists that that must not be understood anthropomorphically as if the Spirit breathed the Word through lips, etc., but understood *divinitus*, in a divine manner. See *De arte cabalistica* 1 (pp. 623ff.).

80. The Sacred Scripture whether written by the instrument of Hebrew or Greek letters is all of Christ *(ista Christi). In septem psalmos poenitentiales hebraicos interpretatio*, fol. a3.

81. *De verbo mirifico* 3.11 (p. 279).

82. It is significant that when Reuchlin spoke of "the three states of the Word" as "God, the Son, and the Incarnate," he does not mention the written word of the Scripture. *De verbo mirifico* 3.4 (p. 242).

(3) Two of Reuchlin's great insights were that the relation between the One Word of God and the words of the Sacred Scripture was miraculous and that Hebrew, like any other language, had highly distinctive traits and characteristics which must be taken into account if the Old Testament writings are to be adequately and properly interpreted. But since Hebrew was the original language of Revelation, Reuchlin concluded that the distinct characteristics of Hebrew were not unconnected with the miraculous relation between the wonderful Word of God and the speech of the Bible.[83] Reuchlin was so deeply convinced of the peculiar nature of each language that he insisted on learning Greek from Greek teachers and Hebrew from Jewish teachers. It is not surprising, therefore, that in order to understand these *idiomata et proprietates* of the Old Testament language he should turn to other Hebrew literature and to the judgments of Jewish scholars, such as the rabbis whose teaching is recorded in the Talmud, or to commentators like Rashi and Kimhi, or to thinkers like Maimonides.[84] But in this extracanonical Jewish literature he found in the Massoretic tradition a slavish reverence for the peculiarities of Hebrew, down to the very points and apexes of the letters. And he found in the Cabbalistic tradition mystical and speculative tendencies which claimed a higher wisdom not given to the multitude in virtue of which the deepest secrets of the sacred writings could be unravelled. Fascinated by this sapiential literature and speculation, Reuchlin could not refrain from probing into the wonderful relation between the Word and the words; so he developed an esoteric philosophy of Scripture which seriously distorted his christological insight into the doctrine of the Word and damaged his influence both within and without the Roman Church.

Reuchlin's peculiar view may be described by saying that he transposed the basic *eikonic* relation between words and what they signified from the *eidetic* to the *acoustic* realm; for it is only in word that God's Word can be imaged or signified. Hence it is through meditating upon the distinctive features of the sacred letters that we discern the *signacula* or *symbola* that aid our hearing the secret speech of God. That is what he called the anagogical method of interpretation, for through it our minds are elevated to the heights where we are in touch with divine reality.[85] This is what he called wisdom, *sapientia, sophia,* a mode of "philosophy" in which he claimed to transcend ordinary knowledge by breaking through the visible world into the invisible and achetypal world of divine patterns in the light of which all else becomes lit up with supernal truth.[86]

Reuchlin's veneration for the *idiomata et proprietates* of Hebrew Scriptures is rather like the veneration for icons that one finds in the eastern church—ex-

---

83. Sacred letters, he held, had a "majesty" about them in which the "divine character" originally imposed upon them could be discerned. *Johann Reuchlins Briefwechsel,* 16; cf. also p. 189.

84. *Der Augenspiegel* 8, and passim.

85. See *De arte cabalistica* 1 (pp. 641f.).

86. Reuchlin's "theosophical" attempt to penetrate more deeply into the relation between the Word and the words has a parallel in modern "sophiology," in which attempts have been made (e.g. by S. Bulgakov) to penetrate behind negatives of the Chalcedonian Christology into a deeper and more positive understanding of the relation between the divine and human natures in the person of Christ.

cept that this involves a meditation through contemplation. Behind both there are latent or Neoplatonic tendencies which can become particularly powerful and damaging to the interpretation of the Scriptures or the formulation of doctrine when it is worked out into some kind of philosophy of eidetic or acoustic representation.

Reuchlin's great contribution to biblical interpretation lies in his insistence that the text must be understood in accordance with the nature of the divine Word mediated to us through it; for behind the speech of the biblical writings there is the Word that eternally inheres in the being of God and is made audible in and through the divine revelation that reached its fulfillment and finality in the Incarnation. It also lies in his recovery of the insight that this Word of God heard in and through the Scriptures is God's mighty Arm, for God's Word has not only being in God but comes forth from him as his creative act and is at work in the church in healing and saving activity—that is, in the healing and saving activity of Jesus Christ. Thus whereas for the Greeks and for the Schoolmen word was primarily an expression of intellectual activity, for Reuchlin word is primarily a dynamic force. God's Word is thus Word which includes his act within it so that in our hearing it he acts upon it miraculously and unites us to himself in a communion that transcends nature. Hence the significance of biblical statements is not independent of the divine utterance that lies behind them and may be reached only through a consideration of the force with which they are laden.

But Reuchlin fell down badly at the very point where he rejected the methods of the Schoolmen. In rejecting their sophistical *quaestiones* and *distinctiones* which they imposed upon the Scriptures, he also rejected the all-important argumentative mode of interpretation in which the reader of the Scriptures does not simply interpret language with grammatical and syntactical rigor, nor simply meditate upon what is written in order to be lifted up to communion with God, but thinks the realities that are denoted by them and allows his mind to be shaped and directed by the inner logic of those realities. Reuchlin came near to doing that in the last book of *De verbo mirifico*, but when he veered off into his abstruse sapiential speculations he deprived himself of the one discipline that would surely have corrected his thinking and prevented him from straying into the fatal morass of hermetic and Cabbalistic fancy. And yet for all that he did insist that he was not expounding the Holy Scriptures in any way contrary to what the church taught, for what the church believed he believed, and by what the Roman Church taught he allowed himself to be guided. He remained therefore an opponent of the Reformation which was to benefit so much from his opening up of the study of the Scriptures in Hebrew.

Reuchlin's influence upon his contemporaries may be judged from the collect composed by Erasmus and published in his *Soliloquies* in the essay entitled "The Apotheosis of Capnio." I give it in the seventeenth-century translation of Sir Roger L'Estrange.

O God that art the lover of mankind, and by Thy chosen servant John Reuchlin, hast renewed to mankind the gift of tongues, by which Thy Holy Spirit from above did formerly enable the Apostles for the preaching of the Gospel; grant that all people may in all tongues, preach the glory of Thy Son, to the confounding of the tongues of the false apostles, who being in confederacy, to uphold the wicked tower of Babel, endeavour to obscure Thy glory, by advancing their own, when to Thee is due all glory, etc.

Luther's Use of 1 Corinthians 14

Robert A. Kelly

In his introduction to the English translation of Gert Haendler's recent book on Luther's ecclesiology, Eric Gritsch says, "Luther's view of the ordained ministry, and its relationship to the ministerial function of the congregation, has been the subject of considerable research and debate."[1] This is indeed the case, and yet the discussion often seems to be going nowhere. The issue that seems to prevent the development of consensus is whether or not Luther held to an "institution theory" or "delegation theory" (also referred to as "transferral" or "derivation") of the ordained ministry and whether or not he changed his mind about the relationship of the called and ordained pastor to the congregation. While we may never be able to settle such a discussion once and for all, it would seem helpful to try a different approach to the question, coming in by a side door, as it were. In researching Luther's views on ecclesiastical authority I noticed that he made use of 1 Corinthians 14 at key points in debates on the ministry with several opponents. Perhaps the study of Luther's use of this chapter from St. Paul can throw some light on the topic of ordained ministry and congregation. At the same time such a study could serve the secondary purpose of developing data which will help further understanding of Luther's hermeneutics.

My method for the background of this study has been as follows. First I surveyed the recent literature on Luther's theology of the ministry and summarized the various solutions to the problem. Next I examined all references to 1 Corinthians 14 in AE and compared the texts to WA. In addition I consulted several references to 1 Corinthians 14 which are not translated in AE. I then arranged these uses by the year in which a treatise was published or lectures or sermons were delivered. Here I present the results of that collation in narrative form.

I

In 1965 Brian Gerrish surveyed previous research on Luther's doctrine of the ministry.[2] He found that the literature focuses on the question whether "the special ministry rests on the common priesthood or on direct divine institution." The delegation theory derives the ministry from the congregation; the institution theory bases the ministry on a direct and special institution. By the early 1960s German

1. Gert Haendeler, *Luther on Ministerial Office and Congregational Function* (tr. Ruth C. Gritsch, ed. Eric W. Gritsch; Philadelphia: Fortress, 1981) 10. In this essay I will cite *Luther's Works* from the American Edition (AE) with volume and page and from the Weimarer Ausgabe (WA) with volume (or volume-part) and page.

2. B. A. Gerrish, "Priesthood and Ministry in the Theology of Luther," *CH* 34 (1965) 404-22.

scholarship, in the work of Wilhem Brunotte[3] and Hellmut Lieberg,[4] had come to the conclusion that only the institution theory appeared in Luther or that the delegation theory was clearly subordinate. Gerrish himself drew the conclusion that "Luther's way of relating priesthood and ministry identifies the functions of each, but makes a distinction between their normal spheres of exercise." While the congregation delegates the right to preach publicly, they cannot delegate the priestly functions. "Ministry and priesthood exist together in the Church as complementary vehicles of the Word." This seems straightforward enough, but Gerrish also finds that Luther's "clarity and simplicity" are marred by inconsistent thinking and terminology. Luther uses words such as "priest" and "clerical estate" in their medieval sense. The "office" terminology is also difficult. In addition, Gerrish finds that Luther at times does attempt to build the office of the ministry out of the priesthood of all believers. Thus Luther's statements about the office of ministry suffer from ambiguity.

Lowell Green attributed the ambiguity found by Gerrish to a change in Luther's doctrine of the ministry.[5] Green posited three periods in Luther's thought: prior to 1519, 1520-1525, and after 1525. During the earliest period Luther's views reflected traditional theology. In the middle period the idea of the priesthood of all believers emerged in polemic against the papist party. Beginning already in 1522, but especially after 1528, Luther places more emphasis on the authority of the office of the ministry. According to Green's interpretation, the change after

3. See Wilhelm Brunotte, *Das geistliche Amt bei Luther* (Berlin: Lutherisches Verlagshaus, 1959), which presents a good summary of German scholarship from the confessional controversies of the 1850's to the postwar reaction to the *Kirchenkampf*.

4. Hellmut Lieberg, *Amt und Ordination bei Luther und Melanchthon* (Göttingen: Vandenhoeck & Ruprecht, 1962). For further discussion see Jan Aarts, *Die Lehre Martin Luthers über das Amt der Kirche*, Schriften der Luther-Agricola Gesellschaft, no. A 15 (Helsinki, 1972); Heinrich Bornkamm, *Das Jahrhundert der Reformation* (Göttingen: Vandenhoeck & Ruprecht, 1960) 185-202; Hermann Dörries, "Geschichte der Vocation zum kirchlichen Amt," in *Wort und Stunde* (3 vols.; Göttingen: Vandenhoeck & Ruprecht, 1970) 3.347-86; Helmar Junghans, "Freiheit und Ordnung bei Luther während der Wittenberger Bewegung und der Visitationen," *TLZ* 97 (1972) 95-104; Hans Liermann, "Amt und Kirchenverfassung," in Friedrich Hubner, ed., *Gedenkschrift für D. Werner Elert* (Berlin: Lutherisches Verlagshaus, 1955) 359-72; Liermann, "Luther ordnet seine Kirche," *Lutherjahrbuch* 31 (1964) 29-46; Peter Manns, "Amt und Eucharistie in der Theologie Martin Luthers," in Peter Blaser, ed., *Amt und Eucharistie* (Paderborn: Bonifacius Druckerei, 1973), 68-173; Regin Prenter, "Die göttliche Einsetzung des Predigtamtes und das allgemeine Priestertums bei Luther," *TLZ* 86 (1961) 321-32; Wolfgang Stein, *Das kirchliche Amt bei Luther* (Weisbaden: Franz Steiner Verlag, 1974); Hans Storck, "Das allgemeine Priestertum bei Luther," *Theologische Existenz Heute*, N.F. 37 (München: Chr. Kaiser Verlag, 1973); Winkler, *Impulse Luthers für die heutige Gemeindepraxis* (Stuttgart: Calwer Verlag, 1983); and Ernst Wolf, *Peregrinatio: Studien zur reformatorischen Theologie und zum Kirchenproblem* (München: Chr. Kaiser Verlag, 1962).

5. Lowell C. Green, "Change in Luther's Doctrine of the Ministry," *LQ* 18 (1966) 173-83. The general idea of change in Luther's statements about the ministry, though not Luther's basic theology of the ministry, is supported by Bernhard Lohse, *Martin Luther: An Introduction to His Life and Work* (tr. Robert C. Schultz; Philadelphia: Fortress, 1986) 182-86. Lohse divides the periods of Luther's emphases on the ministry as 1517–1520, 1520–1523, 1524–1530, and after 1530. He believes that Luther's earlier statements that sound "congregational" must be read in light of his general acceptance of episcopal ministry.

1525 can be seen in three ways: (1) Luther no longer derives the office of the ministry from the priesthood of all believers but sees the two as separate; (2) Luther emphasizes that the *geistliches Regiment* is one of the offices that must be obeyed under the fourth commandment; and (3) *Kirche* replaces *Gemeinde* in Luther's thought. The reason for these changes is that Luther found that the ideas which he had espoused in 1523 when counseling the congregation in Leisnig did not "wear well in the ensuing events."

The views expressed by Gerrish and Green were not long in provoking response. Robert Fischer found both to be in basic agreement about Luther's view of the relation of "special ministry" to the priesthood of all believers.[6] In Fischer's opinion both Gerrish and Green had come to incorrect answers because they had been asking the question incorrectly. Fischer begins his criticism of Green by pointing out evidence which Green had not considered, especially that regarding Luther's distinction between power, which belongs to all Christians, and use, which belongs to the office of the ministry of the Word. Fischer, citing references in 1520 and 1523 to the divine origin of the ministry and objections to the word *Kirche* in 1539, demonstrates that Green's periodization of Luther's thinking does not fit the available evidence. Fischer concluded: "Green is wrong in thinking that Luther's solution was to switch from a 'transferral theory' of the ministry to a divine institution theory."

Fischer's criticism of Gerrish is that his quotations from Luther do not pay close enough attention to the context and historical development in Luther's thought. The point is to appreciate Luther's development without rigid periodization. More importantly, the question about Luther's "theory" of the relation of ministry to priesthood is off the mark. Luther did not hold to any theory, but tried to exposit "the ever-mysterious wonder of *God's* working in and through *men*." This mystery, plus the tension in two uses of the term "ministry of the Word" produces "permanent tension in Luther's view."

Fischer refers the reader to Edmund Schlink[7] and draws the conclusion:

To call ministry and priesthood "*independent* modes of God's working," then, is likely to be misleading. The authority of the ordained ministry is neither independent of the God-instituted church, nor derived from the humanly instituted church, local or otherwise. God does his work through men, but he retains the sovereignty before which both the whole body of the church and the clergy must bow.

In an essay prepared for the Sixth Assembly of the Lutheran World Federation (in Dar es Salaam in 1977),[8] Gunther Gassmann states that Luther emphasizes either the delegation theory or the instutition theory depending on the polemical situation. Luther was not interested in a theoretical solution to the problem of the

---

6. Robert H. Fischer, "Another Look at Luther's Doctrine of the Ministry," *LQ* 18 (1966) 260-71.

7. Edmund Schlink, *Theology of the Lutheran Confessions* (tr. Paul F. Koehneke and Herbert J. A. Bouman; Philadelphia: Muhlenberg, 1961) 229-37, 241-59.

8. Günther Gassmann, "The Ordained Ministry and Church Order," in Vilmos Vajta, ed., *The Lutheran Church Past and Present* (Minneapolis: Augsburg, 1977) 163-84.

basis of ministerial authority but shaped his statements according to the goal of advancing the gospel. "Ministry and general priesthood must be seen together as much as possible and . . . both are based in God's institution." Thus congregational call and ordained office are aspects of the same reality.

In 1977, in the context of the wider study of ministry and vocation, Thomas Wilkens returned to the questions raised by Gerrish, Green, and Fischer.[9] He phrases the question thus: "does ministry—that is, the public ministry—rest for its legitimization on the common priesthood just discussed? . . . Or does the public ministry receive its legitimization from direct divine establishment?" As can be seen from the way that Wilkens phrases the question, he does not agree with Fischer's analysis. He also rejects Green's idea of periodization but finds Gerrish's study convincing. His own view is that "the best attempt to harmonize [Luther's] two views is to maintain that the ministry was instituted by God but is transmitted by man."

In *Luther on Ministerial Office and Congregational Function,* Gert Haendler finds that Luther "took specific positions derived from very particular situations.[10] Specifically, Luther supported the "freedom of pastoral elections in city congregations" and "could not seriously conceive of the possibility of a rural congregation capable of functioning independently and also electing its own pastor." In Haendler's opinion Luther always gave the congregation "a very high priority" and perceived the congregation to be "the protector of the apostolic tradition, from which ministers emerge whenever required." It seems that, in Haendler's view, Luther did not change his mind, but always held that the congregation was prior to the ordained ministry.

With this we have the basic views: (1) Luther held only to the institutional theory; (2) Luther held to the institution theory except when necessity forced him to use the delegation theory; (3) Luther began with the derivation theory and changed to the institutional theory; (4) Luther held ordained ministry and common priesthood together in a dialectical tension; (5) Luther emphasized either theory according to the polemical context; and (6) Luther held to the derivation theory except when necessity forced him to use the institution theory.

II

Luther begins the preface to his first lectures on the Psalms (1513–1515) with a reference to 1 Cor 14:15—"I will sing with the spirit and I will sing with the mind also." This citation introduces a discussion of the hermeneutical importance of distinguishing the letter and the spirit in the Scriptures. In this preface the fourfold interpretation is subordinated to the distinction of letter and spirit. This distinction and the christocentric interpretation which it opens up are a gift to the church from the Holy Spirit.[11] 1 Corinthians 14 is used four times more in the *scholia* of these Psalms lectures. In a marginal addition at Ps 4:1, Luther alludes to

9. Thomas G. Wilkens, "Ministry, Vocation, and Ordination: Some Perspectives from Luther," *LQ* 29 (1977) 66-81.

10. Haendler, *Luther on Ministerial Office,* 20.

11. AE 10.3-5; WA 3.11-12.

14:15—"What is yours? That which comes forth from your spirit and your mind, because you are a human being chiefly according to the soul."[12] At Ps 12:4 Luther uses 1 Cor 14:30 to encourage students not to be stubborn but to listen to the opinion of others.[13] The distinction of letter and spirit is reinforced at Ps 19:4 using 1 Cor 14:8.[14] Finally Luther uses 1 Cor 14:6 to reinforce his definition of doctrine as "moral tradition."[15]

Uses of 1 Cor 14 appear once in the lectures on Romans (1515–1516) and once in the Hebrews lectures (1517–1518). In the Romans lectures the use occurs in a discussion of prayer in the *scholia* to 12:12. There "sung in the spirit" (1 Cor 14:15) is used to refer to a prayer "recited in the simplicity of the heart"; and speaking to God in tongues (1 Cor 14:2) is said to refer to reading the Word of God. Luther then cites 1 Cor 14:15 again to direct students to be attentive to both the emotional and the intellectual aspects of prayer.[16] In the Hebrews lectures verse 15 is again brought forward, this time as a reference in which St. Paul refers to human nature as bipartite.[17]

The first instance in which Luther uses 1 Corinthians 14 to make a point relevant to our specific interest is in his commentary on the proceedings at Augsburg in 1518. There Luther says:

> Furthermore, how many decretals are corrected by later ones! Therefore in time this decretal can also be corrected. Panormitanus, too, in his edition of the *Decretals*, shows that in matters of faith not only is a general council above the pope, but also any believer, provided he uses better authority or reason than the pope, just as Paul does with Peter in Gal 2. This is confirmed also in the following statement in 1 Cor. 14: "If a revelation is made to another sitting by, let the first be silent."[18]

The use of 1 Cor 14:30 to make the point that "lower" persons can correct "higher" persons in the church would become one of Luther's scriptural weapons in the struggle with German papalists.

In fact, it was soon included in lectures on Psalm 2:

> In 1 Cor. 14 Paul clearly teaches that if a revelation is made to one who is sitting by, the first speaker should be silent. In the New Testament, therefore, all superiors are to be heard in such a way that everyone of the lowest degree may be free to judge the thought of the superior in matters of faith. . . .[19]

In his 1519 lectures on Galatians Luther refers to 1 Corinthians 14 twice, both times using the phrase "tongues are a sign to unbelievers" in 14:22 as a reference to allegory. In the first instance he says that allegory is not suitable for

12. AE 10.53; WA 3.46.
13. AE 10.102; WA 3.97.
14. AE 10.229; WA 3.276-77.
15. AE 11.461; WA 4.338.
16. AE 25.459-60; WA 56.466-68.
17. AE 29.166; WA 57-3.163.
18. AE 31.265-66; WA 2.10.
19. AE 14.341; WA 5.68.

elementary instruction,[20] and in the second instance he uses the verse to say that allegory is suitable for the instruction of believers, but is not appropriate for apologetics.[21]

In Luther's many publications of 1520 he cites 1 Corinthians 14 only twice. In "Babylonian Captivity" he calls reading the hours speaking in tongues.[22] In "Why the Books of the Pope Were Burned," Luther uses 1 Cor 14:30 to justify his standing in judgment over the pope, who claims sole authority to interpret Scripture: "[The pope] thereby puts himself above God's Word, dismembers and destroys it, as St. Paul says in 1 Cor. 14, the superior should yield to the revelation of the inferior."[23] Three treatises written in 1521 use our passage for support. "Against Latomus" contains a significant use of 1 Cor 14:29:

> I am commanded to believe the Word of God, not their fancies. There is one teacher, even Christ, and the fathers are to be tested by the judgement of the divine Scriptures so that it may be known who has clarified and who has obscured them. Thus Paul orders us to "test everything; hold fast to what is good." In 1 Cor. 14 he says, "Let two or three prophets speak, and let the others weigh what is said." He commands that all be tested and that there be no exceptions—neither Augustine, nor Origen, nor any man. . . .[24]

Written in the same year, "Misuse of the Mass" uses 1 Corinthians 14 three times. First, Luther uses verses 24-25 to support his idea that "The church does not constitute the Word, but is constituted by the Word." The presence of the Word is a sure sign of the presence of the church.[25] Luther then goes on to criticize the papal idea of priesthood and to develop the importance of the preaching office. In these efforts he cites verses 40 and 27-31.

> We readily admit that not many of you are to preach at the same time, although all have the power to do so. When Paul said in Acts 4: "Barnabas, be still!" was Barnabas therefore not supposed to have the power to preach? "But all things should be done decently and in order" (1 Cor. 14). By this the universality of the office of preaching is not abolished; indeed it is strengthened thereby. For if all men did not possess the prerogative of preaching and only one had the right to speak, what need would there be to command and keep order? It is precisely because all have the right and power to preach that it becomes necessary to keep order.
>
> Let us therefore examine Paul's words, for in this passage with mighty thunderbolts he smashes to bits the pope's lies regarding authority and the power to preach. Thus Paul speaks: "If any speak in a tongue, let there be only two or at most three, and each in turn; and let one interpret. But if there is no one to interpret, let each of them keep silence in church before the people,

20. AE 27.180; WA 2.463.
21. AE 27.310; WA 2.550.
22. AE 36.115; WA 6.566.
23. AE 31.392; WA 7.175.
24. AE 32.217; WA 8.99.
25. AE 36.145; WA 8.491-92.

and pray to God by himself. Let two or three prophets speak, and let the others weigh what is said. If a revelation is made to one among those who are listening, let the first be silent, for you can all prophesy, so that all may learn and be encouraged." What will you say against this, you idols and counterfeits of the pope? Paul says that they can all prophesy, and in an orderly way, one after the other; so that one who is sitting by or listening may rise if a revelation is made to him, and the first, who is preaching, is to be silent and yield to him, and all who preach or lecture are to allow the listeners to judge and be subject to them. Where are you now, Pelagius, with your proud, insolent, slanderous tongue, daring with puffed-up cheeks to say in your fleshly law: "Where the authority is, namely the spiritual authority, there is the right to command; on the rest devolves of necessity the matter of obedience."

The devil himself has proclaimed this through your mouth in opposition to Christ, who is speaking through Paul. By divine might Christ has made you and everything that is yours subject to everyone. He has given to everyone the right and power to weigh and decide, to lecture and preach. Yet you venture on your own wicked authority to subjugate everything to yourself, and to exalt yourself above everyone, like Lucifer. You falsely allot to yourself alone the right to speak and judge, contrary to God and the Scriptures! Away, you villain; all Christians have a good and perfect right to lecture and preach from the Scripture, even if you should burst.[26]

The third use of 1 Corinthians 14 in 1521 was in "Answer to the Hyperchristian Book" in which Luther cites the chapter to refer to the distinction of spirit and letter, much as he had in the first Psalms lectures, but with a rejection of the fourfold sense, rather a subordination.[27]

In the writings from the Wartburg, the Postil contains one use of 1 Cor 14:20-30. There Luther argues that neither pope nor bishop alone should be believed. "Their teaching should rather be subject to the assembly of believers." The congregation judges the theology of the bishops. Just as Mary has precedence over Joseph, though of lesser rank, so the church is "preferred to the preachers."[28]

1 Corinthians 14 plays an important role among the passages cited to support Luther's argument in "That a Christian Congregation Has the Right," written in 1523 for the congregation at Leisnig. Luther's basic thesis in this treatise is that it is the listeners, not the teachers, who have the authority to judge teaching in the church. The congregation is the judge of the preacher, so congregations have the right to call preachers and teachers. Every Christian has the right and power to teach the Word. In situations where there are no other Christians, any Christian can and should take up the task of preaching the gospel.

Luther brings forward 1 Cor 14:30, 31, 39-40 in the next step of his argument. In a situation where there are many Christians, no one should assert himself, but the body of Christians should choose and call someone to preach. If there is a lack of teachers any Christian can teach without call, "provided he does it in a

26. AE 36.149-50; WA 8.495-96.
27. AE 39.180-81; WA 7.652.
28. AE 52.40; WA 10-1.140-41.

decent and becoming manner." If this is true, how much more does a congregation have the right to call a person into the preaching office. "Let this passage be your sure foundation, because it gives such an overwhelming power to the Christian congregation to preach, to permit preaching, and to call."[29]

1 Corinthians 14 plays an even more prominent role in Luther's epistle to the Bohemians, "Concerning the Ministry," written also in 1523. The first citations (to 14:26 and 14:31) occur in a section where Luther is arguing that the ministry of the Word is common to all Christians:

> Paul confirms this in 1 Cor. 14 as he speaks not to the shorn or to a few, but to the whole church and each individual Christian: "Each one of you has a hymn, a lesson, a revelation, a tongue or an interpretation." And further on: "For you can all prophesy one by one, so that all may learn and be encouraged." For say, what is meant by "each one of you"? These passages very strongly and clearly corroborate that the ministry of the Word is the highest office in the church, that it is unique and belongs to all who are Christians, not only by right but by command. Indeed it is not a priesthood if it is not unique and common to all. Nothing can prevail against these divine thunderings, be it numberless fathers, innumerable councils, the custom of ages, or a majority of all the world. For these are but as straws by which the shorn masqueraders strive to establish their priesthood.[30]

Having demonstrated that the function of the Word belongs to all Christians, Luther goes on to show proof that the functions of baptism, the Eucharist, absolution, sacrifice, and intercessory prayer also belong to all. The seventh function of the priesthood is to judge doctrine, and here Luther again returns to 1 Corinthians 14 to buttress his argument, citing verses 30, 32, and 31. The course of the argument is similar to previous treatises where Luther argues for the right and duty of the listeners to judge the teaching of the teacher.[31]

After establishing the right of all Christians to the seven functions of priesthood, Luther then issues a call for good order, citing 1 Cor 14:40. Since all Christians have the rights and duties of priests, no one person may "arrogate to himself alone" what belongs to all. Where there are no other Christians, any Christian may exercise his priestly rights, but in normal situations one or more are chosen to perform the priestly functions publicly. "For it is one thing to exercise a right publicly; another to use it in time of emergency."[32] Thus the context and situation are important factors in deciding questions of the form of the teaching office.

The substance is that the office of priest belongs to all Christians and the office of Word and sacrament is a serving ministry within the community of priests. This ministry is an office and a function, while the whole community of believers holds the authority and dignity of the priesthood. Luther next says, "We have clearly shown that to each one is given the right of ministry in the Word, and indeed that he is commanded to do so if he sees that teachers are lacking or if those in of-

29. AE 39.310-11; WA 11.412-13.
30. AE 40.22-23; WA 12.181.
31. AE 40.32-33; WA 12.188.
32. AE 40.34; WA 12.189.

fice are not teaching correctly, as Paul affirmed in 1 Cor. 14, so that the power of God might be proclaimed by us all." If such a right is given to individual Christians, certainly a community has the right and duty to call qualified persons into the office of the Word.[33]

After several more arguments in this vein Luther brings forward the example of Apollos, who preached in Ephesus without call or ordination. It was only "by the general right common to all Christians, as described in 1 Cor. 14" that Apollos exercised the ministry of the Word. In the same way any competent Christian could fill a need for teaching the Word, without call if necessary, and certainly when called by the whole community.[34]

Luther's final use of 1 Corinthians 14 in "Concerning the Ministry" occurs in a passage where he is assuring the Bohemians that they are a true church. It is not ceremonies, but the Word that marks the church. This is supported by a reference to 1 Cor 14:24-25. Luther says that God is present wherever his Word is present.[35]

In addition to these two polemical writings, Luther used 1 Corinthians 14 in liturgical writings and a sermon during 1523. In a sermon for Tuesday afternoon in Easter week Luther cited verse 31 to state that uninterpreted and private masses were illegitimate.[36] The chapter is used twice in "Concerning the Order of Public Worship." There Luther cites verses 26-31 as requiring that the Word be preached whenever Christians gather for worship, and he cites verse 27 as requiring the interpretation of lessons read in Latin ("tongues").[37] In the *Formula Missae* Luther cites 1 Cor 14:38 to say that the Reformation has now waited long enough for the weak in faith and will henceforth administer the sacrament in both kinds.[38] In the 1524 preface to the Wittenberg hymnal Luther cited 1 Corinthians 14 as the place where St. Paul instituted the singing of psalms in Christian worship.[39]

During this period Luther was not the only reformer using 1 Corinthians 14 to buttress his arguments. Andreas Bodenstein von Karlstadt used the chapter to forbid the use of Latin in worship for the congregation.[40] Luther responded to Karlstadt in "Against the Heavenly Prophets" of 1525. He maintained that Paul does not forbid the use of Latin per se, but only the use of untranslated or uninterpreted Latin. "Tongues" are allowed as long as someone interprets. More

33. AE 40.36; WA 12.190-91.

34. AE 40.37-38; WA 12.191-92.

35. AE 40.41-42; WA 12.194.

36. WA 11.93. *Ita Paulus et apostoli fecerunt, postea diaboli instinctu mutatum, ut latine legeretur Euangelium et Epistola. Nunc fecimus ex hoc opus et occulte Euangelium et Epistola legitur, cum palam et germanice legi debeant, sed haec occulta sunt.* Ad Cor. 14. *Si non est hic, qui interpretetur, taceant. Hic missam abrogavit, ritus vester est contra Paulum.*

37. AE 53.11-12; WA 12.35-36.

38. AE 53.34; WA 12.217. There is a possible allusion to 1 Cor 14:33 in Luther's exposition of 1 Corinthians 7, where he cites words that sound like that verse to Romans 15. Both the WA and AE editors make this suggestion (WA with a question mark).

39. AE 53.315-16; WA 35.474.

40. Cf. *Luthers Sämmtliche Schriften* (St. Louis: Concordia Publishing House, 1881), vol. 20, col. 2306-13; and WA 18.456.

importantly, Luther strikes a new tone in this treatise. Rather than being directed to the congregation, 1 Corinthians 14 is addressed to the preachers. The congregation's duty is to listen.[41] In the exhortation to the Livonians (1525) Luther says that external forms are *adiaphora,* but must be changed—if they are changed at all—with a constant eye to "the edification of the common people, as St. Paul says, 1 Corinthians 14, 'All things should be done to edify.' . . ."[42] *Bondage of the Will* also contains one reference to 1 Cor 14:29, reminiscent of Luther's earlier use of the passage. Here he criticizes Erasmus for refraining to judge the decrees of the church.[43]

Luther's lectures for the years 1526–1528 contain occasional references to our chapter. In the Ecclesiastes lectures (1526) verse 9 is used to elucidate Ecc 5:16.[44] The Titus lectures (1527) use 1 Cor 14:19 to emphasize how the cognitive power influences the conscience.[45] In the lectures on 2 Timothy (1528) Luther cites the chapter to enforce the translation of Latin readings in worship.[46]

The Zechariah lectures of 1527 contain a reference to 1 Cor 14:31 significant to our topic. Here we have a passage that Luther used against Romanist opposition in 1523, but now with a different thrust. What is emphasized is not the right to teach or call teachers but rather order and humility. The preacher rebukes and the simple person obeys humbly.[47]

This use of 1 Corinthians 14 to call the laity to submit to already installed evangelical clergy rather than to call congregations to depose Romanists marks a change in Luther's use of the passage, especially when taken together with "Against the Heavenly Prophets." A letter to Lazarus Spengler of 15 August 1528 indicates another trend that will become more apparent: Luther moves away from verses 26-31 and toward verses 33-40, especially 34 and 40, in his citations from 1 Corinthians 14. As the radical threat grows, orderly conduct becomes much more important to Luther. No longer is he the rebel fighting for legitimacy, but the leader of the church in Saxony struggling to keep his followers in line. In the letter he encourages Spengler to have the city council of Nuremberg preserve uniformity in liturgical practice.[48] In "Confession Concerning Christ's Supper" (1528), Luther uses 1 Cor 14:33 in a similar way.[49] The Isaiah lectures contain one citation and two allusions to our chapter. Both of the allusions are polemics against false prophets who do not know what they are saying, which might refer to 1 Cor 14:9 or 16.[50] The citation is in a reference to the seeds of Isa 28:24 as the varied gifts God gives to his people.[51]

Luther uses 1 Corinthians 14 three times in writings of 1530–1531. In the ex-

41. AE 40.141-42; WA 18.123-24.
42. AE 53.47: WA 18.419.
43. AE 33.23-24; WA 18.604-5.
44. AE 15.91; WA 20.106.
45. AE 29.47; WA 25.39.
47. AE 20.334; WA 23.652-53.
48. AE 49.205-6; WA Br 4.534.
49. AE 37.167; WA 26.265.
50. AE 16.223; WA 31-2.159 (WA has no note, AE a footnote suggesting 14:9). Also AE 17.53; WA 31-2.301-2 (WA notes 14:16, which AE follows, but in the text).
51. AE 16.236; WA 31-32.170.

position of Psalm 117 he refers to the four principal parts of the meaning of Scripture, citing verse 6. While criticizing the medieval fourfold meaning, Luther suggests his own four ways of interpreting.[52] In the preface to the book of Revelation in the German Bible of 1530, Luther speaks of the different types of prophecy.[53] In the "Commentary on the Alleged Imperial Edict" Luther makes what appears to be his last use of verse 30 to claim the right to question the hierarchy: "St. Paul also commands, in 1 Corinthians 14, that if a revelation comes to someone other than the head teacher, then the head teacher shall be silent and obey." In this case Luther is defending his own right to reform the church.[54]

After nine years of occasional use, 1 Corinthians 14 again comes to the fore in the 1532 treatise "Infiltrating and Clandestine Preachers." There Luther gives an interpretation of the chapter—which stands at the conclusion to his argument—that flatly contradicts his interpretation of 1523.[55] Against the Anabaptists, Luther maintains that verse 30 is addressed to "the prophets who are to teach, not [to] the people, who are to listen." Anyone who applies this text to the congregation is guilty of smuggling a foreign meaning into the text.

Here Luther also injects verse 34 as support for denying the office of the ministry to women. It seems that this is the first time in his career that Luther cited this verse, and it is used three times in this treatise. After 1532 Luther makes further occasional use of the verse.[56]

The main point, which Luther returns to, is that St. Paul "is not commanding the congregation to preach, but is dealing with those who are preachers in the congregations or assemblies." The chapter does not allow unauthorized persons to preach, but reminds those who are called to maintain the order Paul commands. It is wicked and arrogant to depart from one's own office and usurp the office of another. "If the incumbents of the office teach wrongly, what affair is that of yours?" 1 Corinthians 14 commands the congregation to listen and does not commission it to preach. The chapter clearly distinguishes the office of preaching from the congregation of listeners. No lay person ought ever to presume the authority to judge the preachers.

Throughout this section Luther is concerned with order. He worries that the church will become a tavern or marketplace and envisions strife and quarrels in the chancel. The point is not to reproduce the Pauline order of ministry or worship but to maintain Pauline decency and order. The "uncouth, undisciplined, shameless people" had to be kept in check so that worship and preaching could continue. This was the force of Paul's words in 1 Corinthians 14. Between 1523 and 1532 this chapter radically changed its character for Luther, no longer serving as a call to the

52. AE 14.36; WA 36-1.254.
53. AE 35.399-400; WA DB 7.406. The 1546 preface at this point is unchanged. WA DB 7.407.
54. AE 34.102-3; WA 30-3.384-85.
55. AE 40.388-94; WA 30-3.522-27.
56. AE 41.154-55; WA 50.633 (1539). See also AE 41.361-62; WA 54.287 (1545). In the printed form of the lectures on Psalm 2 the verse is used allegorically to silence reason (see AE 12.54; WA 40.259); and in the disputation on John 1:14 it is used to silence syllogisms and heretics (see AE 38.240, 252, 258-59; WA 39-2.4, 18, 26).

authority of the congregation but as a summons to order under the authority of the clergy.

In lectures and sermons of the years 1531–1535, 1 Corinthians 14 appears occasionally. Most often the reference is to verse 40 and is a call to maintain good order in the church.[57] There is one reference to tongues as one of the visible signs necessary to convince unbelievers in the first century.[58] The 1534 printed version of the 1532 sermons on 1 Corinthians 15 contains a reference to chapter 14 in which Luther says that a person truly endowed with the Holy Spirit will only teach with a proper call. A pious person who is not called, "even when he hears an error preached . . . proceeds with humility and admonishes the preacher in a friendly and fraternal way. . . ."[59]

After 1535 Luther makes reference to our chapter only a few times. Again verse 40 and the call for orderly worship and church life predominate.[60] The majority of references to 14:34 noted above come from this period. In the Genesis commentary the chapter is cited to support public preaching in worship over against the whispered portions of the canon of the Mass.[61]

III

What conclusions can be drawn from this study? While the narrow focus does not allow generalizations about Luther's total views on authority in the church and on the relationship of the office of the ministry to the common priesthood, it has been clearly shown that Luther's interpretation and use of 1 Corinthians 14 changed significantly in the period 1525–1530. Prior to that time Luther's writings that cited our chapter regarding ministry and authority used verses 26-30 to support the authority of the congregation to judge the quality of preaching and to call and depose preachers. After that time Luther completely reversed himself and used the chapter to require congregations to submit to the authority of the preaching office. The period 1525–1530 is marked by an overlap of the two interpretations. The change in Luther's attitude can also be seen in which verses he chooses to emphasize. Prior to 1525 verses 30-31 predominate; after 1530 verses 34 and 40 predominate.

If his use of 1 Corinthians 14 is any indication, Luther did not have a consistent "doctrine" of ecclesiastical authority but changed his views at the point when he became "the establishment." This study supports those who have held that a consistent doctrine of ministry and office is not to be found in Luther. Certainly there are themes and ideas that occur in all periods, and Luther normally has some consistency in his thought; but, at least in his use of 1 Corinthians 14, Luther did not find a principle to integrate the needs of the reformer and the needs of the established church leader.

57. AE 12.200; WA 40-2.475-76 (1532). See also AE 26.448; WA 40-1.673-74; and AE 27.139; WA 40-2.177-78 (1531/1535).

58. AE 26.374; WA 40-1.571-72 (1531/1535).

59. AE 28.87-88; WA 63.515.

60. AE 41.131, 173-74; WA 50.614, 649 (1539). AE 6.231; WA 44.171.

61. AE 2.333; WA 42.500.

Calvin's Commentary on Hebrews

T. H. L. Parker

For the student of Calvin's commentaries, lectures, and sermons, the year 1549 marks the change from obscurity and conjecture to relative abundance and certitude of information. Unfortunately, the commentary on Hebrews lies just on the wrong side of the dividing line. We do not know whether Calvin lectured on this epistle; and, although it was studied in the *Congrégations* along with the Canonical Epistles from 1549 to 1550, the commentary must have been almost or quite completed at this time and the *Congrégations* cannot have furnished preparation for it.

The commentary on Hebrews therefore has to be taken as independent of previous drafts, whether in the form of lectures, *Congrégations,* or sermons. The first edition[1] has no colophon and therefore no precise date of printing; the title page gives only the year. The nearest we come to precision is the date of the author's dedicatory epistle: "10 Calend. Iunii. 1549"—that is, May 23. This must be the *terminus ad quem.* How long it had taken to write, whether it had just been finished or written some time before and laid aside for some reason, we do not know. From the fact that Hebrews furnished the subject for both *Congrégations* and sermons in 1549 (1548f.?) it is a legitimate guess that the commentary was written at about the same time, that is, from summer or autumn 1548 to late spring 1549.

We leave conjecture for facts. *Hebrews* was included, as a sort of adjunct to the Pauline corpus, in the collected edition of commentaries on St. Paul's Epistles in 1551 and again in 1556 and 1557/1563. The distinction was carefully observed in the titles of all three editions: "The Commentaries of John Calvin on all the Epistles of Paul the Apostle, *and also on the Epistle to the Hebrews.*" As the first edition was carried over into the collected editions changes were made, though we are immediately struck by the lightness of the revision. This becomes the more apparent when we compare *Hebrews* with *Romans. Romans,* Calvin's first biblical commentary, published nine years before *Hebrews,* was both extensively corrected and also expanded by half for the 1556 revision. Not a page survived unaltered, but the largest additions and rewritings were made to the commentaries on Romans 8–11, which were in effect written afresh and at greater length with the use of the earlier material. In *Hebrews,* by contrast, the last edition is little different from the first. Many pages remained completely untouched; in many others the alterations

---

1. Printed by Jean Gérard of Geneva, who had printed all Calvin's commentaries since 1547. It is a book of 215 pages, with a maximum of 42 lines to the page—in all about 70,000 words. The print is crowded and not very clear. Gérard also published the first French edition in the same year, a translation not attributed to Calvin on the title page and therefore probably not by him.

were minor, such as a different form for biblical references (possibly to be ascribed to the printer rather than to the author), or a tiny stylistic or grammatical change, as *his* for *iis* (which occurs several times), *multisque* for *et multis,* and so on. These are interesting both for the light they throw on Calvin as a craftsman in writing and as evidence of the attention he paid to detail in his revising.

Beside the minutiae, there are some places where a word has been changed to effect an improvement in sense, and not a few places which Calvin has amplified, thinking the original explanation insufficient, no doubt. These last, however, occur less frequently and are far less extensive than the similar additions in *Romans;* the longest contains no more than forty-three words. Most are, as I say, amplifications for the sake of clarity or force. Some make an exegetical point, others add a piece of polemic or a reference to another opinion. One alters the direction of Calvin's interpretation.[2] We note also a rarity, a place where something from the earlier edition is omitted without any replacement.[3] Calvin's Latin translation of the Greek text is also carefully revised.

We leave the comparison of the editions of Hebrews and turn to the substance of the book as it is stated in the initial *Argumentum* (and we may mention at once that there are no differences here, apart from the punctuation, between 1549 and 1556).[4] The part with which we are concerned begins at the words: "I now come to the argument."[5]

Calvin first gives as briefly but comprehensively as possible a summary of the essence of the epistle. The matter to be discussed (he is using the technical rhetorical terms, the *status causae*—"the case stands thus"—and the *cardo*—"the point on which everything turns") is christological, but not christological in the sense of proving or demonstrating that "Jesus the Son of Mary is the Christ."[6] It is taken for granted that the Jewish Christians to whom he was writing would already have accepted this fundamental truth; indeed, they would not be Christians unless they had done so. But it would appear from a study of the epistle that "they had not yet grasped the purpose, power, and fruit of his advent."[7] They still retained "a wrong understanding of the Law" and "were clinging to the shadow instead of the body itself."[8] Therefore, what they needed to learn and what Hebrews was written to teach them was "what the office of Christ is."[9] In the commen-

---

2. *Ioannis Calvini Opera Quae Supersunt Omnia* (ed. J. W. Baum, E. Cunitz, and E. Reuss; 59 vols., Brunswick: Schwetschke, 1863–1900) 50.80, lines 1-5 (this work will hereafter be abbreviated CO); CTS 151, lines 3-8.

3. CO 55.92, line 31; CTS 172, line 17: "By the word *Introduction* he signifies . . ." (1549); "By the word *Subintroduction* (for that, in my judgment, is what the compound Greek word *epeisagōgē* amounts to) he signifies. . . ."

4. K. Hagen, in his excellent little book *Hebrews Commenting from Erasmus to Béze 1516–1598,* has translated, expounded, and compared the *Argumenta* of all the forty-five commentaries written in that period. He deliberately concentrates on the problem of the authorship of Hebrews and therefore says little about the *Argumenta* as summaries of the teaching of the epistle.

5. CO 55.6, line 17; CTS 28, line 2.

6. CO 55.5, lines 18-20; CTS 28, lines 3-5.

7. CO 55.6, lines 29-30; CTS 28, lines 14-15.

8. CO 55.6, lines 31-32; CTS 28, lines 15-16.

9. CO 55.6, lines 22-23; CTS 28, lines 7-8.

tary itself this is also paraphrased as "that the Jews might carefully recognize what and how great Christ is" *(qualis et quantus sit Christus).*[10]

We are, in fact, taken into the sphere of the *officium* or *munus Christi,* which the *Institutio* tells us is the threefold prophet, king, and priest.[11] In Hebrews, however, the balance is rather different, as we shall see.

The office of Christ, his quality, and his greatness are not abstractions but are to be explained in their relevance to these Jewish Christians precisely because they believe the truth that "Jesus the Son of Mary is the Christ." This means that they understand something of the Jewish context of Jesus. But by holding on to their own view of the Law as paramount and to the ceremonies of the Law as the way of life prescribed by God, they were unable to appreciate the fullness of the messiahship of Jesus. Moses had to hold his unique position as the lawgiver, Aaron as the high priest, and only into this structure could be fitted Jesus the Messiah. The epistle counters such Judaism, according to Calvin, by focusing all the attention on Jesus Christ, showing his real greatness and significance and his *qualities,* or what he is as the mediator between God and man. In this way Calvin expounds "the office of Christ," or, in other and even more concrete terms, "the purpose, power, and fruit of his advent." The message of the epistle is concentrated into these three correspondent statements.

Calvin divides Hebrews as follows in the *Argumentum:*[12]

1:1–3:6	The supremacy of Christ and his apostleship
3:7–4:13	Exhortations and threatenings
4:14–5:10	The priesthood of Christ
5:11–6:20	Digression—reproofs and exhortations
7–10	The priesthood of Christ
11	The true line of inheritance
12–13	Various precepts on right living

It is the passages 1:1–3:6; 4:14–5:10; and 7–10 which provide the material for "the office of Christ," "the purpose, power, and fruit of his advent," and "the quality and greatness of Christ."

The starting point of the epistle, says the *Argumentum,* is the *dignitas* of Christ.[13] That the word here means greatness in the sense of high rank is shown by the other terms used in the same paragraph: "Christ was far above all";[14] the author "sets the angels below him, that along with them he may force all others into rank *(ordine)*";[15] "the Son of God stands out above all, whether men or even angels."[16] To attain his end the author had to establish the superiority of Jesus Christ to Moses; but he knew that if he attempted to do that immediately and bluntly he would lose his audience. He therefore went to work in a roundabout way, judg-

10. CO 55.35, lines 31-32; CTS 77, lines 6-8.

11. *Institutio christianae religionis* 2.15

12. He leaves the actual dividing points vague, but the chapter and verse references supplied are indicated by his comments.

13. CO 55.6, line 36; CTS 28, line 22.

14. CO 55.7, line 2; CTS 28, lines 28-29.

15. CO 55.7, lines 4-5; CTS 28, lines 30-32.

ing that the Jews would readily accept that one who was superior to the angels would certainly also be superior to Moses.

We perceive that at the same time he is explaining this point Calvin also has another aspect of the matter in mind. No sooner has he mentioned the *dignitas Christi* than in the next clause he speaks of the gospel and in the following sentence of "the doctrine":

> His starting point is the dignity of Christ. For it seemed absurd to the Jews that the Law should be put below the gospel. And first of all he establishes the point in dispute, that the doctrine announced by Christ holds first place because it was the conclusion *[clausula]* of all the prophecies.[17]

And again: "That in the first three chapters he placed Christ in the highest rank of sovereignty *[in summo gradu principatus]* means that when he speaks all must be silent and that nothing must hinder us from giving our whole attention to his teaching."[18]

Calvin has therefore been unobtrusively introducing the subject of the prophetic or apostolic office of Christ. The opening words of the epistle have afforded the opportunity for—or rather, have demanded—this theological inquiry: "God, who at sundry times and in divers manners *spake* unto the fathers by the *prophets,* hath in these last days *spoken* unto us by his Son." On this Calvin comments: "This exordium relates to the commendation of the doctrine of Christ."[19] When the word "therefore" at the beginning of Heb 2:1 is expounded, it leads to a summary of chapter 1 in terms of *doctrina.* "He now declares what his purpose had been in comparing Christ with the angels—that he might establish the supreme authority of [Christ's] doctrine."[20] The passages of exhortation (e.g., 2:1-4) receive their weight from that authority of the doctrine or gospel, which is superior to the authority of the Law as being manifest and not veiled. Similarly, writing on 2:11 ("he is not ashamed to call them brethren"), Calvin moves to 2:12 ("I will declare my name") to bring out the prophetic/apostolic office of Christ: "Moreover we must note what rôle *[partes]* Christ assumed—that is, of proclaiming the name of God."[21]

When therefore, he comes at the beginning of chapter 3 to summing up what has gone before, Calvin speaks as if the previous chapters had dealt fully with the prophetic office:

> He ends the foregoing teaching with a useful exhortation to the Jews to grasp carefully of what nature and how great Christ is. By earlier naming doctor and high priest, he had compared him briefly with Moses and Aaron; but now he comprehends both, for he adorns him with the two titles, even as he bears the dual role *(persona)* in the Church of God. Moses performed the office of

16. CO 55.7, lines 10-12; CTS 28, lines 37-38.
17. CO 55.6, lines 36-40; CTS 28, lines 22-27.
18. CO 55.7, lines 15-19; CTS 29, lines 4-7.
19. CO 55.9, lines 6-7; CTS 31, lines 10-11.
20. CO 55.21, lines 8-11; CTS 51, lines 28-30.
21. CO 55.29, lines 17-18; CTS 66, line 3.

prophet and doctor, Aaron of high priest. Both offices were laid upon Christ. Therefore, if we wish to receive [suscipere] him, we must consider his quality [qualis sit]; he is, I say, to be clothed with his own power [virtute] if we are not to grasp his empty shadow [wraith?—umbra] instead of himself.[22]

As is plain, Calvin uses the terms *prophet* and *doctor* interchangeably in this context, although perhaps not quite synonymously. To these he first adds, following Heb 3:1, *apostle,* less in the sense of being sent than of apostolic activity in proclamation of the gospel: "Here he treats of Christ's apostolate. For there are two parts in God's covenant, the promulgation of the teaching and its so to say real confirmation."[23] *Realis confirmatio* refers to the sacraments and therefore to the office of priesthood, whereas "the promulgation of the teaching" belongs to the apostolate, thus making *apostle* here equivalent to *doctor.*

Calvin afterwards adds yet another title, calling Christ the "legislator":[24]

Since the condition of the Law and priesthood are one, Christ was ordained [creatur] not only high priest but also legislator. Thus the right [ius] of Moses as well as that of Aaron was transferred to him.[25]

But we must be clear what he means by "legislator." He is not setting up a new giver of moral laws after the manner of Moses, although what this legislator says is binding. Nor is the term applied to Christ in his pre-incarnational work of giving the Law through Moses. It is the Moses who delivers the will of God to the people who is thought of here—thus Moses the prophet and doctor. Hence Christ is the legislator as the apostle and doctor, as the proclaimer of the gospel. The *doctrina* which is the gospel is opposed to the *doctrina* which is the (Mosaic) Law.

From this point the *Argumentum* takes up the theme of Christ's priesthood in Hebrews. With this we can deal more briefly, merely indicating those points which Calvin himself emphasizes. After he has said that the priesthood of Christ differs from that under the old covenant, he puts forward three ways in which it was superior. First, it took the place of the other and was also sealed in its establishment by a special oath. Second, it is eternal and is always flourishing. And third, he who executed this office transcended in honor Aaron and all the Levitical priests.

In summarizing chapter 4 Calvin emphasizes one of the issues that he had introduced earlier: "the true and pure knowledge of [the priesthood of Christ] abolishes all the ceremonies of the Law."[26] Indeed, this is the inference drawn at the very beginning of the doctrinal section of the *Argumentum:* "The hinge on which it all turns is to show of what sort Christ's office is; whence it appears that by his coming an end was put to the ceremonies."[27] To this he returns after

22. CO 55.35, lines 31-43; CTS 77, lines 5-16.
23. CO 55.36, lines 29-31; CTS 78, line 32–CTS 79, line 2.
24. Cf. Aquinas: "all these [i.e. legislator, priest, and king] come together in Christ as in the fountain of all graces." *Summa Theol.* 3, Q.22, Art. 1, ad tertium.
25. CO 55.89, lines 15-19; CTS 167, lines 4-7.
26. CO 55.7, lines 27-28; CTS 29, lines 15-16.
27. CO 55.6, lines 22-24; CTS 28, lines 7-9.

the passage on the superiority of Christ. The ceremonies performed by the priests are not to be regarded in their own right but in relation to "the heavenly proto-type," that is, the incarnate Christ. They themselves, now that the reality has appeared, must necessarily cease to possess their only reason for existing (i.e., to stand in place of the absent reality): "After he has discussed the similitude and agreement between the shadows and the truth exhibited in Christ, he concludes that all the rites instituted by Moses have been abrogated by the unique sacrifice of Christ; for the efficacy of this sacrifice is perpetual."[28]

This final point leads us to one of the most important features in Calvin's interpretation of Hebrews. The uniqueness of Christ's sacrifice, expressed in the epistle by *hapax* or *ephapax,* apparently leads, as a first step at least, to the negative statement that therefore it is unrepeatable. This, of course, frequently formed the substance of the attack by the reformers (Calvin among them) on "the sacrifice of the Mass." His commentary on Hebrews, however, takes "once for all" in a positive sense, as indicating the perpetual efficacy of the sacrifice; more, that the sacrificial death itself was a continuous event, not in its physical sense (for then Christ would always be dying and never have died), but in its spiritual power. Thus, in the commentary on 13:20 ("the blood of the everlasting covenant"), he states:

> It seems to me that the Apostle here meant that Christ so rose from the dead that his death was nevertheless not terminated *[abolita]* but kept an eternal vigour. It is as if he had said that God raised his Son, but in such a way that his blood, which once was shed in death, is vigorous after his resurrection to establish the eternal covenant, and it brings forth its fruit precisely as if it were always flowing.[29]

"Once," then, means "for all eternity," and it is only from this positive truth that Calvin makes the negative polemic against the late-medieval concept of sacrifice in the Eucharist: if the sacrifice is eternal and ever active, it does not need somehow to be repeated or reenacted.

To return to the main theme of our paper: The *Argumentum* interprets Hebrews in terms of a twofold office of Christ. He is the prophet, doctor, apostle, legislator, and also the high priest. Is it not interesting that the third office, the kingship of Christ, has no place in the interpretation? Certainly it may be argued that the word *king* comes only a very few times in Hebrews. But an opportunity is offered in 7:2, where Melchizedek, the type of Christ, is called king of righteousness and king of peace. In the *Argumentum* this is ignored. In the commentary, although both titles are applied to Christ to whom they properly belong, the concept is treated as part of the main typology—as part of the priesthood in which Melchizedek was the type of Christ. We are therefore left with a twofold office, and what is more, not the customary twofold office of priest and king but that of prophet and priest. Yet this should not be seen as an inconsistency or aberration in Calvin's work; rather it is an instance of his remarkable fidelity to the document he is explaining.

---

28. CO 55.8, lines 13-17; CTS 30, lines 7-11.
29. CO 55.197, lines 27-34; CTS 356, line 37–CTS 357, line 5.

John Calvin, John Knox, and the Scottish Reformation

W. Stanford Reid

To say that the Scottish Reformation had its roots in the religious reformation on the continent of Europe would be to utter a platitude. Yet not many historians have bothered to show exactly how the two movements are related. Nor have they, although they take his role for granted, sought to indicate the place of John Knox in this process of transmission. When one studies the problem, however, it soon becomes apparent that Knox played a major part as a protagonist of the views of John Calvin, the Genevan reformer, from whom he obtained most of his theological views both by direct contact and by indirect influences. Therefore, to understand both the way in which Calvinism was disseminated in the sixteenth century and the reason for the Scottish Reformation's strong Calvinistic character, we should look closely at the relations of the two men as well as at Knox's activity in the movement for church reform in Scotland.

KNOX'S CONTACTS WITH CALVIN

Although John Calvin preached and taught in Geneva from the pulpit of the cathedral for most of his time in the city, his outreach by this means would have been relatively limited if he had spoken only to the Genevan citizens. With the constant inflow of refugees from other countries, however, he was able to wield an influence much wider than the relatively small area of Genevan political influence would warrant. Many of the refugees stayed for only a time in the city and then passed on to other places, or as in the case of Knox returned to their homelands. In this way they became bearers of the ideas which they had heard expressed in the Protestant "New Jerusalem."

Even more important than his preaching were Calvin's writings. The most important of these was the *Institutes of the Christian Religion,* which appeared first in 1536 as a small book of seven chapters but which Calvin revised repeatedly until it took its present definitive form in 1559.[1] Added to this major work were his pamphlets, many of which were translated soon after their publication in Latin or French into various vernacular languages as widely different as English and Czech. Perhaps as important as these expository and didactic writings were his biblical commentaries in which he endeavored to make plain the meaning of most of the biblical books. Again, although these were published originally in Latin, they were soon translated into French and many other languages.[2] And finally,

---

1. B. B. Warfield, *Calvin and Calvinism* (New York: Oxford University Press, 1931) 373ff.
2. See D. A. Erichson, *Bibliographia Calviniana* (Nieuwkoop: B. de Graaf, 1960) *passim* for the translations of Calvin's pamphlets and commentaries.

Calvin had a very wide correspondence, not only with other theologians and reformers, but with many of the leading political figures and crowned heads of Europe and with humble supporters of the Reformation who sought advice and help. These letters were very often a commentary on his other writings, bringing out points which had been overlooked either by him or by his readers. By these means Calvin wielded a wide influence over the whole movement of reformation throughout his lifetime, and "he being dead yet speaketh."

When we turn to the relationship of Calvin and Knox, we find that it is a little difficult to determine when Knox first came in contact with Calvin's writings. The original Reformation movement in Scotland would seem to have come out of Wittenberg with a strongly Lutheran character.[3] By the middle of the 1540s, however, this influence would seem to have become somewhat weakened; and as we look at Knox's sermon preached in St. Andrews Castle in 1548, we find that the views expressed might be termed generally evangelical, perhaps influenced by Luther, and strongly antipapal.[4] They could hardly be described as Reformed or Calvinistic.

It may be that Knox's first knowledge of Calvin came during his captivity in France when he toiled at the oar of the galley *Notre Dame*. Captured in the Castle of St. Andrews by French forces, he was carried to France where he was sentenced to the galleys for life. During this period he undoubtedly had contacts with French Protestants in Rouen and Nantes, from whom he may well have heard something of Calvin's teachings, for by 1548 Calvinism was beginning to make itself felt in those regions. Released from his captivity in 1549 through English intervention, Knox may have visited Geneva before going to England, for we find him quoting in 1549 Calvin's comments on the Prophet Jeremiah, although they were not published until some years later. It would seem certain, however, that he acquired the 1539 edition of Calvin's *Institutes* and a little later obtained a copy of the 1550 edition. From his statements in letters and in some of the pamphlets he wrote at this time, he gives an indication that he was being influenced by Calvin in his thinking.[5]

With the accession of Mary Tudor to the English throne Knox found it advisable to leave England for Dieppe, where he spent the first few months of his sojourn on the continent. There he devoted his time to writing pamphlets to encourage the English Protestants in their faith and to incite them to make action when possible to restore Protestant freedom.[6] These writings, however, raised questions in his own mind concerning the lawfulness of rebellion and also concerning the right of a woman to rule a country. To satisfy himself on these matters he journeyed to Geneva where he discussed the problem with Calvin and then passed on to consult Viret in Lauzanne and Bullinger in Zurich. One cannot but

3. W. S. Reid, "Lutheranism in the Scottish Reformation," *WTJ* 7 (1945) 91ff.

4. John Knox, *History of the Reformation in Scotland* (ed. W. C. Dickinson; Edinburgh: Nelson, 1949) 1.84ff.; R. Kyle, *The Mind of John Knox* (Lawrence, Kans.: Coronado Press, 1984) 17.

5. V. E. d'Assonville, *John Knox and the Institutes of Calvin* (Durban: Drakensberg, 1968) chap. 1.

6. John Knox, *Works* (ed. D. Laing; Edinburgh: T. G. Stevenson, 1864) 3.157ff., 251ff.

suspect that he was somewhat disappointed in the replies of both Calvin and Bullinger who, advising great caution, insisted upon following constitutional processes according to the laws of each individual country.[7]

Any lukewarmness toward rebellion on the part of Calvin did not, however, deter Knox from his desire to study in Geneva, with the result that when he reached the conclusion that he could do no more from Dieppe he returned to the Swiss city to study Hebrew and other important subjects. But he was not left in peace. Some eight hundred English Protestant refugees had arrived in Frankfurt am Main where they sought to establish a religious colony free from the control of some of the English bishops who had moved to Strasbourg under the threat of persecution from Mary. After some unsuccessful efforts to obtain the services of an English pastor, they asked Knox to take the post. He was not really interested, but when Calvin applied some pressure he relented. His term of office in Frankfurt, however, was not long, for soon after his arrival Richard Cox came from Strasbourg to attempt the takeover of the congregation. In this he was successful, and Knox returned to Geneva soon to be followed by some two hundred of his former congregation. In the struggle which had taken place in Frankfurt over the use of the second Edwardian *Book of Common Prayer,* both sides had appealed to Calvin, who had given firm support to Knox, insisting that he had not been dealt with in a brotherly fashion.[8]

In Geneva, which he termed "the most perfect schole of Christ," Knox became the pastor of a congregation which he felt was truly Reformed. *The Form of Prayer and Ministration of the Sacrament* produced by the congregation under Knox's leadership reflected quite clearly the influence of Calvin's *Forme des Prieres,* but what was equally important was the close contact which Calvin and Knox enjoyed at this time. It was more than the relationship of a teacher and a pupil, for we find indications that it was on a close personal level. When Knox's wife died some years later in Scotland, Calvin commented on her characteristics in a letter, indicating that he must have had close contact with the Knoxes while they were in Geneva. It is also interesting to note that Calvin was one of Knox's sponsors when he was made a burgess of Geneva.[9] Throughout the period from 1555, when the English congregation came into existence, until 1558, when its members departed on Elizabeth's accession to the English throne, Knox and Calvin must have been in constant communication.

We must recognize, on the other hand, that they did not always agree. It was during his Genevan exile that Knox wrote one of his most famous works: *The First Blast of the Trumpet against the Monstrous Regiment of Women* (1558), in which he attacked the view that a woman might rule a country. Although he felt that this was a logical deduction from Calvin's own views on women, neither Knox nor Jean Crespin, the publisher, was willing to take the risk of appending his name to the publication; and later Calvin denied all knowledge of its origin.[10] More in

---

7. Ibid., 3.217; 2.442, 459, 460; Kyle, *The Mind of John Knox,* 250ff.

8. Knox, *Works,* 4.1ff., 59; W. S. Reid, "The Divisions of the Marian Exiles," *CJH* 3 (1968) 21ff.

9. Gènève: Registre du Conseil, 54, fo. 217.

10. Knox, *Works,* 4.357f.

accord with Calvin's views was his attack on an Anabaptist work which sought to refute Calvin's view of predestination. This is Knox's longest, indeed only, theological work and it is pure Calvin through and through. Other writings, pamphlets, and letters sent to Scotland usually had a political objective, but it would seem that Knox felt in the views he expressed in these that he was simply carrying Calvin's ideas on government to their logical and practical conclusions.[11]

With the departure of his English congregation for home in 1558, Knox had no more cause to stay in Geneva. But because of his *First Blast* he could not return to his former congregations, and so Scotland was the only place he could go. By May of 1559 he was back home taking a leading part in the movement for reformation. Yet he seems to have kept in contact with Calvin though absent from Geneva. We find them exchanging letters on the subject of church government, baptism, and the death of Knox's wife. After Calvin's death in 1564, Knox and Beza, Calvin's successor in Geneva, continued to correspond.[12] Knox's personal contacts with Geneva continued until the time of his own death in 1572.

THE DIFFERENT SITUATIONS OF CALVIN AND KNOX

To understand the relationships of the two men and in turn their relationships to the Scottish Reformation, we must look at them and their actual situations somewhat more closely. It is always necessary to keep in mind that they were both rather strong-minded individuals. While they might well agree on some matters, on others they could differ quite widely. Such differences, however, were by no means merely a matter of personality. They were in situations which could only be contrasted rather than compared. These two factors must be kept in mind when one seeks to understand their actions, thoughts, and influences.

One way in which Calvin and Knox resembled each other was that both were trained in law. Calvin, on his father's insistence after a fight with the Bishop of Noyon, had moved from Paris to Orleans where he read law under the direction of Pierre de l'Estoile, and he also spent some time at Bourges attending the lectures of the humanist lawyer André Alcait. He thus had the benefit of the best legal thinkers of the day. Knox, on the other hand, studied law at St. Andrews University, becoming a papal notary on his graduation. His training was not in civil law but in canon law which would perhaps give him a somewhat different perspective from that of the humanist civilian, John Calvin.[13]

The differences in their legal training would show up in a number of ways. For one thing, Calvin, trained as a humanist at Paris, would tend to be philosophical in his thinking about law and its enforcement. True, he was very practical as we can see from his work on the legal reform committee in Geneva in the early 1540s. But he would be interested in systematization and a theoretical understanding of

11. Ibid., 5.9ff.

12. *Ioannis Calvini Opera Quae Supersunt Omnia* (ed. J. W. Baum, E. Cunitz, and E. Reuss; Brunswick: Schwetske, 1878) 18.434ff.; Knox, *Works,* 6.562ff., 613ff.

13. J. Cadier, *Calvin* (Paris: Presses Universitaire, 1966) 17ff; T. Thomson, "Where Was Knox Born?" *Proceedings Society of Antiquaries of Scotland,* Edinburgh (1862) 3.67; P. H. Brown, *John Knox* (London: A. & C. Black, 1895), 1.58-61.

law, as becomes very clear in his commentary on Seneca's *De Clementia,* Calvin's first published work.[14] In contrast to the humanist approach, Knox had little or no contact with the Renaissance in his training and was obliged to be very practical in his preparation of documents and in carrying out the rather mundane duties of a notary.

This difference undoubtedly reinforced Knox's radicalism over against the more philosophical coolness of Calvin. Calvin, a typical Picard, had a love of order and a reflective attitude to all that he did. Knox was different in that he was much more emotional. His reactions to any situation were usually from the heart rather than from the head. He could and did use his mind, but the emotional aspect was always very important. This would seem to be the basic reason for his radicalism and his rebellious characteristics which displayed themselves at times to his disadvantage and at other times to the accomplishment of his purposes.

The differences between the two men make their appearances in the situations in which they found themselves. When Calvin came to Geneva in 1536 on his way to Strasbourg, the Reformation had already exercised a powerful influence in the city owing to the activities of the fiery Guillaume Farel. The latter, however, realized his own deficiencies as an organizer, so when Calvin appeared on the scene he immediately demanded that the young lawyer stay and assist him in organizing a truly Reformed church. Although Calvin had his difficulties at first, from 1541 on much of his time was spent establishing a genuinely Reformed discipline in both Geneva and other places. His work consisted not in initiating the Reformation but in providing it with a viable organization and structure.[15]

Knox's problem was very different from that of Calvin. Although the Reformation had already commenced in Scotland, it was largely an underground movement, with "privy Kirks" in nobles' houses or in the quiet house gatherings of burgesses in the burghs. What he had to do was stimulate the crypto-Protestants to come out into the open and take a stand. This was his problem before he was captured in St. Andrews Castle, when he was acting as a copastor in the Reformed church in Dieppe and when later he was dealing either by letter or in person with the hesitant nobles in Scotland. He had to stimulate the Protestants to action, and in the chaotic political state of affairs which prevailed in the country, such a task could not be accomplished by a cool, rational statement of objectives. As the English ambassador explained in a report to his superiors, Knox was able to put more courage in the Protestants than "five hundred trumpets blustering constantly in our ears."[16] His words give a good picture of Knox's approach, which was very different from that of his Genevan counterpart.

Part of the reason for Knox's somewhat more vigorous, at least outwardly, approach to his task was that he faced a much greater challenge than did Calvin. The latter had the problem of organizing a reformation in a relatively small town with four churches. Knox, on the other hand, had the gigantic task of trying to es-

14. *Calvin's Commentary on Seneca's de Clementia* (ed. F. L. Battles and A. M. Hugo; Leiden: E. J. Brill, 1969) introduction.

15. Cf. E. W. Monter, *Calvin's Geneva* (New York: John Wiley, 1967) for a description of Calvin's work in Geneva.

16. *Calendar of State Papers, Scottish* (ed. J. Bain; Edinburgh, 1898) 1.551.

tablish a Reformed church in a much larger and much wilder country with at the most twelve Reformed ministers to bring this project to fruition. To attain this objective, more than a rational, humanistic approach was required. Vim, vigor, vitality, and plenty of emotion as well as a practical political sense were called for, and these Knox possessed. Furthermore, because of the largeness of his task in attempting to bring about a national reformation, much of his attention focused on France, where the structures of a national Reformed church had already begun to take shape.[17]

It is not strange, therefore, that Knox seemed to follow the example of the French in a number of ways. He had apparently come to know something of the French Protestant movement while in the galley. Later he was active in Dieppe, preached in La Rochelle, and may have visited Poitiers at the first synod of Reformed pastors. Moreover, he undoubtedly saw the draft of the first French *Discipline* which was adopted by the first national synod, held three weeks after he had left for Scotland in 1559.[18] In this way he followed Calvin, but at one remove through the French example establishing a nationwide church organization.

All of the above mentioned factors must be kept in mind when it comes to the actual influence of Calvin on the Scottish Reformation through the agency of John Knox. We must, however, go one step further to see the differences and resemblances of their doctrinal views. Only then will we really grasp the impact which Calvin had on the Scottish religious changes in the sixteenth century.

THE THEOLOGICAL VIEWS OF CALVIN AND KNOX

To understand the theological positions of both Calvin and Knox one has to begin with their doctrine of Scripture, for to both of them the Bible was the foundation of any Christian theology. To Calvin, as he expressed his thinking in the first chapters of the *Institutes,* the Bible was the inspired Word of God. In and through it God had revealed himself to Israel in the Old Testament dispensation, and he now spoke to his people through both the Old and New Testaments. Calvin recognized, however, that God's word to his people was not static but that it was progressive in the sense that it was a gradual unfolding of his redemptive purpose in history. This meant, as Calvin pointed out on numerous occasions, that neither the economic system nor the political structures of the Old Testament were to be copied in the sixteenth century A.D. Rather the Scriptures were the ultimate guide to the church given by God through the prophets and apostles to direct and vivify the church. This work, however, could be accomplished only through the Holy Spirit's enlightening of the eyes of men that they might understand.[19]

While Knox was prepared to accept these ideas, he yet had a somewhat static view of the Scriptures in the sense that he constantly went back to the Old Testament for guidance as to what political actions or structures Christians should favor.

17. For the national organization set up in France see *Documents Protestants Inédits du XVI*[e] Siècle (ed. E. Arnaud; Paris: Grossart, 1872) 6ff.

18. For further details see W. S. Reid, *Trumpeter of God* (New York: Scribner, 1974) 145, 153, 192.

19. D'Assonville, *Knox and the Institutes,* 66.

If one compares his political views as expressed in some of his pamphlets with those of Calvin in Book 4 of the *Institutes* one finds a different approach on the parts of the two men. Furthermore, the views expressed by Knox in his questions submitted to Calvin and others on the subject of women rulers along with his argument in his *First Blast* set forth a definite Old Testament point of view about which Calvin and Bullinger had very grave doubts. To Knox even the oldest parts of the Old Testament were truly contemporaneous.[20]

On the subject of sin both men were in hearty agreement, believing that sin had corrupted man totally, so that he was unable of his own accord to listen to and believe the gospel. Yet even here one notices something of a difference, for Calvin held that man still had some of the image of God left in him by God's grace, which enabled him to establish states and nations, which made it possible for him to produce things of beauty in the world, and which gave him the ability to manifest "civil righteousness."[21] Knox, on the other hand, did not seem to take much cognizance of such an idea. He tended to regard all those who did not accept the gospel as totally, not just relatively, bad under the restraint of divine grace.

It was on the basis of the doctrine of human total depravity and of divine grace that both men followed the Pauline teaching on election, predestination, and reprobation. Here again, however, Knox was somewhat more radical than Calvin, for while Calvin was not prepared to say exactly what lay behind the divine choice of man to salvation, Knox believed that it was a matter of simple divine volition. In his thinking, the divine will was the ultimate arbiter of man's fate, a position which Calvin was never quite willing to take.[22]

Central to both men's theologies was the fact of redemption. Here again one notices subtle differences. On the one hand Calvin laid great stress on the atoning work of Christ. Christ had paid the penalty of sin for his people and they are infallibly brought to faith through the work of the Holy Spirit in their effectual calling. Knox agreed with all of this most heartily, but he also stressed the place of faith, even more than Calvin.[23] He spoke and wrote as the preacher, rather than as the theologian or scholar. Perhaps one might say that this was in fact the basic difference between the two men. Calvin was operating within an already established parameter, while Knox was faced with the necessity of persuading people to take action to change both church and society.

This comes out somewhat more clearly when one examines the attitude of both men toward their theologies. While they agreed on both the preaching of the Word and the administration of the sacraments, as one author has pointed out, Knox tended to be more the rationalist. Calvin was prepared to leave a mystery as a mystery. Knox, on the other hand, in his endeavors to persuade men to accept

20. Ibid., 67; Kyle, *The Mind of John Knox,* 38ff.

21. See L. Nixon, *John Calvin's Teachings on Human Reason* (New York: Exposition, 1960) 53ff.; John Calvin, *Institutes of the Christian Religion* (eds. J. T. McNeill and F. L. Battles; Philadelphia: Westminster, 1965) 1.3ff.; Kyle, *The Mind of John Knox,* 205f.

22. Knox, *Works,* 5.8ff.: "An Answer to the Cavillations of an Adversary Respecting the Doctrine of Predestination"; D'Assonville, *Knox and the Institutes,* 47ff.; Kyle, *The Mind of John Knox,* 102ff.

23. Knox, *Works,* 3.433ff.

his views, was inclined to attempt explanation and reasoning as his instruments for convincing his opponents. In some cases, as in his dispute before the bishop of Durham concerning Romanism, he actually employed typical medieval syllogistic arguments to prove his point.[24]

One is able to see this facet of Knox's thinking by examining his doctrine of the church. Calvin had set forth the church as the people of God, redeemed by him to serve in this world. For this reason the true church had definite marks by which it could be recognized: the faithful preaching of the Word and the proper administration of the sacraments. Knox, finding that the Genevan situation was very different from that in Scotland, accepted Calvin's two marks but also added a third: "ecclesiastical discipline uprightlie administered." The Scots Confession, in whose formulation Knox played a major role, stressed the importance of good works and the binding character of the Old Testament law, expressed in discipline. In this he was following the French model as set forth in the acts of the Synod of Poitiers (1557), and this was certainly required in the lawless society he encountered in Scotland.[25]

In this connection one must note that Knox, in his whole concept of the church and its work, tended to look to the Old Testament even more than the New for his pattern of the church. Here again we see his failure to recognize the progressive character of biblical revelation which Calvin with a better historical sense took for granted. This influenced Knox's idea of the church's character and of its function in society, particularly its relation to the state.

From a practical point of view, he found the French model as projected in the *Discipline* set forth by the Synod of 1559 more in line with his needs as he worked for reform in Scotland. Thus when one examines what was probably the first draft of the *Book of Discipline* one finds the similarity with the French work noticeable. In much the same way, the French confession also served as a model for the Scottish statement of faith, although it was by no means followed slavishly.[26] The Scots had their own ideas and their own needs to be met.

In both the *Confession* and the *Book of Discipline*, however, Knox's view of the relation of church and state show some clear differences from that of Calvin. The question of the relationship of the two bodies was one of the most important the reformers had to face. Calvin insisted that both church and state held independent commissions from God—the one to preach the gospel and to nourish the faithful, the other to maintain justice and equity in public life while at the same time seeing that the gospel was faithfully proclaimed, primarily by financing the church and by making it adhere to its confession. He did not stress a covenant relationship but implied that there was a covenant existing between ruler and subject to which both must adhere as ultimately responsible to God.[27] This provided some basis for the later thought of the Monarchomachs in France, but it was carried even farther by Knox.

24. Ibid., 3.29ff.

25. Knox, *History of the Reformation,* 266; see also *Documents Protestants Inédits.*

26. Cf. W. S. Reid, "French Influence on the First Scots Confession and Book of Discipline," *WTJ* 35 (1972) 1ff.

27. See W. S. Reid, "Calvin and the Political Order," in *John Calvin, Contemporary Prophet* (ed. J. T. Hoogstra; Grand Rapids: Baker Book House, 1959) 243ff.; Calvin, *Institutes,* 4.20.

Knox based his view of the relation of church and state upon the Old Testament concept of the covenanted nation. Once a nation such as England or Scotland had accepted the Reformation it had become a covenanted nation in a position similar to that of Israel under the old dispensation. He held that a double covenant existed, one between the people and their rulers and a second between the people together with their ruler and God. The state, therefore had a solemn responsibility to make very sure that all subjects conformed to the true religion which was set forth by the Reformed church. One gets the impression from what Knox himself states that he carried his thinking to a logical conclusion that Calvin had tended to avoid.[28]

This appears in his doctrine of resistance. Except for the last paragraphs in the *Institutes,* Calvin had steered well clear of advocating anything like armed resistance to a ruler. And even when he sanctioned it, he agreed that only the subordinate magistrates had the right to call upon the people to withstand a godless or persecuting magistrate.[29] Knox at first seems to have agreed with this. But once Mary Tudor ascended the English throne and began to persecute the Protestants, his opinion changed somewhat suddenly. While waiting in Dieppe for news of the happenings in England, he wrote a violent pamphlet in which he called upon the English, as a covenanted nation, to overthrow the persecutor of the true religion. Five years later he summoned the Scottish nobles to overthrow Mary of Guise who was persecuting the Protestants, and then he issued another pamphlet telling the "commonality" that if the nobles would not take action, they had a perfect right, indeed a duty, to do so. These views were supported by his *First Blast* and by the outline of his *Second Blast.* Some nine years later, when Queen Mary had been taken prisoner by the Protestant nobles, Knox called for her execution as an accomplice in the murder of her husband, Henry Darnley. One cannot but doubt that Calvin would have carried matters to these extremes.[30] On the other hand, we have to recognize that Knox's radical approach was not entirely foreign to past events in Scottish history.

As one attempts to compare Calvin and Knox insofar as their theological views agreed or disagreed, it can be said that Knox in general followed Calvin. Indeed, he was quite prepared to acknowledge this. But he was also more radical than Calvin, a tendency which arose partially out of his personality, partially out of his concept of his calling as "a trumpeter of God," and partially out of the actual situation in which he found himself in Scotland. Only one who had a strong sense of calling and a willingness to carry his views through to their full length would have been able to accomplish anything lasting in Scotland of the sixteenth century.

THE CHARACTER OF THE SCOTTISH REFORMATION

Knox felt that Geneva was "the most perfect schole of Christ" he had ever known, and on his return to Scotland he sought to achieve the same objective, only it would not be limited to a city and its environs but would extend to a whole

28. D'Assonville, *Knox and the Institutes,* 73ff.; Knox, *Works,* 4.461ff.; Reid, *Trumpeter,* 110f., 171, 234, 251, 288f.

29. Calvin, *Opera Omnia,* 4.20.32.

30. See C. P. Finlayson, "A Volume Associated with John Knox," *SHR* 38 (1959) 170ff.

country. He was, therefore, quite happy to state in the introduction to the fourth book of his *History of the Reformation in Scotland* that the Scots had the "best Reformed church."[31] This phrase was repeated by others of his following. He and his supporters felt that they had carried the Reformation through more fully and completely than had any of the other reformers: they believed what they said!

It would seem that one of the principal reasons for their confidence was the stress they laid upon the covenant people. Furthermore, Knox insisted that as the covenant people the church had the right to act freely in its holding of assemblies, in its preaching of the Word, and in its enforcement of discipline. It was for this reason that he and many others after him were prepared to take positions which often brought them into direct conflict with regents, queens, and kings who tried to tell the church what it should do.

Knox and the other Scottish reformers did not limit their concept of the covenant people to the church, however. Following the Old Testament example, they believed that Scotland as a nation was covenanted with God to acknowledge Jesus Christ as the ultimate head of the state, to whom the rulers were responsible and by whom they would be judged. Knox emphasized this point to Mary more than once, and Andrew Melville's famous statement in which he called James VI "God's sillie vassal" underlined this covenant concept. Likewise, the whole plan for popular education outlined in the first *Book of Discipline* had its raison d'être in the view that Scotland was a convenanted nation whose citizens had the responsibility of fulfilling their obligations to serve God in every aspect of their lives.[32]

Such thinking carried over into the following centuries, and it exists in some quarters even today. Most important, however, was its influence in the seventeenth century when it provided the ideology of those who opposed the Stuart monarchs from James VI to James VII. From Andrew Melville through William Carstares, Anthony Peden and James Renwick, the Covenanters or Cameronians constantly demanded that Scotland recognize its covenanted position by acknowledging officially "the crown rights of Jesus Christ." This in turn would call for a national act of repentance for sins and a heartfelt manifestation of national righteousness.

The covenant relationship was not thought of merely as national or public but also as an obligation of the individual. Stress was laid upon the idea of calling, in which the individual was to serve God in this life. To fulfill one's calling one needed the best possible training, a view reflected in the plan for universal public education. But education was only one aspect of the individual's responsibility. Hard work, thrift, diligence in political, economic, social, and religious duties were all required. At the same time rest and relaxation were not ruled out. But all was to be done "to the glory of God."

In all of this Calvin's influence can be seen. The theology, the form of church government, the ethical and moral obligations all find their roots in the

31. Knox, *History of the Reformation*, 2. Prefaetio to the Fourth Book; *Works*, 6.544.
32. Knox, *History of the Reformation*, 2.26f.; Jas. Melville, *Autobiography and Diary* (ed. R. Pitcairn; Edinburgh: Wodrow Society, 1842) 270.

Genevan teaching. Part of the thinking came to Scotland from France, but in the final analysis most of it, whether through the prism of the French example or directly from Geneva, reached Scotland through John Knox, who gave it the stamp of his own personality and experience. The result was an amalgam which might be termed "Scottish covenanting Calvinism," a product often more radical, perhaps more extreme, than the original Calvinism, but it was a Calvinism well suited to the intellectual, social, and physical climate of Scotland.

The English Protestant Creed

Peter Toon

In the sixteenth century, the reformed Church of England produced its own, domestic creed in order to make clear its position in the disputed issues of the day. That creed became known as the Thirty-Nine Articles of Religion and to this day it has remained the doctrinal formulary of both the Church of England and a part (but not the whole) of the Anglican communion of churches. Regrettably, however, where it has legal status it is often overlooked and neglected. In 1959 G. W. Bromiley wrote these words:

> The current neglect or evasion or even defiance of the *Articles* is one of the greatest tragedies of modern Anglicanism. As they were conceived in the first instance, they gave hope of promoting both the unity in truth and the freedom under authority which are so necessary to the well-being of the Church. In spite of every obstacle, they have not wholly failed of their purpose. But quite obviously, they cannot today exercise their functions in the fruitful way which could mean so much not only for doctrinal but for spiritual and disciplinary health. No matter is more urgent than that glib misconceptions should be removed, the true historical purpose of the Articles appreciated and the place restored to them in which positively and constructively, as well as negatively and critically, they can discharge their living and salutary function.[1]

It is my hope that Anglican readers of this essay will take to heart what Dr. Bromiley said and will be inspired to work to fulfill his vision.

The Articles authorize the Two Books of Homilies as further sources of Anglican teaching in sermonic form. Regrettably, these are now becoming collector's items for they have been neglected for a long time both in the Church of England and in the other churches of the Anglican communion. In his little book on Archbishop Thomas Cranmer, Dr. Bromiley writes of the "scriptural and evangelical nature of their teaching."[2] And, like me, he will be delighted if readers of this essay were to find a copy of the Homilies and carefully read it. In fact, a modern, critical edition of the Homilies is much needed!

In the Church of England, each ordinand has to make the following declaration of assent before he is ordained. He repeats it before being installed as the rector of a parish.

Preface: The Church of England is part of the One, Holy, Catholic and Apostolic Church worshipping the one true God, Father, Son and Holy Spirit. It

1. Bromiley, in *The Churchman* (June 1959) 65.
2. Bromiley, *Thomas Cranmer* (London: Church Book Room Press, 1956) 66.

professes the faith uniquely revealed in the Holy Scriptures and set forth in the catholic creeds, which faith the Church is called upon to proclaim afresh in each generation. Led by the Holy Spirit, it has borne witness to Christian truth in its historic formularies, the Thirty Nine Articles of Religion, the Book of Common Prayer and the Ordering of Bishops, Priests and Deacons. In the declaration you are about to make will you affirm your loyalty to this inheritance of faith as your inspiration and guidance under God in bringing the grace and truth of Christ to this generation and making him known to those in your care?

Declaration of Assent: I do so affirm, and accordingly declare my belief in the faith which is revealed in the Holy Scriptures and set forth in the catholic creeds and to which the historic formularies of the Church of England bear witness; and in public prayer and the administration of the sacraments, I will use only the forms of service which are authorised or allowed by Canon.

Similar declarations are made in other Anglican churches.

The Church of England and other Anglican churches are not *confessional* churches in the same sense that Lutheran and Reformed churches claim to be; yet dogma and doctrine are important. Thus the Articles are best seen not merely as a sixteenth-century signpost pointing in which direction the church ought doctrinally to go, but also as the lens in the telescope (along with the lens of the earlier catholic creeds) by which members receive or see the Christian doctrinal tradition in which they are placed. In this sense the Articles can never be revised. And the same holds true of the Homilies, which strengthen and expand the doctrinal emphases of the Articles and thus, as it were, make the non-removable lens more clear and powerful.

By using these lenses the members know how to approach Scripture, evaluate and create liturgy, face new questions, and engage in God's mission in the world. Without them they are more prone (as much of modern Anglicanism currently is) to receive from the secularist spirit of the day ideas and practices which are contrary to the gospel, and thereby to be unfaithful, often unwittingly, to their Lord. Merely to have the catholic creeds and prayer books, with the Ordinal, is insufficient in our day for we desperately need the soteriological insights, views of authority, and sacramental principles supplied by the Articles.

Bearing all this in mind, we shall now examine the origin and content of both the Articles and the Homilies.

THE ARTICLES

1. Origins

After the break with Rome in 1534 three statements of faith appeared in order to identify where the Church of England was in the disputes of the time. The three statements were the *Ten Articles* (1536), the *Institution of a Christian Man* (1537), which was known as the "Bishops' Book," and *A Necessary Doctrine and Erudition for any Christian Man* (1543), known as the "King's Book." These represent the way in which the Church of England was being pulled by the old and new religious forces, first in one way then in another, in the changing theological climate of western Europe. However, the *Thirteen Articles* (1538), which were never published at that time, represent a distinctly Protestant statement of faith in the theological agreement arrived at by Lutheran and English theologians. They had met in England with the agreement of Henry VIII because it suited his foreign policy at that time to have a concord with Lutheran princes. What they produced, which owed much to the Lutheran *Augsburg Confession* (1530), may be seen as the first stage of the process which culminated in the Thirty-Nine Articles of thirty years later.

Archbishop Cranmer had many contacts with Lutherans and he was prominent in the agreement involving the *Thirteen Articles*. He was also the major figure behind the next stage of the process, the drafting, authorizing, and publication of the *Forty-Two Articles* (1553). In between his original drafting and the production of the final version the articles were examined by various bishops and advisers to the young king. Yet they had to wait for their appearance until other Protestant publications (e.g., *Prayer Books* and the *First Book of Homilies*) had appeared; and, when they did appear, there was little time to enforce them because of the death of Edward and the accession of the Roman Catholic Mary.

The *Forty-Two Articles* are certainly Protestant—that is, reformed catholic—in their positive teaching on the orthodox doctrines of the Trinity, the person of Christ, and human sinfulness and in their particularly Protestant emphasis upon justification by faith, the Scriptures, and the two gospel sacraments. They safeguard this reformed catholicity by the rejection of a variety of views being propagated by the radical reformers ("Anabaptists"), by the Church of Rome, and by medieval scholastic theology.

With the accession of Queen Elizabeth I in 1558 and her Settlement of Religion (1559), the Church of England reverted to its reformed catholicity as a Protestant church. The production of the Thirty-Nine Articles is to be attributed primarily to Archbishop Parker, a disciple and admirer of Cranmer. He made use of the recently published Lutheran Confession of Wurtemberg (which had been presented to the Council of Trent by the ambassadors of Wurtemberg in 1562), and he took account of the Calvinist ("Reformed") sacramental views.

Essentially, the Thirty-Nine Articles are a revised form of the *Forty-Two Articles* and the former were approved, in virtually their final form, by the Convocation which met in 1562–1563. Eight years later, in 1571, the Thirty-Nine Articles reached their final form, being approved first by the Convocation and then by Parliament. There appeared official versions in both Latin and English, and the bill that went through Parliament required that they be used in English and that they be signed by all candidates for ordination. The full title was *Articles Agreed upon by the Archbishops and Bishops of both Provinces, and the whole Clergy in the Convocation holden at London in the year 1562, for the avoiding of diversities of opinions and for the establishing of Consent touching true religion.* Then in 1628 Charles I added a preface to the Articles in which he stated that they "do contain the true doctrine of the Church of England agreeable to God's Word." As "Defender of the Faith and Supreme Governor of the Church," he required all his "loving subjects to continue in the uniform profession thereof."

2. Doctrine

Before examining the purpose of the Articles, we must supply their titles and, at the same time, provide a brief comment on each in the context of a thematic division of them.

A. The Substance of Faith (1-5)

1. *Of Faith in the Holy Trinity.* Orthodox Trinitarianism, rejecting pantheism and the anti-trinitarianism of radicals and sectarians.

2. *Of Christ the Son of God.* Classic Christology, rejecting docetic views propagated by radicals and sectarians.

3. *Of the going down of Christ into hell (ad inferos).* A brief assertion allowing different interpretations.

4. *Of the Resurrection of Christ.* The bodily resurrection and ascension of Jesus; thereby excluding docetism as taught by some radicals and sectarians.

5. *Of the Holy Ghost.* The full deity of the person of the Holy Spirit, who proceeds from the Father and the Son *(filioque)*, rejecting anti-trinitarianism (as article 1).

B. The Rule of Faith (6-8)

6. *Of the Sufficiency of the Holy Scriptures for salvation.* A clear, Protestant affirmation of the authority and sufficiency of Scripture and a rejection of both the medieval theory of the "Word unwritten" and the teaching of radical spiritualists, who rejected "book-religion." The list of the canonical books supplied here is that of the Hebrew canon only for the Old Testament: the other books of the Vulgate are listed but are said not to have canonical authority and are not to be used to establish doctrine.

7. *Of the Old Testament.* Directed against those radicals who claimed that a Christian has no relationship to the law of the Old Testament; positively asserting that Christians are obliged to obey the moral teaching of the commandments.

8. *Of the Three Creeds.* Wholehearted acceptance of the Apostles', Nicene, and Athanasian Creeds; the catholic and conservative character of the Church of England is asserted.

C. The Life of Faith (9-18)

9. *Of original or birth-sin.* Augustinian doctrine of original sin, rejecting Pelagian notions.

10. *Of free-will.* Augustinian teaching asserting that without the grace of Christ no good works can be performed which are acceptable in God's sight. As in article 9, directed against Pelagian-like teaching.

11. *Of the justification of man.* Clear Lutheran doctrine of justification as being reckoned or accounted righteous before God, for Christ's sake, by faith; rejects the medieval view of justification, understood as a process of being made righteous.

12. *Of good works.* Lutheran doctrine of good works as the fruit of faith is affirmed. Solifidianism is excluded.

13. *Of works before justification.* Rejects the scholastic theory of merit *de con-*

gruo (concerning what is appropriate)—i.e., the doctrine that man, by nature, is capable of good works which please God.

14. *Of works of supererogation.* Rejects the scholastic theory that voluntary good works which are done over and above one's duty are meritorious.

15. *Of Christ alone without sin.* Affirms the sinlessness of Christ and, by implication, rejects the doctrine of the sinlessness (i.e., the immaculate conception) of Mary, his mother.

16. *Of sin after baptism.* By grace, there can be forgiveness after baptism; therefore the Novatianism of certain radicals is rejected.

17. *Of predestination and election.* Seeks to prevent angry controversy on predestination by asserting a positive and clear view of divine election as the choice made by the sovereign God of grace. No decree of election unto damnation is taught.

18. *Of obtaining eternal salvation only by the name of Christ.* Salvation is only offered by God in and through Christ and any alternative method is to be totally rejected.

D. The Household of Faith (19-39)

19. *Of the Church.* The visible church is a company of believing and faithful people, in which society the word of God is preached and the sacraments faithfully ministered.

20. *Of the authority of the Church.* The visible church is to be under the authority of the Scriptures yet has certain authority itself; directed against excessive notions of church authority as were held by Rome.

21. *Of the authority of general councils.* Vindicates the right of the civil power to call councils together and also insists that they may err.

22. *Of purgatory.* Rejects the late medieval doctrine and practices concerning purgatory as repugnant to the Word of God.

23. *Of ministering in the congregation.* Only those who have been properly licensed ought to preach; directed against self-appointed radical and sectarian preachers.

24. *Of speaking in the congregation in such a tongue as the people understand.* Rejects the use of Latin in ordinary church services.

25. *Of the sacraments.* Rejects Zwinglian, Roman Catholic, and sectarian teaching and insists that there are two sacraments ordained by Christ in the gospel and then five "commonly called" but not genuine sacraments.

26. *Of the unworthiness of the ministers, which hinders not the effect of the sacrament.* The gospel sacraments are Christ's and the virtue comes from him and is therefore not prevented (as certain sectarians insisted) by administration from the hands of an evil minister.

27. *Of baptism.* The sign and instrument of regeneration and the confirmation of faith is to be administered to infants. The Anabaptist position is rejected, as also is an *ex opere operato* view.

28. *Of the Lord's Supper.* Rejects both the doctrine of transubstantiation and various medieval practices (e.g., reservation) and also the Zwinglian view that it is merely a sign. In faith there is a true partaking of the body and blood of Christ.

29. *Of the wicked which eat not the body of Christ in the use of the Lord's Supper.* Those who do not receive the sacrament in lively faith do not, in fact, receive Christ spiritually; but they do bring condemnation upon themselves. Written against the medieval view that the wicked do, in fact, receive the real Christ when they receive communion.

30. *Of both kinds.* The cup of the Lord is to be given to the laity.

31. *Of the one oblation of Christ finished upon the Cross.* Christ's offering of himself was a perfect propitiation and satisfaction for our sins; thus the doctrine of the sacrifice of the mass as taught in the late medieval church and Tridentine Catholicism is rejected.

32. *Of the marriage of priests.* Rejecting clerical celibacy; the right of ordained ministers to marry is taught.

33. *Of excommunicate persons, how they are to be avoided.* The right of the church, as a visible society, to exclude unworthy members from the body.

34. *Of the tradition of the Church.* Three points are made: First, there is no need for traditions and ceremonies to be everywhere the same. Second, those persons are deserving of censure who break the traditions and ceremonies of the church, which are ordained by rightful authority. And third, every particular or national church is competent to arrange its own ceremonies and rites.

35. *Of the homilies.* The two books of homilies contain wholesome doctrine and are fit to be read in churches.

36. *Of consecration of bishops and ministers.* The Ordinal contains wholesome teaching, and nothing that is superstitious and ungodly.

37. *Of the civil magistrates.* This deals with four subjects: the royal supremacy, the false papal claims, the lawfulness of capital punishment, and the lawfulness of war.

38. *Of Christian men's goods, which are not common.* Rejects radical sectarian teaching concerning the sharing of goods (i.e., Christian communism).

39. *Of a Christian man's oath.* Asserts the lawfulness of taking an oath in a court of law.

It is now easy to see why, in the title of the Articles, it is claimed that they are "for the avoiding of diversities of opinions and for the establishing of consent touching true religion." In the effort to set forth reformed catholicity, the writers of the Articles set aside troublesome views being propagated by the active sectarians ("Anabaptists"), by the traditionalist Romanists, and by the growing band of Puritans. But they also sought peace among the faithful in their attempts to provide acceptable statements of predestination and the descent into hell. Therefore, from one viewpoint they are pacifying while from another they are denunciatory.

The Articles are certainly not ambiguous (when interpreted historically and contextually), but they are minimal in their requirements, leaving many secondary questions open. They only lay down, in the mid sixteenth-century situation, as much as was necessary to secure catholic faith and ordered life in the Church of England. They do not seek to go past the minimum. On the central issues of the gospel they are full and exact. Yet they are as broad and comprehensive as was deemed to be consistent with theological safety.

Apart from being conscientiously minimal, the Articles are also conscientiously eclectic. As we have noted they make use of the teaching of the patristic period
for doctrines of the Trinity, Christology, and original sin; of the Augsburg and
Wurtemberg Confessions for the teaching on the gospel and justification; and of
the teaching from Geneva and Calvinist and Reformed theology for sacramental
understanding (articles 25-29). As a whole they present the reformed catholocity of
the *ecclesia Anglicana* and are (in the title of the first commentary upon them) *The
English Creeds: consenting with the True, Auncient, Catholique and Apostolique
Church in al the points and articles of Religion which everie Christian is to knowe
and believe that would be saved* (in two parts, 1585 and 1587, by Thomas
Rogers).

Generally speaking, expositions of the Articles from the seventeenth to the
twentieth century have fallen into four types: (1) evangelical and Reformed, (2)
broad church and latitudinarian, (3) high-church and generally Arminian, and (4)
Anglo-Catholic. That there have been and are different traditions of interpretation is generally acknowledged. It should also be generally accepted that the Articles ought to be read in the light of the situation out of which they came and to
which they were addressed, that their words must be taken in the context and the
sense they bore at the time of writing, and that their statements must be construed in the light of the known views, assumptions, and intentions of their authors.

THE HOMILIES AND THEIR ORIGINS

As with the Articles, so with the Homilies: their origins are to be sought in
the reign of Henry VIII and in the reforming zeal of Thomas Cranmer. Inspired
perhaps by his knowledge of Luther's collection of sermons for reading in parish
churches, the archbishop had conceived the plan for a book of homilies as early as
1539. We must remember that the office of preaching was highly valued by the
reformers for they saw it as the divinely appointed way of taking the truth of the
gospel to the minds, hearts, and wills of the people. And if the men who were supposed to preach were ignorant, then they had to be given something good to preach
(read).

In the Convocation of 1542–1543 Cranmer was busy explaining why a book of
homilies was necessary and inviting men to write sermons for it. Not only must the
gospel be proclaimed in all parishes, but also the errors of the ignorant and heretical must be prevented from being disseminated. By the end of the Convocation
some sermons were prepared, but, due to the opposition of the king, the collection
remained in manuscript form. It was not until 1547, following the death of
Henry VIII and the beginning of the reign of Edward VI, that Cranmer was able to
bring his plan to fruition by releasing what we have come to call the First Book of
Homilies of 1547. This book contained at least several sermons recently prepared,
but it appears that the majority of the twelve had been produced in 1542–1543. As
a doctrinal statement, set against the doctrinal publications of Henry's reign (to
which we referred above when discussing the Articles), the Homilies represented
the first coherent statement of the Reformed doctrines of salvation to be set forth
by official authority in England. In particular they presented a clear, unambiguous,

"Lutheran" statement of justification by faith; and they replaced the "King's Book" of 1543 as authoritative doctrine.

The Homilies were published with a preface by Edward VI, whose royal injunctions of 31 July 1547 required every parish church in England to have copies of the whole Bible in English, the Paraphrases on the Gospels and Acts by Erasmus (translated by Nicholas Udall), and the Homilies. The injunctions further required the churches to use these three as the basis for reading, studying, and preaching from the Bible. Thus the Homilies were part of a larger plan to bring the message of the word of God to the people of England.

The titles of the sermons are as follows.

1. A Fruitful Exhortation to the Reading and Knowledge of Holy Scripture (Archbishop Cranmer)

2. A Sermon of the Misery of all Mankind (Archdeacon Harpsfield)

3. A Sermon of the Salvation of Mankind by only Christ our Saviour (Archbishop Cranmer)

4. A Short Declaration of the True, Lively, and Christian Faith (Archbishop Cranmer)

5. A Sermon of Good Works annexed unto Faith (Archbishop Cranmer)

6. A Sermon of Christian Love and Charity (Bishop Bonner)

7. A Sermon against Swearing and Perjury (Thomas Becon)

8. A Sermon how dangerous a Thing it is to fall from God (author unknown)

9. An Exhortation against the Fear of Death (author unknown)

10. An Exhortation concerning Good Order and Obedience to Rulers and Magistrates (author unknown)

11. A Sermon against Whoredom and Uncleanness (Thomas Becon)

12. A Sermon against Contention and Brawling (Bishop Latimer)

Of these, the third was to become most well-known, for it is specifically referred to in article 11 as an authoritative account of justification by faith.

It would be wrong to see these twelve sermons merely as teaching basic biblical doctrine and morality. Taking various themes from the royal preface, John N. Wall, Jr., has suggested that the contents of the Homilies

are, quite specifically, to be read in order, "as they stand in the boke"; in some sense, they form a unit, a collection specifically arranged to move in a progression of argument from a beginning toward a particular end. Second, they emerge as a way to meet specific needs—"the decaye of religion" and "the desire of subjects to be delivered from al errors"—and to achieve specific goals—"to honor GOD, and to serve their kynge and to behave them selfes"—by specific means; "the true setting furth of GODS woorde." The Preface also defines the ends of the work in terms of moving "the people to honor and worshippe almightie GOD, and diligently to serve hym." It describes what this means in terms of honoring God, serving the king "with all humilitie and subjeccion" and "godly and honestly, (behaving) them selfes towarde all men." What is being evoked here is the vision of the *republica christiana,* the true Christian commonwealth, that humanist vision of national life, which goes beyond matters of religious ceremonial or devotional practice to embrace total reform of all aspects of human society.[3]

Both the Christian humanist and the Lutheran soteriological roots of the Homilies need to be seen to capture their original intention.

After being widely used in the reign of Edward VI, the Homilies had no official sanction during the reign of Mary but were effectively reintroduced by the Act of Uniformity of April 1559, since the rubric in the communion service requiring them to be read was unaltered in the modestly revised Prayer Book. Therefore a new edition appeared in 1559 bearing the subtitle "By her Grace's advice perused and overseen, for the better understanding of the simple people" and with the Queen's title changed from Supreme Head to Supreme Governor in the tenth homily. There was a further edition in 1562 whose preface declared that her majesty commanded and charged the clergy to make right use of them.

In the Second Prayer Book of Edward VI of 1552 the following rubric is found after the creed: "After the Crede, if there be no sermon, shal follow one of the homelies already set forth, or hereafter to be set forth by commune authoritie." The young king was at this time looking for the "making of more Homelies." Regrettably he never lived to see them appear.

The Second Book of Homilies was approved by the Convocation in early 1563 along with the Thirty-Nine Articles. However, the Queen and her advisers took a few months to review the twenty sermons (divided into thirty-eight parts), and some alterations were made. The book appeared in the summer of 1563 under the title "The Second Tome of Homilies, of such matters as were promised and intituled in the former part of Homilies: set out by the authority of the Queen's Majesty, and to be read in every Parish Church agreeably."

Apparently Bishop John Jewel (1522–1571), author of the important *Apologia Ecclesiae Anglicanae* (1563), was the editor of this volume of homilies. Some sermons were written solely by him while others were adapted by him from a variety of sources. Both the present and the next Archbishop of Canterbury, Parker and Grindal, made contributions. The titles and writers, as far as they are known, are as follows.

1. A Homily of the Right Use of the Church (Bishop Jewel)
2. A Homily against Peril of Idolatry (Bishop Jewel and Bullinger)
3. A Homily for Repairing and Keeping Clean of Churches (Bishop Jewel)
4. A Homily of Fasting (Archbishop Grindal)
5. A Homily against Glutony and Drunkenness (Bishop Pilkington and Peter Martyr)
6. A Homily against Excess of Apparel (Bishop Pilkington and Peter Martyr)
7. A Homily concerning Prayer (Bishop Jewel)
8. A Homily of the Place and Time of Prayer (Bishop Jewel)
9. A Homily wherein is declared that Common Prayer and Sacraments ought to be ministered in a Tongue that is understanded of the Hearers (Bishop Jewel)

3. Wall, in J. E. Booty, ed., *The Godly Kingdom of Tudor England* (Wilton, Conn.: Morehouse-Barlow, 1981) 91.

10. An Information for them which take Offence at certain Places of the Holy Scripture (partly from Erasmus)

11. A Homily of Alms-deeds (author unknown)

12. A Homily or Sermon concerning the Nativity and Birth of our Saviour Jesus Christ (author unknown)

13. A Homily for Good Friday concerning the Death and Passion of our Saviour Christ (Taverner's Postils)

14. A Homily of the Resurrection of our Saviour Jesus Christ. For Easter Day (Taverner's Postils)

15. A Homily of the worthy Receiving and reverent Esteeming of the Sacrament of the Body and Blood of Christ (Bishop Jewel)

16. A Homily concerning the Coming Down of the Holy Ghost and the manifold Gifts of the same. For Whit-Sunday (Bishop Jewel)

17. A Homily for the Days of Rogation Week (Archbishop Parker)

18. A Homily of the State of Matrimony (partly from Chrysostom; partly from Veit Deitrick, a Lutheran)

19. A Homily against Idleness (Bishop Jewel)

20. A Homily of Repentance (partly from Rodolph Gualter)

In 1571 a further "Homily against Disobedience and wilful Rebellion," written by Archbishop Parker, was added following the rebellion in the north of England in late 1569.

In 1547 Archbishop Cranmer believed that justification by faith was the message most needed to be proclaimed from English pulpits, so this theme is prominent in the First Book. In 1563 Bishop Jewel held that the purity and right ordering of public worship was the most needed message, so this theme is prominent in the Second Book.

To summarize, the Anglican communion of churches (and not least the mother church) needs to cherish and use, as an important doctrinal lens in its theological telescope, the Articles (supplemented by the Homilies) in order to retain and develop its special character as both catholic and reformed. Without this lens, it is in real danger of losing its hold on the gospel and of missing its mission in the world. Further, it will become a society that plays liturgical games based on admirable patristic rules and models and that has little to offer in inter-church dialogue. Anglicans must get back into the habit of printing the Articles at the back of their prayer books (even the modern ones) so that they may be read and may remain of critical importance in the doctrinal heritage. May Geoffrey W. Bromiley's words of 1959 be effectually heard!

Church and Politics in the Reformed Tradition

Eberhard Busch

As a pastor in the Reformed Church in the Swiss Canton of Aargau, I am committed to a church order in whose first paragraph Jesus Christ is called the "Lord and hope" of our church. Its commission is "to live according to the Gospel and to declare to all people the sovereignty of God." According to this, to live *from* the gospel means to live *according to* the gospel, and this means to witness to "the sovereignty of God" to all people. Although it comes a paragraph later, this statement belongs unconditionally to this witness: "the congregation and its members are called by the love of Jesus Christ to work for the solution of political, economic and social questions of the day. They are to intercede particularly on behalf of the weak and disadvantaged for justice and truthfulness in all areas. . . ."

The binding declaration that in the observation of its spiritual commission the church also bears a social responsibility, and that in so doing it is not meddling in someone else's business, I perceive to be a fruit of the Reformed tradition. Now even with such a paragraph our church has hardly arrived at the kingdom of God. Indeed, as we shall see, I believe our Reformed tradition is encumbered with a rather heavy mortgage. Nonetheless, that such a paragraph is found in our church order, and that again and again it plays a genuine role—in discussions on the military and peace, on the banking and financial system, and on the problem of asylum and development, for example—I see as a sign of the liveliness of the Reformed tradition.

If one should ask what has kept this tradition alive all these centuries, I would point not last to the custom in our worship of singing, with a certain partiality, the Psalms which yet today make up the first section of our hymnal. Through them runs a certain unmistakably characteristic tone—a tone of militance toward the mighty and also of solidarity with those suffering injustice—and in that tone a conviction that faith in God and the well-being of the people in justice have a great deal to do with one another. In fact, the tone became so loud in the hymnal that it has etched its mark in the Reformed Church, even its church order—a tone often covered over but never completely drowned out. As we examine the character of the Reformed tradition through its theological foundations in Ulrich Zwingli and John Calvin, we should keep in mind that their understanding in this matter remained alive and was renewed in spite of all opposing and contradictory developments because in its core it was nourished continually by the hymns of praise and confession in the gathered congregation. We will examine this understanding in four sections, from both its bright and dark sides.

THE DISTINCTION BETWEEN PROCLAMATION AND POLITICS

As is well known, Luther emphasized in "On Temporal Authority" (1523) that the tasks of the church and state are of two types and that they are to be distinguished from each other and may not be mixed. Later he failed to see this same point in Zwingli and accused him of being a man seduced by "a devilish rogue," a man who had meddled "seditiously in temporal government."[1] His charge, however, is not at all correct because in fact such a thing was possible neither in Zurich nor in Geneva at the time.[2] More importantly, in 1523, a few weeks after Luther's publication, Zwingli published his own work on the same question, "On Divine and Human Righteousness [Gerechtigkeit]," in which the content of the church's proclamation, God's gracious activity, is designated by that first righteousness (or justice) and that of the earthly state by the second. In this work he stressed the differences between the two tasks in such a way that one immediately suspects his dependence on Luther;[3] the tasks are as different as heaven and earth.[4] But Calvin, too, said at the very beginning of his chapter "On Civil Government" that "Christ's spiritual kingdom and the civil order are two completely different things," and that "we may not—as people commonly do—unwisely mix these two together."[5]

The distinction between church and state in all three reformers is based upon their total separation from the Roman church of the day, for they intended to rebuke it for its assumption of worldly power by its clergy. The distinction reached its highest point in the church's repudiation of mixing its spiritual task with the use of power and force in its own spiritual realm. Calvin's statement in a letter from 1562 is characteristic: it would be a "betrayal of God" were he not to warn against a preacher becoming a soldier, "and it is even much worse when he, hardly down from the pulpit, reaches for his weapon."[6]

One must consider that the reformer's insistence on this distinction was also a reaction to the dramatic changes in the social environment of the day. The political authorities, moreover, had emancipated themselves from the church, but in such a way that they intentionally adapted what had been papal-episcopal laws to the exercise of political power.[7] With their distinction between church and state the reformers approved of this as appropriate, but it was not a process which they were responsible for setting into motion, as has been suggested occasionally. We see, in fact, that they reversed the emphasis completely—just as bishops were not to be worldly princes, so temporal rulers should not go too far and extend their rule into

1. Martin Luther, *An den Rath zu Münster*, vom 21. December 1532, in EA 54.346.

2. Ulrich Gäbler, *Huldrych Zwingli. Eine Einführung in sein Leben und Werk* (Munich: C. H. Beck, 1983) 18; William F. Dankbaar, *Calvin. Sein Weg und sein Werk* (2d ed.; Neukirken: Neukirchener Verlag, 1966) 88ff.

3. Christof Gestrich, *Zwingli als Theologe. Glaube und Geist Beim Zürcher Reformator* (Zurich: Zwingli-Verlag, 1967).

4. Zwingli, *Von göttlicher und menschlicher Gerechtigkeit*, in *Zwingli Haupstschriften* (ed., Fritz Blanke, Oskar Farner, Rudolf Pfister; Zurich: Zwingli-Verlag, 1948) 7.56.

5. Calvin, *Institutes*, 4.20.1.

6. Dankbaar, *Calvin*, 163.

7. Gäbler, *Zwingli*, 22; Dankbaar, *Calvin*, 88f.

the church. This concern was the actual occasion for Luther's "On Temporal Authority," a significant part of which was made up of his warnings against it.[8] Zwingli likewise warned against the "Obere" (authorities) who "lay their violent hand on the Word of God. . . ."[9] In Calvin, the second generation reformer, this warning received even greater urgency, as after the deaths of Luther and Zwingli he saw state-church governments established in the territories in which they had been influential.[10]

One must add that this distinction between church and state in both Zwingli and Luther is connected with a sort of self-defense on the part of the Reformation—but not yet against the "Schwärmer," as is often assumed.[11] Their movement had not actually begun until after these two works were written; indeed, the radicals may have actually been provoked by the doctrines represented in these works. Zwingli saw his reforming activities beset by influential Catholic circles which accused his "Lutheran doctrine as the root of all disobedience against the authorities."[12] With the intent of moving the state to attack the Reformation, the charges were that the Reformation would destroy the state. This accusation put Zwingli, and Luther as well, in the delicate position of proving that one may preach the word of God as long as one does not teach rebellion against the authorities. In this situation the distinction between church and state received the apologetic meaning that the Reformation was of a merely spiritual sort and that it did not enter into the domain of the state, though from the standpoint of faith it could recognize the state as legitimate per se.

For their defense against the charge of destroying the state, Zwingli and Calvin stressed as strongly as Luther the Christian's duty to obey state officials regardless of their worthiness to be obeyed.[13] In their overzealousness to refute the accusation of their opponents, the reformers certainly overstated this side of the argument. This occurred especially in their quickness to distance themselves from the Schwärmer, who the reformers understood to be denying that a true Christian still needs a state authority (a thesis that Luther and Zwingli affirmed in principle).[14] They did this to defend themselves against the Schwärmer's argument that the state is to be rejected because of its profane nature, especially because it is established by force. Over against this, the distinction between church and state signified that each realm has the right to exist and that the state, too, is established by God and thus also is to be respected by Christians.[15] According to Calvin, the Schwärmer reject not only "the authorities, but push God aside as well."[16]

8. Luther, *Von weltlicher Obrigkeit, wie weit man ihr Gehorsam Schuldig sei* in EA 22.82f.

9. Zwingli, *Von göttlicher und menschlicher Gerechtigkeit*, 75.

10. Wilhelm Niesel, *Die Theologie Calvins* (2d ed.; Munich: Christian Kaiser Verlag, 1957) 232.

11. See Oskar Farner, *Huldrych Zwingli* (4 vols.; Zürich: Zwingli-Verlag, 1943–1960) 3.388.

12. Zwingli, *Sämtliche Werke* (Leipzig, 1908) 2.437,3.

13. Zwingli, *Von göttlicher und menschlicher Gerechtigkeit*, 74; Calvin, *Institutes*, 4.20.24.

14. Luther, *Von weltlicher Obrigkeit*, 66, 68; Zwingli, *Von göttlicher und menschlicher Gerechtigkeit*, 55.

15. Calvin, *Institutes*, 4.20.5; Zwingli, *Von göttlicher und menschlicher Gerechtigkeit*, 74f.

16. Calvin, *Institutes*, 4.20.7.

As a result the Reformed fathers emphasized the state's right to use force and the Christian's duty to obey even an "unchristian" government, and they stressed this point so much that they came into conflict with other of their own principles. They resolutely redirected the charge (which was not very applicable to the Schwärmer) of "destroying the State" with consequences not only deadly for the Schwärmer but also troublesome for their own theory and praxis.

Although the Reformation distinction between church and state is embedded in this problem, it is to be said nonetheless that the aversion to mixing the spiritual and worldly, the presumption of the church's own particular duty in the recognition of the state's particular task, is an important and indispensable Protestant understanding. The reformers distinguished between the two even though they presumed (often incorrectly) that they were dealing with a "Christian government." We need not regret their distinction today even though we are no longer capable of these presuppositions. This distinction basically means that the church would be unfaithful to itself and its task were it to understand itself as state and that the state would be unfaithful to itself were it to see itself as church. However close these relations may be here and there, they are meaningful only so long as church remains church and state remains state. More pointedly, this distinction means that the church can recognize the task of the state as meaningful and that it cannot be indifferent to whether the state does its task more or less well. The church can do nothing better, indeed actually can do nothing else, than remain alert and live and act according to its own "law."

The Reformed theologian Karl Barth affirmed the meaning of this distinction for our time as well. The state "must renounce itself if it wishes to be the Church, and the Church, for its task's sake, cannot wish it to cease being the State. It [the State] cannot be the true Church. It could, if it dared such madness, only become a false Church. And all the more must the Church renounce itself should it want to become the State. . . . It cannot be the true State, it can only become a State of clergy . . . with a bad conscience because of their neglected duty."[17]

In this first section I have deliberately presented the common Reformation view first. I wish to understand the differences between the Lutheran and Reformed views as differences within this commonality. I also wish to plead thereby for "tolerance" within the churches of the Reformation as it hardly has been practiced since Luther's time—tolerance not in the sense that these differences are to be considered of no consequence but rather in the sense that the Reformed deviation from Luther will not be seen prematurely as a fall from the heights of the Reformation.

THE RELATION BETWEEN CHURCH AND STATE

The thesis that the tasks of the church and state are to be distinguished but not separated leads us closer to the particular Reformed accent here. The thesis is expressed in the title of Zwingli's work "On Divine and Human Righteousness," with the significant subtitle "How they relate to one another." Even if the two "righteousnesses" are different, as different as heaven and earth, that with which they are concerned can be designated by the *same* concept—"righteousness." Thus

17. Karl Barth, *Rechtfertigung und Recht* (Zollikon: Evangelischer Verlag, 1938) 31.

both "are related." Calvin, too, continues in the above-mentioned chapter, "As we have just now pointed out that the temporal government is distinct from the spiritual Kingdom of Christ, we must also know that they do not stand in contradiction"—at least not fundamentally.[18]

In order to evaluate the particular Reformed emphasis it is good to cite Gottfried Locher's insightful observation that on the whole Zwingli—and this applied to Calvin as well—took a different approach from that of Luther. Zwingli thought like Luther in his aversion to Judaism, legalism, and works-righteousness, but at the same time, and perhaps even more rigorously, he reacted against the danger of secularism.[19] Thus both Zwingli and Calvin stressed not only the justification of the sinner by grace, but also the sanctification of the person by God. They thought more in Old Testament terms than Luther, which in this case meant always in aversion to the other great danger with which particularly the Old Testament struggled—peace with false gods. From the outset they thought more in social terms than Luther, reasoning not so much along the lines of "How do *I* find . . . ," but rather "How does my *people* have a gracious God?"

This emphasis worked itself out in their understanding of the relation of the church to the state. In his approach to matters of law, Luther was prepared to leave the state to the caprice of human reason. One must say that in his skepticism toward all human possibilities he showed great indifference to the question of how the worldly nature played itself out in the state. It is enough that the church limits itself to its own task—to proclaim grace to sinners and thereby to comfort those who are oppressed by the laws of the state—in order that at the same time it might appeal to the conscience of the princes who are also Christians.[20]

Zwingli and Calvin, on the other hand, were always distrustful of a state left to determine itself by its own laws—or at least they were distrustful of the sanctification of Christians who were indifferent to the political structure of human society. There can be no occasion for indifference because there is a *relation* between church and state. Calling special attention to this relation was all the more important to the Reformed thinkers since the emancipation of the state from the church was precisely the political process occurring at that time. It would be approved by the Reformed, but they would not let the matter rest with their approval. Rather, basic to this relation is the fact that it is not the "church" but the *Lord* who is proclaimed in the church who has a "relation" with the state. He is present, of course, even in the state where he is not proclaimed; he is the Lord even over this territory.

Luther says this as well. But while he emphasized that God is present there *in a completely different way* from in the spiritual arena, which the Reformed did not dispute, the latter emphasize more that there is *no other one* than he who is proclaimed in the church. The "doctrine of civil government" is, particularly in Calvin, not so clearly "established by the royal office of Christ," as Wilhelm Niesel claims.[21] Calvin speaks not, like Luther, of the God who governs and is "hid-

18. Calvin, *Institutes*, 4.20.2.

19. Gottfried Locher, *Huldrych Zwingli in Neuer Sicht. Zehn Beiträge zur Theologie der Zürcher Reformation* (Zurich/Stuttgart: Zwingli-Verlag, 1969) 36.

20. Luther, *Von weltlicher Obrigkeit*, 96.

21. Niesel, *Die Theologie Calvins*, 228.

den" beneath the law, but often abstractly of the reigning "providence of God."[22] And, moreover, like Luther, he can separate "Christ's spiritual Kingdom" in the church from the state.[23] The connection between this and his other thought that worldly government is "an image of the royal rule of our Lord Jesus Christ" is not so clear.[24] Calvin can say further that, even before his appearance, Christ, as "eternal King," possessed "all power on heaven and on earth" to rule over all earthly rulers or, if they opposed him, to depose them.[25] Surely because of the unclear relation between the rule of Christ and the providence of God it appears that his talk of "Christ" in this connection more often tends toward the abstraction of his central revelation; Christ appears sooner as the personified "content" of that freely reigning providence—and perhaps at bottom here lies the root of the weakness of Calvin's perspective. Nonetheless, it is clearly his intent to say that the God who is believed in the church is also the Lord of the political realm.

God is particularly present there in the fact that the simple existence of the state can be recognized by Christians as a gift and order of God. Thus Zwingli and Calvin, like Luther, said that the government rests upon divine "ordinance."[26] It is for them, with Romans 13, "God's servant"—indeed, as Calvin so boldly put it, God's minister.[27] The Reformed fathers' emphasis was different, however, and here is their most decisive departure from Luther. To oversimplify, Luther tended toward the idea that the government is God's servant *because and insofar as* it is the *government.* Zwingli and Calvin, on the other hand, tended toward the idea that the government is true government *when and insofar as* it is *God's servant.* Thus the Reformed fathers refused to identify a government directly and automatically with God's will—as Calvin says, "As if God had made over his right to mortal men, giving them the rule over mankind! Or as if earthly power were diminished when it is subjected to its Author!"[28] Thus even if the state rests upon a divine order, it never takes the place of God. Here Calvin corrects a misunderstanding of his view of "government" as God's minister with the critique that it robs "God of his glory" when it wants "so much to take his place" that it demands blind obedience.[29] Having ordained the government, God remains Lord over this ordinance. In any case, it remains "in subjection" to him. Obedience to God and obedience to a temporal government always remain two different things, and obedience to the government always takes second place to obedience to God. If there is no other Lord who reigns in the political world than he to whom the church bears witness, then he is in any case *the Lord* here as much as there— the Lord who, in Calvin's bold words, possesses "the government of the world," indeed has "absolute monarchy in the world."[30]

22. Calvin, *Institutes*, 4.20.6, 30.
23. Calvin, *Institutes*, 4.20.1.
24. See Niesel, *Die Theologie Calvins*, 228.
25. Calvin, *Ezechiel und Daniel* in *Auslegung der Heiligen Schrift* (ed. Otto Weber; Neukirchen: Neukirchener Verlag, 1938) 9.394.
26. Calvin, *Institutes*, 4.20.4; Zwingli, *Von göttlicher und menschlicher Gerechtigkeit*, 74ff.
27. Calvin, *Institutes*, 4.20.4.
28. Calvin, *Ezechiel und Daniel*, 385.
29. Ibid., 435, 413.
30. Ibid., 385.

This viewpoint was at the core of Karl Barth's thought in 1933–1934 in the German "Kirchenkampf" dispute with a Lutheran tradition that equated Hitler's state with "God's servant." Barth asserted the viewpoint already formulated by Calvin: "The Lord is King of all kings who, when he has opened his sacred mouth, must alone be heard; next to him we are subject to those who are in authority over us, but only in him. If they command anything against him, let it go unheeded, it matters not."[31] One can compare as well a sentence from the Dutch Reformed Confession of 1949: "Obedience to the authority of government finds its basis and its limits in obedience to the authority of the Word of God."[32] The classic Bible verse to which the Reformed appeal here is Acts 5:29, "One should obey God rather than persons!"[33] Luther, too, cites this verse in his work on government.[34] But if it remains unclear just what this means for the Christian, the Reformed appeal to the word gives more concretely the possibility of examining whether a temporal government is fulfilling its own office.[35]

Indeed, this viewpoint offers the possibility of seeing that the state is always (not *only*, as Luther saw it) threatened from *below* by the people in that they ignore the divine ordinance of the government; and it also makes it possible to see that the state is also threatened from *above* by those who hold government office in that they demand absolute obedience and thereby transgress against him through whom their office is established in the first place. Chaos, the prevention of which is (according to Luther) the good and divine reason for establishing temporal government, can thus come even from within the government. Calvin expressly said that it was for this reason that he purposed to develop his doctrine of the state: he stood against the double danger of rebellion against the government by the people and the misuse of power against the people by the government.[36] Thus for him any talk of the duty of the "subjects" cannot be meaningful unless one at the same time speaks of the duty of the "authorities" to care for the welfare of all.[37] Zwingli took aim at rebellion from below even earlier, in his work "Who gives cause for Rebellion" ("The Troublemakers," 1524), but he attacked more energetically rebellion from above, by the mighty who are quick to call others rebels even though they themselves are rebels. They are the ones who give occasion for rebellion "from below."[38]

Now certainly Luther was not blind. In his "On Temporal Authority" he complained about the wickedness of the rulers who "do and command only what they want," who "are commonly the greatest fools and worst scoundrels on earth; thus one should always expect the worst from them and must expect little

31. Calvin, *Institutes*, 4.20.32.
32. Otto Weber, ed., *Lebendiges Bekenntnis. Die "Grundlagen und Perspektiven des Bekennens" der Generalsynode der Niederländischen Reformierten Kirche 1949* (2d ed.; Neukirchen: Neukirchener Verlag, 1959) 62.
33. Calvin, *Institutes*, 4.20.32; Zwingli, *Von göttlicher und menschlicher Gerechtigkeit*, 77; Zwingli, *Auslegen und Begründen der Schlussreden* in *Zwingli Hauptschriften* (Zurich: Zwingli-Verlag, 1952) 4.108, 112.
34. Luther, *Von weltlicher Obrigkeit*, 101.
35. See note 33.
36. Calvin, *Institutes*, 4.20.1.
37. Niesel, *Die Theologie Calvins*, 241.
38. Zwingli, *Wer Ursache gebe zum Aufruhr* in *Zwingli Hauptschriften*, 7.170ff.

good of them."[39] It is certainly a mystery that in Luther this complaint is a cry of caution without consequence, and it never led to constructive, concrete criticism of the deplorable state of affairs among the authorities. It is indeed a mystery how in the same breath he could expect these "fools and scoundrels" to do what, according to him, they are supposed to do (in that they are in fact the authorities), namely, protect the good from the evil.[40]

Luther obviously intended to give the matter no further thought because precisely here he rather abstractly assigned the categories of "law and gospel" to the categories of "state and church." The state represents the law, whereby the concept of "law" loses so much of its basic meaning in Scripture that at the core it means a wrath that terrifies people. The state *is* a category of wrath, and thus for Luther the sword is its *essential* mark—so it even is not so bad when it is bad. The subjects, then, must understand and endure it as God's wrathful judgment upon them as sinners, which should draw them to the comfort of the gospel which the church has to proclaim.

Even though the Reformed fathers said this at times as well,[41] their situation was different. That is, they enjoyed the possibility of making concrete criticisms of governmental misuse of power. This possibility also included for them the task of pointing out positively what the task of worldly government is, the mark against which its work must be measured. They had considered the best forms of government—monarchy, aristocracy, and democracy.[42] They preferred a mixture of the last two and were thus in favor of a form of representative democracy. None of these forms was without danger, which is why for them the question of the *form* of government was secondary to the *content* of a political system, however it may be organized.

In determining the task of the state by its content, however, they were prevented from simply dividing "law and gospel" into "state and church" because they could neither separate so widely the law and gospel as testified to in Scripture nor conceive of them as almost opposite expressions of God's will. They too understood the law as the power of wrath insofar as it was isolated from the gospel,[43] but with God the two belong together: his law and his gospel, his righteousness and his grace. Therefore Zwingli could sum up the message of God's grace and commandments in the concept "righteousness." The church cannot simply delegate the notion of law to the state, but rather its proclamation includes both law and gospel. Both are forms of God's righteous grace.

If the two may not be separated in the church's proclamation, how then can the content of the worldly government's task be determined? Here we encounter a major difficulty in the Reformed fathers in which, with disastrous results, they achieved no clarity. Their answer to the question naturally was that a state is

---

39. Luther, *Von weltlicher Obrigkeit*, 62, 89.

40. Ibid., 65.

41. For example, Zwingli, *Auslegen und Begründen*, 98.

42. Oskar Farner, ed., *Aus Zwinglis Predigten zu Jesaja und Jeremia* (Zurich: Verlag Berichthaus, 1957) 269ff.; Calvin, *Institutes*, 4.20.8.

43. Calvin, *Institutes*, 2.7.6-9.

humanly righteous just where "its laws conform to the divine will."[44] But how does temporal government know this divine will? And how may this divine will be binding for the state, which indeed is not the church and is comprised of the unfaithful as well as the faithful? Calvin emphasized that by the will of God he did not mean the Mosaic law exactly as found in the Bible but rather an "ethical law," a "lasting rule of love" upon which even the law of Moses based itself as upon the "eternal standard of righteousness," and which allows for the "freedom" to establish itself in laws formulated differently.[45] But this does not remove the difficulty. Either the "divine will" (that ethical law) to which the laws of the state are to conform is determined by revelation—in which case the government must at least be bound by the word proclaimed in church and to that degree be Christian—or, if one wishes to avoid this, one must make the "will" of God one with the *lex naturalis* which is already to be found in the human heart, as Zwingli and Calvin could actually say.[46] Quite contrary to their intent, however, this means that this element and the gospel are hopelessly separated.

It appears that both Calvin and Zwingli swung back and forth uncertainly between these two possibilities. They could not work their way out of this dilemma to the satisfactory conclusion that the conformity of the laws of a state to the will of God nonetheless cannot prescribe Christianity to a secular government, but rather only that Christianity can participate in the political process. It is not impossible that, given the circumstances at that time, both fathers actually meant the latter. In any case, they assumed that not only believers but unbelievers as well lived in the state. For them the goal of conforming the laws of the state to the divine will was not expressly that the state be "Christian," but rather that it be a *human* state in caring for a life worthy of humanity. For both fathers the state is clearly not the church in that its task is the protection of life and community, whether its citizens are believers or not. And insofar as the state provides for this, its actions, while not identical to, are in conformity with the righteousness and will of God proclaimed in the church, in which he desires not the death of sinners but that they repent and live (Ezek 33:11). Christians recognize a state as more just the more it conforms to this.

This means two things. First, the Christian cannot be indifferent to how the state and how the "authorities" govern. Constant work and cooperation for *improvement* are possible and necessary so that the laws of the state become "more in conformity" with the will of God.[47] As Karl Barth said in 1946, the state is "capable of conformity" and "in need of conformity" in relation to the kingdom of God proclaimed in the church.[48] Second, in this way a truly *positive* determination of the task of the state was possible for the Reformed fathers. The state is in essence not at all an order for punishment and violence. Calvin said against this that

44. Zwingli, *Auslegen und Begründen*, 112ff.
45. Calvin, *Institutes*, 4.20.14.
46. Zwingli, *Auslegen und Begründen*, 114; Calvin, *Institutes*, 4.20.16.
47. Zwingli, *Auslegen und Begründen*, 112ff.
48. Karl Barth, *Christengemeinde und Bürgergemeinde (Stuttgart: Kohlhammer, 1946) 29f.*

kindness is the first gift of the princes.[49] And above all, the primary task of a temporal government is to care for the preservation of life and community—for Zwingli it was to provide for "righteousness and peace,"[50] a formulation used in the Barmen Declaration.[51] Or, as Calvin said, its task is to provide for "welfare and the common peace,"[52] to see that "humanity remains in existence among people."[53]

What Luther considered decisive Zwingli and Calvin did not even deem important—the state's protection of the good from the evil. Rather, their first criterion for the humanness of the state was its protection of the weak from the strong.[54] "True righteousness consists in mercy toward the weak and needy."[55] For them the first mark of the state is not the sword. To be sure, it bears the sword—they never disputed this—but it bears it more as merely an accessory. In 1933 a group of leading German theologians in the Lutheran tradition said (in rather macabre fashion in light of the state's proceedings against the Jews), "The State has to judge, the Church has to save."[56] This would be unthinkable for Zwingli and Calvin. In one way this is to think too highly of the church—that it is the one that "saves" (this is especially so in the case of the Jews, where it never even made an attempt). In another way it is to think too meanly of the state, that it is not to save at all. Its essence is not the sword: mere power does not make a true state. Otherwise might makes right. The authorities, rather, have the right to use force only in a certain function—to provide for "justice and peace" and to protect those suffering violence. The use of civil power must always be tested against this end. Otherwise it will become a state run by violence, which is also a concern of the Reformed tradition.

THE CHURCH'S OFFICE OF WATCHMAN OVER THE STATE

Zwingli himself occasionally called his preaching office a "watchman's office." More frequently he called it the service of a "prophet."[57] Both expressions call to mind the Old Testament prophets in their watchfulness against godlessness and unrighteousness in the life of the people. Calvin readily called preachers shepherds, "pastores," but also said, using an expression from Ezekiel, that they "are placed in the Church as watchmen."[58] Thus for Calvin this dimension also belongs to the church's duty of proclamation.

49. Calvin, *Institutes*, 4.20.10.
50. Erik Wolf, "Die Sozialtheologie Zwinglis," *Festschrift Guido Kisch* (Stuttgart, 1955) 188.
51. Proposition 5 of the Barmen Declaration of May 30, 1934.
52. Calvin, *Institutes*, 4.20.9.
53. Calvin, *Institutes*, 4.20.3.
54. Zwingli, *Auslegen und Begründen*, 112; Calvin, *Institutes*, 4.20.12: The use of force only as the last resort.
55. Calvin, *Ezechiel und Daniel*, 437.
56. Kurt Meier, *Kirche und Judentum. Die Haltung der Evangelischen Kirche zur Judenpolitik des Dritten Reiches* (Göttingen: Vandenhoeck und Rupprecht, 1968) 83.
57. Zwingli, Sämtliche Werke, 2.313.
58. Calvin, *Institutes*, 4.3.6.

What does it mean that the ecclesiastical office of watchman belongs to the Reformed tradition? By the office of watchman I do not intend to replace the biblical sermon with a political speech. Neither of the Reformed fathers ever forgot the difference between church and state. For them, direct involvement in politics did not belong in the pulpit but rather in the appropriate political arena. Zwingli was somewhat active in politics, but as a member of the Zurich Council and as a representative on the civic commission. Thus he spoke as just one voice among others. Calvin was not a member of the municipal government; in many cases he could not get his way with it, and he was unable to stem its (in his opinion too strong) influence on the church. Nevertheless, he had the power of his personality and finally could exercise some degree of influence on the state as a citizen.[59] While the Reformed fathers considered it possible for a Christian to participate in politics, they certainly did not as yet see with the necessary clarity the difference between the realm of the state and that of the church as Karl Barth did in this century. In Barth's view, Christians can participate at the political level but must do so *"anonymously"*; that is, Christians do not claim to act in the name of Christianity but rather they translate their Christian motives into commonly comprehensible arguments.[60]

In any case, the Reformed fathers had already emphasized that one can participate as a Christian in an arena which is not the church. According to them, for example, a Christian can, if necessary, mix in politics by refusing to participate in an unjust government. Indeed, from the very beginning, the doctrine that a government that has become pure tyranny can be "dismissed by God" belongs to the Reformed tradition.[61] The doctrine in this tradition made it possible for the Reformed fathers, as we have seen, to assume that there can be not only a "revolt" from below, by the people against the government, but also a revolt from above, by the government against the people—both of which they considered as disobedience against God. Nonetheless, Zwingli and Calvin had considered that there might be circumstances and ways in which such an extreme measure as the removal of a government could be done legitimately, without new injustice thereby arising but rather so that justice would replace injustice.

A Christian can become involved politically in this or that matter, but that is not yet the church's office of watchman. This office belongs immediately to the church's witness itself, while such political activity is not *directly* a matter of the church's testimony. Zwingli answered the question (and Calvin thought no differently) of what the church of Christ is with the statement, "The one who hears his Word!"[62] To the question of what the kingdom of God is he said, "It is nothing other than the Word of God."[63] And to the question of what the preacher should proclaim he answered, "Nothing other than the Word of God."[64] The proclamation of and witness to this word of God is the whole task of the church,

59. Dankbaar, *Calvin*, 98.
60. Barth, *Christengemeinde und Bürgergemeinde*, 48.
61. Zwingli, *Auslegen und Begründen*, 136.
62. Farner, *Huldrych Zwingli*, 3.367.
63. Zwingli, *Sämtliche Werke*, 2.182.
64. Zwingli, *Der Prediger* in *Zwingli Hauptschriften* (Zurich: Zwingli-Verlag, 1940) 1.187.

besides which it has no other. Here we can answer the question of how the church can influence the state so that its laws conform more to the will of God in the way the Reformed fathers intended: it can do so by nothing other than preaching the word of God. We can expand on Zwingli's points: not only in the sermon, but whenever the church speaks and acts *as* church, it must bear witness only to the word of God.

Of course the Reformed fathers were convinced that if one only applied and proclaimed the unqualified word of God in church according to the whole of Scripture it would also have a political effect. Indeed, this effect will be, in a certain sense, in the best interests of the state; but in certain circumstances it will be quite different from what politicians would desire from the church. Calvin speaks clearly of how politicians and often tyrants desire a religious inauguration so that their "work may have a pious appearance," and so that they may erect temples to themselves. Of course if "one asks what they mean by this, the answer comes: We do this to the glory of God! But in this they seek only their own fame."[65] "Even though they thus despise God in their pride, they still use religion to strengthen their power and . . . to keep their people duty-bound [to them]." Indeed, they do not deny God, but "shut God up in heaven" and desire that he will not "meddle in people's affairs."[66] Calvin saw, moreover, that it is precisely the bad rulers who readily surround themselves with flatterers, and find many who will dance "to the King's pipes" and agree "with great applause."[67]

Insofar as God and his word are always obeyed first and foremost, the duty of the preachers cannot be that of the flatterer or the one who delivers the higher sanction that problematic political programs may seek. Their obedience to God will be a clear protest against this; it will automatically create a critical distance and especially will destroy the desired false religion. This preaching will be a witness to God who, because he is by no means "shut up in heaven," indeed "mixes in people's affairs."

Even beyond this, since God and his word as found in Scripture are first and always obediently applied in the church, one will not only refuse to submit to the misuse of power, one obviously will have to speak out against injustice against the oppressed, and against the causes of injustice and strife. It was along the lines of the Reformed tradition that Karl Barth said in Berlin in October, 1933, "What does the Church say to what is going on in the concentration camps? Or to the treatment of the Jews? Or to all that is done in the name of eugenics? Or to the absolute claim of the State?" Then came the decisive sentence, "Whoever has to proclaim the Word of God must say to such proceedings what the Word of God says."[68] It is characteristic of the Reformed style of confession to speak so "abruptly" (H. Gollwitzer) from the word of God to a concrete political problem. Behind this stands the conviction that where nothing but the word of God is proclaimed, one

65. Calvin, *Ezechiel und Daniel*, 405.
66. Niesel, *Die Theologie Calvins*, 236.
67. Calvin, *Ezechiel und Daniel*, 409.
68. Hans Prolingheuer, *Der Fall Karl Barth. Chronographie einer Vertreibung 1934–1935* (2d ed.; Neukirchen: Neukirchener Verlag, 1984) 18; Klaus Scholder, *Die Kirchen und das Dritte Reich* (Frankfurt/Berlin/Vienna: Propyläen, 1977), 1.687.

will have to address concrete injustice and real threats because the word of God *itself* addresses them. A bit later Barth reproached the church for remaining silent in the face of all manner of injustice, "which the Old Testament prophets surely would have addressed."[69] The reference to the Old Testament is characteristic, as the Reformed frequently used it in their criticism of abuses. Calvin diligently compiled verses precisely from this section of the Bible and held them up before the princes: Do not oppress strangers, widows, and orphans! Do justice to the needy! Save the least out of the hand of the oppressor! Hear the small as well as the great![70]

Thus in its origins the word of God in Scripture had to do with earthly justice in the state. Again, if this "earthly justice" has to do with the enhancement of human life, it is acting in conformity with divine justice as preached in the church, in which God desires not the death of the sinner but that the sinner may live. Should one witness to this divine righteousness in a sermon, this always has something to do, directly or indirectly, with earthly justice. Indeed, if the word of God is truly proclaimed, the word of God itself will ensure that it will have its effect in the area of earthly justice. For, as Zwingli says, this word of God is "so powerful that from that very hour all things will conform to it or . . . be formed by it."[71] This means that the conformity of earthly justice with divine righteousness actually is taken care of by God's word itself—if only it is preached according to all of Scripture.

But whoever does this and does not cease to say to earthly injustice "what the Word of God says" will find anything but "conformity," that is, agreement. Rather, they will, says Zwingli, be sent out by Jesus as sheep among wolves.[72] They will encounter opposition or at least the assumption that one should indeed preach, but "no further than the authorities will allow." The powerful say immediately, "What does that have to do with the gospel?" Indeed, Zwingli answers, "The demons spoke thus from the possessed man; Jesus, what have we to do with you!"[73] Thus one may not give in to this expectation in the church. Calvin also was of the opinion "that we cannot follow God's command without danger to our lives" and that one ruins everything through "cowardice and timidity," but one must sooner "go out and meet death unafraid than disobey."[74]

This is precisely the office of watchman in the Reformed fathers: to be undaunted, to speak the truth according to God's word straightforwardly and plainly, and thus also to call injustice by name without fear of being accused of being a rebel, as Zwingli said.[75] After Zwingli's death, when the young Heinrich Bullinger assumed his position, the city council sought to forbid him in the future from

---

69. Karl Barth, *Zum Kirchenkampf. Beteiligung, Mahnung, Zuspruch* (Theol. Existenz Heute, N.F. 49; Munich: Christian Kaiser, 1956) 34.

70. Calvin, *Institutes,* 4.20.9.

71. Zwingli, *Der Prediger,* 79.

72. Ibid., 231.

73. Zwingli, *Sämtliche Werke,* 2.494; Zwingli, *Wer Ursach gebe zum Aufruhr,* in *Zwingli Hauptschriften* 7.190.

74. Calvin, *Ezechiel und Daniel,* 368, 459.

75. Zwingli, *Auslegen und Begründen,* 109.

mixing in worldly things. He answered that he would not be forbidden to preach what Scripture had to say, for God's word "would also have its discord."[76] Shortly thereafter the Council of Bern made similar demands of its pastors, to which one of the most beautiful Reformed Confessions, "The Synod of Bern," responded, "Because the truth (always also) bites and is sharp," the pastors should spare no one the divine word, "please or displease whomever it will." Even if the authorities should thereby believe themselves unjustly criticized, the pastors should say of themselves, "Better a slanderer whom the authorities can charge with being untruthful than a friend who says yes to everything. For the latter lulls them into a false security, while the former keeps them alert so that they behave all the more uprightly."[77] This is the language of a church in which the office of proclamation discharges the prophetic office of watchman and is not the sacral lacky of the government.

Nonetheless, even when the church speaks to the state in its office of watchman, it must remain clear that the church does not thereby cease to be church and does not somehow put itself in the place of the state. Rather it is the point of this office of watchman that the church thereby presses the *state* to be a *true* state.

THE STATE'S OFFICE OF WATCHMAN OVER THE CHURCH?

Now we come to the truly problematic aspect of the old Reformed view of the relation of church and state. We must add immediately that the problems with this view are not recent but have deep roots that have borne such questionable fruit here that the other, good elements have been overshadowed and historically without much influence. This problematic aspect is the Reformed fathers' recognition of something like an office of watchman in the state over the church.

Now this has nothing to do with the idea that the temporal government may, by the power of its office, meddle in the spiritual task of the church. There is a proper involvement insofar as governmental figures are also members of the Christian community. The contention that members of the government are "praecipua membra" (special members) of the church with special claims to authority in it (as not only the Lutheran but also the Reformed fathers allowed)[78] is certainly not a principle which can be based on the Bible. Since according to James 2:2ff. the wealthy person in the congregation can be only one person alongside others, this must apply accordingly to persons in civil authority as well. Nonetheless, as Christians alongside others they certainly are able to participate in ecclesiastical matters.

But here we have a different matter—that politicians not as church members but as *representatives of the state* are to see that the church fulfills its spiritual task. Just as the church, in exercising its office of watchman, may not take the place of the state but has as its goal that the state be a proper state, so the state may not in its office make itself into the church. Rather it must—and this is emphasized

76. Farner, *Huldrych Zwingli*, 4.509.

77. Gottfried Locher, ed., *Der Berner Synodus von 1532* (Neukirchen: Neukirchener Verlag, 1982) 1.112f., 120f.

78. See Alfred Farner, *Die Lehre von Kirche und Staat bei Zwingli* (Tübingen: Mohr, 1930); Dankbaar, *Calvin*, 93; Niesel, *Die Theologie Calvins*, 232.

by Zwingli and Calvin as well as by Luther[79]—give full freedom to the proclamation of the church and thus in its role toward the church can have as its only goal that the church be true church.

This definition shows that for the Reformed fathers church and state in fact must have in their own interest the well-being of the other side. Zwingli's frequent remark that there can be no better government than one under which God's word is proclaimed most clearly in the church[80] was easily misunderstood to imply that the church was to supply the grease for a smoothly functioning state. Yet the deepest meaning of the statement is that it is also in the best interests of the state when the church does earnestly what the state cannot and may not do, and thus it should desire this and support the church in it. Surely behind this stands the thought of a mutual interdependence—the church depending upon the state for the protection of life and the state relying upon the church to tell *why* this life is to be protected.

If one keeps firmly in mind the difference between church and state stressed by the Reformed fathers, one will be able to affirm these thoughts but refine the conclusion. It is proper for the true state, as evidence of its institution by God, and therefore it is in fact in its own interest, to give freedom to the church in its task and testimony. But we must take into account that the state—even when it calls itself "Christian"—can always grant this freedom for completely different reasons from those the church has for exercising it. Thus one must formulate this concern rigorously, as Karl Barth did over against Hitler's state in 1933. In his words, the church "is the natural border of every . . . State," and it is this "for the good of the people, for *that* good which neither State nor Church can create, but which the Church is called to proclaim."[81] The true state requires limits to which it can consent, so that it will not itself become an "institution of salvation" and an idol—and thus a totalitarian state. But it is only in faith and *in* the church that one knows about *this* meaning of the self-limitation of the state. Thus the church should expect from the state only that it will limit itself to its task and thereby allow freedom for the church. No matter how foreign the state's motives for doing this may be to the concerns of the church, in so doing this the state in fact does what it is to do in seeing that the church is true church.

The Reformed fathers consciously went further in defining the state's concern for the church—apparently because they presupposed a Christian government. One should not rush to say that in their day this presupposition was correct while today we can no longer assume such a thing. Even at that time their assumption was highly questionable and was the starting point for an ominous meddling of the state in the church. What led them astray was not the idea that the worldly government was in fact "Christian," but rather that as true government it is *necessarily* Christian. They were unable to draw a second conclusion from the thought, in itself correct, that earthly justice must use "divine righteousness" as its standard. The

---

79. Luther, *Von weltlicher Obrigkeit,* 82ff.; for Calvin and Niesel see *Die Theologie Calvins,* 232; for Zwingli see his *Eine freundliche Bitte und Ermahnung, . . . dass man das Heilige Evengelium zu predigen erlaube* (1522).

80. Zwingli, *Auslegen und Begründen,* 90, 121, etc.

81. Karl Barth, *Theologische Existenz Heute!* (Munich: Christian Kaiser Verlag, 1933) 40.

Reformed fathers did not take seriously the distinction between church and state here as well; and they did not see from this that "divine righteousness" can influence the formation of "earthly justice" in only very *indirect* forms and can be applied anonymously in the state. Instead, they postulated that in order to act correctly the authorities must have a *direct* knowledge of God's will and righteousness. By the force of this idea they also ascribed to the authorities the competence to see that the church says of the will of God what they need to know of it in order to be able to act correctly.

From here Zwingli developed the thought that for its own sake the true state should desire the existence of the church. His conclusions would require that the entire supervision of the church be entrusted to the state.[82] Thus he handed over to the Zurich Council complete rights over the church—the use of church property, the installation and removal of pastors, the exclusion of certain people from the Lord's Supper, supervision of the pastors and their sermons, the right to carry out or prevent reforms, etc. In this Zwingli had overlooked that already before the Reformation the Council had begun to assume not only the worldly but also the ecclesiastical rights of the bishop—and not out of pure delight in the gospel but rather out of clear interest in power. Thus Zwingli, with the permission of the state, approved of its systematic progress "to make the clergy subject to the State."[83] How could the clergy resist after the external law of the church was handed over to the state? Calvin rightly took Zwingli's solution to task, saying that here Protestant doctrine was "subject not only to power, but even to the mere gesture of a few men—theologically uneducated ones at that: one must speak or be silent according to how they wave their finger."[84]

Here Calvin was not afraid without reason. This danger was not yet acute in Zwingli himself—he was too mighty a prophetic watchman for that. But it did become acute in the territories where his thought was influential in the following centuries. The clergy were made subject to the interests of the state and for centuries had to take an oath on their spiritual office, first to strictly obey the government and second to also preach the word of God.[85] The Reformed church put up with this huge demand which stood the concern of the Reformed fathers on its head. In fact, around 1830 the church submitted when a (by that time) secularized government forbade the use of the Heidelberg Catechism.[86]

With Calvin circumstances were a bit different, but not so different that he could prevent a similar development, despite his criticism of Zwingli and despite his success in securing for the church its own spiritual leadership and organization. Indeed, against the hand of the state, which in his case as well was grabbing strongly at the church, he could not achieve all he had in mind.[87] But his creation for the

82. Gäbler, *Zwingli,* 89.

83. Ibid., 76.

84. Rudolf Schwarz, ed., Johannes Calvins Lebenswerk in seinen Briefen (Neukirchen: Neukirchener Verlag, 1961) 231.

85. *Neu-verbesserte Predikanten-Ordnung Des sammtlichen Ministerii Der Teutschen Landen Hoch-Loblicher Stadt Bern* (Bern, 1748) 121.

86. Jakob Heiz, "Zur 400 jährigen Jubiläumsfeier der Berner Reformation," in Ernst Marti, ed., *Menschenrat und Gottestat, Geschichte der Berner Reformation* (Bern: Büchler, 1927) 19.

87. Dankbaar, *Calvin,* 93, 98.

church of its own leadership was impressive in comparison not only with Zwingli but also with the Lutheran territories where the leadership of the church was handed over to the "sovereign state government of the Church" (the authorities). Calvin believed that representatives of the offices of the church should lead the church according to the model of early Christianity (pastors, teachers, deacons, and elders—this last office, of course, being where the political leadership also sat in church leadership). With this, Calvin paved the way for the important understanding Karl Barth introduced into proposition three of the Barmen Declaration in 1934:[88] that the church may not be left to the state even in its outward form of organization but rather must be structured according to its own nature. Otherwise it will be robbed of its power to confess *to* the state—and, if necessary, *against* it—and it will become to the contrary a structure easily manipulated by state and society.

Nonetheless, not only was Calvin unable to avert this danger, he even helped further it. This resulted precisely from the conclusion he drew from the thought that (as he formulated it) the advancement of God's glory and the humaneness of humanity belong inseparably together, and that the keeping of the second table of the Ten Commandments in the state is impossible without the keeping of the first table as well. If with Calvin as with Zwingli the authorities did not have to exercise the organizational leadership of the church, as the political power they nonetheless had the right and duty to look after the keeping of the first table— and this not only formally for the freedom of the church but also materially for the institution and preservation of true worship and the abolition of false worship.[89] John Knox then took this thought—that rulers are "appointed not only for civil government but also to maintain true religion and to suppress all idolatry and superstition"—into the Scots Confession.[90] Just how dangerous this statement is, is shown in its continuation (even when it is limited by the qualification that the authorities fulfill their office properly): "Therefore . . . those who resist the supreme powers . . . are resisting God's ordinance."

Karl Barth observed correctly that "Spiritual corruption must be overcome by spiritual and not by political power. If the Church fails to recognize this, who can save it, what reforms could be demanded of it one day with political power?"[91] It came to demands soon enough in Geneva, where already in 1537, at Calvin's instigation, the police wanted to force all inhabitants to swear by his Reformed confession of faith.[92] Calvin's complete lack of comprehension of Bullinger's and Capito's criticisms of the proceedings shows that the development was not a mere coincidence but rather was clearly the consequence of his thinking. This then validated in rather infamous fashion the trial of the antitrinitarian Servetus and a series of similar incidents.[93]

---

88. "We reject the false teaching that the church may surrender . . . her Order . . . to the changes of the political convictions of those currently in power."

89. Calvin, *Institutes,* 4.20.9.

90. Scots Confession, Article 24.

91. Karl Barth, *Gotteserkenntnis und Gottesdienst nach reformatorischer Lehre* (Zollikon: Evangelischer Verlag, 1938) 210.

92. Fritz Blanke, "Calvins Fehler," *Reformatio* 8 (1959) 298ff.

93. Ibid., 303ff.

The problem with Calvin's thinking on this point is that it can lead to even greater demands. Once the state was granted the right to mix with political power in the spiritual realm, how could the church protect itself if authorities who no longer saw themselves as Christian chose to hang onto this right? Further, what if Calvin's grounding of the state's authority on the doctrine of providence was completely dissolved from its already loose ties to the doctrine of the reign of Christ? Further still, what if Calvin's favorite verse, Dan 2:21, that the Lord establishes and deposes kings,[94] were to be put into the framework of a general doctrine of providence in history? As long as "the Lord" does not depose the authorities, must not any capricious act toward the church by a long-secularized worldly government be accepted as God-given? It was not coincidentally that later forms of Calvinism granted themselves a "legitimacy" over against the government.[95]

This was particularly the case in German-speaking Switzerland. This is illustrated in the recognition of the principle that the secularized government expressed in 1800: the state protects the church with the qualification that no Christian avoids "his civil duty on the pretext of religion."[96] Here the favorite words of the old Reformed theologians are twisted into just their opposite. It is no longer "One should obey God rather than persons" but rather one should first obey the state (or else the social customs) and then, as far as there is agreement, God as well. Here the Christian faith can not only have no social and political influence, but it has been reduced to a "religion" which can take up just a corner of life when compared with the commonly accepted superiority of the state. Now of course not everything got as bad as all that. Nonetheless, in most cases the observation of the church's prophetic office of watchman was the exception in the Reformed territories. Moreover, in most cases much of what was crucial in the Reformed doctrine of church and state went awry and failed to develop. Under the circumstances, the paragraph in our church order cited at the beginning of this paper is indeed Reformed, but nonetheless it is a miracle. Its consequences are now in a long-term struggle with that just-mentioned Swiss Reformed mentality.

It was indeed an indirect result of Calvin's thought that the way was paved for a consciousness of freedom in other areas influenced by him, and that resistance movements against the capricious use of force developed in Holland, France, and Scotland.[97] Karl Barth was right when he observed in Calvin what, mutatis mutandis, applies to Zwingli as well: "his political attitude is distinguished by the same light, but also by the same shadows, which are characteristic of his theology."[98] Calvin's and Zwingli's important, and no longer to be surrendered, discovery of the church's "prophetic office of watchman" over injustice by the state was moved into the shadows by Calvin and Zwingli themselves. They allowed the primary obedience of the Christian to God, which is the basis of the office of watchman, to be limited by granting the state the right to watch over this

---

94. Calvin, *Ezechiel und Daniel*, 386; *Institutes*, 4.20.26.
95. Otto Weber, "Calvinismus," *EKL* 1.663.
96. Jakob Heiz, "Zur 400 jährigen Jubiläumsfeier," 22.
97. Gerhard Gloede, "Calvin," *EKL* 1.656.
98. Karl Barth, "Calvin als Theologe," *Reformatio* 8 (1959) 318.

obedience. The light in this matter will shine only when this shadow with which they have burdened their enlightened understanding is restrained. Their light shines only when one subjects their concession of a limitation of Christian obedience to God by an order of the state to a thoroughgoing criticism. Only then will Calvin's closing statement in his chapter on temporal government (and indeed in the Institutes in general) have real meaning. Christ has bought and redeemed us at such a great price "that we should not enslave ourselves to the evil desires of humanity, and much less should we submit to godlessness. Glory be to God!"[99]

99. Calvin, *Institutes*, 4.20.32.

Toleration, Nonconformity, and the Unity of the Spirit: Popular Religion in Eighteenth-Century England

James E. Bradley

The Act of Toleration of 1689 is often described as a "grudging concession," since the penal legislation that followed the Act of Uniformity was not repealed by it.[1] Toleration, however, did exempt the Presbyterians, Congregationalists, Baptists, and Quakers from the penalties inflicted by the former legislation, and it clearly signaled the beginning of modern denominationalism in England. It permitted the Nonconformists freedom to worship if their ministers took the new oaths of allegiance and subscribed to thirty-four of the Thirty-Nine Articles.[2] The Dissenters' doctrinal compatibility with the Anglicans was emphatically underscored by their willingness to subscribe to the remaining articles. Nonconformists did not chafe under this requirement until late in the eighteenth century when the drift into Unitarianism was becoming widespread, particularly among the Presbyterians. The "penalties" of the Test and Corporation Acts, however, were not among those from which Nonconformists were exempted, and they were required in addition to meet in unlocked buildings, pay tithes, and register their assemblies with the bishop, archdeacon, or justice of the peace. Despite these restrictions, Lord Macaulay was undoubtedly correct when he wrote that the act "removed a vast mass of evil without shocking a vast mass of prejudice."[3]

The Act of Toleration did not permit, therefore, any church or group of churches to qualify as a rival to the established church. Presbyterians with their proposed scheme of national synods became congregational in polity; the distinguishing mark of Presbyterian polity was hereafter a difference in name only. This had

1. See E. N. Williams, *The Eighteenth Century Constitution, 1688–1815: Documents and Commentary* (Cambridge: Cambridge University Press, 1970) 6. Russell E. Richey, "Effects of Toleration on Eighteenth-Century Dissent," *JRH* 8 (1975) 352-53, argues persuasively for a unified tradition of Nonconformity that was more important than individual denominational labels; the distinctive social institutions common to the Dissenters were congregation, academy, ministerial association, deputies, trusts, and a party of leadership. Denominationalism was first popularized and practiced in the eighteenth century, though the concept was worked out theologically by Independent divines, particularly Jeremiah Burroughes, in the mid-seventeenth century. See Winthrop S. Hudson, "Denominationalism as a Basis for Ecumenicity: A Seventeenth Century Conception," *CH* 24 (1955) 32-33. I wish to thank Dr. John D. Walsh of Jesus College Oxford for reading this essay and drawing my attention to several additional references.

2. 1 W. & M., c. 18. The full title makes these points clear: "An Act for exempting their Majesties protestant subjects, dissenting from the church of England, from the penalties of certain laws." Articles 20, 34, 35, and 36 on rites and ceremonies, the traditions of the church, and ordination were not required, and Article 27 on infant baptism was not required for Baptists.

3. Lord Macaulay, *The History of England from the Accession of James the Second* (ed. C. H. Frith; 6 vols.; London: Macmillan, 1913–1915) 3.1390. Macaulay eloquently notes the inadequacies, indeed the outright contradictions, in the law but on the whole applauds it.

the effect of endearing them to the Congregationalists and Baptists, and in the period following 1689 the "three denominations," as they were commonly called, considered ways to unite in the common cause. Much has been written on the various efforts at cooperation among the denominations at the highest levels of ecclesiastical life. For example, Presbyterian and Congregationalist ministers in London united in 1691 under "the Heads of Agreement" for the purpose of assisting small congregations. A second ministerial association encompassing the Baptists was formed in 1702 taking the title "The General Body of Protestant Dissenting Ministers of the Three Denominations in and about the City of London and Westminster." Later, in 1732, the Nonconformists organized the Dissenting Deputies to act on behalf of the three denominations in their efforts to repeal the Test and Corporation acts.[4] There were also several attempts at reunion with the established church. After the abortive Rebellion of 1745, Dr. Samuel Chandler of Old Jewry, London, engaged the bishops of Norwich and Salisbury in conversations on comprehension. Similarly, Thomas Herring, the Archbishop of Canterbury, entered into discussions with Philip Doddridge in 1748 concerning a possible scheme of comprehension. Herring and Doddridge agreed that a "perfect coalition" would be impractical, but that an occasional exchange of pulpits might be admissible.[5]

These and other attempts at comprehension are well documented, but practical expressions of "the unity of the Spirit" at the local level of chapel life and experimentation in cooperative efforts between Nonconformists and Anglicans have not received the attention they deserve. The Dissenting elite and denominational historians have had a tendency to highlight their own denominational distinctives, and in the interest of definition they have neglected those elements that are common to eighteenth-century Christians. In addition, the various expressions of tolerance that have been studied are almost invariably attributed to the emergence of theological liberalism.[6] The Act of Toleration in fact resulted in in-

4. The Congregationalists of London started their own fund in 1695. See the exhaustive studies by Bernard Lord Manning, *The Protestant Dissenting Deputies* (ed. Ormerod Greenwood; Cambridge: Cambridge University Press, 1952); N. C. Hunt, *Two Early Political Associations: The Quakers and the Dissenting Deputies in the Age of Sir Robert Walpole* (Oxford: Clarendon, 1961); and Richard B. Barlow, *Citizenship and Conscience: A Study in the Theory and Practice of Religious Toleration in England During the Eighteenth Century* (Philadelphia: University of Pennsylvania Press, 1962).

5. Ernest A. Payne, "Toleration and Establishment: 1, A Historical Outline," in Geoffrey F. Nuttall and Owen Chadwick, eds., *From Uniformity to Unity, 1662–1962* (London: SPCK, 1962) 264. High Anglicans traditionally resisted all such schemes. See Geoffrey Holmes, *Religion and Party in Late Stuart England* (London: The Historical Association, 1975) 12. On the divisions between evangelical churchmen, Dissenters, and especially Methodists, and on their hopes for unity, see Roger H. Martin, *Evangelicals United: Ecumenical Stirrings in Pre-Victorian Britain, 1795–1830* (Metuchen, N.J./London: Scarecrow, 1983) 2-22.

6. Richey, "Effects of Toleration," 353-54, 361; Edward Carpenter, "Toleration and Establishment: 2, Studies in a Relationship," in *From Uniformity to Unity*, 293. Donald Davie clearly sees that the common association of toleration with theological liberalism is largely a result of reading the history of eighteenth-century Nonconformity through the roseate lens of Unitarian beliefs. See Davie, *Dissentient Voice: Enlightenment and Christian Dissent* (Notre Dame/London: University of Notre Dame Press, 1982) 94, 98-99, 117.

numerable instances of cooperation between the three denominations quite unrelated to the new theological vogues, and it established a new relationship between "old Dissent" on the one hand, and the Quakers, the Methodists, and the Anglicans, on the other.

The modern study of popular Christian experience in eighteenth-century England lags far behind research in popular religion on the continent of Europe.[7] The detailed examination of local records and diaries has just begun, and before new generalizations can be made such research will require the amassing of numerous illustrations of the behavior of specific individuals. One neglected source that will contribute to this research is deposited in Dr. Williams's Library in London. This library contains the work of Josiah Thompson, a Baptist minister in London in the last quarter of the eighteenth century, who complied a massive five-volume manuscript entitled "A Collection of Papers containing an account of the original Formation of some hundred protestant dissenting Congregations; the Succession of their Pastors, and Remarkable Providences . . . taken from their Church Books, the Testimony and Report of old People, private Papers, and other Authentic Records."[8] From internal evidence, it can be shown that the collection was begun in 1772 and continued as late as 1784. Even though these volumes bring together in a single collection an incomparable mine of local church records, modern scholars have almost completely overlooked them. Thompson preserved many examples of cooperation, not only among Dissenters, but also between Nonconformists and Anglicans. By supplementing these records with information from the collection of chapel histories at Dr. Williams's Library, we can get a much fuller grasp of day to day interdenominational activities.

7. No study of Nonconformity compares to the work of Norman Sykes on eighteenth-century Anglicanism. On popular religion, see the essay by R. C. Trexler in Kaspar von Greyerz, ed., *Religion and Society in Early Modern Europe, 1500–1800* (London: Allen & Unwin, 1984). Two good examples of recent work on Britain that deal mostly with nineteenth-century religion are James Obelkevich, *Religion and Rural Society: South Lindsey, 1825–1875* (Oxford: Oxford University Press, 1976); and S. J. Conolly, *Priests and People in Pre-Famine Ireland, 1780–1845* (New York: St. Martin's, 1982).

8. Josiah Thompson, ed., "History of Protestant Dissenting Congregations" (5 vols.; 1772–1784), MS. 38.7-11, microfilm copy from Dr. Williams's Library, London (hereafter cited as Thompson, "History"). The title of this work, "History of Protestant Dissenting Congregations," was assigned by Kenneth Twinn et al., comps. in *Nonconformist Congregations in Great Britain: A List of Histories and Other Material in Dr. Williams's Library* (London: Dr. Williams's Trust, 1973) 1. The allusion to "the Testimony and Report of old People" suggests that this was one of the earliest efforts to reconstruct the past on the basis of what has come to be known as oral history. Additional information in this essay is drawn principally from four other sources from Dr. Williams's Library. Josiah Thompson's List of Protestant Dissenting Congregations in England and Wales (1772–1773), MS. 38.6, microfilm copy (hereafter cited as the Thompson List, 38.6). This list was printed in partial form under the title, "A View of English Nonconformity in 1773" in *CHST* 5 (1911– 1912) 204-22, 261-77, 372-85. There is another manuscript copy of the Thompson List with information from a list of 1715 and slight alterations (hereafter cited as the Thompson List, 38.5). John Evans has also compiled a List of Dissenting Congregations in England and Wales (1715–1729), MS. 38.4, microfilm copy (hereafter cited as the Evans List). And finally, "A View of the Dissenting Interest in London . . . from the Year 1695 to the 25th of December 1731" (1731), MS. 38.18, microfilm copy (hereafter cited as "A View of the Dissenting Interest in London").

Writing in 1774, Thompson depicted the differences between the various Dissenters in Cambridge in terms of their polity. "The Cambridge Nonconformists were a mixture of a sort, the largest part were for *independent* Church government of which sort were many at Cambridge.—a *Second* part were for a Presbyterian government. These were not numerous, but they were rich. . . . A *Third* sort were Baptists. These at Cambridge were mixed with the Independents till 1726 when they also formed a separate church." Thompson concluded that the three denominations differed from each other only in "discipline," a term broad enough to include the form of polity, the ordination of ministers, and the administration of the sacraments.[9] How important were differences in "discipline" to eighteenth-century Dissenters, and how important were differences in doctrine?

The "Age of Reason" was not nearly so placid theologically as is sometimes supposed, and the Dissenters were involved in many doctrinal disputes throughout the eighteenth century. Calvinism continued to divide the Baptists, but while there were divisions at the denominational level and while individual chapels might still be split over Calvinism at the local level, the three denominations were not divided primarily on a doctrinal basis.[10] Presbyterians and Congregationalists were not as riven as the Baptists, though there was little unanimity within these denominations. Theology was often more important to the Dissenters than denominational label, but in all three denominations a broad spectrum of Calvinism could be found.[11] Essentially the same observation applies to the Trinitarian controversy, for it, too, was no respecter of denominational walls. In the aftermath of the meeting of ministers at Salters Hall in 1719, numerous Dissenters avowedly had accepted Arianism but still stopped short of Unitarianism. Mature Unitarianism gained many adherents throughout England in the course of the century, but a Unitarian denomination was not formally organized until 1774. A liberal tendency

9. Thompson, "History," 1.152. It was quite common for Dissenters to base their own self-definition on these two broad categories of doctrine and discipline. See Thompson, "History," 4.183.

10. The distinction between General and Particular is not consistently made in the Evans and Thompson Lists, but the denominations were carefully distinguished, and one must add the small Seventh Day Baptist denomination to them. Thompson, writing on Norfolk, said: "It is somewhat particular that in this part of Norfolk there should be 3 Baptist congreg[ations] very near together and all 3 of different denominations" (see the Thompson List, 38.6, 25). In London in 1731 there were twenty-five Baptist chapels; of these, fifteen were Particular, eight General, and two Seventh Day (see "A View of the Dissenting Interest in London," 100). For variations among Baptists see the Thompson List, 38.6, 13, 25; Thompson, "History," 3.17; 4.171. On the doctrinal dispute over law and grace in the antinomian controversy see Michael Watts, *The Dissenters* (Oxford: Clarendon, 1978) 293-96, and on the Caffyn controversy among the General Baptists see pp. 298-300.

11. See "A View of the Dissenting Interest in London," 8; Thompson, "History," 4.179; the Evans List, 88. Watts argues that Congregationalists were stricter with respect to admission to the Lord's Supper than Presbyterians were (*The Dissenters*, 291). He examines the abiding differences between the two denominations in liturgical practice and hymn singing (308); differences in the practice of ordination (315-17); and differences in the practice of discipline (321-25); see also 377- 79. But he overstates the extent of the denominational division resulting from the antinomian controversy, though he does concede that local expressions of cooperation continued (296-97).

could be found in each of the denominations, though it was more prevalent among Presbyterians than among Congregationalists and Baptists.[12]

For all of the differences in doctrine the Dissenters were fond to display, and for all of their disagreements over discipline and polity, the underlying unity was more important in shaping their history. Contemporary Nonconformists spoke appropriately of "the Dissenting Interest" when describing the three denominations; in the manuscript source this phrase, or the phrase, the "Protestant Dissenting Interest," is found time and again.[13] The relationship of the three denominations to several other religious traditions contributed to this cohesion.

Eighteenth-century Dissenters defined themselves in relationship to their several denominational distinctives but also in relation to the Anglicans. Traditionally the Presbyterians were least offended by the establishment, while some Congregationalists and Baptists were nearly rabid in their rejection of Anglicanism. Some Dissenters refused to make any distinction between Anglicans and Roman Catholics; others had no scruples about receiving the sacrament in the Anglican church. Similarly, within the Anglican church, opinion about dissent varied widely. Gilbert Sheldon, the principal author of the "Clarendon Code," sought to construct an unbridgeable gulf between Dissenters and Anglicans. On the other hand, John Tillotson, converted Nonconformist and untiring advocate of comprehension, wished to see the barriers between them utterly destroyed: both men served as Archbishop of Canterbury (1663–1677 and 1691–1694 respectively). Thus any generalization about the relationship of Dissenters to Anglicans, and how the first were defined vis-à-vis the second, must be heavily qualified. Moreover, if the relationship varied from person to person, then it also changed from age to age. After the Hanoverian accession, for example, tensions were eased, but during the American and French Revolutions, strife was common. Finally, Dissenters and Anglicans got along differently in different geographic areas: where high church sentiment was rife, as in the northwest of England, there was always considerable friction. Nevertheless, when all of these qualifications have been made, the evidence for cooperative efforts at the parish level and for intercommunion between chapels is still considerable.

INTERCOMMUNION AMONG THE THREE DENOMINATIONS

The common theological heritage of the Dissenters, together with their shared political experience under the Stuarts, shaped them into a single, well-defined religious tradition. Though instances of infighting and strife are not unknown, the unifying agents of law, theology, and experience led naturally to much intercommunion at the local level. Illustrations of practical cooperation found in the details of everyday parish life will show how the Dissenters understood each other,

12. See Thompson, "History," 2.68; "A View of the Dissenting Interest in London," 64; the Thompson List, 38.6, 25. The debate over Arianism was in some ways felt more at the local level than at the national level. Richey, "Effects of Toleration," 363; but on the denominational question, see the fine discussion in Watts, *The Dissenters,* 378-80.

13. "A View of the Dissenting Interest in London," 2; the Thompson List, 38.6, 1; Thompson, "History," 2.67, 74; 3.82-83.

and how they defined themselves in relationship to the Anglicans, the Quakers, and the Methodists.

The Dissenters of different denominations sometimes met together for worship. In fact, the practice was widespread, and one can find examples of Presbyterians meeting with Congregationalists, and each of these denominations meeting with Baptists. The joining of Presbyterians with Congregationalists for public worship is not, perhaps, surprising, since the two denominations largely agreed on polity. The failure of the Presbyterians to organize synods contributed to the cooperation; for example, the pastor of the Congregational church at Barnstaple, Devonshire, was a Presbyterian, and he "never instituted any regular order of church government."[14] A note in the church book of the Congregational chapel at Hertford indicates that contemporaries recognized a denominational barrier but sometimes transcended it in the interest of Christian fellowship: "November 3rd, 1708. Agreed to admit of members of a Presbyterian Church to occasional communion with us if they desire it."[15] In addition to polity, the two denominations agreed on infant baptism, and there were many alliances that resulted from these common bonds. In the minutes of the Bury St. Edmunds Congregational Chapel for 8 July 1758 there is an interesting allusion to confraternity between Presbyterians and Congregationalists. "Will[iam] the Son of the Revd Mr. Lincoln [the Presbyterian minister] Bapt by Thos. Savil" the Congregational minister.[16] In Suffolk the Dissenting church at Walsham was poorly attended after 1728. Then, "the bulk of that Congregation united itself to that at Wattisfield." However, "they being of 2 different denominations, viz. Presbyterian and Independent, a [Presbyterian] lecture was once a month beg[u]n at Walsham . . . which continues to be preached there to this day."[17] In this case the alliance was temporary. But the Presbyterians and the Congregationalists at Leicester met "in one meeting" early in the century; other examples of common worship have been found at Canterbury, Chester, Chesterfield, and Worcester.[18] The most important list of Dissenting congregations for the eighteenth century, the Evans List, repeatedly blurs the distinction between Presbyterian and Congregational churches; and the Thompson List, compiled fifty years later, drops this terminology altogether. Distinctions among the denominations did exist, but the outside observer sometimes had difficulty in telling them apart.[19]

The fraternity between the paedobaptists and Baptists is somewhat more noteworthy since the Baptists in many cases had not advanced as far up the social

---

14. Thompson, "History," 2.9. For instances of cooperation between the two denominations in the seventeenth century see Watts, *The Dissenters,* 289-90.

15. William Urwick, *Nonconformity in Hertfordshire* (London: Hazell, Watsun, and Vivey, 1884) 544.

16. J. Duncan, "The History of the Congregational Church in Bury St. Edmunds," (1962) typescript in Dr. Williams's Library, London, 149.

17. The Thompson List, 38.6, 33.

18. The Evans List, 64; for the last four references see Watts, *The Dissenters,* 297.

19. One could argue that the distinction between Presbyterian and Congregational chapels had become merely a nominal one, and that such instances of communion are really not significant. W. Densham and J. Ogle note that the chapels at Weymouth and Melcombe Regis and at Wareham and other places in the county went by the name Presbyterian but were in fact Congregational, since they were assisted by the Congregational Fund Board. Similarly,

scale as the other two denominations. Moreover, the debate over infant baptism was far from a theoretical question for most believers. Despite these differences, the denominations met together on occasion. The two Baptist churches at Slapton and Eschott were "mixt, as to Baptism," that is, there were some paedobaptists who met with the Baptists for worship.[20] Throughout the county of Bedford the vast majority of the Dissenting congregations were Baptist, and therefore "almost every one of them admit of free Communion."[21] Both "free and "mixed" communion meant that believers of different denominations were not excluded from the Lord's Table. In the borough of Bedford the paedobaptists met with the Baptists, and such instances of mixed communion can be multiplied.[22] Occasionally the Dissenters met together, shared the same sermon, and then regathered for separate communions.[23] At Reading the close fellowship between the Baptist and Congregationalist chapels resulted in a common Sunday evening worship service in the latter half of the eighteenth century.[24]

In some cases these alliances grew out of a transitory need, for example, in those settings where there were too few qualified ministers. A drop in attendance also contributed to this kind of temporary merger.[25] Cooperation, however, was not always based on need. A single congregation might be blessed with the services of two ministers from different denominations. At Soham, Cambridgeshire, a Presbyterian and a Congregational pastor worked together in the 1720s "in good friendship." From about 1715 at Bunyan's church in Bedford the minister was a paedobaptist, "tho[ugh] more than one half of the society have been of the Baptist persuasion." Finally, Dissenters of "all denominations" could be found at the Presbyterian church in the famous western resort of Bath, Somersetshire.[26]

Robert Halley observed that in Lancashire and Cheshire the distinctions between the two denominations has been all but obliterated. Densham and Ogle, *The Story of the Congregational Churches of Dorset from their Foundation to the Present Time* (Bournemouth: W. Mate, 1899) 372; Halley, *Lancashire, Its Puritanism and Nonconformity* (2 vols.; Manchester, 1869) 2.384.

20. The Evans List, 88. On the debate over open communion in the 1770s, see Martin, *Evangelicals United,* 18-19.

21. The Thompson List, 38.6, 1.

22. The practice may be found at Greenwich and Woolich, Kent, and probably in some of the other congregations that met together for worship (the Thompson List, 38.6, 18). The College Lane Chapel, Northampton, allowed open membership, i.e., they accepted both infant and believers baptism (see Watts, *The Dissenters,* 319). Watts discusses the tendency of Baptist chapels with open membership to become Congregational. But there is an account of a change in discipline in the opposite direction at Ridgmont, Bedfordshire. "Hitherto the society had adhered to their original engagement and the principle of mixed communion on which they were first formed, but May 31, 1770, they unanimously agreed to review that agreement and thence forward to make adult baptism by immersion an indispensable term of admission to Communion." Thompson, "History," 1.95.

23. For examples at Wantage, Berkshire, and Broad Mead, Bristol, in Gloucestershire see the Thompson List, 38.6, 2; and Thompson, "History," 2.148. For variations on a theme see Thompson, "History," 2.13, 156; 1.117; 4.198; the Thompson List, 38.5, 9; the Evans List, 103.

24. Leslie W. Harman, *The History of Christianity in Reading* (add. material by Keith R. Brymer; Reading: Bradley & Son, 1952) 68.

25. Thompson, "History," 1.117.

26. Ibid., 175; the Thompson List, 38.6, 5; Thompson, "History," 4.172.

Such instances of cooperation among the denominations were often temporary expedients. There were, however, churches that changed their denominational
affiliation permanently, a circumstance that was sometimes occasioned by a
change in the convictions of the minister. At Bideford, Devonshire, "the church
was formerly governed by the strictest discipline. The last Mr. Bartlet relaxed its
severity and it is now a compound of independency and Presbyterianism."[27] In the
village of Bourton-on-the-Water, Gloucestershire, a chapel was founded on the
principle of "mixed communion," and then it gradually changed complexion,
first under the direction of a paedobaptist and finally a Baptist minister.[28]

Perhaps the most thoroughgoing expression of ecumenism among the
denominations occurred when there was a permanent merger of two churches. At
Shrewsbury, Shropshire, "a congregation of protestant Dissenters of the Independent persuasion . . . desired to join with the Presbyterian congregation and be
united with them as one church and Nov. 5, 1741 the churches were united." A
similar merger between Presbyterians and Congregationalists occurred at
Barnstaple, Devonshire; and at Ludlow, Shropshire, all three denominations
formed a church.[29]

Cooperation, then, among the denominations was occasionally practiced at
the broadest level of the church's life. There is further evidence of unity, significantly enough, even at the clerical level. Cooperation among the Dissenting
ministers of London is probably the most well-known example. Beginning in 1727
and continuing through 1776, each of the three denominations in London peri-
odically turned in a list of their approved ministers to the central body of the
Protestant Dissenting ministers in London and Westminster, and these lists were
then recorded in the Minute Books.[30] The denominational affiliation of each minister was carefully distinguished, and each of the denominations had their own
basis for approving ministers.[31] The Congregationalists, for example, decided
against making subscription to the Savoy Declaration a requirement for approval
and decided instead to list any minister who himself chose to be included.[32] The

27. Thompson, "History," 2.11. The same thing happened at Eastcheap, London. "A View of
the Dissenting Interest in London," 64.

28. Thompson, "History," 2.135. Sometimes meeting houses changed hands from one
denomination to another, as at Headcorn, Kent, in 1750, when the Baptists took over a former
Presbyterian building. They made repairs and built a gallery and a baptistry. Thompson, "History," 3.28. See also the case of Milborne Port, Somersetshire. Ibid., 4.182.

29. Ibid., 4.155; 2.9; 4.163.

30. *Minute Books of the Body of Protestant Dissenting Ministers of the Three Denominations
in and about the Cities of London and Westminster,* 2 vols. (11 July 1727–11 April 1797),
MS. 38.105-106, microfilm copy from Dr. Williams's Library, London, 1.3-12, 34-38, 147-53,
162-74, 200-206; 2.57-61, 85-88, 176-80.

31. When on 6 January 1729 John Evans, the compiler of the Evans List, reported on an up-
dated list of approved ministers, five names had to be dropped from the Presbyterian list because
they chose "to be ranked on the Congregational list." Ibid., 1.18.

32. "London Congregational Board," *CHST* 2 (1905–1906) 50. In 1735 it was decided that to
be maintained on the list one must preach at least once every two years, and in 1761 the ministers decided that to be admitted to the list they must be recommended by five ministers who were
already approved and then be agreed on by a two-thirds vote. Ibid., 54, 59. According to these
minutes, about the only order of business of the Congregational Board was determining who
belonged on the list. The Particular Baptists, however, were more demanding in their approval

lists were carefully reviewed every five to six years, and when a minister died or moved away, this fact was duly noted in the minutes. The importance of these lists for this discussion is found in the Dissenting ministers' determination to maintain their denominational distinctives and yet work together cooperatively.

Ministerial cooperation involved a facet of ecclesiastical life that is often carefully isolated by denominational barriers, namely, ordination. When William Medcalf was ordained at Kingston, Surrey, in 1760, Josiah Thompson observed that "some of each denomination assisted on that occasion allmost the only instance of the like nature ever known among Protestant Dissenters."[33] This event was not, in fact, quite so unique as Thompson supposed. Thomas Harmer recorded that when he was ordained in 1735 in the Congregational church of Wattisfield, Suffolk, pastors from both the Presbyterian and Congregational churches were present.[34] Meredith Townsend was ordained at Dagger Lane Congregational Church, Kingston-upon-Hull, in 1749, and the Rev. T. Walker, Presbyterian pastor of Mill Hill, Leeds, preached the sermon.[35] At the ordination of Mr. Waldegrave in the Whiting Street Congregational Church, Bury St. Edmunds, the Presbyterian minister, Rev. William Lincoln, took part in the service (11 July 1771); and at the installation of the Rev. John Driver in the Presbyterian church at Bury (13 September 1792), the minister of the Friars Street Congregational Church at Sudbury, John Mead Ray, was present.[36]

In addition to ordination, a variety of other chapel celebrations elicited ministerial cooperation. When the Vicar Lane Congregational Church of Coventry was opened for public worship on 14 October 1724, the sermon was preached by John Fleming, a Presbyterian. At the centenary of the Dissenting chapel at Wattisfield Suffolk (25 September 1754) both Congregational and Presbyterian ministers participated.[37] Such episodes of intercommunion have been too readily dismissed as merely happy social occasions of convivial fellowship among pastors.[38] But the frequency and widespread incidence of denominational cooperation in ordination services suggests that the frequently discussed distinctions in the doctrine of ministry between Presbyterians and Congregationalists[39] need to be reinterpreted in the light of the actual practice of ordination. The perceptions and the practice of ordinary ministers must be weighed against the distinctions made by contemporary Dissenting theologians.

In spite of the extensive cooperation among the three denominations, with

---

of a minister. For example, an approved minister had to believe in the Trinity. "The Baptist Board Minutes, 1724–June 27, 1820," *BHST* 5 (1916–1917) 208.

33. Thompson, "History," 4.293.

34. Ibid., 256.

35. W. Whitaker, *One Line of the Puritan Tradition in Hull. Bowl Alley Lane Chapel* (London: Philip Green, 1910) 102. On the other hand, the Congregationalists at Hull would tolerate fellowship with neither the Methodists nor the "Anabaptists." C. E. Darwent, *The Story of Fish Street Church, Hull* (London: William Andrews & Co., 1899) 201-2.

36. Duncan, "The Congregational Church in Bury St. Edmunds," 73-74.

37. John Sibree and M. Caston, *Independency in Warwickshire* (London: Ward & Co., 1855) 58; Duncan, "The Congregational Church in Bury St. Edmunds," 65.

38. Richey, "Effects of Toleration," 356n.13.

39. Ibid., 355-56; Watts, *The Dissenters,* 377-79.

few exceptions their meeting houses were designated as either Presbyterian, Congregational, or Baptist. Rivalry between them was by no means uncommon. Churches did split over points of denominational distinction, and one finds a dreary record of schism after schism.[40] A few examples will illustrate the kinds of problems the churches faced. A Baptist minister was preaching at a Congregational church at Over, Cambridgeshire, about 1755. Because he was a Baptist, "they could not unanimously agree to settle him for their pastor," and as a result there was a schism which "weakened if not dissolved" the church.[41] Whenever a minister changed his opinion regarding infant baptism, there could be serious repercussions, often leading to disruption if not outright division. Confusion, and apparently a loss of numbers, was the result of such a change at Smarden, Kent.[42]

Just as with baptism, the issue of polity could result in unity, as noted above, or it could produce division. Nonconformists at Bridport, Dorset, split into two assemblies in 1742, one Congregational, the other Presbyterian.[43] Differences over polity at Cambridge resulted in the separation of Hoghill Congregational Church from Green Street Presbyterian Church.[44] Schism over church order was therefore by no means rare in the eighteenth century. Predictably, local congregations also divided over the issue of Arianism.[45]

NONCONFORMISTS, QUAKERS, AND METHODISTS

The Dissenters of the three denominations carefully separated themselves from Quakers and Methodists. There is no evidence of the three denominations combining with Quakers for worship in the seventeenth or eighteenth century. Both in doctrine and practice Quakers were far removed from the three denominations. In the political sphere, the Friends established their own separate organization to work for relief from the burden of tithes.[46] At the local level of English politics, the Quaker vote was sometimes analyzed along with the three denominations which implies that they would normally act together on the side of the Whigs. In one list of Dissenting congregations, however, their presence is noted for only four county and three borough constituencies.[47]

40. In every age of the church there have been divisions over such minor issues as personality. It was no different in the eighteenth century. Thompson, "History," 1.155.

41. Ibid., 173. For other instances of baptism producing schism, see ibid., 4.52; the Thompson List, 38.6, 116.

42. Thompson, "History," 3.33; "A View of the Dissenting Interest in London," 18.

43. Thompson, "History," 2.69.

44. Ibid., 1.154. The Congregational church split again, however, in 1722 over the issue of who their pastor should be. Ibid., 155.

45. T. Timpson, Church History of Kent: From the Earliest Period to the Year MDCCLVIII (London: Ward & Co., 1859) 335.

46. The pastor of the Congregational church in Norwich wrote several tracts against the Quakers. Thompson, "History," 4.21.

47. Their vote is carefully analyzed in the Evans List for Berkshire, Cumberland, Hampshire, and Hertfordshire. The number of auditors is noted for Westmorland, and voters for the boroughs of Hertford and Durham. Their wealth and strength is noted for Bristol, but altogether this is a very fragmentary account. See the Evans List, 5, 105, 49, 122, 35, 147. They are not listed at all by

The three denominations interacted a good deal more with the Methodists than with the Quakers.[48] The Dissenters viewed the Methodists with a wary eye, since in many communities Methodist gains meant losses for the Dissenters. Where the congregations of old Dissent were already weak and dwindling, the Dissenters' response to the Methodists veered over into hostility. The Methodists seemed to them a strange paradox: their fiery zeal was a rebuke to Nonconformists who had grown staid and complacent, yet their connection with the establishment put them in the same class as the Anglicans. Unlike the Quakers, the Methodists experienced none of the legal proscriptions of the other denominations until late in the century. The Dissenters' attitude toward this new brand of evangelism was sometimes hopeful, sometimes critical, and very often ambiguous.

An interesting example of these various responses, which also graphically depicts the advances that Methodism was making, is found at Bideford, Devonshire. The pastor of the Dissenting congregation, Mr. Sedgeley, had seen the church grow substantially in the 1730s. "No man was more beloved and esteemed, till an indiscreet act set him at variance with his people. The occasion of it was this. When Mr. Whit[e]field visited Bideford Mr. Sedgeley warmly espoused his cause and permitted him to preach in his pulpit, condescending himself to be his clerk. The consequence of which was, the people's regards were in a great measure withdrawn from their own minister. They were all on fire,—and all Mr. Segeley's attempts to extinguish it, enflamed it the more." Sedgeley was obliged to remove to Newbury.[49]

Occasionally the Dissenters benefited from the aggressive evangelism of the Methodists. For example, Thompson noted that "this Congregation at Melbourn [Derbyshire] and 4 or 5 others in Leicestershire owe their rise to Mr. Whitefield and Mr. Wesley's preaching above 30 years ago, but they have been formed into regular orderly dissenting congegations for upwards of 25 years." By "dissenting congregations" he meant Baptists.[50] Similarly, at Greenwich (Kent), Great Yarmouth and Mattishall (Norfolk), and Barton in the Beans (Leicestershire), the denominations of old Dissent, and especially the Congregationalists and Baptists, brought believers into their churches who were converted by Methodist preachers.[51] In these and numerous other cases, preachers of "the Methodist complexion" or persons "methodistically inclined" brought real growth to the Dissenters. Instances of competition and rancor, however, were equally numerous.

At Battle, Sussex, the Dissenting meeting in the years 1746–1774 was "sunk

---

Thompson. In the early part of the century there was one Quaker meeting voting with the Tories at Hertford. Romney R. Sedgwick, ed., *The History of Parliament: The House of Commons, 1715–1754* (2 vols.; London: Her Majesty's Stationery Office, 1970), 1.261.

48. On the relation between Dissenters and Methodists, see Watts, *The Dissenters*, 440-45; and Donald Davie, *A Gathered Church: The Literature of the English Dissenting Interest, 1700–1930* (New York: Oxford University Press, 1978) 37-54, who illumines some literary battles but also touches on theological and practical wrangles.

49. Thompson, "History," 2.11.

50. The Thompson List, 38.5, 8.

51. Ibid., 18; the Thompson List, 38.6, 20, 25. For Methodists and Baptists at Barton in the Beans see Adam Taylor, *The History of the English General Baptists* (1818) vol. 2.

and declined greatly, and the methodists increased in proportion."[52] This pattern was often repeated. Dissenters of the three denominations were converted to Methodism at Sandwich (Dorsetshire), Martock (Somersetshire), Kingston (Surrey), Morley (Yorkshire), and numerous other places.[53] The same drift into Methodism was discerned at Shrewsbury, Shropshire, and a bewildered observer commented, "how long this will continue or how it will affect the Dissenting Societies is uncertain."[54]

Besides these outright gains and discouraging losses, the Dissenters occasionally mixed with the Methodists. In the 1740s the Methodists threatened to split the Dissenting congregation at Ludlow, Shropshire, by encouraging the people against their pastor, but the threat came to nothing. Then, in the 1770s when the church seemed "sunk past recovery," it was revived by Lady Huntingdon's students who came there to preach. In 1776 the attendance was stabilized and still comprised principally of Baptists and paedobaptists, but at this date Methodists were officiating.[55] Numerous other instances of intercommunion could be cited.[56]

Methodists were, of course, rapidly displacing old Dissent, and by the early years of the nineteenth century they would far outnumber them. This displacement is graphically seen wherever the Methodists took over deserted Dissenting meeting houses.[57] The minutes of the Wesleyan Conference held in August 1773 listed 27,726 "societies" in England and eighty-seven "preachers."[58] In the vast majority of cases, the distinction between old Dissent and the Methodists was maintained, at least as late as the 1780s. While Josiah Thompson was disturbed by Methodist inroads among the Baptists, he was not the only one who insisted on maintaining denominational integrity.[59] His correspondent, Thomas Harmer, concurred by saying of the believers at Denton, "I cannot but rank them rather among the Methodists than our assemblies."[60] In the eighteenth century the Methodists were still conformists, and Presbyterians, Congregationalists, and Baptists were normally not willing to claim them as their own.

NONCONFORMITY AND THE ESTABLISHED CHURCH

Despite the legal handicaps the Dissenters bore, after 1689 they often cooperated with the Anglicans. Following the repeal of the Occasional Conformity

52. Thompson, "History," 4.321. The same thing was happening in Derbyshire. The Thompson List, 38.6, 11.

53. Thompson, "History," 2.71; 4.179, 294; the Thompson List, 38.6, 41.

54. Thompson, "History," 4.158.

55. Ibid., 163.

56. As at Lincoln, Lincolnshire; Kibworth, Leicestershire; and Carffwood, Devonshire. See Ibid., 3.118; the Thompson List, 38.6, 20; "A View of English Nonconformity in 1773," 213.

57. This occurred at Nantwich, Cheshire; Denton, Norfolk; Bilson, Staffordshire; Minehead, Somersetshire; and many other places as well. The Thompson List, 38.5, 5; the Thompson List, 38.6, 25, 36; Thompson, "History," 4.176.

58. Appended to the Thompson List and found in "A View of English Nonconformity in 1773," 385.

59. Thompson repeatedly insists on the distinctiveness of the old denominations. An old Dissenting meeting, reopened by Methodists at Harleston, Norfolk, was not to be included among the Dissenting congregations. Thompson, "History," 4.10. See also ibid., 174, 228; and the Thompson List, 38.5, 19.

60. Quoted in the Thompson List, 38.6, 5.

and Schism acts in 1719, relations between them improved even further. In the eighteenth century there was sometimes very little distinction made between Anglicans and Dissenters. In certain circumstances the Dissenters had attained a degree of respectability that endeared them to the establishment. Interrelations between Anglicans and Dissenters were carried on at various levels, ranging from the most informal contacts to elaborate schemes of comprehension.

One of the commonest points of contact between the confessions was the practice called occasional conformity, that is, attendance at an Anglican church to receive the sacrament according to the usage of the Book of Common Prayer. Occasional conformity is usually discussed in the context of qualification for public office under the Test and Corporation acts. Many Nonconformists considered this practice hypocritical and pronounced judgment on anyone who would compromise his conscience for worldly advancement. In Daniel Defoe's memorable phrase, it was like "playing bo-peep with God Almighty." The concept, however, should be lifted out of the context of qualification for office and broadened to include communion with Anglicans at levels other than the sacrament. When the concept is broadened, it will be seen that occasional conformity was sometimes practiced with pure religious motivation. Such a view had been advocated for years by Richard Baxter, and in the early eighteenth century Thomas Tenison supported the practice. In 1703 when debate raged in both Houses of Parliament over the issue of occasional conformity, the famed low church bishop, Gilbert Burnet, made an eloquent plea against harsh legislation, since many Dissenters, he claimed, retired to the church not out of selfish interest, but as an act of religious devotion.[61] Few will argue today that this purer form of occasional conformity was a frequent occurrence, but it did happen, and it does provide a new and distinct perspective on the political practice.

From the first, the lines the law had drawn between Anglican and Dissenter were not satisfactory for some. In Bristol a group of Dissenters separated from the Church of England in 1640, but the church book records that "they continued their attendance at sermon (but not the prayers) at the parish church in the morning of every Lord's Day." The manuscript does not indicate how long this practice continued, and shortly after 1640 the church was undoubtedly no longer the "parish church." In the same city over a century later, a certain Mr. Holland said that he was "a member of Mr. Thomas['s] Church in Bristol and only a hearer in the chapel."[62] This was, of course, an instance of complete conformity, and to many Dissenters such behavior was nothing short of apostasy. Henry Ward, minister of the Congregational church of Woodbridge, Suffolk, from 1709 to 1734, was a "very firm and noble pillar" of the Dissenting interest there, but at the same time "he always retained an esteem of respect for such of his conforming brethren as were men of virtue and goodness."[63] In the same county the pastor of Framlingham Presbyterian Church, Richard Charley, left the ministry because of old age, increasing blindness, and the doctrinal contentions in his church. In the 1730s "he joined in lay-communion with the Church of England, to which he had been

---

61. G. V. Bennett, "Conflict in the Church," in Geoffrey Holmes, ed., *Britain after the Glorious Revolution, 1689–1714* (London: Macmillan, 1969) 168.

62. Thompson, "History," 2.144; the Thompson List, 38.6, 5.

63. Thompson, "History," 4.76.

inclin[e]d many years, and which inclination was not lessen[e]d by the preceding behavior of some of the warmer people of the congregation he had served. In this connection he finished his days; but retained very friendly regards to the Dissenting ministers about him, who frequently visited him to the last."[64] These two examples depict a facet of the Dissenters' life that is not often remembered in denominational histories.

William Kingsbury, pastor of the Above Bar Congregational Chapel, Southampton, carried on a close friendship over a period of years with many Anglican clergymen. Walter Taylor, a wealthy deacon in Kingsbury's chapel, followed the example set by his pastor and went a step further. In a neighboring village adjacent to his own private property, Taylor supported a curate of the established church, and the chapel historian assures us that although he "entertained favourable views of that section of religion," he remained a Dissenter.[65] Mr. Millar, vicar of Harlow, Essex, was esteemed a "very mild, benevolent man" and was observed often walking "arm in arm" with the local Dissenting minister."[66]

The American Revolution did stir up latent antagonisms. Thomas Davis, pastor of the Reading Baptist Chapel, was apparently under some pressure from the local Anglican clergy during the Revolution. Davis wrote in 1776: "The world rages, the devil roars, and the doctor of our parish said he would silence me if he went to the King in person, and the Bishop of London is his friend. I said they might tell him, if he had a mind to silence me he must take out my tongue." Historians of the revolutionary period have naturally focused attention on such conflict, but this tells only half of the story. The Congregationalist minister at Reading, Thomas Noon, was said to be held in great esteem by the clergy of the Church of England at Reading, and we have noted above the ongoing evening fellowship between the Baptist and Congregational chapels.[67]

More evidence for intercommunion is found earlier in the century in Thomas Secker's 1758 visitation return for the diocese of Canterbury. Edward Carpenter located frequent references in this document to Dissenters and Methodists coming to church "regularly," though with the former it was occasionally qualified with the notation "except on Sacrament Sunday." Theodore Delafaye, rector in the parish of St. Mildred, Canterbury, wrote "there are 3 or 4 presbyterian families but they scruple not to attend the church service, whenever their own is intermitted," and in another parish where thirteen "anabaptist" families resided, the incumbent observed that they attended the church once a month.[68]

Perhaps more remarkable are several instances of Dissenting pastors ministering in Anglican churches. Kirkstead Abbey in Linconshire was described as "a sort

---

64. Ibid., 235.

65. S. Stainer, *History of the Above Bar Congregational Church, Southampton, from 1662 to 1908* (Southampton: The Southampton Times Co., 1909) 88-89.

66. Cited in Carpenter, "Toleration and Establishment: 2," 305.

67. Wiliam Legg, *Historical Memorials of Broad Street Chapel, Reading* (London: Hamilton, Adams & Co., 1851) 50.

68. Carpenter, "Toleration and Establishment: 2, Studies in a Relationship," 307. For other instances of Dissenters attending church in the morning and the chapel at night, see Obelkevich, *Religion and Rural Society*.

of privileg[e]d place, where Dissenting ministers were allow[e]d to preach, and where some particular liberties were indulg[e]d them."[69] In the county of Suffolk there were at least three Anglican churches where the impropriators—that is, lay patrons of livings—were men of "very moderate principles." In Walsham-in-the-Willows, Barkin, and Badwell-Ash the impropriators allowed Dissenting ministers to preach; and it appears that at Walsham the minister, while technically ejected, stayed on until his death. In 1699 Richard Charley, the "eminent" Presbyterian minister noted above, came to Walsham and preached the funeral sermon of a Mr. Salkeld, an ejected minister who had been preaching in the parish church with the consent of the impropriator, apparently since 1662. Mr. Bury of Bury preached the funeral sermon of Mr. Fairfax in Barkin Church. Thompson, the chronicler, adds that "one however if not both these gentlemen thought it requisite to write a respectful apologetical letter to Bishop Moore who was then Bishop of the diocese on account of the liberty that had been taken, who pass[e]d over the affair in silence." The same thing probably occurred at Badwell-Ash, and Thompson concludes, "this kind of liberty was frequently taken by the ejected ministers whether by their immediate successors, I do not know. It however is not a singular instance of the kind."[70] These illustrations prove that the relationships between the Dissenters and Anglicans could be, and often were, congenial, at least in the period of the Restoration.

Despite such displays of intercommunion, and despite the many instances of occasional and complete conformity, there was a widespread suspicion of the Anglican church among the Dissenters. In locations where there was both a church and a chapel, the most common pattern was competition, not communion. When Dissenters gained a few converts from the Anglican church, they were delighted;[71] and when they lost a believer to the establishment, they immediately laid it up to Anglican intrigue or artifice.[72] Instances of Anglican dislike of Dissent can also be found, so hostile sentiment cut both ways.[73]

Cases of Dissenters' complete conformity to the church, especially when this occurred among ministers, were sometimes used to point a moral. Just as ejection was a badge of honor, conformity was considered betrayal, or even apostasy. In many cases the fate of a conforming minister was used to bring home the lesson that fidelity to the cause was the more excellent way. One minister's conformity was brought about through the persuasions "of a proud wife," and another's conformity was made to appear to contribute to his senility. One minis-

69. Thompson, "History," 4.23.

70. Ibid., 257.

71. As at Artlingborough, Northamptonshire, and Hinchley, Leicestershire. The Thompson List, 38.6, 26, 20. Mr. Medcalf, Thompson's correspondent, attributes the Dissenters' gain at Hinchley to the "ignorance" and the "idleness" of the Anglican clergy. The same thing is recorded in Yorkshire and Sutton Colfield, Warwickshire. The Thompson List, 38.5, 42; the Thompson List, 38.6, 37.

72. The cause of the weakness of the Dissenting congregation at Shepton Mallet, Somersetshire, is easy to find: "inter- marriages with bigotted Church people have had the most fatal effect of all." Thompson, "History," 4.185. There is another story of competition between Anglican and Dissenter at Wallingham, Cambridge. Ibid., 1.177.

73. Ibid., 1.130.

ter who conformed was granted an Anglican living and became as a result, "allmost a beggar." It was said that William Nokes, having been turned down as pastor of a Congregational church, "afterwards conform[e]d, became a clergyman and being taken ill suddenly in the Street expir[e]d on the steps of St. Andrews Holburn [sic] London." A certain Mr. Jokes failed to win the affection of his people, then conformed, but was frustrated in his attempts to win preferment in the church.[74] In no case is the sorry fate of these conformists explicitly called the judgment of God, but the implication is present. In the area of religious intercommunion the lines between Anglican and Dissenter were fairly rigidly drawn and carefully preserved. Their cooperation in the political sphere, however, considerably altered this picture.

An illustration of how moderate some churchmen were and how they defined themselves with respect to Dissent is found in the parson at Dorking, Surrey. Josiah Thompson, writing in 1784, noted that "it is remarkable that the Revd Mr. John Brian, a clergyman of the Church of England, who resided for some considerable time in Dorking, by his last will bequeathed an annuity of £20 p. annum to the Dissenting minister of this congregation for ever. The unfavorable disposition of the court towards the Dissenters in the latter end of the reign of Queen Anne and the conviction he had that they deserved a much better treatment were the declared motives for his making such a generous bequest to a denomination of Christians to which he did not himself belong."[75] This incident also illustrates the persistence of the alliance between Dissenters and low church Anglicans begun in the 1670s. With clergymen like Brian, it is little wonder that Dissenters and Anglicans together were sometimes referred to as "the low church."

One of the most noteworthy examples of confessional fraternity in eighteenth-century England occurred in Cambridge. Early in the 1760s a young Baptist preacher, Robert Robinson, began his ministry in the local chapel. Robinson would in time become one of the most well-known Baptist ministers in England and is justly famous for his hymns, including "Come Thou Fount of Every Blessing." Upon arrival at Cambridge, Robinson found that the church covenant was very strict: the formula forbade any contact with the Church of England. The Baptists, in fact, were required "formally to abjure the established church."[76] Robinson himself had received his training in the Anglican church and he thus refused to become their pastor unless the people agreed to forego such a strict discipline. Happily, the congregation agreed to his stipulation, and the results, as told by Robinson, were gratifying. Many of the university students were won over to the Dissenters, and, said Robinson, "blessed be God, Church men are seen at Meeting, Dissenters at

74. Ibid., 2.9, 5, 11.

75. Thompson, "History," 4.287. He also bequeathed £20 per annum to the Dissenting congregation at Guilford. Under Guilford, Thompson adds that Brian was a "Serious Clergyman" and that his estate in land was worth £40 per annum and was to be used for the Dissenting interest in the county, "which continues to be regularly pas[se]d to the present time." Ibid., 290n.a. The annuity continued at least through 1774.

76. Robinson relates the story in the sermon he preached on 3 January 1773 entitled "A Becoming Behavior in Religious Assemblies," written out in full in Thompson, "History," 1.196-99.

Church, and people begin to act as if they thought the religion of Christians a religion of love."[77]

Such occurrences were rare: the law on the Baptist church book was the rule, and Robinson's brilliant and gracious leadership the exception. Still, the story depicts a kind of sincere occasional conformity that was more common than is often realized. More importantly, Robinson's concern for the unity of the Spirit was expressed in 1773, long before he began to drift into Unitarianism. As with most of the examples cited in this study, his appeal for practical cooperation among Christians of different denominations was based on the conviction that Christ taught his disciples to love one another, not on a latitudinarian acceptance of others' opinions bordering on indifference or heresy. At the local level of parish and chapel life, and among the common people of England, many instances of cooperation and intercommunion in the eighteenth century emerged from the belief that the religion of Christians was a religion of love.

***

For more than twenty-five years of graduate level teaching, Geoffrey W. Bromiley encouraged his students to understand and value the treasures of their own denominational heritage, even though in most cases they belonged to denominations that dissented from the Anglican tradition. When the subject of church history turned to the Anglican reformers, Professor Bromiley taught with even more than his usual authority, but when he moved on to the Presbyterians, the Quakers, and the Methodists, students found in his lectures the same evenhanded respect for their own traditions that they had found in his treatment of Anglicanism. To his students, Dr. Bromiley exemplified broad churchmanship at its finest while he always warned against the folly of theological reductionism. He helped us see that the true unity of the church cannot be served by compromising one's theological convictions, and that neither is the unity of the Spirit to be equated with the kind of bland uniformity that veers away from the traditions of the church, even for the best of causes. In his ministry of teaching, in his publications, and in his pastoring, Professor Bromiley has inspired a generation of younger scholars to guard the unity of Spirit while at the same time he has shown us the importance of serving the church of Jesus Christ as the pillar and bulwark of the truth.

77. Ibid., 198.

The Role of Theology in Ecumenical Activity

J. K. S. Reid

We need today to be clearer about the role of theology in ecumenical activity. Let me put it summarily: we cannot have too much theology, but we can and do have too much theological impedimenta. I hazard a literary illustration. In Sir Walter Scott's *Guy Mannering,* Colonel Mannering hears with astonishment a sermon in Greyfriars Church, Edinburgh (the time is the mid-18th century): he "had seldom heard so much learning, metaphysical acuteness and energy of argument brought into the service of Christianity." His companion told him that the preacher and his colleague in office led different parties in the church without losing regard and respect for each other. The Colonel asked: "And what do you think of their points of difference?" and received the answer: "Why, I hope a plain man may go to heaven without thinking about them at all." Without in the least condoning intellectual indolence, who would wish to contest the truth of the reply? But to accept it argues the need for some distinction within theological activity, a little more sophisticated than that of Mannering's interlocutor.

FIDES EXPLICITA AND IMPLICITA

The illustration had to do with soteriological matters, and it divided what was requisite to secure salvation from what was not. Roman Catholic theology maps out this area neatly. I venture to put it in my own way—dogma is the part of theology that achieves canonization and is articulated in definitions. This is then proposed by the church or magisterium as a divinely revealed object of faith and as necessary for salvation. *Fides explicita* is the acceptance by the individual believer of as much as he can reasonably be expected to understand and hold, the minimum being usually regarded as scripturally laid down in the two truths of Heb 11:6—that God exists and that he rewards those who search for him. *Fides implicita* is the extension of the same acceptive disposition to all that God has revealed and the church proposes. This may be enjoined in a more or less authoritative manner: either as necessary submission to the authority of God as declared by the church or as acceptance by an individual member of the body of Christ of what that koinonia as a whole believes.

For my part I think the churches of the Reformation may well learn a lesson from this. We cannot emphasize too often that the individual believer is a *member* of the believing body of Christ—a person in his or her own right certainly, but one who *belongs* to the people of God.[1] The body has indeed no right to exact belief

---

1. Paul makes versatile use of the member-body theme in 1 Cor 12 (v. 20 "many members, one body", v. 27 "the body of Christ, particular members") to show variety of function and to prohibit enmity. Underlying all he says is the double-sided basic truth: the Christian koinonia

in an authoritarian manner (submission), but only to commend it (acceptance). But on their side individuals must exercise restraint in pressing upon the koinonia of which they are member quite idiosyncratic views (even if to them they are matters of conscience) to the point of distressing or offending or even of disrupting it.[2] On the other hand Protestant churches can hardly accept the distinction as so defined. In any case there are trends within the Roman Church that evidently move against it. John Paul II calls Vatican II "the Council of the laity," and notes that the distinction at point, *ecclesia docens—ecclesia discens,* makes an appearance.[3] J. M. Todd speaks of the laity since Vatican II being integrated into the whole *laos;*[4] and again John Paul in Great Britain more than once emphasized "bishop, priest, or laity" as on a certain equality. If the mood here coming to expression should prevail, it may be that the neat but causistical distinction between *fides explicita* and *fides implicita* is unlikely to prove satisfactory indefinitely.

ORDINARY AND OFFICIAL FAITH

If some distinction within theology is necessary for ecumenical purposes, Karl Rahner should be heard. He says: "the faith of the practising Christian is much the same in all churches; and it is this living faith, not the agreed speculative conclusions of the theological consciousness, that must be the seed from which the fulness of unity can flow."[5] The distinction made is between ordinary working faith and the products of the self-conscious and expert deliberation upon Christianity conducted by theologians. "Ordinary working Christian faith" is "much the same"; it is not affected by denominational separation; and from this, ecumenical advance must proceed. The implication is that theological "speculation" introduces a differentiation not conducive to ecumenical advance.

J. M. Tillard says much the same thing when he argues "that the official faith of any church is different from its actual faith (what even committed members actually believe); that the latter is more alike in different churches; and that it has an important part to play in the movement towards Christian unity".[6] Here the distinction is between "actual faith" and "official faith," but the point being made is the same: the ordinary believing members of one church, with their limited ability to articulate what they believe and to understand fully what theology says, can join hands in fellowship with the ordinary believing members of other churches. But theology as it discharges its task of explicating and defending the faith disrupts that fellowship: what ordinary belief joins together theology puts asunder. Theology

---

is characterized by a diversity, which is totally resistant to division. Cardinal Ratzinger finds the source of Protestant individualism in the "sola scriptura principle," from which he infers that "faith arises from one's individual perceptions." *The Ratzinger Report* (Leominster: Fowler Wright, 1985) 157.

2. Irenaeus's "no reform can compare with the harm of schism" is at least worthy of consideration.

3. Karol Wojtyla, *Sources of Renewal* (London: Collins, 1980) 339.

4. In a recent issue of *The Tablet.*

5. Karl Rahner, *Theological Investigations* (tr. Margaret Kohl; London: Darton, Longman & Todd, 1981) 17, chap. 16.

6. J. M. Tillard, *The Month* (August 1981) 285.

must ask itself: if there really is a oneness at the level of ordinary believers that spans the denominations, how does it come about that denominational barriers arise? Must we draw the conclusion that the gospel unites while theology divides? Or, rather, how can this frightening conclusion be avoided?

Tillard restates the distinction and then draws certain ecumenical consequences. Here are his words: "There are two 'moments' in the Yes of faith. There is the global Yes given in baptism: through the sacrament this incorporates a man into Christ. There is (further) the Yes given to dogmas, doctrines, and theological traditions that are the explication of the first Yes." Here again is the distinction between ordinary and official faith. On the one hand, the baptismal Yes is no more than trust in; on the other, the theological Yes is assent to. But gradations span the gap. In infant baptism I should not be averse to crediting the child with an incipient faith included in an unquestioning trust he reposes in his mother, and so too in the universe and God. After all, Calvin could say: Who can say that the infant has no faith? Roman thinking holds that the virtue of faith is already present in the infant. But of course there is growth in the apprehension of that in which trust is placed. It acquires an increasingly cognitive character; and this, when articulated, is expressed as acknowledgment of doctrines to which assent is accorded. Actual faith and official faith is distinguished not in essence but in degree: there is faith only inchoately articulated, and there is official faith fully, or in various stages of fullness, explicated.

Tillard turns this consideration to a double ecumenical use. "The ecumenical problem consists in knowing *id quod requiritur et sufficit,* in order that the second Yes does not involve betrayal of the intention or the essential content of the first." It is to be noted that some degree of betrayal has already taken place. The churches have reached a remakable degree of unanimity concerning baptism: it is agreed that "the Yes of baptism incorporates a man into Christ." One practical outcome of this agreement is the Common Baptismal Certificate used in some countries by both Roman and Protestant churches. Each church thereby acknowledges that what the other church does in baptism is essentially the same as what it does, despite any difference in practice or even theological expression. Moreover, this mutual acknowledgment is accorded to a rite already to some extent compromised by denominational influence: the administration of the rite is not unified but already denominationally splintered. It is effected not by the one church of Jesus Christ, but by different and separate denominational churches of Jesus Christ which between them share out all the membership of the one church without remainder.[7] You become a member of *the church* by a baptism administered denominationally—a baptism that simultaneously and inescapably makes you a member of a denominational part of that church. Further, this denominational pattern imprinted on baptism when administered, far from diminishing at other levels, unhappily increases. Such oneness as is achieved in baptism is quite lost by the time the other dominical sacrament is reached. When the faithful come to the Lord's Supper they are streamed off to communicate at separate tables. What at baptism is required and sufficient to constitute basic oneness comes to be augmented, with dis-

7. Baptism is like jam: you cannot have jam in general. If you want jam you must take it in a particular kind. You do not spread a Platonic idea on your bread, but you apply strawberry or blackcurrant or some other kind of jam.

astrously divisive consequences. The anxious question arises: Is all such augmentation required? Does it exceed the sufficient?

The principle of the required and the sufficient has a second application. "One should not impose on another Church as condition for entry into a communion with the Catholic Church anything beyond this *id quod requiritur et sufficit.*" Mutatis mutandis this applies to all ecumenical conversation. (Tillard himself expressly repudiates "ecumenism of the return.") The proposal constitutes a severe but controlled reductionism. Theology is practiced largely in denominational compartments, traditionally sealed off from one another, but now happily increasingly leaking into one another. From what theology on this basic pattern proposes, a quintessence has to be distilled whose content is required or indispensable and whose extent is sufficient or irreducible. That quintessence constitutes the theological basis on which churches may recover their unity. Here a simple diagram may help. Imagine two eccentric circles so positioned that they partly overlap. In the overlap will be contained what is required and sufficient—that on which the churches are agreed. But whatever is in that overlap will not constitute all that any one church believes or practices. In the sections not overlapping the churches will be entitled, without prejudice to the oneness they enjoy, to retain beliefs and practices, and certainly interpretations, that are proper in themselves alone and are not mandatory for others. The circles need not overlap more than is necessary, but they must sufficiently overlap to justify and exhibit the churches' oneness.[8]

It would be gratifying and certainly agreeably simple if the required and sufficient were found to be self-authenticating. But this of course is not the case. When we ask, Required by what? Sufficient for what? no self-evident and immediately agreed criteria emerge. What one church regards as required may seem to another quite dispensable; the agreement deemed sufficient by one church may seem quite inadequate to another. There are no ready-made answers to the questions of what should go into the overlap and what may be left outside.

This is not surprising. During the four centuries of separation the churches have each gone their own way and so of course have come to think and to do things differently. The complexity is daunting, but not quite overwhelming. For ecumenical purposes, we do not have to examine the entire range of theological material from canonized dogma to individual theological speculation. Rather we have to focus attention on the points where churches chiefly differ. The ecumenical movement obliges us to scrutinize these differences with the object of sorting them out. Some are, or presently seem to be, divisive, causing division and justifying the perpetuation of division. On the other hand, some are not so divisive. Of the first class

---

8. The reformers discerned this truth when drawing up the confessions that formed so salient a feature of their theological activity. When at their most percipient, they saw the confession as including as one element all the content of the ecumenical creeds, and indeed as flowing from them. A second element comprised what the Reformation had enabled them to discover or recover concerning Christian truth; and this they felt obliged to testify, declare, and commend to other churches. There was also a third aspect: they gave expression to certain other elements that belonged to individual confessing churches, a patrimony not necessarily shared even by all Reformation churches, e.g., by bishops in Swedish Lutheranism.

we must ask: Can they be resolved? Of the second we must declare: These are permissible variants, capable of accommodation within a united church in which they would constitute licit diversities.

CONCEPTUAL TOOLS

In the course of recent ecumenical exchanges, certain concepts have emerged as tools for conducting such a scrutiny of the differences lying between the churches. I will mention four here.

(1) I turn first to the celebrated distinction made by John XXIII. In the Opening Allocution to Vatican II, on 11 October 1962, he declared: "the substance of ancient doctrine of the deposit of faith is one thing, and the way in which it is presented is another. For the truths preserved in our sacred doctrine can retain the same substance and meaning under different forms of expression."[9] Of course the principle is not a novelty;[10] but it was given here express formulation by authority in quite special circumstances; and its implications are being all the time realized in the thought of all churches.

One can hardly quarrel with a principle that has clear exemplification in Scripture itself. Within the canon, when Paul takes over the transmission of the gospel, the term *messiah* is phased out in favor of *Lord* (*Son of God* appears only 15 times, *kyrios* 184 times); yet no one will suppose that a different gospel is being preached. Again the postapostolic age did not expressly formulate the principle, but it was nonetheless guided by it, as Greek categories and modes of thought were employed to transmit the gospel—categories and modes which were often deliberately adapted to do the job.[11] Around every corner lurked the danger of *traduttore traditore*—the translator is traitor—but the church proceeded on its way undeterred. The desideratum is not exactness of repetition but rather equivalence of transmission. The principle accords a proper and today widely recognized importance to the historical factor in all thinking: substance is invested with form, and that form cannot be other than time-conditioned. That "the Bible is phrased in the changeable conceptions of a given epoch" can today be said without any fear of the validity and authority of the Bible being destroyed or impaired.[12] As for doctrine, "the Roman Catholic Church has admitted that its past

9. Abbott, *The Documents of Vatican II* (London: G. Chapman, 1966) 715.

10. Leo the Great spoke of "the need to proclaim the same faith, however many theologies be involved."

11. Examples can be found within the Gospels themselves: "The very existence of diverse traditions of the words of Jesus reflected in the four Gospels testifies to the fact that his followers understood his words to be so time-conditioned and so locale-conditioned as to require adaptation as they were transmitted to new times and places." This is formally acknowledged by the Roman Church in Instruction of the Roman Pontifical Commission on "The Historical Truth of the Gospels"; see R. E. Brown, *The Critical Meaning of the Bible* (London: Cassell, 1982) 12f. Similar examples may be found within the Pauline corpus itself: "deutero-Pauline works (the Pastorals, Ephesians, perhaps Colossians and II Thessalonians) are joined canonically to the indisputably genuine Pauline writings," so that "we have a larger view of how the Pauline theology develops and was adapted," ibid., 31. In the case of the OT, the best known case is Deut 5:21, which appreciated more highly the position of wives than did the earlier Ex 20:17.

12. Ibid.

magisterial statements have been enunciated in 'the changeable conceptions of a given epoch.'"[13] And Rahner declares "I would undertake to prove that even the apostolic confession of faith is conditioned [mitbedingt] by a particular theology of a particular time."[14]

John XXIII enunciated the principle to facilitate the detection through the ages of doctrinal identity under changing forms: the *homoousios* is neither biblical nor apostolic, but it does convey a truth that is both biblical and apostolic. Similarly, what was affirmed in terms of substance in the fourth century is in the twentieth century better conveyed in personal terms. Just as important, however, is the application of the principle to ecumenical affairs: it prompts the urgent and unavoidable question whether there is doctrinal identity behind the different forms in which the different churches have invested the doctrinal substance. Different ecclesiastical traditions may be carrying identical doctrines whose identical character is masked by the different forms accorded to them. The whole field of difference between churches is opened up for discovery and reassessment. Thus the churches are warned to be on guard against "identifying the objective content of the faith with its expression, its organisation, its perception, with this or that theology, this or that piety, this or that religious sensibility; this would be to sin against catholicity and so against unity." And it is further observed that "another temptation is to identify the truth of faith on which agreement is necessary with one or more (of the) formulations it has been given in the course of history."[15]

13. Ibid.

14. Rahner, *The Month* (July 1974). Additional documentation, Vatican II, papal, and unofficial, can readily be supplied.

(a) The phrase "the changeable conceptions of a given epoch" is itself from the Sacred Congregation's Mysterium Ecclesiae 1973.

(b) Vatican II Uni Red 4 declares: "while preserving unity in essentials, let all members of the Church, according to the office entrusted to each, preserve proper freedom . . . even in the elaboration of revealed truth" (Abbot, *The Documents of Vatican II*, 349).

(c) Paul VI, asserting that visible union requires "identity of faith and participation in the same sacrament and . . . organic harmony of a single ecclesiastical control," yet added that "this allows for a great variety of verbal expressions." Secretariat for Promoting Christian Unity: Information Service (hereafter SPCU Info Serv) no. 36.11.

(d) Later papal evidence is provided by John Paul II in words less well-known but even more pragmatic. Recognizing that the circumstances of discord and dispute impart their own flavor to theological thought, he accordingly recommended that we "go behind the habit of thought and expression born and nourished in enmity and controversy, to scrutinise together the great treasure, to clothe it in the language at once traditional and expressive of an age which no longer glories in strife, but seeks to come together in listening to the quiet voice of the Spirit." *The Month* (August 1982) 275.

(e) So too at greater length the Mysterium Ecclesiae of the Secretariat for the Doctrine of Faith (later Congregation) 1973: "The dogmatic formulas of the magisterium have been suitable from the beginning to express revealed truth, and remaining unchanged they communicated that truth to those who interpreted them properly. But it does not at all follow that every one of them has or will always have this aptitude to the same degree. . . . As occasion arises, new expositions or enunciations may be added to preserve or clarify their original sense. Moreover it has happened that even in the habitual usage of the Church certain of these formulas have given way to new modes of expression which, proposed and approved by the magisterium, have presented the same meaning more clearly and fully" (SPCU Info Serv 47.115).

15. Cardinal President, SPCU Info Serv no. 47.115.

That churches do not easily resist the temptation was strikingly illustrated by certain responses evoked by the *Final Report* of the Anglican-Roman Catholic International Commission (ARCIC). An official response, *Observations,* came from the Sacred Congregation for the Doctrine of Faith. In responding at all the Congregation was making history by taking such notice of a document drawn up jointly by Romans and non-Romans. Among other responses, three of particular interest emanated from the conservative-evangelical wing of the Anglican church—those of James Atkinson, R. T. Beckwith, and John Stott. The truly remarkable thing was the pattern observable in all four responses. While welcoming coolly the *Final Report,* the Sacred Congregation intimated its objections by retreating to the archives and quoting from Trent and Vatican I,[16] while the three Anglicans, reaching back to the armories of the Reformation, complained that the *Final Report* failed to do justice to the Reformation principles of *sola scriptura* and *sola gratia.*

ARCIC is concerned with the substance of the faith. Is it to be discerned in recognizable identity under the different historical formulations current in the two churches? The Roman and Anglican responses I have cited (of course not all are of this kind) each demand, in complete contrast, that its formulation and its alone conveys the substance of the faith. And both take up their stance upon the embattled positions characteristic of a pre-ecumenical era. This can only lead to the perpetuation of the historical deadlock.

This deadlock of history is slowly passing away. The contentions concerning *sola scriptura* and *sola gratia* are being seen in a different light. Witnesses should be called and heard. J. Ratzinger says: "It is important to note that (in Dei Verbum 9) only Scripture is defined in terms of what *is:* it is stated that Scripture is the word of God consigned to writing. Tradition, however, is described only functionally, in terms of what it *does:* it hands on the word of God, but is not the word of God."[17] How far is this from what the reformers were saying?

As for the *sola gratia,* Lambeth spokesmen have often declared that between Rome and Canterbury "no disagreement remains over this doctrine." On the Roman side, Bishop B. C. Butler declares: "I do not think, in the light of modern scholarship and theology, that there is more than verbal disagreement (if that) between the heirs of the Reformation and the Catholic Church on the subject of justification by faith."[18] And K. Rahner even more expansively says: "the three solas of the Reformation have been enfranchised in the thought of the Roman Church."[19]

16. Specifically the Congregation complained of the treatment accorded to the propitiatory value of the eucharist (section B.I.1) and to the adoration of eucharistic elements (from Trent) (B.I.3); and similarly to the treatment accorded to the primacy of the Pope (B.III.2) and to the use made of indefectibility (Vatican I) (B.III.3).

17. J. Ratzinger, *Documents of Vatican II 3.194; Brown, The Critical Meaning,* 21n.48.

18. *London Times,* 10 June 1982.

19. If these centuries-old doctrinal barriers are collapsing, what remains to divide Rome from Geneva and Canterbury? Paul Avis in his important *Ecumenical Theology* (London: SPCK, 1986) sees "no insuperable doctrinal barriers between the Anglican and Roman Catholic Churches" (xii); but, though he advocates intercommunion, no "full union is even remotely attainable" (105). This is because profound differences remain concerning "approach to Christian truth" (34) and about the "methods, norms and sources of theology" (xii). The issue here is bluntly authoritarianism. Even here, I judge, there are signs of hope. The extraordinary Synod

(2) *Relativizing the differences.* Scrutiny of the differences does not go far before it is apparent that *differences differ*. In other words, differences vary in importance. The calibration of the variations is illuminating. John Paul II on an informal occasion declared: "the sense of continuity can preserve us from naive and presumptuous illusions that the generation to which we belong is the first to discover certain truths and to live certain experiences. The sense of the relative, which has nothing to do with scepticism, teaches us to discern what is essential. A certain number of difficulties in faith, of individual or collective crises, are due to relativising the absolute and absolutising the relative."[20]

It is not unreasonable to expect that something can be done to relativize the theological differences that estrange the churches. After all the essence of the gospel is that God accepts us unconditionally for Jesus Christ's sake. This might appear to have as an immediate corollary that all believers unconditionally accept each other. If this does not happen, some alien factor has intervened to distort the situation. But it remains true that the absolutely unconditional character of gospel acceptance must relativize whatever it is that so disturbs the situation as to displace acceptance with mutual alienation and rejection. How much this principle can do is sometimes exaggerated. It does not abolish the differences; it does no more than relativize them. That is, while the principle renders all differences in the last resort relative, it does not throw immediate light upon how we *can* relativize them. Relativization in this connection can only mean the demotion of differences from the position in which they impose separation upon the churches. Their demotion means their transference to the category of permissible diversities. (We will take up the matter of diversity later.) Note how Professor J. P. Mackey of Edinburgh proposes that the principle be used. Churches in conversation through appointed representatives are constantly submitting for judgment by the appropriate authorities agreed statements or consensual documents on matters hitherto thought to be divisive. When and if approval is accorded, there will still remain other matters and areas not covered by the agreements in which difference persists. It is here that a process of relativization can operate. Mackey declares that "much rapprochement between various . . . theologies has already been achieved. To insist on waiting for more, rather than relativize the remaining differences, would be a betrayal of Jesus' own great sacrament of unity, pardon, peace and generosity."[21]

(3) *Hierarchy of truths.* That differences vary in importance is a principle derivable from the constitution of many churches. The Church of Scotland is representative of many Presbyterian churches that owe allegiance to the Westminster Confession of Faith. It declares itself to be guided and judged ultimately by Scrip-

---

of Roman Catholic bishops in November 1985 seems to have reached two decisions of outstanding importance: first, that the Roman Church must go forward from Vatican II; and second, that less attention should be paid to the *Romanitas* of the Church and more to its character as *communio ecclesiarum*. Is a celebrated idiom in process of being rephrased to read: *Roma locuta, causa aperta est*?

20. John Paul II, Taizé Vigil, Dec. 1980; SPCU Info Serv no. 45.14.

21. J. P. Mackey, in *New College Bulletin*, Oct. 1981.

ture. But it also recognizes a "subordinate standard" in the Westminster Confession; and those that bear office are obliged to subscribe to it. The difficulties of testifying adherence today to a document three centuries old and (in view of what has already been said) motivated and profoundly influenced by concepts belonging to the particular epoch from which it emanated are indeed formidable. Accordingly the church has spoken evasively of "recognising liberty of opinion on such points of doctrine as do not enter into the substance of the faith." Moreover, it affirms its right and ability to modify this subordinate standard (powers of which it has up till now not availed itself); but any modification is required to be "in agreement with the Word of God and the fundamental doctrines of the Christian faith contained in the said Confession, of which agreement the Church itself shall be sole judge."[22] The guidance offered here is probably hopelessly equivocal and obscure.[23] But this at least is clear: a distinction is being made between what belongs and what does not belong to "the substance of the faith" (which may or may not be identical with "the fundamental doctrines of the Christian faith").[24]

In fact the distinction in Presbyterianism has usually operated introspectively rather than externally—to define the mind of the church rather than to illumine relations between churches. But it has a ready application to ecumenical affairs: a church would feel obliged to include within the overlap of agreement those things deemed to be fundamental, and allow to be removed to the peripheral areas of the two circles the things not so understood.

Roman teaching on the "hierarchy of truths" has a similar intention. Vatican II's Unitatis Redintegratio makes its statement specifically within the ecumenical context when it declares that "Catholic theologians engaged in ecumenical dealings . . . , while standing fast by the teaching of the Church and searching together with separated brethren into the divine mysteries, should act with love for truth, with charity, and with humility . . . when comparing doctrines, they should remember that in Catholic teaching there exists an order or 'hierarchy' of truths, since they vary in their relationship [aliter: proximity] to the foundation of the Christian faith."[25]

Non-Romans are not quite clear what exactly is intended here. Unitatis Redintegratio itself understands the discriminatory principle that orders truths in the hierarchy to be their relation, that is, their varying proximity, to the "foundation

22. Ordinal 1931, Ordination of Ministers.

23. See my contribution in *The Westminster Confession of Faith for Today* (Edinburgh: St. Andrew, 1962).

24. The evasiveness rightly complained of appertains solely to the role of the Confession and the "fundamental doctrines . . . contained in" it. It is not a weakness but a strength that no attempt is made to list which products of "liberty of opinion" are valid and which invalid in advance of or in preparation for their appearance. Such anticipatory action would be proper for a philosophical system, but Christian doctrine—even Systematic Theology—is not systematic in a closed sense. Rather it is a living organism that responds to the changing circumstances and environment in which it operates. The world discharges a hermeneutical function in the development of doctrine; or, as Augustine said, the church expounds doctrine *non sponte sed coactu*—in response to a particular situation or a specific challenge, and under the living guidance of the Holy Spirit.

25. Unitatis Redintegratio 11.354.

of the Christian faith." But a different understanding is also offered: "a heirachy of doctrines is not only permissible but recommended, since whatever God has revealed is true and whatever we conclude from his revelation is also valid. But some truths are more in the limelight than others, are more immediately pertinent than others, and therefore more pastorally worthy of attention."[26] Discrimination on this view is pragmatic: situational relevance rather than inherent importance is the criterion.

As in the case of the Westminster Confession, the projected use seems to be internal rather than external, domestic rather than ecumenical. But Vatican II deliberately formulated the principle in an ecumenical context, and it surely ought to be ecumenically employed. Tillard recognizes and confirms this when he says: "the fact that a church is unable to acknowledge certain Catholic doctrines does not *necessarily* call into question the possibility of a communion of faith between that Church and the Catholic Church. There is need to ascertain what place such doctrines hold in the hierarchy of truths."[27] A particular case where application of the principle might have been expected occurred in connection with ARCIC's *Final Report*. The document formulated a view of papal primacy it could approve; it confessed to great difficulty with the Marian dogmas; and it had virtually nothing to say about eucharistic adoration of the elements. Clearly in the mind of ARCIC these three doctrines varied in importance—that is, they stood in different degrees of proximity to that "foundation of the Christian faith" of which Unitatis Redintegratio spoke. But the response of the Secretariat's *Observations* (A.2.ii) was abrupt: in these areas, "for example eucharistic adoration, papal primacy, the Marian dogmas, it would not be possible to appeal to the 'heirachy of truths.'" Such a rebuff, in an area that looked tailor-made for using the principle, is difficult to understand or accept.

(4) *Diversity*. The concept of diversity has already been mentioned: diversity of expression may convey identical substance; and again, in things of relative importance diversity in understanding and practice is permissible. The hierarchy of truths similarly seems designed to permit diversity of interpretation in the case of truths standing less proximate to the foundation of the faith. Diversity has thus proved useful in scrutinizing the differences between churches.

But diversity is not always employed so as to yield beneficial effects; and this is particularly true of "reconciled diversity."[28] The term is of Lutheran provenance and was used as a working principle in the deliberations that resulted in the Leuenberg Agreement. This provided the groundplan for the reconciliation of the Lutheran and Reformed traditions on many historically divisive issues.

Using the key of identity of substance and diversity of form, Lutheran and Reformed representatives reassessed the traditional eucharistic differences and,

26. J. A. Hardon, *The Catholic Catechism* (Dublin/London: G. Chapman, 1975) 21.

27. Tillard, *The Month* (August 1981).

28. "There is the typically Protestant concept of unity: starting from the real situation, this sees unity as reconciled diversity" (quoted by Bishop Torrella at Meeting of Delegates of National Ecumenical Commissions, Rome, Nov. 1979; see SPCU Info Serv no. 42.34). But we must deny the allegation that this is "typical."

in the light of modern theological developments, found that they no longer required separation. But the Agreement was conceived in meager terms. It made no provision for interfusion or blending of the traditions or for any period of real growing together. Hence, though it encouraged intercommunion where none existed before, it did little to change the eucharistic habits of the ordinary membership of the two churches. Earlier "unions" between Lutheran and Reformed in Germany (1817, and rather differently 1945 EKD) merged structure without emphasizing eucharistic communion. Leuenberg advocated a common altar, but it took no steps to implement agreement at the structural and congregational level. No perceptible change took place in the aspect the churches presented publicly. The Agreement created a genial climate in which, however, the churches remained frozen in the postures they had assumed four hundred years earlier, and the movement toward real unity was aborted.

The signatories at Leuenberg were not alone at fault in their manipulation of diversity. Oppressed by dread of uniformity, many church people are ready to applaud the notion of diversity, provided it is dispersed among the churches in such a way that any individual church need do nothing about it. Then the church as a whole may pride itself on accommodating diversity to the glory of God, while individual parts thank God that no change is demanded of them. In practice they cheerfully remain trapped luxuriously in the impregnable uniformity their limited tradition has imposed on them.

Yves Congar supplies striking confirmation of the rightness of this diagnosis. He says, "I think the prime theological problem raised by ecumenism today is that of specifying as far as possible what differences are compatible with the establishment of full communion. What diversity can authentic organic unity admit?"[29] For this reason he resolved to explore in a course of lectures "the problem of Reconciled Diversity"; the results of this exploration appeared in *Diversity and Communion* (1982; tr. 1984).[30]

Unity and diversity are not opposites; rather unity is complementary to diversity, and indeed accessory to it. Diversity, the Roman Church maintains, can be properly nourished, its frontiers fully occupied, and its resources fruitfully exploited precisely when alongside of it there is a focus and center of unity which itself is impregnable and unassailable. The *Final Report* of ARCIC admits this: there is "need for a focus and centre of authority in the visible church—pastoral in purpose and intention, but also unavoidably juridical. We should even want to say that the more diversity was cherished, the greater the need for such a centre and focus." There is a certain kind of unity that prohibits genuine diversity, that is, the uniformity of the sect: "those who are most concerned to defend rightful diversity may find that only within an accepted visible unity can diversity be developed and defended against sectarian tyrannies: those most concerned with a visible authority and unity may find that, without acceptance of diversity, unity shrivels

29. Yves Congar, *Voices of Unity* (Geneva: WCC, 1981) 31.

30. The Forum on Bilateral Dialogues, Oct. 1980 (SPCU Info Serv no. 47.137), provides further corroboration. The churches have "the task of deciding how far differences that remain can be regarded as legitimate diversity within the framework of a fundamental agreement." There is "need to be clear as to what is necessary for unity and what is needed to guard its richness."

into a narrow sectarianism and denies itself the power of growth and development." Such visible focus the Roman Church of course possesses. But the non-Roman churches need not be destitute of it. Reverting to the diagram of eccentric circles, if the overlap is filled with that which is required and sufficient, a rich diversity can be accommodated in the area of the circles not overlapping. Thus one may hope that the pervasive dread of uniformity can be exorcised and replaced by an acceptance of diversity-in-unity.

THEOLOGY AND EUCHARIST

"What differences are compatible with the establishment of full communion?" Congar's question deserves the fullest consideration. Doctrine and eucharistic fellowship have frequently appeared in close conjunction in recent ecumenical exchanges. The ecumenical objective has come to be defined as *one faith and one eucharistic fellowship* or, alternatively, *common understanding of the apostolic faith and full communion in the eucharist.* The eucharist requires a measure of agreement in the faith, and no more extensive or detailed measure is required than what suffices to make full communion possible.

The situation is that some of those who accept the dominical eucharistic invitation to "come" discriminate in the very same breath among the others who accept between those whom they will and those whom they will not sit beside. The free hospitality of the Host of the Table relativizes the differences that tear us apart, but I do not find that it resolves them. All it does is give us an invincible assurance that the differences can be overcome.

At the Reformation eucharistic differences were crucially important (though strictly speaking they were eucharist-related differences). The reformers deemed the teaching and practice of the church from which disruption took place to embody an erroneous understanding of what happens in the Lord's Supper. The interpretation of Christ's presence in terms of transubstantiation appeared to them to be injurious to the resurrected and exalted Christ and so detrimental to his *person;* and the sacrificial terminology and theology of the Mass seemed to imply the repetition of the sacrifice of Calvary, and so to contradict the sufficiency of Christ's *work.* Alas! united in their repudiation of such understandings, the reformers fell out among themselves as they attempted to formulate a proper definition of the first of these matters, how Christ may be said to be present at the eucharist.

The situation today is very different. Reassessment of precisely those differences has brought common understanding closer: they have not been completely bridged, but they have been significantly abridged. On the one hand, Leuenberg declared that the eucharistic issues that separated the churches at the Reformation are no longer divisive. On the other hand, Roman and non-Roman churches have moved convergently toward each another. In briefest summary, the churches of the Reformation have come to see that the eucharist can and must bear a sacrificial interpretation; on the Roman side there is now "almost universal repudiation that the mass either repeats or supplements the sacrifice of Christ."[31] As for divergent understanding of

31. E. L. Mascall, *Dictionary of Christian Theology,* 118.

Christ's eucharistic presence at the Reformation, representative Romans and Protestants together have today found it possible to dismiss the divisiveness of transubstantiation in a single six line footnote.[32]

In the more relaxed climate in which it is widely realized that such Reformation issues are no longer primed with the same disruptive force, discussion can with better hope attempt some kind of answer to Congar's question. Can the four tools of which we have spoken help us to feel our way toward defining the required and sufficient measure of agreement? The tools bluntly remind the denominations: (a) you may have your own quite proper formulation of a Christian truth—but do not imagine that it is exclusively right; (b) since grace is unconditional and one, our differences are sapped of their power and relativized; (c) some elements in formulated Christian faith are more important than others, and while consensus is necessary in some it is not necessary in all; and (d) as much diversity is permissible as is compatible with reconciliation and unity. Quintessentially the message conveyed is as follows: *since differences differ, consensus is not necessary about everything.* Can this rule of thumb be used in responding to Congar's challenge?

It is this mode of thinking that determines the pattern in which *Baptism, Eucharist and Ministry* presents the eucharist for consideration by the churches.[33]

(a) There are basic affirmations on which there is general agreement:

—that Christ is at the center of the eucharist (E 14);

—that the eucharist is about the presence of Christ (13);

—that Christ's presence is connected with the eucharistic elements under the rubric of "becomes" (15).

(b) *Baptism, Eucharist and Ministry* simply regards other issues (principally in the Commentary section) as issues not possessing disruptive force, and it proposes they be placed on the agenda for further discussion by the churches:

—the fact of the real presence being affirmed, how is it to be theologically stated?—that is, what is the nature of the presence? (C15);

—the fact of Christ being in some relation to the elements being accepted, how is the relation to be defined? (C13);

—the fact that the eucharist is in some sense sacrificial, how is Christ's sacrifice related to the communicants? (C8).

Baptism, Eucharist and Ministry deliberately leaves these issues unresolved, and it invites the churches to consider them in order to determine:

—how properly each variant interpretation presents the reality to which it refers;

—whether any interpretation has implications injurious to proper understanding of the person or the work of Christ;

—whether all interpretations are equally licit, or whether one or some are better than others.

Baptism, Eucharist and Ministry does not pretend that the ecumenical billet of business is settled. It rewrites it, distinguishing between the issues that have

---

32. ARCIC, "Final Report," 14n.2.

33. *Baptism, Eucharist and Ministry,* Faith and Order Paper no. 111 (Geneva: WCC, 1982).

been settled, or are on the way to settlement, *and* those relatively less important where diversity may properly flourish.[34]

THE ROLE OF THEOLOGY IN ECUMENICAL AFFAIRS

I do not suppose that acceptance of what has been said here will precipitate large scale redundancy in the ranks of theologians. Of course their activity must continue, always respecting Rahner's triple rubric: that all theological statements fall short of the reality to which they refer, that all statements are time-conditioned, and that all statements are accordingly in need of updating.

Theology has the right and duty to carry explication to the limits of the possible and the proper. But of what it says in the arcane regions, the question is rightly asked: does this lie beyond the "that which is required and sufficient"? Does it not really find its place in the nonoverlapping sectors of the eccentric circles, where the licit rather than the mandatory exercises rule? Should "ordinary faith" that has so much in common continue to submit to being dragooned into separate ecclesiastically shaped eucharistic compartments; and should it submit to being held incommunicado there by theological activities which of course "official faith" must neither arrest nor discourage? The engineers labor on the fortifications and outworks, and the combat troops send out patrols to gather intelligence to see how far advance is possible into the uncharted territory ahead. This activity makes it possible for the citizens of the city itself to be sitting beside one another in koinonia, to draw their rations from a common source, and to consume them together at the same table. So the theologians and the people of God.

The Christian church entered the second millennium relatively united—1054 was still in the future. Not long from now it will enter the third millennium. Perhaps by that time the churches will have taken significant and irreversible steps to overcome the consequences of a millennium of division, to harvest the riches imparted by the Holy Spirit to the several churches during the years of separation, and to realize and concretize in visible form the unity they have always spiritually enjoyed. If they have not done something along these lines, what will they offer as an excuse, and where will they look for forgiveness?

---

34. The principle looks simple enough, but its application in practice seems to be no easy matter. One presbytery of the Church of Scotland enthusiastically acclaimed the presentation in *Baptism, Eucharist and Ministry* of the relation between Word and Sacrament: it was the resolution of a major divisive Reformation issue. It then complained about the term *eucharist* and objected to the recommended frequency of celebration. The impression given was that it stood against the report for these two quite peripheral reasons. Similarly an individual declares that "all are agreed that [the eucharistic bread and wine] become something that they were not before" (in terms of E15). Then the individual takes objection to the use of the word *epiklesis*—why not an English alternative? But of course it is clear that agreement consolidated upon common understanding concerning the essence of the eucharist cannot possibly be disrupted, or even dented, by diversity in the use of terms designating a component of the celebration. Here again the agreement and the disagreement do not belong to the same league.

Theological Pluralism and the
Unity of the Spirit

Jacques Ellul

It is my intention to present here a reflection on a theme that is currently of major interest to French Protestantism but which is, perhaps, less crucial in the United States, where the problem poses itself in a somewhat different manner. Nonetheless, it is a theological question that the church has encountered continually during the course of its history and has resolved in different ways in each epoch.

I

It is typical of our times to view religion as always calling forth intolerance. Indeed, when one surveys the history of certain religions, one finds an intolerant attitude toward all other forms of religion or of understanding. When the church exercises power in this way, or when it shares in political power, it tends to avail itself of coercion to combat divergent theological views and to exclude them. It is sufficient to our purpose to call to mind the Inquisition (which was not quite as dreadful as frequently imagined) and all the manifold condemnations of heretics, while emphasizing that the Catholic church has not been alone in its intolerance—for such doctrinal rigidity can also be encountered in the Protestant churches. In addition, intolerance is characteristic not only of the churchly authorities but equally of entire populations, as witnessed by the pogroms against the Jews. And in Islam today it is clearly the crowds that are most unyielding in their intolerance. This attitude is not, however, spontaneous: the course of events is almost always the same. First there is a formulation of dogma, then the dogma is expounded theologically, this theology inspires the preachers, and these provide the faithful with the simple formulae of an absolute religious creed. The faithful will then tolerate no other view. When the authorities then take repressive measures against heretics or against those who practice another religion, it is done in agreement with popular sentiment. The irreligious, in turn, accuse *all* religions of creating intolerance, of inciting the populace in its antagonism to novelty, and of instigating a spirit of persecution.

Why does this intolerance arise? The explanation is very simple: each religion claims to have received or comprehended truth. Everyone conceives this truth to be both absolute and universal. First, it is absolute inasmuch as all that opposes it is error and untruth. Truth must combat untruth. Those who hold to this truth ought to serve it by eliminating those who do not accept it. Bear in mind that we already encounter a problem here, the confusion of spiritual conviction with power or authority. Yet such power is not spiritual but rather political or organizational, or perhaps intellectual in the sense of apologetics. The question, then, is whether the core of this revelation of truth is compatible with the exercise of this power. Here I see a distinction between Islam and Christianity. In the Koran there is a massive confusion of the Islamic religion with power; in the gospel on the contrary there is a distinction between the revelation that God is love and the exercise of power, the claim of a temporal superiority. Nonetheless, in the final analysis both religions conceive of truth as universally exclusive of error, and this view of truth manifests itself in the formal establishment of a dogma—in other words, the elaboration of a particular point of doctrine, sanctioned as a necessary truth by the chief authority of the church, and regarded henceforth in and of itself as an incontestable truth. From this point forward, all of those who dare to be different fall under the condemnation of the authorities.

Second, this truth is by definition universal. It is impossible for there to be more than one truth in the world and, because of this, all those who faithfully hold such a truth are conscious of the duty placed upon them to spread it abroad and to combat all that is obscure, erroneous, and false in other cultures. The conjunction of these two attributes of truth, its absoluteness and universality, leads thus to the problem of intolerance and is an integral part of the history of religions. It remains for us to explore the problem and to raise questions concerning the internal contradictions within the Christian faith.

II

At the present time it is not, on the whole, so much a disposition toward intolerance that confronts us. Instead, I see around me a broad tolerance reigning everywhere except within the "sects." It does not appear, however, to be a positive tolerance and a progress of the human spirit beyond the intolerance of the past but rather what I would call a "tolerance by default." That is to say, when we consider the reaction against intolerance in the preceding centuries, we are perturbed by the vast number of ideologies, by the scientific critiques, and by the uncertainties of life in the modern world; and we adopt a rather skeptical attitude, somewhat disabused of previous illusions and, even in the churches, somewhat agnostic. There is nothing absolute, there is not a jot or tittle in the Bible of which we can be sure, there is nothing left of absolute truth. As a consequence we can "tolerate." This attitude implies an absence of doctrinal formulations (for example, the incredible theological poverty and mediocrity of the "theologies of liberation"!).

As for dogmas, we consider them unworthy of interest because, at bottom, they are nothing more than opinion. A diversity of opinion seems entirely acceptable, and this "tolerance by default" is as much evident in the theological sphere or among ministers of the churches as it is among the faithful. A point that appears very significant to me in the intellectual sphere is research into the encounter of Christianity with other religions. I in no way mean to include Christian ecumenism here—that is something quite different—rather, I speak of dialogues between Jews, Moslems, and Christians, and more recently, those dialogues in which Buddhists also have been included. I have been present at many round-table discussions of this kind. What was most striking was the way in which the Christian participants attempted to dispense with the particularity of Christianity. For example, at a colloquy on the topic "The Oneness of God," agreement was reached on the issue of monotheism without mention of the name Jesus Christ and without any statement of the core of the Christian faith, the doctrine of the Trinity. At a colloquy on the topic "Religions of the Book," the specificity of the New Testament was ignored for the sake of pursuing the points of agreement between the various religious books and in particular for the sake of stressing that the principal point of agreement was the reference of each religion to *a single* revealed book!

Among Christians who are not trained in theology, this same attitude of agnostic tolerance translates itself into the complete abandonment of evangelization and its replacement with "service." To render service to your neighbor, to assist him socially and economically, suffices as Christian witness and as the expression of our "faith." Service to one's neighbor replaces worship and the study of the Bible—and we value this service as truth, even as an act of love. In other times we have spoken too much of love without practicing it. Now we practice it without speaking of it. But it is necessary to add that this dominant tendency to replace witness with service is one of the causes (together with the position of the French Reformed Church and the World Council of Churches on politics) of the gradual alienation of a large number of the faithful, who need spiritual and intellectual nourishment for their faith and can no longer find it. They endeavor to find nourishment in neighboring churches or in enthusiastic sects.

Political involvements, much as the "theology of service," can never account for the revelation of God in Jesus Christ or for the fact that this revelation is the very truth. One can neither conceal it nor pretend that such revelation is accomplished in social commitments. The claim of truth has been made. How then can this truth be affirmed without returning us to the former situation and its intolerance? It has been frequently said in France during the past two decades that the church ought to be "pluralistic," but such statements have never been given a theological foundation and the limits of this pluralism have not been defined. This is the issue I propose to deal with here.

III

Whether we like it or not, all Christianity rests on the revelation of one truth and on no other. The commandments flow forth from this truth. And this truth has a history: it has revealed itself progressively to Israel, culminating in Jesus Christ who could state, "I am the truth." Herein we encounter the first, and intellectually insurmountable, difficulty: the truth has been identified with a person. For Jesus did not say I show you the truth, I tell you the truth, or I teach the truth. He is not a propounder of truth. He is the truth. This is essentially incomprehensible.

The first blow to our intellectual composure immediately demonstrates the vanity of dogmas. I do not mean to imply the vanity of a dogmatics that is an intellectual discourse constructed *on the subject* of the truth. Barth has used this title well: we must not allow anything other than a "Church Dogmatics," that is to say, a dogmatics intended for the use of the church and rooted in its function in the condition of the church at the given moment. Formulated in any other way, dogmatics can become liable to an initial error consisting in the identification of the dogmatic certainty of the church with the truth—and then there begins the drama in which the church wishes to impose the (legitimate) conviction of the moment as if it were truth. (We shall return to this point.) But this error rests, in fact, upon a second, more fundamental, error: the identification of the church with the Holy Spirit. This error is not, of course, formulated so "brutally" but is implicit in the persistently held view that if the Gospels and the epistles are Holy Scripture it is only because they have been received and adopted as such by the church. In other words, it is the church that adjudicates the authenticity of the inspiration of Scripture. This claim transforms a historical process into a metaphysical truth. On the other hand, if such is the case, then as a consequence whatever the church should recognize and adopt as revealed truth will carry the same weight and have the same value as Holy Scripture. Such is the problem of tradition (which, for example, finds its extreme form in the dogma of papal infallibility). We have here the precise identification of the church with the Holy Spirit. It is, moreover, the conjunction of these two errors that leads to intransigence and intolerance: to resist the word of the church is to resist God himself.

We return now to the first problem. Surely we ought to recognize that all of Scripture is inspired and, consequently, that it truly contains, in its entirety, revealed truth. We must observe, however, a limit on this idea of revelation. I have just now said *"revealed"* truth. That is to say, God has graciously determined, for the sake of our salvation, our faith, our love, our hope, to reveal his truth to us. We dare not step beyond this formulation—in other words, we dare not claim, as theologians have too often done, that there is a perfect identity between what God has revealed to us concerning himself and what he *is* in himself, in his fullness, in his being, in his absoluteness. Since God has revealed to us his Trinity, that revelation is, as a result, indispensable to us. But we can affirm neither that the ultimate being of God is Trinity nor that this teaching exhausts the fullness of God. We are not able to say anything because apart from the revelation there is no enlightenment for us, because if indeed God is God we are unable to know it, because we must—apart from revelation—practice a "negative theology" that cannot make any genuine advance toward God on the foundation of our reason and our knowledge. It is this fact that bars the way to any analogy or proportion between God and our ways of knowing. We must remain on this side of the revelation and refrain from speculations concerning the identity of God with his revelation. It is true that Jesus said that "the Spirit will lead you into all truth" (John 16:13). But I do not think that he meant to provide in this statement an adjunct to the definitive formula that Jesus is the truth; it appears to mean only that it is the Spirit who will enable us to grasp the whole of that truth which the apostles were not able to grasp except superficially.

A major problem still confronts us. When we identify the *whole of the revelation with the truth,* we discover two distinct elements in the identification: there is the movement of the revelation toward us, which implies a self-disclosure of God for our benefit, but there is also our own ability to receive this revelation. This revelation comes to us through a witness: it has, therefore, been interpreted by a human being who, however faithful he may be, has placed his own imprint upon it. (This is why each book of the Bible has its own distinctive tonality.) And this witness is written, but, as has often been affirmed, this writing must be transformed into Word. It must, therefore, be interpreted. There will surely be major divergences between the various methods or inspirations underlying this interpretation. Finally, we each receive this interpreted Scripture for ourselves: in other words, according to our individual capacity, our individual abilities and limits. And when we have thus received and heard the Scripture, we must still express it in our words. It cannot remain a secret in my heart, but must be expressed in a hymn, in a prayer, in a sermon, in a theology. The particular form does not matter.

Am I able to claim that I have received and have expressed the fullness of the truth in this series of interpretive acts? If I believe that revelation genuinely conveys all of the truth that God wills to give to me, I must recognize also from experience that I do not know the whole Bible and that I have grasped its whole meaning still more imperfectly. I recognize the difference between external acquaintance with the text and the event that at certain times produced the text, and that has rather suddenly and sharply made that text become indisputable truth for me. In theological terms this is what we mean by revelation by the Holy Spirit. But then an incredibly sharp distinction is established between *this* text—illuminated, profoundly known, become for me both point of reference and command—and, by way of contrast, all of the other biblical texts. I know objectively that these latter texts have the same import and the same potential for the revelation of the Word, but for me they cannot be placed on the same level. Thus, in each effort of the theologian, there is one or more text that serves as a point of reference and as an explanatory key for all the others.

We recognize the importance for Luther of "the just shall live by faith." The parable of the talents (Matt 25:14-30) functions similarly for the theologians of "service" or "stewardship"—and, likewise, the first beatitude in Luke for liberation theologians. In truth, I ought to recognize that I cannot *entirely* understand the revelation of God or the Bible itself. Complete understanding (given the multiplicity of possible meanings for each text) would mean that a human mind is capable of grasping and assimilating the entirety of revelation, which would be to say that a human mind is capable of a thorough understanding of God! And even if, in the church, we still find some people who confront us and who enjoin us, each bearing his own version of the truth, even if we place ourselves in agreement with a formulation that appears to express most precisely what we have grasped, are we entitled to assume that we have now conveyed all of the truth, all of the Word and will of God? This has been the great error of the past ages of the church and of the various churches, whether Catholic or Protestant. It is necessary to recognize that each one of these faithful is able to perceive a small piece of this truth—and this is truly marvelous—a facet of God's diamond.

Because of this fact I am unable to pass judgment on another Christian or another church; I cannot declare another person heretical, but I must first examine what he understands, on his part, to be a fragment of the truth, another facet of the diamond. This may appear theologically unacceptable, but it is confirmed equally by the history of dogma and by the history of the church. There has been an unceasing development of theologies, and our understanding has continually been renewed by the biblical text. This is to say that at no time has any theologian or even the whole church understood the fullness of the truth of God.

These considerations put forward the well-known distinction between "the church sending" and "the church sent forth." The church sending ought to have the humility to recognize that she sends what today appears to her to be the truth but what ought also be recognized as relative. In another act of humility, she ought to admit that in the church sent forth, a particular believer or group of believers are themselves also able to have an insight into a particular aspect of the truth. Moreover, this relativism ought not be understood only in terms of the impossibility for the human spirit of grasping the entirety of revealed truth, but also in terms of the fact that we belong to a certain time and place, to a given cultural situation, and that our interpretation inevitably depends, whatever effort we may make to escape, on the intellectual context, the ideologies, and the methods of our time and place. An anecdote may illustrate this point. In a Reformed church of the Calvinist persuasion, a pastor was actually called to task by the authorities for having said that if a believer failed to attend worship, did not read the Bible, did not pray, and participated in no aspect of the life of the church, he put his salvation in danger. This view is genuinely Calvinistic and would hardly have shocked anyone in the last century. Today, however, considering the theological and moral laxity we know too well, where there is no longer any worry over sin or the possibility of damnation, such a view scandalized the authorities in the church! There are obviously considerable differences in approach depending on time and place.

If I ought to exercise a considerable degree of tolerance because I recognize the limits of what I and my church have discerned as the truth, it is also necessary for me to point this recognition in two directions: theological formulation and complementarity. It belongs to our piety that we cannot avoid formulating intellectually what we have received by revelation. Though a culture may be rude, it is very important that our understanding of the truth be received in the forms of expression used by that culture; and no one ought to be surprised if the African expression of theology is not the same as that which issues forth from Greco-Latin or Hebraic culture. We have only the duty to ask whether the essentials of the faith, the profound meanings, the "truth" are respected—without confusing these things with the formulation given them by the European church.

But all theological formulations have the tendency to close themselves and to exclude whatever does not correspond formally with their own patterns of expression. It is at this point that we must have an eye to our humility by recalling what I have already described. We must, therefore, take notice of the other direction indicated above, complementarity: since we have not been able to grasp more than a fraction, a flash of the truth, we can also conceive that a fellow believer or group of believers has also received the truth, but a different glimpse, and that it will be beneficial to us to receive from them what they have understood. To be sure, this does not imply that there is "a little bit of the truth" on all sides, but rather that I ought never to consider myself as the exclusive custodian of truth, or that I ought to have an attitude of tolerance and receptivity prior to any testing of issues. Alongside this tolerance there must be, equally, an expression of the seriousness of my faith. If I am very certain of what I believe, if I do not fear for the revelation, if I am founded on Jesus Christ, the sole firm foundation, I do not have to be fearful in the presence of formulations of truth that differ from mine, and I am able to receive them in complete tranquility of spirit. In reality, intolerance, exclusion, and judgment on others are all testimonies of uncertainty about the subject of truth—and of the defiance of that subject by my faith. If I am fearful for this truth, if I desire to defend it by violent means—whether by a violent physical defense or a violent intellectual apologetics—that is due to my own fragility: it is the expression of disbelief. This is how we must view the means used by the church and by Christians throughout history for the defense and diffusion of the faith. These means were the opposite of the truth of the gospel, and they testify not only to a contradiction but above all to a profound disbelief. The tolerance of which I now speak is thus the opposite of the tolerance to which I made allusion at the beginning of this essay. It is, I should now say, a "tolerance out of excess," in other words, a tolerance based upon an absolute certainty that the revelation of truth I have received will never be taken from me, and that the Lord is irrevocably on my side.

I should like to compare all that has just been said to the apostle Paul's words to ministers of the church: the church is perhaps a body, but no one of us can claim to be the body. Each one is a member of this body, and all are useful and indispensable. Each one has his place, each his function. None is superior or inferior. And none is able to judge another. The eye has no right to judge the foot, and so forth. But in historical reality, this body became an institution (just as the revelation was changed into dogmatics), and, inasmuch as we live in a society, we cannot avoid this development. Just as theological discourse tends to close upon itself, so does the institution. And this institution, upon closing its ranks, now decides which ministers are useful and what their hierarchy will look like. The Spirit no longer acts and the decision cannot be compared to inspiration. It is necessary to mistrust all institutionalization, as all dogmatization, while recognizing that it is useful, inevitable, and always subject to revision! If we hope to be faithful to the revelation of the truth, it is crucial that we maintain a great degree of flexibility both in our intellectual and in our institutional programs. We must have a tolerance and a receptivity that do not induce us to precipitate ourselves into all innovations or to accept all interpretations of the truth! But we must be attentive and preserve as a truth the important declaration of the wise Gamaliel: "If this plan or this undertaking is of men, it will fail; but if it is of God, you will not be able to overthrow them. You might even be found opposing God!" (Acts 5:38-39). Thus tolerance, but vigilance also!

IV

An essential question has thus been posed: Is this receptivity, this recognition that neither I nor my church has grasped the entirety of revealed truth, and, based on this, is this positive acknowledgment of theologies other than the one I hold to be correct (as in accord with my church)—is this all such that it implies the acceptance of any belief whatsoever under the name of Christian theology or as a confession of Christian faith? Throughout the course of its history, the church has experienced this confrontation. We know that most frequently the proclamation of a dogma has resulted in a need to take a position against any new theology that is judged unfaithful to the revelation. To be sure, it is certain to me that we cannot accept just any belief whatsoever under the pretext that it is a new inspiration of the Holy Spirit, while still proclaiming "Lord, Lord"! This is the great problem, over which we have no control, that arises in the context of differing theological orientations, each of which claims the inspiration of the Holy Spirit.

Let me make three points about this issue. The first is that the control that we can attempt to exercise ought not to be of a philosophical or theological kind (for example, the application of "scientific" methods to the reading of the Bible in order to produce a thoroughly correct interpretation of Scripture). The error has always been to judge new theologies in terms of intratheological criteria, whereas Jesus teaches us that we should recognize the tree *by its fruits*. The question that poses itself for us is, therefore, very simple: What is the behavior, what is the deportment of the faithful who follow Jesus' teaching? The issue is not merely their moral program, but rather the actual conduct of their lives. It is evident that the deportment of most millenarian movements has been scandalous from *all* points of view. The same is true of many sects. Paul clearly provides us with the list of spiritual gifts (which is a simple elaboration of the two great commandments) and also gives us some indications of the kind of works that come forth from Satan. But these are only examples that must not be transformed into a law. They serve, nonetheless, as useful criteria, on the condition that they are also applied to our own conduct and are used in the examination of our own consciences at the same time that we try to understand in what way the conduct of those who say "Lord, Lord" but who fail to do the work of God arises from a false understanding of the gospel. It is certain that a theology cannot be just that is congenial to us because it takes account of the poor but that at the same time presses believers toward class conflict, violence, the acquisition of power, and the exclusion of certain members from the church for political reasons. Neither can the theology of the nineteenth century, which allowed employers to exploit their workers—the patronage of "divine right"—and to justify themselves by good works, be just. Errors of behavior derive from fundamental theological errors.

The second point is that all Christians ought to agree upon *one* formula that is the center, the pivot, of their Christianity: "Jesus Christ, the only Lord, the only Savior"—nothing more, nothing less. Jesus, the Christ: by this all Christian thought that pretends to be content with the Jesus of history, not considered as the Messiah, is called into question. The only Lord: by this all thought that recognizes, implicitly or explicitly, another Lord is challenged—whether the state, riches, or the proletariat. The only Savior: by this all theology that multiplies mediators between us and the Father is rejected. Finally, if a person accepts this formula, he is forcefully drawn to recognize that the Christian God is genuinely one but also trinitarian. This declaration seems to me to be a sufficient criterion—but all that I have already said concerning the interpretation of Scripture bears upon its application. We are incapable of determining, in a way that is at once complete, exact, and sufficient, the sense of the words just now set forth on the subject of Jesus. We are incapable of *the fullness of the meaning* of words like Christ, Savior, and Lord, which are placed infinitely "beyond all that we conceive" (Eph 3:20). We shall never finish drawing out the consequences and the implications of these words. And we must take seriously any theology that places these three proclamations at its core, however different it may be from what we believe.

Conversely, even if we have some affinity with a new intellectual current, we cannot view it as "Christian" if it sets aside one of those designations of Jesus Christ. We may draw two examples from recent theology. First, when we rightly place the historical man Jesus Christ at the center of reflection, we may also be led to consider whether his resurrection was made effectual in the fact that his disciples continued to have faith in him. Second, we may consider whether he was, par excellence, the poor of the earth, so that henceforth those are the poor who, living on this earth, *are* Jesus. I can therefore say that, in the presence of new intellectual currents, of theologies, of new spiritual groups, I have not had to trace limits or barriers in order to affirm that on this side is truth and on the other, error. Rather, I have considered *the center,* the central issue from which all other issues arise. And whatever divergences might exist, if one claims to be or to speak as a "Christian," this central point can surely be nothing other than Christ, even if we do not always know exactly what this name means! We do know, however, that Christ expressly said all that he had to say to his disciples: in other words, his teaching was at once popular and "simple," exoteric.

As a result, we ought to mistrust esoteric teachings totally. We challenge what cannot be definitely condemned or excluded. Jesus often prayed; but all that we can know of his prayers (and, in addition, of the way that the apostles prayed) is that he prayed clearly, not ecstatically, not obscurely. Because of this, we ought to beware of any movement, for example, that in imitation of Hinduism is characterized by a trancelike existence or by the obliteration of intelligence through indefinite repetition, in a yoga position, of the name "Jesus"—replacing the traditional "Om."

Finally, there is the third point to be made about our reflections. I have noted that the church, throughout its history, has often been led to formulate dogmas in opposition to "heretical" movements. In some cases there has been good reason for this. In other cases we have realized several centuries later that the effort was terribly mistaken. The reaction against the heresy of Arius and the quarrel over the *Filioque* seem now utterly eclipsed and perhaps vain. There are those who would say that when the church is led to formulate dogma in a rigorous way it is because she totally understands the truth of a point of revelation. These people are perhaps correct about the movement in which the formulation occurred, but such formulations ought not to become a "truth," secure and unshakable for all time. Thus in the case of Arius the reaction of the church was correct, but the whole debate was false because it revolved around conceptions of God—of essence, substance, and begetting—that were utterly limited to a particular epoch and which are not the truth.

V

In order, however, legitimately to join together an attitude of receptivity and a priori acceptance of a new explanation of Scripture on the one hand with the vigilance and prudence necessary to prevent an adulteration of the truth on the other, one must take one further step. It is neither the unity of doctrine nor the organization of the church that creates Christian unity, but rather the unity of the Spirit. While we do not apprehend more than a fragment of the truth, the Spirit understands the entirety of the truth. Though we have different ministries, they are all inspired by the same Spirit. "Now there are varieties of gifts, but the same Spirit; and there are varieties of service, but the same Lord; and there are varieties of working, but it is the same God who inspires them all in every one. To each is given the manifestation of the Spirit for the common good" (1 Cor 12:4-7). Paul proceeds to examine these gifts, all different, but all coming forth from the same Spirit. And among these gifts are the gifts of wisdom and understanding, which assuredly agrees with Paul's expression of revealed truth—"All these are inspired by one and the same Spirit, who apportions to each one individually as he wills" (1 Cor 12:11). And further, "There is one body and one Spirit" (Eph 4:4). This is very important. The Spirit enlightens each one differently but he maintains, beyond our intellectual, bodily, and organizational limits the unity and existence of the one body. He fashions a *unity before God* from all of these parts that can appear so scattered and contradictory—even if this unity is not perceptible to us. He creates a sort of "patchwork." And this is why we ought to be attentive.

I have said that each person is incapable of grasping more than a facet of the diamond of truth. If we accept this, we have become tolerant and able to hear what others proclaim as *the* truth (but which is, itself, but a facet). And we ought to note that very often those whom we have regarded as heretics or sectarians have succeeded in bringing again to light, in carrying to the forefront, an aspect of revelation that we and our churches have forgotten. Several recent examples are relevant. Pentecostals have rightly emphasized the Holy Spirit, his gifts and his freedom at a time when the churches have either totally forgotten the Spirit or have only pretended to appropriate his work. Adventists have rightly emphasized the question of eschatology, the return of Jesus and the new creation, at a time when the church sleeps and no longer lives in the expectation of the end. Death of God theologies have rightly highlighted the vanity of our culturally conditioned representations of God, at a time when the churches channel and vulgarize the name of God. The error of *all* these movements is to claim that *their* understanding of the truth is the only, the unique, and the universal over against all of the others.

The tolerant and receptive attitude that I believe to be just can, however, also lead to an error: if we are convinced that everyone has received a fragment of the truth, should we not all reunite—should we not merge Calvin and Luther, the Great Awakening and Methodism, and so forth? In other words, should we advocate syncretism and make for ourselves the "patchwork" that I conjured up a moment ago? Or is this impossible and will it lead to nothing but a confusing mixture of ideas and the loss of the truth? All have to proclaim what they have received, with respect for the hearing of others (here the Jews must be included!) and without wishing to master others entirely. The Holy Spirit alone is the one who creates a unity from all these elements—the church, all the various theologies and pieties, the whole people of God. This Holy Spirit, who works all in all but who is at the same time the Spirit of unity, establishes the communion of saints. As a result, given the multiplicity of interpretations of revelation, we should not pretend to play the role of the Holy Spirit, but we should also no longer prevent him from playing his role as spiritual gatherer and as the differentiator of truth from falsehood. Nor should we erect barriers to change when the Spirit points toward union.

In France at the present there is a great rapprochement between Catholics and Reformed, between Reformed and Adventists, Baptists, and even Pentecostals. We must not deny this by holding to rigid doctrines. This reconciliation is not an abandonment; rather it is the recognition that certain theological debates of the past that were legitimate in other times are no longer important. From this point onward, we must open ourselves to brotherhood without ceasing to be ourselves, and we must accept these encounters as genuine gifts of the Spirit. The mere fact that we can have a fraternal dialogue on theological issues that were formerly divisive, the fact that each one recognizes that the other cannot be totally wrong, the fact that each one studies in the other whatever might complete his own interpretation of revelation—all of this ought to be accepted as a genuine work of the Holy Spirit.

In the same way, moreover, the institutional churches must not reject these gifts of the Holy Spirit, the charismatic and renewal movements, for the sake of a particular interpretation of revelation. They ought to accept them as different witnesses to this activity of the Holy Spirit, and at the same time they should be ready to transmit their own heritage of truth, which many others have neglected. But between us all, it is always the Holy Spirit who, in so many different situations, elicits and arouses new callings and who produces unity at the same time that he brings about fraternal dialogue and mutual hearing. This Spirit, however, is also, reciprocally, the one through whom the discernment of spirits is made possible. That is to say that not all innovation in piety, in theology, and in community is necessarily good. The point is to understand from which spirit the innovation comes—and only the Holy Spirit can tell us this. It is very evident that "evil spirits" are always at work. But I am not able, without the discernment of spirits that is a special gift of the Holy Spirit, to say that someone else is inspired by an evil spirit and that his interpretation of Scripture and his theology extols the "devil." Above all, this discernment cannot be the work either of a tribunal of the church or of a legal act (as if it were "representative" of the people of the church).

We are given only two guides in this matter: "No one speaking by the Spirit of God ever says 'Jesus be cursed!' and no one can say 'Jesus is Lord' except by the Holy Spirit" (1 Cor 12:3). Everything thus rests upon the place that we give to Jesus in our theology and in our witness. It is truly he who is the touchstone of authenticity for our discourse and its truth. All the rest is incidental. Nonetheless, it is obviously necessary to take into account the entire breadth of meaning of these two formulae with all of their implications—something that I cannot do in this essay, for this by itself would demand a whole theological treatise. For the present we can only note that Paul uses simply the name "Jesus": thus it is a historical man, someone who lived (and not an idea, or the Christ, or the resurrected One), that we have to recognize as Savior. It is "the little wandering Jew," with all that he did and said, as has been related to us in the Gospels. There is nothing recorded that ought to lead us to curse him. This is the criterion that ought to enable us to identify all that pretends to be Christian or to supercede Christianity. (In the name of this standard we should powerfully reject Islam, which makes Jesus into a mere prophet; and we should equally reject the Jehovah's Witnesses.)

There is one other aid in discernment, one that concerns the interpretation of Scripture according to the "analogy of faith." "Since we all have different gifts . . . let the one who has the gift of prophecy exercise it according to the analogy of faith" (Rom 12:6). Barth interprets this by saying that Christian teachings ought to be tested by their ability to produce *conformity to Christ,* a conformity that never arises out of one's self and is always problematic (*Church Dogmatics* 1/1, 12-16). This in turn implies an analysis of the relationship between belief and understanding. According to Augustine, belief ought to precede understanding inasmuch as it is faith resting on the Word of God. But faith ought to follow understanding inasmuch as it is faith that must be ratified by the word of man (the prophet). "Faith considered as *faith in God* rests upon itself and provides a foundation for understanding. Faith considered as the *faith of man* has a need for this understanding and is only ratified by this understanding" (*Church Dogmatics* 1/1, 17-18). Thus this analogy of faith ought to be the criterion for our understanding of Scripture, of all theology of the faith. It presupposes a relation of each text to the whole of Scripture and a constant interrelationship between various passages of Scripture that have been understood in faith in order that each text may be controlled (but not rigidly) by all the others and in order that all texts may be construed together and all carefully examined. Each text is capable of prophetic proclamation (but no one can call himself a prophet).

These two orientations—discernment of spirits and analogy of faith—remind us very clearly that we must not *judge.* If today we concede a particular formulation in ethics, we concede still less in the political sphere, and for believers we concede nothing at all in matters that concern preaching and teaching theology. In all our work, as we state firmly whatever we have believed and received as the truth of God—that is, after we have prayerfully attempted the discernment of spirits and exercised the analogy of faith—we should be attentive to what is said by our brothers in Christ. We ought in all cases to recognize the presence of the Holy Spirit in the possibility for fraternal dialogue between Christians of different demoninations and of different theological assumptions.

I shall endorse once more a frequently noted judgment: new methods of exegesis (after historical-critical analysis and linguistic structural analysis) are called scientific. We witness quite often a twofold reaction in the church: the "scientific minds" scorn the pietistic or hortatory sermon of the "mediocre" pastor, and they leave the faithful behind in what they perceive to be superstitious ignorance. They are incapable of discerning the truth of the faith and the distance that separates them from the revelation. Equally so, the faithful often judge these "searchers" to be impious, inasmuch as they dare to lay a hand on the "sacred texts," and find them utterly incomprehensible since their arguments depart from customary patterns. This double judgment is a mortal blow to the church. It is necessary for the scholars to submit themselves to the law of the analogy of faith and for the faithful to find in these new scholarly arguments a new discovery about the identity of Christ the Lord.

Such reciprocal hearing is made possible by the Holy Spirit. Some would say that when we refuse this reciprocal hearing the Holy Spirit is not present. But it is never the Holy Spirit who stops ears and provokes judgments. This reciprocal listening ought, moreover, to involve, by means of the confidence we have in the unity of the Holy Spirit, a reciprocal *obedience*. This obedience should be totally separate from the administrative authority of the church, but it should be able to lead a "superior" to be of service to an "inferior." It should be an obedience in the minister, in the theologian, and in the doctor that pauses to listen to the faith of the simple believer who himself could also have received the gift of the Spirit. Everything that I have written here is but an expression of the love that establishes the bond between all members of the church. It is particularly important that a congregation of the faithful be ever ready to hear another word—and to hear it with the receptivity or openness that conveys love and that is opposite to the closedness of so many groups of Christians that are turned in upon "their truth." This readiness and openness will lead that congregation farther along their way than would a unique truth preserved once for all time but in reality no longer received as truth because of excessive repetition.

Karl Barth and T. S. Eliot on Tradition

Bernard Ramm

I

It may appear strange to link together the names of Karl Barth and T. S. Eliot. What they have in common is that each was a towering figure in his own specialty in his own country. Barth was a dominant figure in theology on the continent and Eliot was a dominating figure in literature in England. Yet there is another tiny tendril connecting them. John Baillie and Hugh Martin decided to publish a series of essays on the theme of revelation, a topic at the center of theological discussion at that time.[1] They requested an essay from Karl Barth and he responded. They also thought that an expert in European culture should write an introductory essay that would explain the culture in which the book would circulate. They asked T. S. Eliot to do so and he did. It can be hoped that Barth read Eliot's introduction and that Eliot read Barth's essay. Both men also contributed to the *Christian News Letter,* but if there are other contacts between them I have not found them.

My aim is to attempt to show that although Barth and Eliot had very divergent careers and interests, they did have much in common when it came to the concept of tradition. Tradition was not a secondary concept in their thinking and writing but was for each of them part of the central core of their working assumptions.

II

Insofar as Eliot was almost unknown in theological studies and while his person and writings are fading away as the historical process moves on, something must be said biographically of this man in order to understand his concept of tradition and its importance in the understanding of both culture and theology.[2]

Eliot belonged to the Harvard Eliots who were also known for their Unitarianism. It is a story with more than passing interest how a Unitarian Eliot eventually became a High Church Anglican. The common explanation is that he had a Roman Catholic nanny who took him to mass and also instructed him as much as could be expected at that young age in the fundamentals of Roman Catholicism. Eliot remarked later in his life that he could not understand why

---

1. John Baillie and Hugh Martin, *Revelation* (London: Faber and Faber, 1937).

2. It must be said Eliot was (and still is in English departments) a controversial figure. Two biographies sympathetic to Eliot are Robert Sencourt, *T. S. Eliot: A Memoir* (ed. Donald Adamson; New York: Delta, 1971); and Russell Kirk, *Eliot and His Age* (New York: Random House, 1971). Representative of a critical interpretation is T. S. Matthews, *Great Tom: Notes Towards the Definition of T. S. Eliot* (New York: Harper & Row, 1973).

philosophers had such troubles with proofs for the existence of God. He observed that his nanny had recited them to him when he was a child and they were perfectly obvious as valid logical arguments.

Our story, however, begins neither with Roman Catholicism nor with Harvard. Eliot's grandfather believed that St. Louis was going to be the metropolis of mid-America. He moved the family to St. Louis and founded the Messiah Unitarian Church; he was also instrumental in founding Washington University and Smith Academy. Eliot's father did not follow in the academic tradition of the Eliots but became a successful business man in St. Louis.

Young Eliot suffered from a hernia, so while the boys of his own age played their outdoor games, he sat curled up on a big chair forever reading books. One may presume that this was one of the reasons he returned again to the academic tradition of the Eliots. For three years he studied at Smith Academy, where, among other things, he learned Greek, Latin, German, and French. His knowledge of Italian came later with his studies of Dante. He spent his fourth preparatory year at Milton Academy in Massachusetts. He then entered Harvard, and although he majored in philosophy, he virtually had a second major in literature. The Harvard faculty of philosophy presumed that after finishing his education he would join the philosophical faculty, so they sent him to Paris to hear the lectures of Henri Bergson, who at that time was one of the most famous philosophers in Europe. Taking advantage of the situation, Eliot refined his knowledge of French, plunged into current French literature, and eventually was able to write poetry in French.

He spent the next two years after his return from Paris as an instructor at Harvard. In those years he also studied Oriental religions but admitted that he could never get on their wave length. The faculty sent him next to Germany (Marburg) where Rudolf Eucken was lecturing. He had hardly unpacked his bags when World War I broke out. Sometime before, Eliot had bought a copy of *Appearance and Reality*[3] by F. H. Bradley, whom many scholars thought was the sharpest philosophical mind England had produced in the nineteenth century. Eliot was so impressed by Bradley's book that he decided to write his dissertation on some phase of it: consequently it appeared to him that the only thing to do was to go to Oxford and work with Bradley on his dissertation. But when Eliot arrived there he was in for two surprises: he learned first that Bradley hated students and second that he was too sick to work with anybody. So Eliot worked with Bradley's assistant, Hans Henry Joachim.

He finished his dissertation and mailed it to Harvard. The Harvard faculty received it with enthusiasm; but Harvard followed the rule that no degree could be awarded in absentia and Eliot did not return to Cambridge to accept it. His biographers are divided over why he did not do so. One view is that he was so much in love with London as a city—and was just finding his way into the inner circle of great literary personalities there—that he did not see any value in leaving to accept his degree. Another view is that crossing the ocean during World War I was dangerous and Eliot refused to take the risk. He had earned his Ph.D. as far as academic requirements were concerned, but because of the technicality of the in

---

3. F. H. Bradley, *Appearance and Reality* (Oxford: Clarendon, 1916).

absentia rule he never formally received it. Yet his dissertation was finally printed as a book in 1964.

Stranded in England, Eliot had a difficult time in finding employment, but he finally found a place with Lloyd's bank. The war had created all kinds of problems in international banking, and because Eliot was a bit of a linguist, he got the job of working on foreign accounts. In the process of working through these accounts he became thoroughly acquainted with the politics and economics of Europe. He became so skillful at his task that the bank asked him to prepare a weekly report on the political and economic conditions in Europe. In doing this kind of reporting, he was one of the few people (along with Karl Barth) who was aware of the dangers of Hitler before they became more publicly known.

In between the wars he edited a small journal called *The Criterion*. Although its largest run was nine hundred copies, it was the journal of the intellectuals, and it exerted a far greater influence than its circulation might suggest. *The Criterion* has been considered such a valuable resource for that period that the entire run of the journal has been reprinted and made available to the world of literary scholars.

In 1927 Eliot issued his famous life-committal statement. He announced that in politics he was a royalist; in education he was a classicist; and in religion he had joined the Anglican Communion, associating himself with the high church or the Anglo-Catholic branch of the church. In due course Eliot was considered the greatest poet and playwright in the English speaking world. He also became famous for his lectures and his shrewd ability to analyze culture. He was one of the few persons chosen to lecture in Germany after World War II to help revive the spirits of the crushed German people.

III

We are now prepared to examine Eliot's concept of tradition. One of the reasons the concept emerged in his thinking and writing was his attempt to find some wisdom on how life is to be lived in a culture created by science, technology, and industrialization, which in turn creates the continuous and rapid change of society. Some writers use the word *rapidization* to express this cultural acceleration. Eliot's question concerned how a person can live authentically and stably in a culture undergoing such rapidization. There are many ways one could address this problem, but we shall limit ourselves to three emphases found in Eliot's writings. Of course we are all living at the same edge of time, so we are not thinking of some sort of time machine. Rather we are considering how people internally program themselves in order to cope with rapidization and not be overwhelmed by it.

The first possible solution would be to live in the past, both mentally, emotionally, and culturally. A priest who is distressed by the rapidization going on within his own parish might retreat to the high-water mark of the Middle Ages, when at least in idea church, state, education, philosophy, theology, and culture formed one harmonious civilization. His Protestant counterpart is the pastor who finds his rest, security, and stability by reliving the sixteenth century. And there are others who continue to dream dreams of the age of the Puritans.

But to Eliot, this would be an evasion of the problem, not a solution. Healthy solutions realistically confront the present, while to retreat is to fossilize intellectually and culturally.

IV

Another method of coming to terms with the distress rapidization creates is to drift with the changes—one simply becomes a trendy cultural drifter. Such people follow cultural changes much like some of the wealthy of the world follow the latest fashions from Paris or Milan. Such people boost their egos by vacationing where the jet set does. This sort of mentality can be found even among philosophers and theologians: Bertrand Russell was one such philosopher. The worst indictment is to accuse a theologian of taking up the theology of the last book he read; this is akin to the ridiculous scene in the days of the youth rebellion when ministers with snow white hair marched with college students. Another cheap side of this solution is that of playing gamesmanship with the latest journal articles one has read. No doubt such tactics reward the person with a sense of "being with it," but there is no depth, no character, no substance in such a constantly shifting collection of theological opinions.

Eliot's solution to the problems created by rapidization, whether in culture, philosophy, or theology, hinges on his concept of tradition. So central is tradition to his thinking that Sean Lucy has dedicated an entire book to an elucidation of it.[4] The author states that his aim is

> to show the theme of tradition is one of Eliot's constant preoccupations, and is central to both his criticism and to his creative work. . . . [I]n all aspects of our lives *we are our past* both personal and historical, and it is only by accepting, realizing, rectifying and vivifying that past that we can attain to a life of significant essential discipline for significant identity.[5]

Two important theses are contained in these words. The first is that the past is not dead, inert material stuffed away in the books of history in our libraries. The past is powerfully in the present. For example, it is because Alexander the Great wanted not only to conquer the world but also to Hellenize it that our New Testament is in the Greek language. Hundreds of theological students every year commence their learning of Greek due to this one ancient decision of Alexander. Moreover, the languages spoken in North and South America are the languages of the conquerers—hence we have French spoken in Quebec, English in the rest of Canada and in the United States, Spanish throughout Central and South America, and Portugese in Brazil. In Eliot's mind, this continuous impingement of the past on the present is a significant part of the definition of tradition. This understanding of the connection of history, tradition, and the present has a great deal to do not only with the kinds of decisions we make as individuals but also with the policy statements of nations.

4. Sean Lucy, *T. S. Eliot and the Concept of Tradition* (rept.; New York: Barnes and Noble, 1960).
5. Ibid., viii. Emphasis added.

The second thesis is even more important than the first: it is by the study of tradition (yet to be defined) that we learn the wisdom whereby we can live authentically in the present. Romantically returning to the past does not solve our problem, nor does spineless conformity to the present. Only in the wisdom gained by tradition can we live authentic lives in an international culture undergoing rapidization. And the use of such wisdom is applicable to the decisions of states as well as to those of persons.

Eliot does not give the word *tradition* the same common meaning it is given in ordinary conversation. He meant by tradition that which we might call the cream of tradition as understood in the popular sense. Tradition is that body of material able to sustain itself through the centuries because of its inherent truthfulness and because of the profound depth of its content. The person who has learned his tradition, in Eliot's definition of the term, is the one who can live an authentic and fulfilling life in the midst of the constant eddies of change. He has criteria whereby he can separate wheat from chaff.

Two subtheses must be appended to this. First, understanding tradition does not grant infallibility; but it gives us the best possible basis for living our lives in a meaningful way. Second, some things survive that are not substantial tradition, but Eliot thought that given enough time such material would inevitably drop out of existence since they did not contain enough inherent substance to maintain themselves. Eliot was not provincial in his view. He came very close to the Great Books theory inasmuch as books give us the easiest access to tradition. But he recognized that other forms of culture, such as music and art, were also carriers of tradition. What is more, he did not have in mind only European classics or European Great Books: if a person were Chinese, he would and should read classic Chinese literature.

There is another dimension of Eliot's view of tradition that is almost uniformly bypassed in so many books on him. During his early traning there was a revolt among many of the younger neo-Hegelian philosophers against their heritage and a growing openness to the newer scientific philosophies. One must remember that Eliot was first of all a philosopher, destined to be on the Harvard faculty of philosophy. Both Bertrand Russell and Alfred North Whitehead had lectured at Harvard when Eliot was a student. These two men coauthored the famous work on symbolic logic, *Principia Mathematica,* which became the Bible of the new emerging scientific and positivistic philosophies. One does not just read a book on logic, but Eliot worked his way deeply into this volume until he decided that its philosophical presuppositions were too alien to his way of thinking. I cannot overstate how much of a sheer intellectual feat it was for Eliot to make his way through most of this book.

Around this same time, the new and powerful scientific philosophy originally called logical positivism was gaining influence, and Eliot familiarized himself with it. One of the central themes in logical positivism and its descendants is that of verification or verifiability. We commonly think of a hypothesis as verified or falsified by proper laboratory work. Although not the simplified procedure laymen think it is, the methods used by scientists are always designed to verify their hypotheses. This is all well and good as far as science is concerned; but what kind of verification do we have for philosophies or political theories or economic assumptions? The routine methods of verification in the sciences do not apply. In what possible way can we speak of a political theory being true that could never be verified in a scientific sense? According to Eliot, tradition is the principle of verification in these non-scientific territories. To put it succinctly, trivial theories have a short life span, and substantial theories live through the centuries. A theory in political science or a philosophy will endure if it has merit and substance. Pop ideologies have no such merit and hence no durability.

Eliot applied the criterion of tradition to theology. He was an orthodox Christian because the churches of orthodoxy (the Anglican communion, the Roman Catholic church, and the Eastern Orthodox church) had passed the test of tradition and hence, as far as it could be said of such institutions, they had been "verified." Eliot admitted that if he had lived in France he would have been a Roman Catholic—but hardly a Baptist in Germany, since the first German Baptist church appeared in 1812! For a number of reasons he had an extreme dislike for English liberalism (the *Modern Churchmen's Union*). On one occasion he set time aside and read a number of its theological texts and found them wanting. But the most fatal flaw of all for liberalism was that no tradition could be built up in a theology scarcely a hundred years old—it lacked even the shadow of verification.

V

Helmut Thielicke stands as a very interesting connecting link between Eliot and Barth: he poses the identical problem that Eliot does only within a narrower theological circle. As a theologian he mediates the gap between Eliot, the man of letters, and Barth, the man of theology.[6] Thielicke poses the problem of how we can be theologians with our roots deep in the past (tradition) and yet speak meaningfully to our own generation. That he has actually done this is witnessed by the great number of volumes of his preaching that have been published, with a goodly number of them translated into English.

Thielicke discusses three different groups of theologians that each take a different tack to solving the problem of addressing the present while remaining rooted in the past. First there are those theologians who in their theology and preaching anchor themselves to their great Lutheran history, its creeds, and its theology. They are the repeaters of history. They correspond to Eliot's first class of people who find peace of soul by a retreat to a past period of imagined glory. Thielicke calls them betrayers because they force the listener to learn their vocabulary; this is a betrayal of the duty of the preacher or theologian to reframe the Christian message in the vocabulary and thought patterns of the current generation.

The second group is composed of theologians who are overly anxious to conform to their own generation. They overtranslate the Christian message. Schleiermacher, Bultmann, and Tillich are prime examples. What they have done, in the

6. Helmut Thielicke, *The Evangelical Faith*, vol. 1, *Prolegomena: The Relation of Theology to Modern Thought Forms* (tr. Geoffrey W. Bromiley; Grand Rapids: Eerdmans, 1974).

end, is to translate the gospel out of existence. This corresponds to Eliot's second group who lose their integrity by never challenging the contemporary culture.

The third group are the theologians who have accepted the theology of their fathers and seek to communicate it to the modern generation. The center of this tradition is the gospel, and the center of the gospel are God's actions for the redemption of the world—the mighty acts of God (see Acts 2:22). This corresponds to Eliot's third group who have learned to live in the present and to anticipate the future because they have learned the past—tradition—so well.

In moving from Eliot to Barth via Thielicke, it would be a cardinal error to look up the word *tradition* in the index volume of Barth's *Church Dogmatics*. At the right time that procedure is valid, and we have done so. The primary question here, however, is not whether Barth used the word *tradition* in the same sense that Eliot did; rather it is this: Is there an element of Barth's theology that corresponds to Eliot's concept of tradition? The answer is historical theology. It is interesting that there is one passage where Barth uses *tradition* in the same sense as Eliot's definition and mentions historical theology as a synonym.[7] Otherwise Barth uses the word in the customary theological sense.[8]

VI

Presuming for the moment that Eliot's concept of tradition is very similar to Barth's concept of historical theology, we must give some attention to historical theology as such. There is a difference between a general and imprecise notion of history and a modern, more or less scientific understanding of history. As far back as there has been writing, there has been history in the first sense. This sort of history can be found in the Old and New Testaments, among the Greeks (e.g., Herodotus), among the Jews (e.g., Josephus), among the Romans (e.g., Tacitus) and among the church fathers (e.g., Augustine and Eusebius).

The first probings into the nature of history in the second sense commenced during the Enlightenment (e.g., with Voltaire and Hume). It is generally admitted that the concept of a scientific history was forged in the nineteenth century among German and English historians (e.g., von Ranke and Lord Acton). In that historical theology is a subdivision of history, it had to wait for the more formal definitions of history before it could formulate a conception of its own nature and task. The first work in historical theology is attributed to S. G. Lange's *Ausfürliche Geschichte der Dogma* (1796). However the two great names in historical theology are Friedrich Loofs and Adolf von Harnack.[9]

7. Karl Barth, *Evangelical Theology: An Introduction* (tr. Grover Foley; New York: Holt, Rinehart and Winston, 1963) 37-47.

8. Karl Barth, *Church Dogmatics* (tr. G. T. Thompson and Harold Knight; Edinburgh: T. & T. Clark, 1956) 1/us2, 546- 54.

9. Friedrich Loofs, *Leitfaden zum Studium der Dogmengeschichte* (5th ed., ed. Kurt Aland; Halle: Veb Max Niemeyer Verlag, 1953). Adolf von Harnack, *History of Dogma* (7 vols., 3d ed., tr. Neil Buchanan; New York: Dover, 1961).

VII

We know that Barth had been exposed in depth to historical theology. When he left Switzerland and went to Berlin to continue his theological studies, he commenced work with Harnack, who is considered the greatest historian of dogma ever. It was Ernst Troeltsch who did the most to correlate a scientific study of history with Christian theology, and Troeltsch was one of the scholars Barth studied in much detail. Barth's *Protestant Theology in the Nineteenth Century* evidences this correlation and provides a magisterial interpretation of theology in that time period.[10]

However, when Barth began to publish his huge volumes of the *Church Dogmatics* it was obvious that historical theology was one of the central pillars in his theological methodology. Some scholars are of the opinion that if Barth had specialized in the history of dogma he would have surpassed the great Harnack. Since our thesis is that tradition functioned in Eliot's system in the same way that the history of dogma functioned in Barth's system, a closer look at Barth's theology is necessary.

It is an underlying thesis in all of Barth's writings that competence in historical theology is necessary for competence in theology. I shall argue this point again in another context. In Eliot's language, a knowledge of the theological tradition of the church is necessary for theologians who write for the church. Barth did not mean that historical theology was to dominate the theologian nor, even worse, that it was to limit the theologian. A theologian has the right to express himself in the manner he wishes. But the right to have one's say in the church is purchased by a knowledge of historical theology. For example, one can gather how lean liberal theology became by reading some representative books like Douglas Clyde Macintosh's *Theology as an Empirical Science*.[11]

In some liberally oriented seminaries, theology has been replaced by ethics. Although this exchange may be able to make the students feel very relevant, it does so at the expense of providing the students knowledge of the theological heritage of the church. Other seminaries replaced theology with philosophy of religion, as James Collins has clearly detailed.[12] Similarly, one of the glaring weaknesses of the theology of fundamentalism is its lack of interaction with historical theology, except at a very superficial level. It has a few favorite names on its list, such as Augustine, Luther, Calvin, and some of the members of the old Princeton school, like the Hodges and Benjamin Warfield. But in the area of historical theology it is bankrupt.

The same is even more true of the Pentecostal movement. In *The Pentecostals,* the so-called encyclopedia of Pentecostalism, Walter Hollenweger laments how little Pentecostal theology interacts with historical theology.[13] In its emphasis on the

10. Karl Barth, *Protestant Theology in the Nineteenth Century* (tr. B. C. Cozens and H. H. Hartwell; Valley Forge: Judson, 1968).

11. D. C. Macintosh, *Theology as an Empirical Science* (New York: Macmillan, 1919).

12. James Collins, *The Emergence of Philosophy of Religion* (New Haven: Yale University Press, 1967).

13. Walter J. Hollenweger, *The Pentecostals* (London: SCM, 1972).

experience of the Holy Spirit, it hardly knows what to do with justification by faith. Pentecostal theologians include justification in their theology, if for no other reason, because it was at the center of the Reformation. They are equally at a loss to interact properly with the doctrine of the Trinity and the more complex facets of Christology; but again, they accept both doctrines as part of the necessary truth to which evangelical Christians are committed.

The parallel between Eliot and Barth at this point is obvious, namely, one must drink deep drafts of historical theology if one wishes to be competent in theology. Eliot said that a poet could do very well the first twenty-five years of his life by his sheer powers of imagination and talent. But after that he shall soon dry up unless he systematically renews himself by constant reading of his literary tradition. It is not stretching the point that Barth would say the same about theology. A good grasp of historical theology is a necessity for fruitful theological writing in the latter part of one's career.

VIII

We now turn to the second reason why Barth put such an emphasis on historical theology. Exod 20:12 is the commandment to honor our fathers and mothers. Besides being a moral injunction, the verse contains implicit instruction in the writing of good theology. A theologian stands, as it were, in the river of theology and its theologians. He has his theological fathers and mothers in the faith. Before a theologian may speak to the church he must show honor to the theologians who have gone before him and who prepared that land on which he stands. It is in the study of historical theology that the young theologian honors his fathers and mothers. Eliot would have little trouble in turning this around a bit to say that only those people who learned the tradition have the preparedness and depth to add to the tradition.

So before the young theologian wishes to express himself he must first honor the past and listen to what has been said in the church. It was Barth's firm conviction that no one theologian and even no one generation of theologians could write the definitive theology. Hence he makes the unfinished character of *Church Dogmatics* a virtue, for it truly reflects the pilgrim character of theology, matching our own pilgrimage through life. The principle of honoring our forefathers (as we do when we study historical theology) is not in this context just a matter of gaining competency. It is rather a rule of responsibility. The failure to meet this responsibility—dishonoring our theological fathers and mothers—can be seen in the manner in which so many American charismatic movements, fundamentalist movements, and parachurch movements ignore historical theology and give the impression (whether they are aware of it or not) that one may safely jump directly from the day of Pentecost to the twentieth century and suffer no losses.

The last impression Barth wanted to give was that historical theology was to be a heavy lead glove on the hand of the theologian, a constraint that would restrict him to writing only the theology of past ages. But there is also the danger of the *neophyton* (a word used of newly planted plants)—the novice who does not know his way around the complex geography of theology. But if we have gone through the weathering of historical theology and have ceased to be neophytes, then we may suggest views that do differ from our theological fathers and mothers.

A good example of how Barth carried out such a program is the manner in which he arrived at his doctrine of election. He studied Calvin at length on this doctrine, and he also reviewed the Canons of Dort in the original Latin text. He has thus honored his theological forefathers. But he could not accept Calvin's version of election: disguise it in any manner you wish, it still is a form of theological determinism. Yet Barth also had no taste for either Pelagianism or Arminianism. He considered Arminianism the origin of the theology of liberalism. If a theologian could determine his salvation by standing in a circle and giving his own ultimate decision about his salvation, he could also claim juridical rights to accept or reject any other doctrine.

Being a theological child of Calvin, however, Barth had to have a doctrine of election. That was a theological obligation. His only recourse was to assume that after studying the doctrine and analyzing its history he would be justified in writing out his own version of election, showing that he honored his father and mother in theology but was not bound to simply repeat them.

IX

Another facet in Barth's conception of historical theology is his opinion of the ecumenical movement. He considered its understanding of ecumenicity too narrow. It was composed of the living talking with the living. The international gatherings of the ecumenical movement are of course composed of living people. Yet according to Barth, true ecumenicity is the meeting of the whole church from Pentecost to the present. Naturally we cannot raise them from the dead and ask for their opinion, so we have to settle for second best, namely, we have to read their literary remains.

Barth so firmly believed this that the books in the study rooms in his house were arranged in historical order beginning with the magnificent German translation of the fathers. By consulting this gallery of theologians from the early church until the present, Barth was a true ecumenical theologian: in his mind historical theology was our method of conversing with the Christians of the past. That accounts for the great number of references Barth makes to the theologians of the past. If a theology is to have any claim to being ecumenical theology, it must have elaborate connection with the theologians of other ages that we can make only from our studies in historical theology. (Unfortunately he was not consistent in this himself and wrote many pages of the *Church Dogmatics* with no attention to historical antecedents.)

One of the values of the study of historical theology is that it gives the theologian a sense of proportion. It prevents theologians from giving too much authority or attention to one period of church history over against all others, and it keeps them from valuing one single theologian above all others. The study of historical theology keeps reminding theologians of the total spectrum of Christian theology and theologians. This point is very obvious in modern studies of the

Gospels. One can read many volumes written by modern specialists in the New Testament and never find a reference to a church father or a council or some theologian in the long history of theology. The specialists are so encapsulated in their own new methodologies that they do not believe anything significant has been said on the subject until the modern period.

If the Christology of the early church was founded on a mistake (such as making a very good man into a deity, or using some mythological terms that do not mean the same to the Gospel writers that they mean to us) then all the intervening centuries have no importance for modern christological studies. Or, as one correspondent wrote, there is no value in historical theology if the Nicene Creed is wrong. Similarly, historical studies falter if the serious study of Christology really only begins with Hermann Reimarus (1694–1768), who first suggested that the historical personage of Jesus was very different from the Jesus Christ of the creeds. These positions mean, as far as the subject of Christology is concerned, that there is no meaningful ecumenical dialogue based on studies in historical theology. If I may attempt again to put words in Barth's mouth, I think he would say something like this: We cannot take the opinions of our current brood of New Testament specialists as the definitive speakers in Christology, because the study of historical theology itself teaches us that in another thirty years we shall have another brood of scholars who might completely reverse the stance of the current brood and once again make the study of historical theology central to the study of Christology.

There is yet another very important strand in Barth's use of historical theology. It is related to the presupposition virtually universal in its reception that in matters of science and technology later discoveries are far truer than those of earlier centuries. There is little or no virtue in retreating to the medical and dental practices of two hundred years ago. But when we come to such issues as God, morality, and philosophical insight or wisdom, it could be that some person of previous centuries may have written or spoken something that is more relevant or truer than that which passes as modern wisdom today. The writings of Plato and Aristotle provide a classic illustration of this viewpoint. Alfred North Whitehead said that the history of philosophy is a series of footnotes on Plato—five huge volumes in the standard English translation. If nothing else, this means that Plato has much more intrinsic worth than a library of modern philosophy. And if one takes up the study of ethics or poetics or politics, some of Aristotle's writings are yet the most valid point of departure.

Barth believes that this principle applies fully to theology. When he anchored his theological methodology, he chose Anselm of the Middle Ages rather than some contemporary theologian. In the same way, he finds Luther and Calvin closer to the scriptural truth than anybody in our modern crop of theologians. He also appeals from time to time to the excellence of the Swiss dogmaticians of the seventeenth century. Similarly, the famous German Lutheran theologians, Helmut Thielicke and Werner Elert, thought that Luther came closer to the meaning of the New Testament in virtue of his theological genius than does the modern scholar armed to his teeth with the latest of critical materials. This is not far from Eliot's view of theology. He thought, for example, that the classic Anglican theologians of the seventeenth century were far superior to modern theologians, and that one would perhaps find more substantial theology in the writings of Dante and Milton than in current liberal theology.

In sum, both Eliot and Barth are counted among the greater minds of the twentieth century, even outside the narrow range of their specialties. In spite of their great difference of language and national identity, both at root used very similar, if not identical, methods in the argumentation of their cases. Both were valiant knights in attempting to turn the tide of consensus back to the great wisdom of the ages and away from the current fad, whether it be in ethics, philosophy or theology. While Bishop Butler said that probability is the guide of life, Barth and Eliot would say that tradition is the guide of life.

Neither Eliot nor Barth wanted to give the impression that the past, as tradition or as historical theology, was to be a leaden glove on the hand of the philosopher or theologian, limiting theology, philosophy, and literature to worthless recitals of the past. On the contrary, both historical theology and tradition were to function in just the opposite way. They freed theologians and philosophers from the tyranny of the spell of the present and enabled them to be better historians, philosophers, theologians or literary artists. It is the neophyte among us, who has not gone through the weathering of the past, who offers us theories that are not only untested but potentially dangerous.

The Anatomy of an Evangelical Type: An American Evangelical Response to Karl Barth's Theology

Howard John Loewen

S. W. Sykes observes that "in a survey of American religion published in 1945, the Dean of Harvard Divinity School wrote Barth off as a reactionary and 'much too sophisticated for the average American layman.'"[1] Although in Great Britain the English-speaking world had begun to read Barth seriously after World War I, in America he was only starting to be read primarily in the post–World War II period, and usually not very thoroughly. As late as 1969, Robert Jenson complained that "almost nothing of what people have spoken of in America or England as 'Barthianism' has much to do with the thought of the man from Basel."[2] This, despite the fact that a transitional phase had occurred in Barth studies in the English-speaking world in the decade following the early 1950s with the translation of Barth's *Church Dogmatics,* Volume 1, Part 2 and the publication of T. F. Torrance's seminal works.[3]

Within the context of this rather reluctant acceptance of the theology of Barth, American evangelicalism also began to forge its own response to him following World War II. Accordingly there is a body of literature that emerged from the late 1940s through the 1960s, and even beyond, that interacts with Karl Barth's thought but generally rejects the validity of his theology.[4] This American evangelical interpretation of Barth was seen by some Barth interpreters, even then, to be somewhat amiss of Barth's real intentions.

Strong objections, for example, were raised against Cornelius Van Til's treatment of Barth in his then influential books, *The New Modernism* and *Christianity and Barthianism,* the two most detailed critiques of Barth in American evangelicalism. G. C. Berkouwer felt that "Van Til's analysis does not correspond to the deepest intents of Barth's theology." The result was some "audacious utterances" about Barth.[5] Likewise, the Catholic theologian, Hans Urs von Balthasar assessed Van Til's response to Barth in the following manner: "The situation is even more ridiculous ten years later (1947), when Cornelius van Til *(The New Modernism)* tries to explain the whole theology of Barth and Brunner on the basis

---

1. S. W. Sykes, "The Study of Barth," in *Karl Barth: Studies of His Theological Method* (ed. S. W. Sykes; Oxford: Clarendon, 1979) 8.

2. See Robert W. Jenson, *Alpha and Omega: A Study in the Theology of Karl Barth* (New York: Nelson and Sons, 1963), as an example of a more perceptive assessment of Barth.

3. See T. F. Torrance, *Karl Barth: An Introduction to His Early Theology, 1910–31* (London: SCM, 1972).

4. In the documentation throughout this study representative citations are made from this corpus of literature.

5. G. C. Berkouwer, *The Triumph of Grace in the Theology of Karl Barth* (Grand Rapids: Eerdmans, 1956) 384-93.

of their earlier positions and in terms of the philosophical principles that are sup-
posedly at the root of their system."[6] Finally, Barth himself was appalled at the
treatment he received in Van Til. G. W. Bromiley stated that "Van Til's study is
so strained that Barth has apparently seen in it almost a willful caricature."[7]
Berkouwer concurred when he stated that "it does not surprise me that Barth
says in amazement that he cannot recognize himself at all in *The New Modernism*."[8]

Others considered the evangelical response to be a critique that was given more
to refuting Barth than to comprehending him. It was seen as going around Barth
rather than through him. Although the evangelical response to Barth has not really
provided grist for the theological mills in Barth studies internationally, the rejection of his theology nevertheless represents a comparatively consistent and influential front in American evangelicalism from the the 1940s through the 1960s, and
even beyond that. The discrepancy between this "typical" American evangelical
response to Barth and the corresponding concern expressed by leading Barth
scholars about the nature of that response provides an opportune occasion to
engage in a more careful analysis of the anatomy of this evangelical type in the
light of its response to Barth.[9] It is important for evangelical theology today to understand and evaluate this chapter of its post–World War II history in light of
the current questions regarding its theological foundations and historical identity.
The American evangelical response to Barth represents an important case-study in
modern evangelical history in that it clearly brings to the surface the infrastructure
of a theological type that continues to pervade evangelical theology in the
present and to profoundly affect its agenda.[10]

6. Hans Urs von Balthasar, *The Theology of Karl Barth* (New York: Holt, Rinehart and
Winston, 1971) 45, 71.

7. Geoffrey W. Bromiley, "Karl Barth," in *Creative Minds in Contemporary Theology* (ed.
Philip E. Hughes; Grand Rapids: Eerdmans, 1966) 52.

8. Berkouwer, *The Triumph of Grace*, 388. It is significant to note that in spite of
Van Til's strong, and often strained, polemic against Barth, he is remarkably close to him
from the standpoint of his location in the fideist rather than in the rationalist Christian apologetic
tradition. In this sense Van Til does not fit neatly into the evangelical type being analyzed in this
study. However, his vigorous critique of Barth was foundational and formative for the larger initial evangelical response to Barth. In principle, Van Til had a more moderate rather than a foundational use of empirical or logical techniques of apologetic discourse.

9. This study represents a major expansion and refinement of the first chapter of my doctoral
dissertation, "Karl Barth and the Church Doctrine of Inspiration: An Appraisal for Evangelical
Theology" (2 vols.; Graduate School of Theology, Fuller Theological Seminary, 1976), which
focuses particularly on Barth's *Church Dogmatics*, Vol. 1, Parts 1 and 2. This study was written
under the guidance of Dr. Geoffrey W. Bromiley, who introduced me so well to the thought of
Barth. For a major American evangelical response to my dissertation see Carl F. H. Henry, *God,
Revelation and Authority* (Waco, Tex.: Word, 1979) 4.256-71.

10. When one surveys the array of literature written by and about evangelicals in the past
decade, one overarching concern quickly surfaces: identity—the rediscovery of the historical and
spiritual roots of evangelical theology. This study is made with the conviction that Barth's massive theological endeavor can serve as a critical resource in the current evangelical quest for
theological identity.

ANALYSIS

The major American evangelical response to Barth finds its locus in the question of the epistemological role of Scripture and evangelicalism's concern for the certainty of rational, objective revelational knowledge. We must approach this central issue from a threefold perspective. In keeping with the philosophical infrastructure of the American response, I will probe the question metaphysically, ontologically, and epistemologically.

Philosophy

Metaphysically speaking, the first concern for American evangelicalism relates to the formal issue of philosophy: it is claimed that Barth refuses to allow philosophy primary status in theological reflection, thus raising the question of the "objective" basis to Barth's theology. This formal issue requires comment from several perspectives. First of all, Barth is primarily criticized for his separation of philosophy from the sphere of theology. "The fundamental issue is the basis on which Barth rigidly segregates theology and philosophy . . . since he neglects the inescapable logical conditions that structure man as man."[11]

For evangelicalism the following consequences ensue. To begin with, theology's own integrity is at stake when one separates sharply from it the disciplines of philosophy, science, and history. Theology, for evangelicalism, must be viewed as a system-building science. Rejecting axiomatic theology with an explicit orientation to philosophy leads to a stop-gap view of theology. Moreover, theology has no point of contact with the outside world when you separate philosophy from its domain. Nor does theology have any universally valid criteria to test its truth claims and those of revelation when there is a refusal to abide by the law of noncontradiction, which is so fundamental to philosophical reasoning. Interestingly enough, however, American evangelicalism is quick to point out that Barth nonetheless does make alliance with nineteenth- and twentieth-century religious theory and its philosophical presuppositions.

Methodologically, Barth is primarily criticized for not freeing himself from the presuppositions of continental critical philosophy, and for possessing as a consequence of that the philosophical bias of Kierkegaard, Schleiermacher, Kant, and even Plato. The crisis theologians are "still under the dominance of Kant and modern philosophic idealism . . . and . . . epistemology more than they are true to the historic Christian faith."[12] For evangelicalism, this earmarks Barth's theol-

11. Henry, *God, Revelation and Authority,* 1.190; see also 1.57, 188, 189-90, 191, 194, 200, 203-10, 248; and 2.317; Henry, "Dare We Renew the Controversy?" *CT* 1.15-18; "The Theological Situation in Europe—Decline of the Bultmann Era?" *CT* 8.1089-92; "The Enigma in Barth," *CT* 6.888-89; Gordon H. Clark, "Special Report: Encountering Barth in Chicago—April 23-27, 1962" (report on Barth's lectures at the University of Chicago) *CT* 6.795-96; Harold Kuhn, review of Clark's "Karl Barth's Theological Method," *CT* 7.950; H. Daniel Frieberg, "Reflections on Karl Barth's Lectures," *CT* 6.847- 48; H. D. McDonald, "The Conflict over Special Revelation," *CT* 6.304.

12. Henry, *Remaking the Modern Mind* (Grand Rapids: Eerdmans, 1946) 295. See also Henry, *God, Revelation and Authority,* 1.191-92; "Chaos in European Theology: The Deterioration of Barth's Defenses," *CT* 9.15-19; "Revelation in History," *CT* 9.177-79 and *CT* 9.229-

ogy fundamentally as a liberal theology, since its presuppositions are essentially neo-Protestant ones;[13] as a speculative theology, since its mode of thinking is primarily non-biblical in nature;[14] as a consciousness theology, since its methodology is strongly critical and dialectical in character, being grounded in the autonomous individual with an epistemology of correlativity; and as an anti-metaphysical theology, since its attitude and bias is strongly antirational if not irrational. "It must be plainly stated that Barth's position is as subjective . . . rejecting the 'old orthodoxy' . . . [and continuing] still in the wastelands of consciousness theology with its relativism and subjectivity."[15]

Therefore, Barth is primarily criticized for his doctrine of subjectivity. Formally speaking, this is the fundamental issue for American evangelicalism. The consequences are as follows: there is no strong metaphysical base, no genuine objectivity; there is an epistemological dualism that reflects a revolt against reason and revelation; there is a deemphasis on emperical reality—on history, nature, reason, conscience, ethics; and there is an irrationalism that characterizes his entire theology. For evangelicalism this last point is the metaphysical issue—the rationality and historicality of revelation. For unless Barth "assigns a higher role to consistency and coherence, he cannot hope to preserve any distinction whatever between truth and untruth in theology."[16]

31; "Revelation as Truth," *CT* 9.335; "The Pale Ghost of Barth," *CT* 15.466-67; Gordon Clark, "Philosophy in the Sixties," *CT* 4.11; Cornelius Van Til, *The New Modernism* (Philadelphia: Presbyterian and Reformed, 1946) xv, 92, 130, 218-21, 336-57; Francis A. Schaeffer, "Neo-Orthodoxy and Its Progeny," *CT* 7.1180. See Bernard Ramm's review of *The Battle of Barth with Bultmann,* in *CT* 3.34-37, for a more ameliorating view on Barth.

13. Henry, "The Enigma in Barth," editorial in *CT* 6.889. See also Henry, "Dare We Renew the Controversy?" *CT* 1.15-18; "Barth Among the Mind-Changers: Some Unresolved Issues," *CT* 4.33; "Between Barth and Bultmann," *CT* 5.188; Francis A. Schaeffer, "Neo-Orthodoxy and Its Progeny," *CT* 7.1180; Leonhard Goppelt, "Dare We Follow Bultmann?" *CT* 6.726; K. Runia, "What Evangelicals Believe About the Bible," *CT* 15.213 (first of a two-part series); P. E. Hughes, "Review of Current Religious Thought," *CT* 1.38. But note also those evangelicals writing in *CT* who see a sharp distinction growing between the theologies of Barth and Bultmann: G. C. Berkouwer, "The Changing Climate of European Theology," *CT* 1.3-4, 16; and G. W. Bromiley, "Crusade Against Demythologization," *CT* 4.34-36.

14. Henry, "The Dilemma Facing Karl Barth," *CT* 7.336. See also Henry, "Has Winter Come Again?: Theological Transition in Europe," *CT* 6.270; "The Predicament of Modern Theology," *CT* 6.320; "Basic Issues in Modern Theology," *CT* 6.320; "Basic Issues in Modern Theology: Revelation as Truth," *CT* 9.334; *God, Revelation and Authority,* 4.393; review of C. Van Til's *Christianity and Barthianism* in *CT* 7.303; Gordon Clark, "Special Report: Encountering Barth in Chicago," *CT* 6.795-96; Francis A. Schaeffer, "Neo-Orthodoxy and Its Progeny," *CT* 7.1178; Harold Lindsell, "The Christian Source of Truth," *CT* 20.249; K. Runia, "The Modern Debate Around the Bible," *CT* 12.972; Winston M. Sherwick, "Heresies and Hearsays," *CT* 10.121-22. For a contrasting perspective see B. Ramm, "The Battle of Barth with Bultmann," *CT* 3.34-37.

15. "What of the New Barth?" *CT* 3.7. See also Van Til, *The New Modernism,* xiii-xv, 40-42, 77, 110, 122-23, 129-30, 143, 159, 212-13, 244; Van Til, *Christianity and Barthianism* (Philadelphia: Presbyterian and Reformed, 1962) 113, 117, 175, 206-208, 224, 265.

16. Henry, *God, Revelation and Authority,* 1.211. See also 1.212, 215, 229, 233, 240-41; Henry, "Revelation and the Bible," *CT* 2.6; "Barth Among the Mind-Changers: Some Un-

Revelation

Ontologically speaking, the second concern relates to the central issue of revelation: it is held that Barth refuses to define revelation in conceptual and propositional terms, thus raising, for American evangelicalism, the question of the "objective" basis for verification in Barth's theology and the question of his use of a philosophical construct after all. This foundational issue requires a twofold observation. First, for evangelicalism the decisive ontological issue is between dialectical disclosure and historical and conceptual revelation. "Barth's dialectical theology unfortunately encouraged the contrast between the personal and propositional, and his later efforts to reinforce the cognitive aspects were too long delayed and too guarded to repeal his non-cognitive emphasis."[17] American evangelicals see in Barth the dialectical and existential redefinition and restatement of revelation reflecting the speculative trends that can be traced back to Kierkegaard, Schleiermacher, Kant, and Plato. The primary issue for evangelicalism is to reject that dialectical dogma, for it undermines the ontological significance of reason, the objectivity of divine revelation, and the cognition of religious experience. It forces the central elements of Christian revelation into a speculative, dialectical model. For evangelicalism, divine revelation is objectively given in historical events and in intelligible concepts and words, historically and scripturally. Thus the decisive issue is the identity of revelation with the words of Scripture.

Second, the primary objection to Barth's understanding of the nature of revelation concerns his dialectical premise in which God is wholly other or transcendent

---

resolved Issues," *CT* 4.410; "The Theological Situation in Europe: Decline of the Bultmann Era?" *CT* 8.1089; "Basic Issues in Modern Theology: Revelation as Truth," *CT* 9.335; "Justification by Ignorance: A Neo-Protestant Motif?" *CT* 14.301; *The Drift of Western Thought* (Grand Rapids: Eerdmans, 1957) 66; *Frontiers in Modern Theology* (Chicago: Moody, 1969) 154-55; "Divine Revelation and the Bible," in *Inspiration and Interpretation* (ed. John F. Walvoord; Grand Rapids: Eerdmans, 1957) 268; G. Clark, "A Heritage of Irrationalism," selections from his *Karl Barth's Theological Method*, in *CT* 9.19. See the reviews of the following books: G. C. Berkouwer's *Conflict with Rome*, in *CT* 2.34; G. C. Berkhower's *The Triumph of Grace in the Theology of Karl Barth*, in *CT* 1.34. See G. H. Clark, *Karl Barth's Theological Method* (Philadelphia: Presbyterian and Reformed, 1963) 54-57, 59, 61-62, 71, 75, 96, 123, 135-36, 138, 144, 149-50, 225; C. Van Til, "What of the New Barth?" *CT* 3.6; *The New Modernism*, xiv, 104-5, 137, 215, 217-18, 368, 372, 376-78; *Christianity and Barthianism*, 113, 145. For contrasting perspectives see William Hordern's comments in "Faith, History and the Resurrection," an editorial by Henry in *CT* 9.655; and G. W. Bromiley, "Barth: A Contemporary Appraisal," *CT* 3.9-10.

17. Henry, *God, Revelation and Authority*, 2.179-80; 322-23; Henry, "Revelation and the Bible," *CT* 2.6-7; "Chaos in European Theology: The Deterioration of Barth's Defenses," *CT* 9.17; "Revelation in History," *CT* 9.32-33; "Revelation in History," *CT* 9.230; "Has Winter Come Again?: Theological Transition in Europe," *CT* 5.140-41, 188-89; and 6.270; *The Protestant Dilemma: An Analysis of the Current Impasse in Theology* (Grand Rapids: Eerdmans, 1949) 88, 149; *Fifty Years of Protestant Theology* (Boston: W. A. Wilde, n.d.) 37; *Frontiers in Modern Theology*, 34, 36, 78, 82; "Faith, History and the Resurrection," *CT* 9.655; Samuel J. Mikolaski, "The Nature of Atonement: The Cross and the Theologians," *CT* 7.623; Van Til, *The New Modernism*, 140; John M. Frame, "Scripture Speaks for Itself," in John W. Montgomery, ed., *God's Inerrant Word* (Minneapolis: Bethany Fellowship, 1973) 194, 195, 197; G. H. Clark, "A Continually Developing Theology," a review of Barth's *Humanity of God* in *CT* 4.32.

and his view of revelation which, according to evangelicalism, is limited to personal confrontation and thus is not conceptually and verbally expressible. The first area of concern is the epistemological transcendence of revelation. According to many evangelicals there are several related dangers into which Barth's theology of transcendent revelation leads us: skepticism, subjectivism, and irrationalism. One danger is that revelation as primarily transcendent Word leads to skepticism. Barth "erred in expounding God's epistemological transcendence to mean that divine activity in the universe is hidden, that God is not revealed in nature and history, nor even conceptually to the mind of man."[18] The qualitative distinction between God and persons leads to skepticism regarding revelational knowledge. Revelation in Barth is identified with external super-history, so that only the transcendent Word is in fact revelation. There is no being of revelation. Thus evangelicalism sees it as a reactionary doctrine of extreme transcendence, for there is an extreme disjunction between eternity and time. Barth's is a docetic notion of revelation. It basically represents a reduction of a comprehensive view of revelation in that it denies general revelation and affirms a naturalistic, mechanical, non-teleological view of nature. Barth's comprehensive doctrine of time, through which he attempts to reinforce the unity and contemporaneity of God's threefold revelation, only reinforces the concern. It is based on what many consider to be a dubious distinction between *Geschichte* and *Historie.*

Another danger of Barth's view is that revelation as primarily personal encounter leads to subjectivism. Barth's view of revelation is seen as "personal, paradoxical and internal and not rational and objective."[19] His religious theory thus makes knowledge of God dependent on repeated personal decision. The internal personal response alone becomes the locus of divine disclosure. The Spirit alone is the locus of revelation together with our obedient response. God meets us personally and we receive him through our submissive response. Thus revelation becomes a recurring miracle, being inherently redemptive. It is anchored in our personal decision in the context of God's time-event with us. For American evangelicalism this view promotes a sharp contrast between personal and propositional revelation. Moreover, revelation defined in terms of personal confrontation allows for no point of contact between God and persons and between gospel and world.

The danger is that revelation as primarily transcendent Word and personal event

18. Henry, *God, Revelation and Authority,* 2.53; see also, 1.49; 2.75, 80, 216; 4.84; see also Henry, "Revelation in History," *CT* 9.33; "Justification by Ignorance: A Neo-Protestant Motif?" *CT* 14.303; "The Pale Ghost of Barth," *CT* 15.466; "Dare We Renew the Controversy?" *CT* 1.15-18; "Chaos in European Theology: The Deterioration of Barth's Defenses," *CT* 9.15; Van Til, *Christianity and Barthianism,* 431; James D. Spiceland, "God Is Transcendent—But Is Language?" *CT* 22.24-25.

19. Henry, *God, Revelation and Authority,* 2.127-28; see also 2.12, 88, 178-79, 242, 281, 284; "Has Winter Come Again?: Theological Transition in Europe," *CT* 5.188-90; "Chaos in European Theology: The Deterioration of Barth's Defenses," *CT* 9.15, 17; "Revelation in History," *CT* 9.31; "Basic Issues in Modern Theology: Revelation in History," *CT* 9.229-31; "Where Is Modern Theology Going?" *CT* 12.527-28; *Frontiers in Modern Theology,* 103; G. H. Clark, *Karl Barth's Theological Method,* 162; Van Til, *The New Modernism,* 375-76; *Christianity and Barthianism,* 121; see also James I. Packer, "Contemporary Views of Revelation," two parts, *CT* 3.3-4 and 15-16; Fred H. Klooster, review of Colin Brown's *Karl Barth and the Christian Message,* in *CT* 11.37.

leads to relativism and irrationalism. Barth's view of revelation seems to be shorn of all forms of objectivity. It thus makes totalitarian claims for itself by renouncing objectifying metaphysical assertions. Even though the later Barth attempts to add some objectifying facets to his theology, in the eyes of American evangelicalism this only exemplifies the dilemma of his basic approach. It is too late to be able to make any significant changes. Evangelicals see Barth's view of revelation relating only tenuously with history and reason; it is simply not adequately grounded in ordinary history. Speaking about the *Geschichte Jesu Christi* rather than about *Heilsgeschichte* he avoids the historical objectivity of the Resurrection through his questionable yet commonly accepted European distinction between *Geschichte* and *Historie*. For American evangelicalism the kerygmatic character of Christian faith in Barth is simply not related to the realm of objective knowledge. His *anti-Heilsgeschichte* view is basically antimetaphysical and thus irrational.

While the first area of objection with the dialectical premises of Barth's view of revelation related to its epistemological transcendence, the second area of objection relates to the non-conceptual nature of revelation. Thus is the basic unacceptable conclusion denounced because of its unacceptable premise. The evangelical response to Barth here can be portrayed by a series of negations which it uses repeatedly throughout its literature concerning Barth's view of revelation: it is non-biblical because basically it is not derived from Scripture;[20] it is non-historical because it is not rooted empirically in history;[21] it is not general because it denies natural revelation;[22] it has non-being because it is conceived purely activistically; it is non-universal because it cannot be validated generally;[23] it is non-objective because it has no metaphysical basis;[24] it is non-verbal because it downgrades language and verbalization;[25] it is non-intellective because there is no content to

20. Henry, *God, Revelation and Authority*, 2.147; see also 2.145-46, 159; "Revelation and the Bible," *CT* 2.7; H. Kuhn, review of G. H. Clark's *Barth's Theological Method*, in *CT* 7.950.

21. Henry, *God, Revelation and Authority*, 2.311; see also 2.277; "Between Barth and Bultmann," *CT* 5.690; Review of Van Til's *Christianity and Barthianism*, in *CT* 7.303; "Chaos in European Theology: The Deterioration of Barth's Defenses," *CT* 9.15-19; "Basic Issues in Modern Theology: Revelation in History," *CT* 9.229-31 (13); *The Protestant Dilemma*, 116; *Frontiers in Modern Theology*, 39, 61, 67-68; Van Til, "What of the New Barth?" *CT* 3.5-6; Review of Barth's *Christ and Adam*, 34-36; Mikolaski, "The Nature of Atonement: The Cross and the Theologians," *CT* 7.623; P. E. Hughes, "Myth in Modern Theology," *CT* 5.950; see also B. Ramm for a more sympathetic perspective in "Review of the Battle of Barth with Bultmann," *CT* 3.36.

22. Henry, *God, Revelation and Authority*, 2.89; see also 2.43, 96, 143.

23. Henry, *God, Revelation and Authority*, 2.145; see also Henry, "Revelation in History," *CT* 9.31.

24. Henry, *God, Revelation and Authority*, 4.222; see also 2.161, 277-78, 298; "Has Winter Come Again?" *CT* 5.189; "Chaos in European Theology: The Deterioration of Barth's Defenses," *CT* 9.15; "Revelation in History," *CT* 9.32; "Faith, History and the Resurrection," *CT* 9.655; "Evangelicals and the Bible," *CT* 16.35; G. H. Clark, "Special Report: Encountering Barth in Chicago—April 23-27," *CT* 6.796. For a different understanding of objectivity in Barth, see B. Ramm, "Review of the Battle of Barth with Bultmann," *CT* 3.35.

25. Henry, *God, Revelation and Authority*, 2.144; see also 4.54; "Has Winter Come Again?" *CT* 5.189; *Evangelical Responsibility in Contemporary Theology*, 58; *The Protestant Dilemma*, 119; G. H. Clark, *Karl Barth's Theological Method*, ch. 7, "Verbal Revelation"; Robert P.

the *imagio Dei* thus splitting revelation and reason and leaving revelation anti-conceptual and irrational;[26] and it is non-conceptual since it is also anti-propositional.[27] For American evangelicalism the most basic issue ensuing from this view is that the Bible for Barth is not revelation. It only becomes revelation in correlation. This has most serious implications for the doctrine of Scripture.

Scripture

Epistemologically speaking, the third American evangelical concern relates to the functional issue of Scripture: it is argued that Barth refuses to identify Scripture with revelation—that is, he does not accept a rationally coherent and inerrant Bible. This raises the question of the "objective" basis for verification on the grounds of a philosophical paradox in Barth—namely, Scripture as errant and Scripture as the Word of God. Rationality and irrationalism is the basic issue here. The question is not whether there is an appeal to divine revelation as a basic axiom of Christian faith or whether Scriptures are mediated through chosen writers. The basic issue is whether divine revelation is mediated in the form of truths by which biblical writings communicate accurate information about God.[28] The concern about Barth is his dialectical evasion of the rational and verbal coherence—that revelation does not exist in its cognitive-verbal teaching or does not involve rational communication. The critique is that Barth is deriving two incompatible positions from the appeal to divine revelation. He is violating the law of non-contradiction by affirming at the same time that the Bible is the Word of God and that the Bible is errant. Thus for evangelicals the Achilles heel of Barth is the way the Bible relates to revelation, namely, as a witness. The non-identity of the Bible with revelation leaves biblical truth with no objective authoritative basis.

The evangelical critique focuses on both the distinction and the correlation between Scripture and revelation in Barth's theology. Both are inadequate. In regard to the distinction, Barth is criticized for refusing to subsume the Bible under the category of revelation. "Barth . . . in contrast to both Lutheran and Calvinistic theologians of the past, detached revelation and the witness of the Spirit from the Bible as the objective Word of God."[29] He distinguishes the Word of God from

---

Lightner, *The Savior and Scriptures* (Philadelphia: Presbyterian and Reformed, 1966) 104-24. Following a lengthy critique of Barth's view of Scripture, Lightner states the central issue: "*Inspiration not verbal:* This is the crux of the issue and with such a view neo-orthodoxy blatantly contradicts the high view of Scripture held by Jesus Christ" (p. 121).

26. Henry, *God, Revelation and Authority,* 1.399; see also 1.395-96; 2.53-54, 310; "Justification by Ignorance: A Neo-Protestant Motif?" *CT* 14.303; *Frontiers in Modern Theology,* 138; *Evangelical Responsibility in Contemporary Theology,* 57-58; G. H. Clark, *Karl Barth's Theological Method,* 224-25; Thomas D. Hersey, "Karl Barth," *CT* 6.1064.

27. Henry, "Revelation and the Bible," *CT* 9.337; *The Protestant Dilemma,* 119; Gordon R. Lewis, "The Triune God: Revelational Bases of Trinitarianism," *CT* 7.329.

28. Cf. G. H. Clark, "Barth's Critique of Modernism," *CT* 6.315; Norman L. Geisler, "Philosophy: The Roots of Vain Deceit," *CT* 21.924.

29. Henry, *God, Revelation and Authority,* 4.278; see also 4.82, 149, 151, 250, 457; "Revelation and the Bible," *CT* 2.5-7; *CT* 2.16; "The Dilemma Facing Karl Barth," *CT* 7.336; "Evangelicals and the Bible," *CT* 16.35-36; *The Protestant Dilemma,* 72, 79, 84; *Fifty Years of Protestant Theology,* 101-2; *Evangelical Responsibility in Contemporary Theology,* 59; *Frontiers in*

the Bible as such. *Deus dixit* and *Paulus dixit* are two different things. Thus the Bible is not seen as revelation itself. It is not an instrument of direct impartation because revelation is seen to supersede the written Word. Accordingly verbal revelation becomes a kind of barricade to control the Bible. Playing off the Word of God against its verbal character, Barth's view no longer guarantees the truth of language, for it denies the objective interpretation of texts. According to American evangelicalism, Barth has no intention of affirming the permanent truth of Scripture, for by separating Scripture from the Word of God he in principle undermines the theological significance of Scripture by defining it as an errant human product. Likewise, he undermines the actual existence of the revelation of the Word in our world.

Barth's view of the relation between Scripture and revelation is characterized in the following manner. First, there is the functional correlation of Scripture with revelation. Barth "understands 'scriptural authority' in functional terms."[30] In other words, the revelational quality of Scripture is to be found in Scripture's accommodation of a confrontation with the transcendent Word of God. Thus the revelational center of Scripture is made up of events not truths and concepts. The inner unity of the scriptural text as a fixed tradition is not in its doctrinal structure but in its identity-description of the acts of God as a single agent. Consequently, it is authoritative not in an epistemological sense but in a functional sense. The Bible is then an instrumentality through which God sporadically communicates his paradoxical Word. It is more inspiring than inspired. The doctrine of inspiration is redefined dynamically.

There is, moreover, a problem in Barth's view of the epistemological role of the Spirit in Scripture becoming revelation. "Barth tries to loosen inspiration from what he calls its 'rigid' and 'narrow' connection with the written Scriptures."[31] The subjective response to the Holy Spirit working in us alone achieves direct identification of revelation and the Bible. For evangelicalism the epistemological role of the Spirit in Barth obscures the objective validity of biblical truth and issues in uncertain subjectivity. Barth detaches revelation and the witness of the Spirit

Modern Theology, 127; G. H. Clark, "Special Report: Encountering Barth in Chicago—April 23-27," *CT* 6.796; *Karl Barth's Theological Method*, 187-88, 193-94, 203; Montgomery, *God's Inerrant Word*, 13; Harold Lindsell, "The Christian Source of Truth," *CT* 20.13; Oswald T. Allis, "Christian Faith and the Supernatural," *CT* 9.119; Robert D. Knudsen, "What is Orthodoxy?" a review of Hordern's *Case for a New Reformation Theology*, in *CT* 2.34-35; "Brilliant Encounter," a review of *Barth's Protestant Thought*, in *CT* 3.42; H. Daniel Frieberg, "Reflections on Karl Barth's Lectures," *CT* 6.847-48; Thomas D. Hersey, "Karl Barth," *CT* 6.1064; James Daane, review of Arnold B. Come's *Introduction to Barth's Dogmatics for Preachers*, in *CT* 7.1149; review of Barth's *God Here and Now*, in *CT* 8.847; G. H. Clark, review of Klaas Runia's *Karl Barth's Doctrine of Holy Scripture*, in *CT* 6.998; K. Runia, "The Modern Debate Around the Bible," *CT* 12.972-73; 12.1072; "Karl Barth, 1886–1968: His Place in History," *CT* 14.217; "What do Evangelicals Believe about the Bible?" *CT* 15.211, 214; 15.264-65; James I. Packer, "Contemporary Views of Revelation," *CT* 3.3.

30. Henry, *God, Revelation and Authority*, 4.84-85; see also 4.93, 148.

31. Ibid., 2.256-58. The entirety of chap. 2 of Henry's book—"The Spirit and the Scriptures," 256-71, is devoted to an analysis of my doctoral dissertation, "Karl Barth and the Church Doctrine of Inspiration: An Appraisal for Evangelical Theology." See also L. Goppelt, "Dare We Follow Bultmann?" *CT* 6.729.

from the Bible as objective Word. Evangelicals see him as correlating the truth of revelation with a super-conceptual inner response, thereby doing a disservice to the classic doctrine of Scripture.

Finally, there is the wordless character of revelation in contrast to Scripture. Barth rejected "the propositional-verbal nature of revelation" and correlated "the truth of revelation instead with a superconceptual inner response."[32] Barth postulates a nebulous revelation behind Scripture and denies that Scripture as such is the proper and final basis of Christian knowledge. Evangelicalism maintains that Scripture for Barth emerges from a supra-verbal divine event and must return to a wordless divine event. For him the revelation of Scripture belongs to a supra-historical sphere which cannot be brought under the norms of history. This in turn fosters a revelation mysticism, if not a Gnosticism and another kind of truth. This superior personal and non-verbal revelation represents a dangerous subjectivizing by centering on event and encounter. A wordless revelation has no conceptual content and is ultimately anchored in the heritage of irrationalism.

Since American evangelicals have read Barth primarily from a epistemological perspective, the implications of their analysis of the functional issue of Scripture are largely epistemological in nature. Moreover, they relate essentially to the role of Scripture, since for American evangelical theology the Bible itself has the key epistemological role. For evangelicalism, therefore, the Bible in Barth's theology authorizes theological proposals only indirectly; such theological proposals can be neither confirmed nor denied by historical-critical exegesis.[33] Thus there is a limited function for the historical-critical method in any form. On the other hand, for American evangelicalism the doctrine of Scripture epistemologically controls all other doctrines of the Christian faith, and the Bible itself authorizes theological proposals directly.

The basic issue is a functional versus an epistemological role of Scripture in the knowledge of revelational truth. This issue finds its antepenultimate roots in the epistemological problematic of the lack of identity between Scripture and revelation; its penultimate roots in the ontological problematic of the failure to define revelation in conceptual terms; and its ultimate roots in Barth's refusal to allow philosophy a primary status in theological reflection. Thus the American evangelical critique centers on the question of the separation of reason from revelation and knowledge from faith. It raises the supreme question of the nature of theological rationality and objectivity. Its fundamental problem with Barth is his doctrine of subjectivity, particularly as it is expressed in the doctrines of revelation and Scripture. It is these three areas that we must now address in our appraisal—subjectivity, revelation, and Scripture.

APPRAISAL

It is my contention that the evangelical response to Barth places too great a burden on the epistemological role of Scripture itself as a conceptual and rationally

---

32. Henry, *God, Revelation and Authority,* 4.312. See also G. H. Clark, *Karl Barth's Theological Method,* 174.

33. Henry, *God, Revelation and Authority,* 4.396; see also Henry, "The Predicament of Modern Theology," *CT* 5.321.

objective deposit of revelation without considering sufficiently other dimensions of theological reality relating to the apprehension of objective knowledge. We must assess this claim in the light of Barth's theology and current Barth studies. In parallel fashion to the preceding section we will evaluate the issue metaphysically, ontologically, and epistemologically.

Methodology

First, we must address the doctrine of subjectivity by dealing with the formal issue of methodology. One of the major problems stems from the tendency in American evangelicalism to read Barth almost exclusively through the grid of modern critical philosophy, and to reconstruct him in light of it. This factor contributes to a fundamental misreading of Barth which must be understood at several levels. First, Barth is read and evaluated too much in terms of his early theology. The later and more mature developments are not sufficiently recognized. Moreover, Barth is evaluated primarily in light of methodological questions that involve revelation as the primary arena of discussion. The epistemological role of Scripture is the basic grid for American evangelicalism's questions to Barth. Other theological centers in his thought are not explored. The inner structure of evangelical response reveals much about evangelical presuppositions regarding the task of theology and the function of Scripture. We will comment on this later. Furthermore, Barth is evaluated too exclusively through a philosophical line of questioning that evangelicalism brings to him, and primarily in light of modern philosophical presuppositions against which he is reconstructed. Finally, Barth is read too monothematically. He is evaluated essentially in terms of a single issue which has the effect of reading him reductionistically.

The preceding observations lead us to make another claim: methodologically, no one center controls Barth's theology. Accordingly, there is no "magic key to unlock all the doors of Barth's theology, . . . for he is not a systematic theologian in the sense that he works out his ideas from a single principle or even a group of principles." Therefore, "I do not think we can do justice to Barth by trying to explain his whole theology by one principle."[34] Thus one cannot give Barth an unconditional endorsement or rejection. To the degree that one does it represents a misreading of him; yet to a large extent American evangelicalism has done that. Although the conceptual control of some themes in Barth is high (such as Christ, the Trinity, or the grace of God), there is no one single center of theology in his thought.[35] Therefore, no one factor is the single reason for what might be wrong with his theology, for he is both compelling and alienating in a much more complex way than evangelicalism's methodology allows.[36] Thus Barth's refusal to produce a philosophical theology does not disqualify his theology from serious

34. T. H. L. Parker, "Barth on Revelation," *SJT* 13 (1968) 368. See also S. W. Sykes, "Barth on the Center of Theology," in *Karl Barth—Studies in His Theological Methods*, 46. Since the American evangelical response to Barth is oriented primarily toward questions of theological methodology, Sykes's collection of essays is one of the most useful studies against which to test an American evangelical reading of Barth's theology.

35. R. D. Williams, "Barth on the Triune God," in *Karl Barth—Studies of His Theological Methods*, 159.

36. Ibid., 192.

consideration. In fact, it represents the greatest challenge of his thought in that he more than any contemporary theologian has attempted to call into question the assumptions of modern theology and philosophy. American evangelicalism has never sufficiently understood that critique and therefore should also be advised to start with Barth and go through him (rather than around him) before seeking to discover what theology will be like beyond him.[37]

Therefore, the metaphysically related criticism that Barth's theology is anchored in a doctrine of subjectivity is substantially weakened by evangelicalism's methodological deficiency in its reading of Barth. Since there is no one center to Barth's theology there can be no single-themed critique of him, as American evangelicalism has basically given. Methodologically speaking, the charges of subjectivism and irrationalism are stated too strongly and simplistically and must be seriously challenged.

Objectivity

This brings us to the second area of our evaluation: the doctrine of revelation. Here we are dealing with the foundational issue of the nature of theology. It is my contention that evangelicalism tends to read Barth too much from a certain understanding of objectivity. It falls prey to the dangers of an objectivism that is primarily conceptually and cognitively based. It tends to be a rationalist critique of Barth's notion of subjectivity, anchored too heavily in the law of non-contradiction and the empirical concern for logical coherence. The use of empirical or logical methods are given foundational status. There is a strong tendency to develop abstractive and analytical modes of thought which are not sufficiently determined by the inherent rationality in the revealed truth itself. On that basis American evangelicalism holds to a concept of objectivity established primarily in and through the arena of historical and philosophical reasoning and anchored essentially in a verbal/conceptual view of revelation whose expression in the doctrine of inerrancy symbolizes the locus of epistemological and ontological certainty.

Evangelicalism thus tends to overload the doctrine of inerrancy as the basis for objectivity. It is made to carry all the epistemological freight in order to assure theological objectivity. However, it is certainly open to question whether the church has ever been able to call on this doctrine effectively to be such a delivery system for epistemological certainty. In any case it should not really be the central issue in accepting or rejecting Barth. At times it seems that for evangelicalism it is more important that Barth is rational than that he is biblical. Its critique issues forth from within a philosophical construct that at points appears to be as alien to the Bible as it accuses Barth's theology of being.

American evangelicalism perhaps sees correctly some of the existentialist splinters in Barth's theological vision, but it does not see the rationalistic and objectivistic beam in its own. It possesses an unbalanced phobia of subjectivity and an uncritical eye to its own rationalistic objectivism. It appears to have a basic inability to see objectivity associated with a paradigm of relational dynamics in

---

37. R. Crawford, "Theological Method of Karl Barth," *SJT* 25 (1972) 321; see also John Baillie, *The Sense of the Presence of God* (New York: Scribner, 1962) 255.

which the biblical and theological realities of covenant relationships and faith-obedience are more at center stage. True objectivity for evangelicalism exists primarily in rational consistency issuing from the beingness of God, and in no significant sense from the dynamic and relational activity of God among his people. For Barth revelation must be understood in terms of the being and becoming of God.

The preceding observations lead us to the conclusion that ontologically Barth's theology of revelation cannot merely be rejected as a brand of dialectical subjectivism. That critique overlooks significant elements of his view, of which I will note three. First, there is the actuality of revelation in Jesus Christ. For Barth the structure of the humanward movement of the Word of God begins in a primary revelatory occurrence, the determinative speaking of the Word in the Word-made-flesh. "The structure of this man-ward movement is, as Barth sets out in Section 4 of his first half-volume ('The Word of God in its Threefold Form'), manifold."[38] Therefore the humanward movement from God is one from actuality to possibility. "Theology starts with actuality (God making himself known) and proceeds to possibility whether he has made himself known i.e. the existence of God will appear *a posteriori* and in the course of the exposition of Faith."[39] The question of the reality of God is most important to Barth. For Barth God exists, acts, and speaks with freedom. Barth nowhere begins by establishing the existence of God apart from Jesus Christ's self-revelation, and he holds that "the proper pathway for theology is to follow the Word of God spoken in Jesus Christ." Moreover, "theology is the function of the church which exists to make Jesus Christ known."[40] Thus his starting point is the actuality of Christ.[41] For him this is the biblical starting point. No *a priori* philosophical constructs regarding the possibility of such a reality are needed.

The second important element in Barth's theology of revelation is the objectivity of faith-knowledge in covenant obedience. From this understanding of the act of revelation Barth proceeds to the construction of a trinitarian theology. We should note that although the conceptual control of the Trinity is high in Barth, it is not the only center of his theology. For him the trinitarian scheme is tightly interwoven with the whole conception of the life of faith. Faith-knowledge is determined from the side of its object, or, better, God the Subject, and thus is genuine and objective knowledge—a point that American evangelicalism has difficulty grasping from its perspective. Barth "holds that knowledge of God is determined from the side of its Object" and "that this faith-knowledge is genuine and objective."[42] Therefore he breaks through the relation between the knower and that which is known, not from the side of the knower but from the side of him who is known, namely the God of Abraham, Isaac, Jacob, and Jesus.[43] For Barth the I-Thou relation is not alien to God. The "I-Thou relationship is exploited by Barth

38. Williams, "Barth on the Triune God," 149.
39. Crawford, "Theological Method," 321.
40. Ibid., 323.
41. Parker, "Barth on Revelation," 381.
42. Crawford, "Theological Method," 325.
43. Frederick L. Herzog, "Theologian of the Word of God," *TToday* 13 (1957) 323.

to the full."[44] He therefore contributes significantly to the relational dimension of revelational faith-knowledge and the covenant obedience that issues forth from this understanding of the God of Scripture. The root metaphor of understanding humanity as "covenant-partner" with God can give us insight into his entire theology. On these grounds Barth is able to develop a comprehensive view of theological obedience in his dogmatics.[45]

Third, there is the receptivity of faith in the original hearing and in our hearing. For Barth experience as faith-obedience and covenant promise is "the correlate of his doctrine of God's action" among us.[46] God acts through promises by making them contemporary, and the Christian experience of the promises is the exposition of faith. "Faith comes through hearing." God's speech in his Word and Scripture is the original hearing which precedes our hearing of the Word.[47] Therefore Barth's doctrine of Scripture is a function of his doctrine of God's being in his action. Scripture is and becomes the Word of God because God makes himself known through this original hearing to our hearing. Thus Scripture is preaching; it is a mouthpiece.[48] The Word awaits our hearing in the words of Scripture (Scripture is the Word of God as such) in the context of our obedient response of faithful hearing (Scripture becomes the Word of God also for us). For Barth the church's freedom to hear the Word of God stands "within the relation of obedience."[49]

Therefore, "Barth's doctrine of the Word of God, his concept of revelation, is an account of the present action of God in the world, an action which has strict reference to his action in Israel and Christ," and therefore in the church.[50] Scripture, and therefore theology, is anchored, not in "an objective law external to the subject" but in the doctrine of God and thus in the history of God's actions in Israel and Christ in the context of the covenant obedience of the faith community. This is "a free and whole hearted obedience, and, ultimately, a gift of grace and of the Holy Spirit."[51] Scripture is therefore the exchange of these dealings between God and his people,[52] yet not only a record of these exchanges but also "the sign of God's presence in the community" of his people then and now. Scripture is a sign like the sacraments, a historical "vehicle for God's present action."[53] It has

44. Crawford, "Theological Method," 335.

45. Stuart D. McLean, "The Root Metaphor of Covenant in Understanding the Church Dogmatics of Karl Barth," paper presented at the American Academy of Religion meetings, December 19-22, 1981, San Francisco, California. See also McLean's *Humanity in the Thought of Karl Barth* (Edinburgh: T. & T. Clark, 1981), especially section III.D., "Man in His Determination as the Covenant-partner of God."

46. Timothy Gorringe, "In Defense of the Identification of Scripture as Word of God," *SJT* 32 (1979) 305.

47. Ibid.

48. Sykes, "Barth on the Center of Theology," 51-52.

49. Williams, "Barth on the Triune God," 189.

50. Gorringe, "In Defense of Scripture as Word of God," 305; see also Crawford, "Theological Method," 335-36.

51. Sykes, "Barth on the Center of Theology," 45.

52. Avery Dulles, "Scripture: Recent Protestant and Catholic Views," *TToday* 37 (April 1980) 8.

53. Gorringe, "In Defense of Scripture as Word of God," 306.

a signifying function. Like the prophets and apostles it is a faithful testimony to God's redemptive actions.

We conclude, therefore, that the primary ontologically related criticism that Barth's theology is anchored in a doctrine of non-conceptual personal revelation and that it is thus subjectivistic in nature needs substantial modification by apprehending the broader notion of objectivity that Barth offers. American evangelicalism needs to appropriate a more broadly based understanding of theological rationality which involves the ability to think through the nature and function of theology and Scripture in relationship to the nature of its object, or, more accurately stated, its Subject. It must recognize that "the 'rational' knowledge of the object of faith is derived from the object of faith and its knowledge is ultimately derived from Truth, that is, from God and from his will."[54] This Subject is the living God of Scripture who has revealed himself in Jesus Christ in the context of faithful hearing and continues to do so among his people and in the world everywhere. Ontologically speaking, evangelicalism is therefore challenged to gain a deeper understanding of the reality of God and the nature of theological objectivity deriving from that reality, from which the concepts of revelation and Scripture take their basic orientation. Ontology and epistemology are inseparably connected, and this linkage is inadequately developed from a theological perspective in American evangelicalism.

Epistemology

We come now to a final area in our assessment: the doctrine of Scripture and its relationship to the functional issue of epistemology. A major problem here is that evangelicalism tends to read Barth too much in terms of the epistemological question rather than the question of the nature of theological reality. Therefore it falls prey to a theological paradigm that has the question of epistemological certainty at its center. It prioritizes concept over covenant and statement over story, thereby portraying a cognitively oriented "objectivist" conception of truth. It clearly adopts a correspondence model of truth over against a more consensually oriented model of truth. Therefore it gives epistemological priority to an inerrant Bible, only a secondary epistemological role to the Holy Spirit, virtually no epistemological function to Christian experience, i.e., to faith-knowledge, and none to the community of faith. With its strong emphasis upon the rational capacity of human nature it vigorously reinforces a modernistic form of natural theology and tends, in developing its theology of knowing, to seriously underestimate the noetic effects of sin. Consequently it lacks a certain epistemic modesty.

Moreover, it frequently confuses the epistemic effects of sin, emphasized in Barth's theology, with Kantian epistemology, which is reputedly governing his thought.[55] As a result it incorrectly sees Barth's epistemology as being largely "subjectivist" in nature when in fact Barth has taken into account very seriously the epistemic limitations of human nature. Therefore, "the issue between Barth and those who wish to resuscitate natural theology is on the understanding of man" in which "it is not primarily an epistemological issue at all but concerns the

---

54. Sykes, "Barth on the Center of Theology," 36-37, 49-50.
55. Parker, "Barth on Revelation," 374.

doctrines of grace and creation."[56] In our judgment evangelicalism has not developed sufficiently the epistemological, and even more so the soteriological, implications of "seeing through a glass darkly." In effect it works with an inadequate understanding of the theological relationship between epistemology and ontology, and it tends to separate them in its theological method.

This separation is rooted in a deeper theological problem in American evangelicalism, namely, the separation of God's being and God's act. It is reflective of an incipient dualism governing the structure of evangelical theology in which God's intervention in time and history through Jesus Christ, and the wholeness of God in him, has seriously minimized its ability to work out an integrated theological method. The dualism of Kant appears much more evident in evangelicalism's theology than in Barth's. This dualism in evangelical thought—the separation of the being of God from the acts of God, of ontology from epistemology, of the theoretical from the empirical—leads to a more fundamental tendency of separating the Incarnation from the atonement, and the consequent inability to adequately ground one's theological method christologically and soteriologically.

The contemporary issues surrounding the doctrine of inspiration and inerrancy tend also to arise from such a propensity toward a dualist framework of thought. Therefore, American evangelicalism's rejection of Barth's doctrine of Scripture on the grounds that it is contradictory and subjectivistic—since it is God's Word and errant at the same time—reflects a much too narrow, if not fundamentally flawed, assessment of Barth's position. The epistemological strength of his theology must be assessed on a much broader basis than the canons of inerrancy. It must be viewed from the standpoint of his understanding of the nature of theological reality as a whole, anchored in the action and being of God as self-disclosed in Jesus Christ. We must bring three general perspectives to bear on our understanding of Barth at this point: God as subject, revelation through signification, and Scripture as story. We must now consider the importance of subjectivity, signification, and story telling for Barth's epistemology and ontology.

Theological Reality

In connection with God as subject one must understand Barth's critique of the assumptions of the modern epistemological debate—sometimes empiricist, sometimes Kantian, sometimes reductionist.[57] Modern epistemologies generally characterized the object of knowledge in terms of the way in which it is known by the human knower, not by the nature of the object known.[58] Here Barth's focus on the nature and reality of God as Subject is foundational. God himself is the starting point of his revelation. God himself is the content of his self-communication and self-giving. Accordingly, "the scandal for post-enlightenment epistemology" is Barth's "concentration on God rather than on ways of proving God, a position

---

56. Gorringe, "In Defense of Scripture as Word of God," 308.
57. D. F. Ford, "Conclusion: Assessing Barth," in *Karl Barth—Studies in His Theological Methods,* 194.
58. Gorringe, "In Defense of Scripture as Word of God," 317.

which is often incomprehensible to his critics" including American evangelical critics.[59] In this Barth is not simply privatizing God (subjectivism), because for him faith is primarily knowledge, a recognition of revelational facts, not only decision.[60] Above all faith is received as a gift of grace. Therefore, for Barth God is present and communicating as the Subject, whom we receive in the life of the Holy Spirit through faith-obedience.[61] However, we must be careful not to confuse this notion with the modern notion that personal religious knowledge does not have the status of true fact and primary knowledge.[62] American evangelicalism gravitates toward this modern reductionist school and therefore is unable to fully comprehend Barth's profound critique of the enlightenment understanding of religious knowledge.

Barth's understanding of the reality of God as Subject contributes directly to his concept of revelation through signification. Here we are dealing with the principle of analogical thinking. The epistemology of the *analogia fidei* or the *analogia relationis* is the basis of Barth's critique of modernity. We know God on the basis of the partial correspondence of analogy. There is a basic recognition that "the human form is inadequate to express the divine content. . . . It is a partial correspondence, the correspondence from God's side only."[63] Now "the basic principle in which Barth operates his analogical thinking is in 'act', rather than in 'being'."[64] God is an acting subject not a static object. Therefore, Barth's is a dynamic and acting ontology. He reacts against any static ontology. Therefore the specific form of the epistemological struggle is between an adequate theological understanding of biblical faith and inadequate medieval and modernistic uses of reason. In Barth we have the triumph of *analogia relationis* over *analogia entis*. Faith has priority over reason.[65] This is a theological rationality, created by God and given to humanity by the grace of God.[66]

For Barth this orientation liberates Christian faith from the fetters of metaphysical speculation. It is important here to note that this emphasis becomes increasingly more dominant in the later Barth,[67] though we should note that Barth's rejection of the analogy of being for the analogy of faith does not mean he denied "every form of ontological presupposition" as long as the former was based on the latter.[68] Consequently, the language and the theology of the later Barth is more analogical than dialectical. It is characterized more by the mode of revelational signification than by that of dialectical paradox. American evangelicalism mainly overlooks the importance of the development and centrality of the *analogia fidei* in Barth,

59. Ford, "Conclusion: Assessing Barth," 195.

60. Williams, "Barth on the Triune God," 186.

61. Ibid., 191-92.

62. Crawford, "Theological Method," 335.

63. Jung Young Lee, "Karl Barth's Use of Analogy in his Church Dogmatics," *SJT* 22 (1969) 141.

64. Ibid., 146.

65. Ibid., 147.

66. Crawford, "Theological Method," 322.

67. Joseph C. McLelland, "The Authority of the Canon," *CJT* 5 (1959) 41.

68. Lee, "Barth's Use of Analogy," 150.

and it bases its critique too much on reading Barth from the perspecive of his ear-lier dialectical tendencies.[69] Moreover, it fails to adequately acknowledge and ap-preciate the truly theological grounding that Barth has given to revelational objec-tivity in the face of deficient medieval and modern epistemologies.

Understanding the reality of God as acting subject and apprehending the truth of revelation through signification relates directly to Barth's theology of Scrip-ture as story. Here we are dealing with the hermeneutic of biblical narrative. Barth deliberately ignored a good part of the post-Kantian debate surrounding the problem of subjectivity. His alternative was to give epistemological expression to a hermeneutic of biblical narrative.[70] Barth's prolegomena in the *Church Dog-matics* are throughout concerned with hermeneutics.[71] But Barth is concerned with a hermeneutic which inquires after the self-interpretation of God in Jesus Christ (a dynamic act) not the conceptualization of historical propositions per se (static being). In this hermeneutic one attempts to say the same thing in other words—with the understanding that it is God in his revelatory action in Christ (as under-stood within the context of the church as a believing community of faith) who con-trols our language.[72] In this connection we must remember that "Barth's doctrine of Scripture is a function of his doctrine of God's being in becoming," that is, his being in his revelatory actions in the history of Israel and the church.[73] In this sense, and only in this sense, "Scripture becomes for us the Word of God be-cause God makes himself known through it."[74]

Accordingly Barth's dominant hermeneutical approach focuses on the inter-pretation of central biblical narratives that signify God's revelatory actions in Is-rael and the church in the covenant context which has been initiated with them through Christ.[75] Since the heart of Barth's theology is in his reflection on biblical narratives, objective scriptural content comes to mean "the total impact" that the story makes on us—Scripture taken as whole not only through the conceptualiza-tion of its propositional content.[76] As narrative rendering God as agent, the Bible is never an independent verification of revelation, nor of other doctrines, nor of itself.[77] As the Word of God it is self-authenticating, a point on which Barth stands firmly with Reformation theology. This theological approach contrasts with the American evangelical approach of having the Bible itself stand as an inde-

69. Ford, "Conclusion: Assessing Barth," 210.

70. David H. Kelsey, *Uses of Scripture in Recent Theology* (Philadelphia: Fortress, 1975) 32-55.

71. Tom Provence states that "to fail to understand the connection between his doctrine of Scripture and his hermeneutic theory is to miss one of the most important elements in Barth's thought." "Karl Barth's Hermeneutics: The Sovereignty of the Object," *Studia Biblical et Theologica* 10 (1980) 45.

72. Ronald R. Ray, "Jacques Ellul's Innocent Notes on Hermeneutics," *Int* 33 (1979) 279.

73. Gorringe, "In Defense of Scripture as Word of God," 305.

74. Ibid. See also Carl F. Starkloff, S.J., "Barth and Loyola on Communication of the Word of God," *SJT* 27 (1974) 148.

75. D. F. Ford, "Barth's Interpretation of the Bible," in *Karl Barth—Studies of His Theologi-cal Method,* 55-87; see also Gorringe, "In Defense of Scripture as Word of God," 312.

76. Gorringe, "In Defense of Scripture as Word of God," 315.

77. Parker, "Barth on Revelation," 370.

pendent epistemological criterion for establishing theological certainty. Thus for Barth, Scripture is used to "authorize" doctrinal conclusions "almost exclusively by providing the data for theological arguments."[78] This hermeneutic of biblical narrative is consonant with Barth's primary motif of hearing the Word of God which is grounded in his doctrines of God and revelation. In effect, Barth provides a more comprehensive and rigorous doctrine of revelational and biblical authority than does American evangelical theology in that, through its very use as the Word of God in and by the church as a theological community, its authority is attested, independent of the need to establish external criteria of verification.

Barth's theological orientation contrasts sharply with the explicit American evangelical approach of having the Bible itself stand as an independent epistemological criterion for establishing theological certainty. Consequently, evangelicalism lacks sufficient appreciation for the profound way in which Barth's theology contributes to reclaiming the theological reality of revelational and biblical authority in the context of post-Enlightenment rationalism. Therefore, the primary American evangelical epistemological criticism that Barth's theology is anchored in a doctrine of Scripture that refuses to identify revelation with Scripture—thereby removing an objective basis of verification—needs to be seriously challenged in view of Barth's hermeneutic of biblical narrative, his principle of analogical thinking, his doctrine of God as acting subject, and his basic critique of modern philosophical assumptions. In effect this conclusion challenges the validity of the very notion of theological objectivity that Barth is criticized for not possessing. We must conclude, therefore, that the evangelical response to Barth places too great a burden on the epistemological role of Scripture itself as a conceptual and rationally objective deposit of revelation without considering sufficiently other dimensions of theological reality in establishing an adequate view of objective theological knowledge. Its dualistic tendency to separate epistemology and ontology, God's act and being, leads to a less-than-adequate theological position.

CONCLUSION

I have argued that the American evangelical assessment of Barth must be significantly modified if not altogether altered in light of a more comprehensive consideration of Barth's theology. Yet the appraisal of the evangelical response to Barth must not obscure the fact that there is also in his theology a certain preoccupation with the epistemological question. Although we must be careful not to read Barth exclusively in terms of this problem, as I think American evangelicalism has done, there is, nonetheless, an epistemological preoccupation with the actuality of the revelatory event and its necessity.[79] The *Church Dogmatics* is permeated with a deep concern about the modern question relating to the knowledge of God, and Barth tends to address it from within a certain structure of epistemological assumptions, which he does not always readily acknowledge.[80]

78. David H. Kelsey, "Appeals to Scripture in Theology," *JR* 48 (1968) 15-16.
79. Ford, "Conclusion: Assessing Barth," 198-200; see also Williams, "Barth on the Triune God," 184.
80. Williams, "Barth on the Triune God," 172-73, 179, 181.

Consequently there is a tendency for persons with their ability to know or not know to occupy "the center of the stage."[81] The difference between Barth and American evangelicalism on this question is that the latter expresses a much greater confidence in the rational capacity of human nature to know God, whereas the former, acknowledging more the epistemic and noetic effects of sin, insists on the need for humanity to participate in the revelational event itself in order to know God. Therefore, for Barth the main question tends to be one of certain knowledge with the possibility of a person being included in the act of revelation.[82] He brings together more effectively than evangelicalism his epistemology and his ontology.

In Barth there is the promise of freedom within the context of obedience; yet it is worked out in the context of a preoccupation with ontologically secure knowledge. This factor is especially discernable in the earlier Barth but, notably, not nearly so much in the later Barth. So even though Barth has a comprehensive view of theological obedience (ethics) running throughout his thought, it tends to be oriented to the question of theological certainty (epistemology), sometimes at the expense of dealing with questions relating to covenant faithfulness.[83] The comprehensive "evangelization" of contemporary human thought in Barth is not always sufficiently extended into an emphasis on the "evangelization" of human action. Barth's powerful emphasis on the objective accomplishment of God's activity in Jesus Christ at times tends to minimize the importance of the concretization of that act in the life of God's people. However, in contrast to American evangelicalism, the nature of that certainty for Barth is not tied up in dogmatic propositions per se but "in the absolute dependability of God as acting subject."[84] Yet, as we have seen, the pervasiveness of the epistemological problem, as it relates to the question of certainty of knowledge, comes around to roost with a much greater presence on the doorstep of American evangelical theology.[85] The problem with the evangelical critique of Barth is that it has not been able to assess Barth constructively beyond its disagreement with him on that question and, more importantly, that it has not realized that the existentialist splinter it has seen in Barth's theological vision may well be related to a rationalistic beam obstructing its own.

81. Ibid., 174.
82. Ibid., 188.
83. Ibid., 187.
84. Ibid., 187-88.
85. The epistemological problem referred to here also extends into Barth's doctrine of Scripture. He conceptualizes Scripture in terms of an analogy to the divine-human nature of Christ (McLelland, "The Authority of the Canon," 41). To a large extent this incarnational analogy underlies his theology of inspiration (see Gorringe, "In Defense of Scripture as Word of God," 312; and Ford, "Conclusion: Assessing Barth," 199). However, a complete analogy for Scripture as the Word of God not only involves the unity of God and humanity in the Incarnation but also the relation of the Spirit of God in Christ to the people of God, Israel, and the church (see McLelland, "The Authority of the Canon," 43; and Gorringe, "In Defense of Scripture as the Word of God," 310). Barth does not adequately develop the pneumatologically and ecclesiologically related analogs for his theology of Scripture. Therefore the weakness in his thought lies not only at the point of the question of theological certainty but also in its limited ability to apprehend and affirm the concrete reality of spiritual community and its epistemological rule. The prominence of the former is related to the deficiency of the latter, a deficiency that is even more prevalent in American evangelicalism's theology of Scripture.

It has been my thesis here that the paradigm of ontological certainty that governs this genre of evangelical theology, which has been analyzed and appraised in relation to the questions of God, revelation, and Scripture, is seriously challenged when evangelicalism gives Barth a more sympathetic and balanced reading than it has given him in the past. Moreover, it is my contention that although Barth's theology also tends to be preoccupied with the question of epistemological certainty, it is much less so than is the theology of American evangelicalism. In addition, I believe that Barth's theology has fruitful lines of thought that can be creatively pursued in the critique and construction of doctrine.[86] That, however, has not been the purpose of this study in which we have given our attention to analyzing and appraising the anatomy of an evangelical type that has not found Barth's theology useful in its own theological constructions but rather has often defined itself in opposition to him. We have tried to evaluate the shape of that response and hope that it will serve as an encouragement to explore further one of the most fertile theological minds of the century and, indeed, of the church's history.

***

In his Barth seminars, his work with graduate students, and his numerous published essays, Geoffrey Bromiley has demonstrated an unparalleled mastery of Barth's thought; and more than any other modern scholar, his understanding has been governed by a remarkable ability to read Barth in a constructive critical manner. Dr. Bromiley's approach to the *Church Dogmatics* represents the best of that discerning attitude with which Barth must be examined today if we are to continue in the needed reconstruction of major areas of evangelical theology that are still all too often controlled by constricting theological paradigms.

86. See Ford, "Conclusion: Assessing Barth," 200; see also Bernard Ramm, *After Fundamentalism* (San Francisco: Harper & Row, 1983) as an excellent recent example of a constructive reading of Barth for shaping the agenda of evangelical theology. The creative edge of evangelical theology in recent years has frequently found Barth to be an ally rather than an adversary in dealing with the critical theological issues facing the church in a post-Enlightenment context.

Doxophany:
A Trinitarian Eschatological Vision

Daniel A. Tappeiner

The purpose of this essay is to provide a theological vision about the ultimate meaning of creation and history. I use the word *vision* because of a conviction that all *vital* theology must be rooted in an inner spiritual perception of reality. I use the qualifying word *theological* because of an equal conviction that any legitimate Christian vision of reality must be mediated through an analysis of the form and content of divine revelation in Scripture. The ultimate meaning proposed will be in terms of the eschatological category of "Doxophany," which, as the word itself suggests, refers to the final, perfect revelation of the glory of God in the eschaton.[1]

In biblical usage the concept of "glory" is very rich. Here "glory" is especially understood in terms of the mystery of the inner trinitarian reality of the love of God as Father, Son, and Holy Spirit. The whole of creation, history, and consummation can be viewed as a movement proceeding from the infinite, eternal inner love of God as triune into a state of exhibition and manifestation of that hidden, inner reality in a new creation and a new humanity, through the Incarnation, atonement, and exaltation of Jesus Christ. My intention is to present in this theological vision a series of historical observations followed by a set of theses.

I

Historical Observations

Theology is man's effort at entering into the reality of God revealed in Jesus Christ and authoritatively witnessed to in holy Scripture. As such, there are infinite possibilities of development in the understanding and consciousness of the church. As Philip Schaff put it in his Theses for the Times,

> Christianity in itself is the *absolute* religion, and in this view unsusceptible to improvement. We must not confound with this, however, the *apprehension* and *appropriation* of Christianity in the consciousness of mankind. This is a progressive process of development that will reach its close only with the second coming of the Lord.[2]

One of the earliest theological visions of the ultimate purpose of creation and redemption is found in the writings of Irenaeus in the second century A.D. Nowhere

---

1. The word comes from *doxa* which means "opinion, appearance, glory" and *phanein* which means "to manifest." I first encountered this word in Ethelbert Stauffer's *New Testament Theology* (tr. John Marsh; London: SCM, 1955) ch. 19.

2. Philip Schaff, *The Principle of Protestantism* (tr. John Nevin; Philadelphia: United Church Press, 1964) 221.

do we find an explicit exposition of his theological vision in an orderly essay—most of it has to be extracted from polemical writings against the gnostic heretics of his time. Yet his contribution provides an important beginning point for our purpose. Irenaeus does not provide the most fundamental framework for the comprehension of the ultimate *telos* of God's ways in creation, history, and consummation. He does, however, present some conceptions which are important to such a framework. In particular, he takes as his starting point the fall of humanity, and he sees the salvation of humanity through Jesus Christ as both a deliverance from the power of Satan and a participation in the divine nature. He focuses on Jesus Christ as the one who "re-capitulates" the history of the race—undoing the tragic effects of the fall and, advancing humankind beyond Adam, also bringing about the perfecting of the race. "Because He who formed us in the beginning and sent His Son at the end is one and the same, the Lord . . . both destroyed our adversary and prefected man in the image and likeness of God."[3] This triumph over Satan and transformation of humankind was rooted in the union between God and humanity accomplished in the incarnation of the Logos. "The Logos of God, our Lord Jesus Christ, who on account of his great love became what we are that he might make us what he is himself."[4]

In Irenaeus we discover two key elements important to a theological vision of God's ultimate purpose: first, the notion of the union of God and humankind through the incarnation of the Logos and, second, the notion of the *transformation*, indeed, the *apotheosis*, of humanity as a central effect of the saving work of Jesus Christ.[5] We discover no particular emphasis on the glory of God or an inner trinitarian love of God in Irenaeus's vision.

A further advance is found in the medieval discussion of the absolute purpose of the Incarnation, that is, that the Incarnation was independent of the fall. We first meet this issue in the work of Alexander of Hales (d. 1245). In part three of his "Body of Theology," commissioned by Pope Innocent IV, he treats the question "Whether if human nature had not fallen through sin there would still have been reason and fitness for the incarnation of Christ?"[6] This he affirms. Many later scholastic theologians, including Albertus Magnus, Thomas Aquinas, and Bonaventura, discuss the question, the former affirming it, the latter two ultimately denying it, preferring to connect the Incarnation with the fall. Yet Thomas Aquinas, in his early commentary on the sentences of Peter Lombard (Sent III Dist 1 Q1 p. 3), comments sympathetically on the affirmative side:[7]

> Others however say that since by the Incarnation of the Son of God there was accomplished not only the liberation from sin, but also the exaltation of human nature, and the consummation of the whole universe, for these reasons even if

3. Irenaeus, *Against Heresies* 5.21.2.
4. Ibid., 5, preface.
5. This theme becomes almost a commonplace in later theology, e.g., Athanasius, *On the Incarnation of the Word*, 51 (*autos gar [ho tou theou logos] epēnthrōpēsen hina hēmeis theopoiēthōmen*), quoted in B. F. Westcott's essay "The Gospel of Creation," in *The Epistles of St. John* (London: Macmillan, 1892) 319.
6. See Westcott, "The Gospel of Creation," 294-95. Thomas would later deny this in the *Summa*.
7. Ibid., 299.

sin had not existed the Incarnation would have taken place. And this can also be maintained with good reason.

Note here the same concepts found in Irenaeus, of liberation from sin and Satan and the transformation of humankind linked to a framework of divine purpose broader than simply redemption of fallen humanity. B. F. Westcott, in his very instructive essay "The Gospel of Creation," writes:

> . . . at least it cannot be said that a belief in the absolute purpose of the Incarnation is at variance with Scripture. . . . [M]uch is gained by the thought that from the first it was the purpose of God to gather up all things in the Son of His love.[8]

In this essay Westcott seeks to establish that the Incarnation was independent of the fall. He sees in the Incarnation a larger connection than simply the redemption of lost humankind. There is for him an archetypal significance in the Incarnation that reveals both the full divine notion of man in the Archetypal Man, Jesus Christ, and also the highest destiny of humankind as made for a mediated union with God. This significance has an impact on and transforms the whole of the created order. This constitutes a material advance toward the maximum cosmic understanding the biblical revelation will allow concerning the *telos* of God's ways in creation, history, and consummation.

In the Reformed tradition we find an explicit discussion of the ultimate divine purpose in creation. Jonathan Edwards in his work "Dissertation Concerning the End for Which God Created the World" concludes his lengthy reasonings as follows: "Thus we see that the great and last end of God's works . . . is indeed but *one;* and this *one* end is most properly and comprehensively called, THE GLORY OF GOD. . . ."[9] He describes the meaning of the "glory of God" as "the emanation and true external expression of God's internal glory and fullness."[10] He further elaborates on the significance of God's "internal glory": "The whole of God's internal good or glory, is in these three things viz. his infinite knowledge; his infinite virtue or holiness, and his infinite joy and happiness."[11]

Edwards was at pains in his treatise both to reject the counterposition that the final end in creation was the conferring of divine benevolence on the creation and to answer arguments that his positions presented God as selfish and self-centered. In answering these objections he provides a glimpse of the inner theological vision underlying his somewhat dry and detailed rational arguments. He writes, "It is such a delight in his own internal fulness and glory, that disposes him to an abundant effusion and incarnation of that glory. . . ."[12] Edwards does not penetrate into this inner "delight" of God to express his glory. Nor does he touch upon the key biblical dictum that "God is love" (John 4:14) or upon the sig-

8. Ibid., 327-28.
9. Jonathan Edwards, *The Works of President Edwards* (New York: Robert Carter & Brothers, 1869) 2.253.
10. Ibid.
11. Ibid.
12. Ibid., 215.

nificance of the intratrinitarian relations within the Godhead in relation to that dictum.

One more historical position relative to the *telos* of God's ways is of interest—that expressed by C. S. Lewis in his rapturous vision of the "Great Dance" found in *Perelandra*. Marvelous, indeed, is the theological poetry presented to us in the "Great Dance"—and precise! Lewis presents creation and redemption as expressions of the unimaginable inner richness of God.

He has immeasurable use for each thing that is made, that His love and splendour may flow forth like a strong river which has need of a great watercourse and fills alike the deep pools and the little crannies. . . .[13]

Note the conjunction of God's love and glory ("splendour") here. The "Great Dance" is a personal expression of the inwardness of God's love and delight.

Referring to the fact of the Incarnation, Lewis says "In the Fallen World He prepared for Himself a body and was united with the dust and made it glorious forever."[14] This is the "apotheosis" theme of Irenaeus and the Greek fathers. He continues, "This is the end and final cause of all creating, and the sin whereby it came is called Fortunate. . . ." Here Lewis sees the eternal intention of God to unite himself to humankind ("dust") in the Incarnation apart from the fall, but it was in fact accomplished through the fall. It is the *felix culpae,* the sin called "Fortunate." At the end of the vision he describes entrance into the mystical silence of adoration and worship at the mystery and glory of God's "Great Dance."[15] He describes "a simplicity beyond all comprehension, ancient and young as spring, illimitable, pellucid" which drew Ransom, his protagonist in the trilogy, "into its own stillness." It is a silent doxology of creaturely worship evoked by the mystical revelation of the doxophany of God in the "Great Dance."

In these historical observations we find the elements of a comprehensive theological vision of the *telos* of God's ways in the grand unfolding drama of creation, redemption, and consummation: (1) the exalted destiny of humanity for mediated union with God through the Incarnation; (2) the manifestation of the inner glory of God as the end result of God's works *ad extra;* and (3) the inner dynamic of love within the triune Godhead as the driving force behind creation and the revelation of that love as its final purpose. We are now ready to develop a precise theological exposition of a trinitarian eschatological vision centered on doxophany.

II

Thesis 1: Eschatology is pictorial final purpose

The title of this essay speaks of an *eschatological* vision. It does so because we must look to the eschatological revelation in Scripture to discover the *telos* of God's ways. Human beings, as Frankl points out, have a "will-to-meaning," which must be satisfied if they are to live in their full capacity as human. Humans have

13. C. S. Lewis, *Perelandra* (New York: Macmillan, 1968) 217.
14. Ibid., 215.
15. Ibid., 219.

always been concerned with the future because of their needs for security, meaning, and even because of simple curiosity.

Modern unbelieving people have developed their own eschatological mythologies, sometimes optimistic and evolutionary, sometimes pessimistic and apocalyptic. Modern science—and science fiction as an extension of modern science—is often the key source of such contemporary eschatological visions. Scriptural revelation presents a radically different vision—another cosmology, another end point for both human experience and the universe.

It is the end result of a process that determines the purpose of that process. Since this is so, if we can discern what, in fact, is the end result of the vast pageantry of creation, history, and final consummation as we find it in Scripture, we will gain an understanding of the final purpose of God and our individual place in it.

In biblical revelation we encounter pictorial, visionary material describing both the origin and the conclusion of the created order. We encounter vivid pictures of divine purpose in the eschaton. What, in fact, is presented as the final result of the great drama of creation and history? We look to a renewed heaven, a renewed earth, and a Spirit-filled creation totally under the dominion of the will of God, so that the kingdom of God manifests itself perfectly in every sphere and in every aspect of existence. In the Spirit-filled creation we find a Spirit-filled people walking, serving, loving, worshiping, and rejoicing in God. God becomes humanity's God fully and truly, and humanity becomes God's people, wholly redeemed.

All of this can be summed up in two words: *doxophany* and *doxology*. The manifestation of the glory of God in all of created reality and the creaturely response of recognition of that glory is an unending doxology to God. As Stauffer puts it so eloquently, "The antiphony of universal history leads to a symphonic doxology. At last God has attained the *telos* of his ways: the revelation of the *gloria dei* achieves its ends in the hallowing of his name."[16]

Thesis 2: The Cause of all things is the eternal love of the triune God

The high point of biblical revelation is found in John's simple words "God is love" (1 John 4:16). This statement unveils to humanity the deepest inner nature of God. The meaning of love is defined by the very nature of God as he is in himself. Everything we know about love as human comes only by virtue of the fact that we are created as *Imago Dei* and experience love in a created and human way.

As we contemplate the mystery of God's eternal existence as love—apart from the creation of the universe—we encounter the truth that God is not an isolated being in himself. God's essence is love, and therefore he has always been love even apart from creation. This is possible because God is not simply *a* person but, as Scripture reveals, is tri-personal—as Father, Son and Holy Spirit—from eternity. This is how God is love from eternity. God has never been alone but has always, with an inner infinite richness, been a community of love within himself. The love of the Father for the Son and of the Son for the Father and the flow of that eternal love in the Holy Spirit have always been the innermost nature of

16. Stauffer, *New Testament Theology*, ch. 19, "The Final Glory of God."

God himself. Undifferentiated Being in an absolute monad is not the biblical revelation of God in Jesus Christ. Neither is God simply a person.

Of this mystery of his being we can only use what must be called theological poetry to describe it. There is a fiery warmth within God himself. The very heartbeat of God's existence is a flow of self-giving from Father to Son, of receiving from Son to Father, a flow back and forth of self-knowledge in the Father and the Son by the Holy Spirit. There is an infinitude of richness within God that is beyond our comprehension—of acceptance, compassion, understanding, giving, caring, communication, intimacy. There is an intimacy threefold, an intimacy on a level and in a dimension beyond our capacity to grasp. Herman Bavinck writes eloquently of God as love in these words:

> In God love far transcends the love of creatures. For the love of God is independent, unchangeable, simple, eternal, and omnipresent. It does not depend upon us, nor is aroused by us, but flows free and pure from the depths of the divine Being. It knows no variation, neither falls nor rises, appears nor disappears, and there is not even a shadow of turning about it. It is not merely a property of the divine Being alongside of other properties . . . but it also coincides with the divine Being Himself. God *is* love: He Himself, wholly, perfectly, and with His whole being. This love is not subject to time and space, but stands above it and comes down out of eternity into the hearts of the children of God. Such a love is absolutely reliable.[17]

The revelation of God as love is the highest truth that we have of God. It tells us that the heartbeat of eternity and of the created order is the heartbeat of divine love. The ultimate reality, over and above everything else that we see or know or understand, is holy love, the holy love of the triune God, who from eternity flows within himself as Father, Son, and Holy Spirit in unvarying glory. That flow of love is the inner glory of God. It is his inmost substance, his reality, his weightiness, his glory. Indeed, the basic meaning of *Kabhod,* the Hebrew word for "glory," is "weightiness, richness, substance." The glory of anything is its weightiness, its substantiveness. This eternal flow of triune love is the hidden glory of God. It is a glory that, apart from creation, was contained wholly within God himself, in the infinite perfect consciousness that is God as Father, Son, and Holy Spirit, in the intense unity of the *perichorēsis euallēlos,* that is, the mutual interpenetration *(mutua inexistentia)* of the three persons in virtue of the simultaneous subsistence in the numerical oneness of the divine *ousia.*[18]

Thesis 3: The plan of the ages is the inclusion of all things into the eternal flow of divine love in the Trinity

Once we have clearly recognized that the heartbeat of eternity and of creation is the eternal love of the triune God, it becomes possible for us to grasp more fully and profoundly the plan that was set in motion through creation and history.

17. Herman Bavinck, *Our Reasonable Faith* (tr. Henry Zylstra; Grand Rapids: Eerdmans, 1956) 138-39.
18. See Polanus's exposition of this concept in Heinrich Heppe, *Reformed Dogmatics* (tr. G. T. Thompson; London: Allen & Unwin, 1950) 113.

God, in his freedom, in his infinite love and depth, chose to create a universe of things visible and invisible. He initiated a plan through creation so that the internal flow of his love might overflow its boundaries and enter into that which he had created, that which he had spoken out of his heart of love, that which he had spoken out of his perfect wisdom, that which he had spoken out of his unlimited power.

The destiny of the created order is this divinely planned purpose of participation in the inward glory of God's love and the consequent exhibition of that glory. In this way doxophany and doxology combine to fulfill the highest imaginable end—the supreme exaltation of God—and to accomplish the diffusion of the greatest good for the created order—union with God in his inward glory of love.

We note here that a genuine, holistic grasp of this point settles some of the concerns raised by those who object to the "selfishness" of God in making himself his own end in creation. Edwards seeks to deal with this in his own way in section 4 of his essay. The proper heart cry of all created reality is to be found in the creaturely sense of absolute dependence upon God and is perfectly expressed by the Psalmist, "Not unto us, O Lord, not unto us, but to thy name give glory" (Ps 115:1). And yet attendant upon the highest end of God's glory is the highest gift of love to the created order—participation in his love through inner union.

Thesis 4: The process of this plan is its unfolding in human history and the consequent transformation of that history

Biblical revelation begins with the creation of all things climaxing in the creation of human beings as *Imago Dei*. The focus of that revelation is the human race, its fall and God's consequent gracious, loving covenant with it—first with Adam, then with Abraham and Moses, and finally in the New Covenant in Jesus Christ. A review (from the perspective of Theses 2 and 3) of what God has been doing in human history makes it clear that the process of all things is aimed at a progressive manifestation of God's eternal love in the created order. It is a process by which that which is inward and hidden in God himself is made available in a unique and wonderful way to humanity and the whole of creation so that the whole of humanity and creation can be brought into intimate union with that inner flow of God's love. A key result of God's covenanted relationship with humankind, which culminated in Jesus Christ, was the transformation of human history by the introduction of the reality of the final glory of the age to come into this present age in a definite, real, and yet partially hidden manner.

Thesis 5: The method of this plan is the mediation of the eternal flow of God's love by means of a union and relation accomplished in the domain of history through the Incarnation of the eternal Word of God, the Second Person of the Trinity

The introduction of the ontological reality of the final glory into this age is conditioned by three basic concepts: mediation, incarnation, and atonement.

It is critical to the biblical revelation that union with God and participation in the eternal flow of God's love is not direct; neither is it an already existing fact of creation simply to be "realized" by humankind. Mediation contradicts all false mystical notions of the self-deification of humanity. Indeed, any such direct, un-mediated union with God is simply a philosophical-religious expression of the *hubris* of the original human sin to seek to be as God. This point is especially im-portant in view of the present movement in Western thought toward Eastern pan-theism and mysticism. The great truth of all false mysticism is that there *is* a genuine union with God to be obtained, a union compatible with the human nature and destiny as *Imago Dei*. But this union is not direct or given in such a way as to allow human beings anything other than the creaturely experience of absolute de-pendence upon God in that union. And it is fully and totally gracious in nature—not even natural to human beings as originally created.

The second key concept is "incarnation." The method of the plan is first the ob-jective (that is, the "actual") union of God the Word, the *eikōn tou theou* (Col 1:10) with humanity, the created *eikōn*. The Incarnation provides a prototype of a new humanity. The inner principle and dynamic of this new life is the mediated union with the flow of God's eternal triune love in a form appropriate to the crea-turely reality of humankind as *Imago Dei*. This reality is only made available to us, however, through the death, resurrection, ascension, and session of the Man of Heaven and the working of the Holy Spirit incorporating humanity into that reality.

At this point the question of the absolute nature of the Incarnation again comes into view. Thomas Aquinas, Bonaventura, and Calvin, with a keen sense of the biblical materials, are certainly secure in seeing the fall and humanity's redemption as the clearly stated context and immediate cause of the Incarnation. It is also clear from a larger theological analysis of the effects of the Incarnation and the final goal of creation that the Incarnation transcends its immediate context of the fall and redemption. The Incarnation, in this light, is a fulfillment and completion of God's *telos* in creation. The final destiny of humankind as doxophany and doxology in bearing the image of the Man from Heaven expresses an eternal purpose of God to unite humankind to the reality of his inner life of trinitarian love.[19]

We must never lose sight, however, of the fact that the Incarnation is not effec-tive apart from atonement through the cross of the incarnate Icon of God. The fall, in fact, disrupted the basic goodness of the created order and estranged human beings from their proper destiny. The Incarnation is clearly accomplished with a view to atonement. Any denigration of the atonement in favor of the inde-pendent significance of the Incarnation is contrary to the emphasis of the New Tes-tament. None of the glory of God's love could be made available to humanity apart from the atonement, nor could it be implemented in human experience apart from the historical facticity of the atonement and the ministry of the Holy Spirit.

Thesis 6: The final purpose of all things is doxophany—the manifestation of the eternal triune love of God as divine glory beyond history

We now come full circle, back to the final state of glory. The *telos* of God's ways is doxophany. The *Soli Deo Gloria* comes to its highest possible expres-sion as the unimaginable richness of the inner life of God as love fills and trans-forms all of created reality. The transformation of the ages is complete. The

19. A careful review of John 17:24-26 and Eph 3:17-19, among other passages, indicates clearly this eternal perspective in conjunction with God's love and participation in that love.

knowledge of the glory of God fills all things as the waters cover the seas (Num 14:21; Isa 11:9; Hab 2:14).

In this thesis we come to the most comprehensive framework for theological understanding. All other purposes which may be discerned in Scripture for creation, redemption, and consummation find their proper significance only in relation to this final cause of all things. Creation, humanity, the fall, sin, history, the Incarnation, atonement, salvation, the kingdom of God, the church—all are illuminated by this final purpose of God.

Creation and the new creation are the purposeful overflow of God's holy love expressed with his perfect wisdom and accomplished by his infinite power. Man, humanity, is now understood only as we understand *The Man,* Jesus Christ, who is the full, final perfect exposition of what it is to be human—to live the *Soli Deo Gloria* both as doxophany and as doxology.

The fall is now clearly seen as an interruption of the process leading to the final goal of doxophany which yet, in divine wisdom, adds a radiance and intensity to the final outcome. History can now be only directional, pointing beyond itself, finding meaning only by being rooted in God's eternal purpose. The Incarnation is now understood as the genuine center of the process of all things by which God carries out his final purpose. It is the "plan for the fulness of time, to unite all things in him, things in heaven and things on earth" (Eph 1:10).

The meaning of the atonement is enriched as a surpassing expression of God's love, not merely in taking upon himself the consequences of sin and fallenness, not merely in restoring humanity's original relationship of creaturely innocence, but in opening up the channel to the ultimate intention of mediated union with God in his eternal flow of love. Salvation now takes on a grandeur beyond all expectation. No longer is it simply a matter of personal deliverance from sin, death, and hell. Now it is understood in its true light as participation by the Holy Spirit, through faith, in the ultimate reality and purpose of the universe.

The kingdom of God and the church come into their own when viewed in the light of doxophany. The inner life of the church transcends the categories of sociology, psychology, and history. The church is rooted in the kingdom of God, which is simply the manifestation of God's glory in a transformed created order. The church is a colony of the age to come. Its present reality is a true participation in the final glory. The church is the burning bush of the presence of the final doxophany. It is the sign and firstfruits of God's final purpose.

Doxophany demands doxology from the created order. C. S. Lewis's "Great Dance" is an artistic recognition of this demand for creaturely response. The "Great Dance" is the exhibition and celebration of the eternal love of God in its infinite richness, variety, and unity of theme: the splendor and the glory of God.

The visions of the Apocalypse are the eloquent testimony of this doxological imperative in scriptural revelation. "Worthy" is the continual cry of the four living creatures, the twenty-four elders, the myriads of myriads of angels, and "every creature in heaven and on earth and under the earth and in the sea, and all therein" (Rev 5:13). In their beings, transformed to be perfect doxophany, and in their free loving response of doxology, all fulfill their highest possible function and existence in one eternal coruscation of the glory of God.

God Is Personal Being

Paul King Jewett

In the year of Grace, 1654,
On Monday, 23d of November, Feast of St. Clement, Pope and Martyr,
and of others in the Martyrology.
Vigil of Saint Chrysogonus, Martyr, and others,
From about half past ten in the evening until about half past twelve.
FIRE
God of Abraham, God of Isaac, God of Jacob, not of the philosophers and scholars.
Certitude. Certitude. Feeling. Joy. Peace.
God of Jesus Christ
Deum meum et Deum vestrum.
"Thy God shall be my God."
Forgetfulness of the world and of everything, except God.
He is to be found only by the ways taught in the Gospel.

Pascal's Memorial.

1. GOD AND THE PHILOSOPHIC ABSOLUTE

Of the fifty "ideas" listed in the Synopticon of the *Great Books of the Western World,* ideas which have "given western civilization its life and light," there is no entry allotted more space than that of "God." Virtually all the authors of the 443 works in the series have something to say on the subject, for it is a theme profoundly affecting our understanding of the universe as a whole and human life in particular. The last author to speak, Sigmund Freud, harbingers the present when he dismisses the idea of God as an illusion, a cosmic projection of the human father, who serves to satisfy humanity's infantile dependence. While perhaps less crass in their conclusions, many thinkers since Freud have agreed with him, though they have often lamented this loss of a transcendent deity. "God is silent," says Sartre; "that I cannot deny, yet everything in myself calls for a God and that I cannot forget. . . ."[1] The "silence of God" (Sartre), the "absence of God" (Jaspers), the "eclipse of God" (Buber), even the "death of God" (W. Hamilton)— these themes that turn up again and again indicate that although many religious thinkers may no longer be "very sure of God," as their forebears were, neither are they very sure that the world is better off without him.

While this lamented modern Götterdämmerung has impinged on Christian theology (for theology is never done in a historical vacuum), its effect has not been as devastating as one might suppose. This is so because theology, insofar as it is

---

1. Sartre, quoted in Wilfred Desan, *The Tragic Finale: An Essay on the Philosophy of Jean-Paul Sartre* (New York: Doubleday, 1960) 179.

truly Christian, does not rest upon an "idea" of God postulated by speculative thought but rather upon God's self-revelation in Jesus Christ. In fact, far from postulating an "idea" of God, Christian theology has ever struggled against it, and in its best moments has resolutely opposed the tendency to substitute a philosophic idea—the "Unmoved Mover," the "Absolute," the "Ground of Being"—for the one, true, and living God who addresses us as our sovereign LORD.

This struggle has its roots in the encounter between biblical revelation and Greek thought. The God of revelation is not the impersonal Being of metaphysics, the Being with which the philosopher is concerned in the science of ontology. It is true that the term *Spirit,* used in the Old Testament to describe God, translates the Hebrew *ruach,* which means literally "wind," a concept which in itself is impersonal. The Hebrews, it would seem, spoke of God in this way because they conceived him in his essential being as the invisible Power (Energy) behind all that is, the creative Breath by which the living creature, indeed the whole universe, is animated. Yet in the context of the Old Testament as a whole it is evident that this animating Power, this creative Breath, is not understood as an impersonal force but rather as a living Subject. The personal Energy which God is in himself, the Breath by which he calls worlds into being (Ps 33:6) is, in the first instance, the Energy by which God wills to be who he is. He is who he is by his own act; that is, his being is *personal* being, being that can be understood only as a self-determined "self," an "I."

By contrast, the gods of the Greek world, into which Christianity came, were ultimately the fundamental Forms of reality, whether they were set forth as the heroes of myths (as in Homer), or as final unifying principles (as in Ionian physics), or as the Ideas of the philosophers.

> In the circle of the philosophy of religion (in classical Greece) God became increasingly the designation of impersonal-metaphysical powers and entities. Consequently the term was frequently reduced to such neutral categories as the Divine, Fate, or even the Good, the Real, the One.[2]

Plato, whose thought greatly influenced early Christian thinkers, used the mythology of the gods to illumine the philosophic quest, but the final Reality, which sustains all, is the impersonal, unindividualized idea of the Good. Likewise for Aristotle, God is essentially the final, necessary, and all sufficient "Condition" of a world order. The Greeks could say Love is God, but never, as the apostle John did, God is Love. This exchanging of the subject for its predicate expresses the difference between Greek philosophy and Christian theology.

Even in Neoplatonism, in which religion and philosophy merge in a kind of natural theology, the situation is not fundamentally different. All is of the One *(hen)* and returns to the One. This line of reasoning culminates in Plotinus's

---

2. Kleinknecht, *Theos,* "Der griechische Gottesbegriff," *TWNT,* 3.68. "Even in Homeric poetry the mythical world of the gods is in retreat and eventually . . . mythology is overcome by the concept of 'Being' in Greek philosophy (Dilthey). For the Greeks, to change was to pass away. Hence in the concepts of 'true Being' and 'the highest Good' the Greeks found the fixed center in the change of appearances and of human endeavors. . . ." Gunter Howe, *Mench und Physik* (Witten and Berlin: Eckart-Verlag, 1963) 15.

metaphysical concept of the One which is the Source and Ground of all. It is out of this Ground of Being (also called Father, *patēr*, and Primary God, *prōtos theos*, as the substance and reality of deity) that the world is formed. Hence there is no meaning to prayer save as an exercise in self-reflection, a return of the soul to its Origin.

The God of Scripture, by contrast, is the God who speaks to us and tells us his name—I am who I am—and thereby brings us into fellowship with himself. In brief, the God of the Bible is a personal God and hence all theology must begin with the affirmation that we know God only as he makes himself known to us; we can say about God only what he has first said about himself.

True, the general term for God in Hebrew, El (*'ēl*), appears to be a primal word in the religious vocabulary of the Semites to designate the POWER which transcends all human powers. Hence power was the basic concept by which the Semites understood the divine. But this POWER was never conceived in the Old Testament impersonally; God is not Power but the powerful One, the LORD God Almighty. The personal character of God is an axiom of biblical revelation, everywhere assumed and therefore never argued. This can be seen from the fact that the generic designation of God in Hebrew (*'ēl, 'eloah, 'elohim*) is throughout the Old Testament found alongside of and exchanged with God's individual, personal name Yahweh. See, for example, the usage of Genesis 2 and 3, where we find Yahweh Elohim, commonly translated "the LORD God." In other words God (*'ēl*) is Yahweh and Yahweh is God.[3]

That God is a personal God is a truth more prominent in Scripture than in formal theology. This is so because theology has derived its conceptual tools largely from philosophy. While it could hardly have been otherwise, the union between philosophy and theology has not always proven a happy one, especially in this area of the doctrine of God. Philosophy, as we know, has been traditionally concerned with ultimates, with truth that is general and abstract. Hence, in using philosophic terms, theology has sometimes been enticed away from its proper subject and become concerned with questions about God in his abstract essence, the God of pure Being rather than the God who has revealed himself in redemptive history as the God and Father of our LORD Jesus Christ.

While acknowledging that God is spoken of in personal terms in Scripture, theologians too often have viewed such usage as devotional in nature, language appropriate to worship rather than to the rigors of the critical thought that should mark serious theological effort.[4] Given such a philosophical approach to theology, the concept of the personal is rejected as descriptive of God because it implies an individuality which cannot be subsumed under a general category such as the Absolute or the Infinite. If it be replied that God is an *infinite person*, this appears to the philosophical mind to be a contradiction in terms. For philosophy, an infinite Being is ultimate, general Being, Being that is without limitation and therefore not

---

3. See Quell, *Theos*, "El und Elohim im A.T.," *TWNT*, 3.89-90.
4. Some, of course, have emphatically disagreed. "The personhood of God is not an anthropomorphism; rather the personhood of man is a theomorphism." E. Brunner, *Dogmatik* (Zurich: Zwingli-Verlag, 1960) 1.143.

susceptible of that definiteness and uniqueness which belongs to personal Being, to one who is an "I" over against a "thou."

It is, of course, true that the language of devotion and worship differs from that of theology, and this difference is not without significance. (When we say that the distinction between the language of worship and the language of theology is not without significance, we have in mind perceptive remarks like that of Ferdinand Ebner: "The pronoun of the first and second persons distinguishes no sex. 'I' and 'thou' . . . are sexless.")[5] This difference, however, does not compel theology to abandon the personal dimension for the abstract conceptuality of philosophy. The language of theology no less than the language of worship is personal. But these languages differ in that in worship we speak *to* God as "thou" whereas in theology we speak *about* God as "he." The language of worship, then, is the primary language of the Christian community; the language of theology, its secondary language. (By talking *with* God rather than *about* him Augustine achieved in his *Confessions* a theological masterpiece that is sui generis.)

Some have sought to make their peace with philosophy and at the same time retain the language of the personal in speaking of God by insisting that just because God is personal, he must be limited. The concept of a finite God is defended in such works as F. R. Tennant's *Philosophical Theology;*[6] William James's *Pragmatism;*[7] and Edgar Sheffield Brightman's *Philosophy of Religion.*[8] The case for a finite God is sometimes given a fillip by the argument that a God who is wholly good, though limited in power, affords a clue to resolving the vexatious problem of evil. Such a view of God gives us assurance that our own efforts to foster truth and goodness are meaningful because they are a part of the larger moral progress which is the leitmotif of human history, a progress of which God himself is the ultimate champion. The several arguments for a finite God, however, have had little appeal to the common people. Their God is the God of the Negro spiritual: "He's got the whole world in his hands." People do not propose, in other words, to take their problems to a God who has problems of his own.

It was Pseudo-Dionysius, above all others, who infected medieval theology with the impersonal approach to God. Starting with a Neoplatonic conception of the Divine, he described God as the Being who transcends all being and existence yet is the beginning and end of all existence; the Unknowable, yet the Source of all reason and knowledge; the Nameless and Inexpressible (Pierre Van Paassen's "Great Anonymous of the Burning Bush"), yet the giver of names to all; the ultimate Unity causing variety in all.

Many systematic theologians in more recent times have turned away from this impersonal approach to God. With their rejection of German Idealism and their use of biblical theology with its emphasis upon the God who acts they have reaffirmed the truth that God is a personal God, the God who speaks to us and so reveals himself as subject. In so doing they have restored to dogmatics its proper

5. Ferdinand Ebner, *Das Wort und die Geistigen Realitäten* (Innsbruck: Brenner Verlag, 1921) 195.

6. F. R. Tennant, *Philosophical Theology* (Cambridge: Cambridge University Press, 1928–1930).

7. William James, *Pragmatism* (New York: Longmans, Green, 1931).

8. E. S. Brightman, *A Philosophy of Religion* (New York: Prentice Hall, 1940).

subject, for there is no more fundamental affirmation about God that can be made than this: the one true God is a personal God, the Subject who says, "I am the LORD your God." This affirmation is a theological axiom.

Theology, then, has as its proper subject, not the God who is *"Prima Causa,"* "Unmoved Mover," "Ground of Being," "Sum of Human Ideals," the "Vital Urge in the Evolutionary Process," the "Ultimate Integrating Principle," but rather the personal, living God who speaks to us: "I am the LORD your God." The God of Scripture is not defined in terms of abstract thought but is disclosed in personal encounter. The writers of Scripture know nothing of a "God-IDEA"; rather, they speak of God in the analogy of a living person. He is the God who calls his people by name, who sees all that they do, who hears all that they say, who knows all that they think. And as he considers all that they think and say and do, he is moved with anger, is filled with pity, and yearns over them with a love that is everlasting. If theologians speak of these affirmations as anthropopathisms, this is not to condemn such usage as primitive and unworthy but to confess that the truth of God is greater than all we can say about him, even when we speak in personal terms.[9]

"That the word 'person' has a certain fitness in statements about God may be suspected," notes Helmut Thielicke, "from the fact that some theologians are so emphatic in banishing it from the field."[10] Thielicke cites as examples from the nineteenth century A. E. Biedermann and D. F. Strauss. "Personal being," avers Biedermann, "[in contrast to the Divine] is the specific substance form of the *human* spirit as *finite*."[11] In this century the most influential theologian to take exception to the language of the personal when speaking of God is Paul Tillich, who especially questioned Brunner's insistence that the divine/human encounter can be conceived in no other way than as an I/thou encounter. "Personal God," he feels, "is a confusing symbol."[12] In his sermon "The Courage to Be," he states:

> The God above the God of theism is present, although hidden, in every divine-human encounter. Biblical religion as well as Protestant theology are aware of the paradoxical character of this encounter. They are aware that if God encounters man, God is neither object nor subject and is above the scheme into which theism has forced him. They are aware that personalism with respect to God is balanced by a trans-personal presence of the divine.[13]

9. As for the loss of the personal in speaking of God, Barth complains that the order of dogmatics which begins with God's nature and attributes and only then speaks of the Trinity of Persons is partly to blame. This order tended, in the era of Protestant scholasticism, toward an abstract view of the divine nature which was equated with such superlatives as the *ens perfectissimum* and the *summum bonum*. Such an approach made easy the task of the so-called "Enlightenment" theology in which the God concept is reduced to "the Eternal Truth of the theoretical-practical-aesthetic Idea of human reason." By the same token it made it difficult for the theologian to escape Feuerbach's maxim: "all theology is anthropology." See Barth, *Die Kirchliche Dogmatik* (Zollikon: Evangelischer Verlag, 1958) 2/1, 322f.

10. Helmut Thielicke, *The Evangelical Faith* (tr. G. W. Bromiley, 3 vols.; Grand Rapids: Eerdmans, 1977) 2.170.

11. A. E. Biedermann, quoted in Brunner, *Dogmatik,* 1.142.

12. Paul Tillich, *Systematic Theology* (Chicago: University of Chicago Press, 1951) 1.245.

13. Tillich, *The Courage to Be* (New Haven: Yale University Press, 1952; rpt. New York: Fontana Library, 1962) 180.

Observing Brunner's profound dislike of the theology of Schleiermacher, whose transpersonal, mystical categories, when applied to our knowledge of God, contradict Brunner's own personalistic emphasis, Tillich asks him "whether it is possible to establish the divinity of the divine in merely personalistic terms and whether both classical medieval and classical German philosophy of religion were not right in combining biblical personalism . . . with basic ontological categories like Being, Life, Spirit and so on. I think they *were* right."[14]

I, on the contrary, think they were *not* right. Indeed, they could hardly have been more wrong. The God of classical German philosophy of religion is not the God of Abraham, Isaac, and Jacob, nor of Sarah, Rebecca, and Rachel.[15] In my judgment, it is simply an obfuscation when Tillich observes: "It should not be forgotten that classical theology employed the term *persona* for the trinitarian hypostases but not for God himself."[16] It is obvious that classical theology conceived the hypostatic distinctions in God as *personae* just because God was perceived as the personal God.

As for the "transpersonal, mystical" categories used by Schleiermacher to describe our knowledge of God, and their corollary that the important thing in religion is feeling, G. Ernest Wright quotes Schleiermacher's familiar dictum, "God is immanent in the human soul as it rises into perfect self consciousness." He then goes on to reflect that Schleiermacher was

so indoctrinated with this point of view in his younger years, that even now he does not feel that he has worshipped unless his emotions have been stirred up and his eyes become watery. God, in such an experience, is an indescribable Something, a great Blur, hazily perceived through dripping eyelids, the experience of whom, nevertheless, causes one to feel deeply. But to feel what? That is something which cannot be described.[17]

The God of Scripture, by contrast, is not an "indescribable Some*thing*," but a Some*one* who describes himself in that he names himself and thereby discloses himself to us.

2. THE NAME OF GOD

In the Old Testament, the name of a person is not simply a designation of convenience; rather, as one is named, so *is* he. Jacob is the supplanter (Gen 27:36); but when God takes possession of his life, he makes him a new person and so gives him a new name. He now becomes Israel (Prince, Ruler with God) because he had wrestled with God and prevailed (Gen 32:27-28).

What is true at the human level is preeminently true of God: his name is him-

---

14. Tillich, "Questions on Brunner's Epistemology," *The Christian Century* (October 24, 1962) 1284.

15. For a penetrating critique of Tillich's thought in this regard see Kenneth Hamilton, *The System and the Gospel* (Grand Rapids: Eerdmans, 1967).

16. Tillich, *Systematic Theology,* 1.245.

17. G. Ernest Wright, *The Challenge of Israel's Faith* (Chicago: University of Chicago Press, 1944) 50.

self, manifested in his ways and works. Whenever God is known and revealed as a *personal presence,* there his name is. He *sends forth* his word; but where his name is, there he presents *himself.* Hence the phrase "*thy name* is called over us" (Jer 14:9) is simply another way of saying: "Thou art in the midst of us."[18] The children of Israel are thus blessed when the LORD is in their midst to bless and keep them, to make his face shine upon them and to be gracious unto them; they are blessed when he lifts up his countenance upon them and gives them peace. This triune blessing of the LORD's presence is said to be a putting of God's name on Israel (Num 6:24-27). The association of God's "face" and "countenance" with the putting of his "name" upon Israel is natural enough. As only persons have names, so only persons have faces. And as the name designates the person, so the face discloses the person. Hence the face of God is the very presence of God himself as he is revealed to his people to bless them. For this reason, Paul speaks (as a Jew and a Christian) of the ultimate in divine revelation as "the light of the knowledge of the glory of God" which is as given "in the *face* of Jesus Christ" (2 Cor 4:6).[19]

H. Braun, who rejected the dimension of the personal as inadequate to describe the biblical view of God, once thought to embarrass L. Goppelt in a radio discussion by asking him to translate the word *person* into Hebrew. Without hesitating Goppelt suggested the Hebrew word *name (shēm).*[20] Properly speaking, only persons have names, and one's name expresses one's personal identity, an identity which cannot be defined in terms of anything else because each person's identity is unique. Therefore God, as the personal God, cannot be known in terms of anyone or anything other than himself, for he is absolutely unique. If we are to know who he is, he must speak to us, he must identify himself; and he has done that in that he has told us his name. In an overwhelming theophany, God revealed his glory to his servant Moses saying, "I will make all my goodness pass before you, and will proclaim before you my name 'The LORD' [Yahweh] . . ." (Exod 33:19).

God's name, in other words, is interchangeable with himself. For this reason, to seek, to love, to honor, to thank, to praise, as well as to desecrate, to despise and to blaspheme—to do any of these to the name of God is to do it to God himself. By the same token, God's name is a refuge. "A mighty fortress is our God," sang Luther; "A strong tower is the *name* of the LORD," declares the Old Testament proverb (Prov 18:10).

The prophet Isaiah was told to name his son Mahershalalhashbaz ("the spoil speeds, the prey hastens") in anticipation of the imminent ruin of Damascus and Samaria by the Assyrians. In their effort to emulate this scriptural precedent and to avoid all pagan names as well as those of Roman Catholic saints and martyrs, the Puritans' zeal knew no bounds. Some of the biblical names of which they were

18. See C. F. Oehler, *The Theology of the Old Testament* (New York: Funk and Wagnalls, 1883) 126-27.

19. By the same token, throughout the Bible there is, because of human sin, a dialectic of longing for God's face—"hide not thy face from me" (Ps 27:9)—and fleeing from his face— "hide us from the face of him who sits on the throne and from the wrath of the Lamb" (Rev 6:16).

20. See Thielicke, *The Evangelical Faith,* 2.107.

fond are still with us, including Hope, Faith, and Grace. It was especially between 1580 and 1640 that they turned biblical watchwords and even theological phrases into Christian sobriquets. "A jury empanelled in 1658 included such worthies as Faint-not Hewitt, Redeemed Compton, Becourteous Cole, Search-the-Scriptures Moreton, Kill-sin Pimple, Fight-the-good-fight-of-faith White, Weep-not Billing and Steadfast-on-high Stringer."[21]

The most celebrated worthy in this class was Praise-God Barebone. Two of his brothers are said to have been called Jesus-Christ-came-into-this-world-to-save Barebone and If-Christ-had-not-died-for-thee-thou-hadst-been-damned Barebone. We are told that, since the morals of the latter were not above reproach, and since his acquaintances were wearied with the length of his name, they abbreviated it to the more curt than courteous, Damned Barebone.[22]

In modern America, black Baptist congregations have shown an arresting originality in naming their churches. Along with such stalwarts as Second Baptist and Trinity Baptist, the following names appear in the Church Service Section of the February 15, 1981, issue of *Church and Community News* for Los Angeles, California: St. Peter's Rock Missionary Baptist Church, All Nation Bibleway Missionary Baptist Church, 1 Timothy Missionary Baptist Church, and Echos of Heaven Missionary Baptist Church. The term "star," the symbol of the light of truth and the sign in the heavens of Jesus' advent, seems especially popular. There is a Morning Star, a Rising Star, an Evening Star, a New Star, and a Greater Bright Star Missionary Baptist Church in Los Angeles.

The New Testament Data

As the equivalent of his person and work, God's name remains as central in the New Testament as in the Old. But in the New Testament that name is bound up with the name Jesus. Jesus' mission as the Christ was to make God's name known (John 17:26); and because he was faithful in this mission, God has given him a name that is above every name. Indeed, the name which he is given is the name by which God himself is known in the Old Testament, that is, "LORD" *(kyrios)*. "Therefore God has highly exalted him and bestowed on him the name which is above every name, that at the name of Jesus every knee should bow . . . and every tongue confess that Jesus Christ is LORD . . ." (Phil 2:9-11).

The name Jesus, of course, was given him at his birth (Matt 1:21), and the names LORD and Christ at his resurrection (Acts 2:36). But the personal identity of him who was born, lived, and died as Jesus with him who was raised as LORD and Christ was always assumed by the early Christians as self-evident. That they knew nothing of the distinction—and especially the use sometimes made of the distinction—between the "historical Jesus" and the "kerygmatic Christ" is evident from Peter's Pentecost sermon as reported in Acts. In this first Christian sermon, Peter affirms that the name on which one must call for salvation is the name of the "LORD" (Acts 2:21, *to onoma kyrion*). But the one to whom he is referring is—to the amazement of his hearers—none other than the man who lived in their midst

---

21. W. F. Moulton, *The History of the English Bible* (London: Kelly, 1911) 285.
22. See C. W. Bardsley, *Curiosities of Puritan Nomenclature* (London: Chatto and Windus, 1880).

as Jesus of Nazareth (Acts 2:22) and whom God has raised from the dead (Acts 2:32), so making him to be "LORD" and "Christ." And because the name Jesus remains when he is exalted as LORD—Stephen, in the throes of death, cries, "LORD Jesus" (Acts 7:59)—Christians have always understood the name Jesus as a kind of shorthand for the name of God and all that that name implies.

Of the many hymns celebrating the name of Jesus by the worshiping people of God, note the following: "Jesus, Name All Names Above," ascribed to Theocritus of the Stadium, c. 890, and translated by John J. Mason Neal (1818–1866); "Oh, For a Thousand Tongues," containing the stanza "Jesus! the name that charms our fears," by Charles Wesley (1707–1788); and "How Sweet the Name of Jesus Sounds in a Believer's Ear!" by John Newton (1725–1807). Note also the many hymns that begin with the name Jesus, ranging all the way from Anna Warrens's "Jesus Loves Me! This I Know," to Wesley's "Jesus, Lover of My Soul."

As the early confession behind the text in Phil 2:5-11 implies, the risen Christ was perceived and worshiped from the beginning as the *LORD* Jesus. So he not only is the one who reveals God but is himself revealed as God and one with God. Thus his name is hypostatized as was God's name in the Old Testament. When the disciples left the Jewish Sanhedrin after a beating, they rejoiced that they have been counted worthy to suffer dishonor for the *Name* (Acts 5:41). Salvation is believing in the *Name,* and apart from such faith one stands condemned (John 3:18); "for there is no other name under heaven given among men by which we must be saved" (Acts 4:12). Hence Christians are people who do all that they do in the name of the LORD Jesus (Col 3:17), because it is he whom they confess to be the Christ, the Son of the living God. Inasmuch as the Son has the same name (LORD) as the Father does, the revelation of God in the New Testament unites this Son with the Father and with the Spirit, by whom he was anointed, in a common name: the trinitarian name of the Father and of the Son and of the Holy Spirit, the name into which Christians are baptized (Matt 28:19).

We cannot now explore the meaning and implication of this triune name, but we must say a word about the name LORD *(kyrios).* If "Father, Son, and Spirit" is God's full and final name (as Christians who are trinitarian confess), LORD is his primary name. Occurring some 6,700 times in the Old Testament, it is by no means displaced in the New. Indeed, the name LORD is the common name of the God of Israel who becomes the God of the Christians. While ordinarily used in the New Testament of the Son, the Father and the Spirit are also called LORD (Rev 11:15; 2 Cor 3:17). In fact, some dogmaticians regard the trinitarian name, Father, Son, and Holy Spirit, to be the exposition, as it were, of the personal name LORD.[23]

The Name Yahweh/*Kyrios*/LORD

The Greek *kyrios* (LORD) renders the Hebrew Yahweh, the sacred, personal

---

23. So Barth, who begins his treatment of the Trinity with the affirmation, "God's word is God himself in his revelation. For God reveals himself as the *LORD* and, according to Scripture, that means, so far as the concept of revelation is concerned, that God is Revealer, Revelation and Revealedness in an inviolable unity and also in an inviolable diversity" (*Die kirchliche Dogmatik,* 1/1, 311).

name of the God of Israel. It is admittedly not a literal translation.[24] It does, however, convey the essential thought that in naming himself LORD, God relates to us, not as an equal, but as he who is sovereign over all his creatures. By his will we live, move, and have our being, and by his word we are to order our lives. Even in human relationships, one who is lord exercises authority as master, and one who is servant acknowledges that authority in submission. In the case of God and humankind, the relationship is grounded in God's mighty acts of creation (Genesis 2) and redemption (Exod 20:1-3). To confess that God is our Maker and Redeemer is to acknowledge that he is our LORD to whom we willingly submit in all of life. And as his authority is not sheer power, which is tyranny, so our submission is not abject resignation, which would be slavery. This submission is rather the freedom of which Augustine spoke when he said: "The essence of freedom is bondage to thy will, O God."

Hence LORD is the name by which Christians know and confess, not God in general, but their God in particular, the God who has revealed himself through Moses and the prophets and finally in the person of Jesus Christ.[25] Hence also, in the New Testament as in the Old, LORD is the name of him who is Maker of heaven and earth (Matt 11:25) and at the same time, and in the most concrete and specific sense, the name of him who is our Savior, the LORD Jesus Christ. In him the personal God, who spoke by the prophets, has spoken his final word; indeed, in him the personal God, whose name is Yahweh, the "I AM WHO I AM" (Exod 3:14), is present in a personal way, present in this person, Jesus, who is God manifest in the flesh.

> The prophetic word is that which points to the Lord, but it is not his very presence, hence not his actual Lordship. The latter happens where he who exercises Lordship is himself present as in former times his word was present; present as a Self who is here revealing himself. Here where the *basileia tou theou ephthasen,* where the real exercise of Lordship is present, here also, the Lord is fully revealed as the Lord. Therefore in the New Testament the title, Lord, is given to Jesus. He is the *kyrios* because in him God, in revelational presence, exercises his lordship no more in a delegated and indirect way through the word of prophets but directly and immediately through him, who himself possesses kingly plentipotency and in his own person can say: "You call me Lord"; [or again] "But I say to you. . . ."[26]

---

24. *Kyrios* literally translates the Hebrew *'adon* rather than *Yahweh*. In English translations the distinction between the two Hebrew words is sometimes preserved by the typographical device of upper and lower case: Yahweh is rendered LORD; *'adon,* Lord. In my view, the desire of some to use another term such as "SOVEREIGN" in order to escape the sexist overtones of LORD is understandable. The problems with the various substitutes, however, are not easily resolved. Hence my decision to remain with the traditional translations of the biblical terms.

25. For a contrasting position, see John Hick, *God Has Many Names* (London: Macmillan, 1980).

26. Brunner, *Dogmatik,* 1.152. In the same vein Otto Weber notes (*Grundlagen der Dogmatik* 1.462) that Jesus is never called the Son of Yahweh or the Son of the LORD but just the LORD.

Concerning the Tetragrammaton

It appears that for the people of the ancient Near East, knowing the name of the god or gods whom they worshiped was crucial to their happiness because this knowledge secured the privilege of invoking the deity in the hour of need. Sometimes this invocation shaded off into magic whereby the devotee sought to manipulate the gods in his own self-interest. To know the name of a god meant to have power over the bearer of the name. While such magic was never sanctioned in Israel, knowing the name of God was of capital importance, for as we have seen it was in the disclosure of his name that God revealed himself to Israel. Indeed, God's name became so identified with himself that it was, so to speak, a "double of his being" (Von Rad) and therefore most sacred. Hence to take God's name in vain was for the Israelite, as it is for the Christian, a kind of *lèse majesté* (Exod 20:7; Matt 6:9).

As we have seen, this sacred name is Yahweh, rendered by the Septuagintal translators as *kyrios* (LORD), a fact bearing significantly on the early Christian usage whereby Jesus is called *kyrios* (LORD). Indeed, Paul says that no one can call Jesus LORD except in—or by—the Holy Spirit (1 Cor 12:3).

Because this memorial name of the God of Israel has become the name of the God of the Christians, the question of what it means has always interested theologians. To answer this question they have traditionally turned to the account of Moses' call at the burning bush (Exod 3:13-14). "Then Moses said to God, 'If I come to the people of Israel and say to them, "The God of your fathers has sent me to you," and they ask me, "What is his name?" what shall I say to them?' God said to Moses, 'I AM WHO I AM [*'ehyeh 'asher 'ehyeh*]. . . . Say this to the people of Israel, "I AM [*'ehyeh*] has sent me to you."'"

It would surely appear that the enigmatic phrase *'ehyeh 'asher 'ehyeh* (I AM WHO I AM) is intended to be an elaboration of the Tetragrammaton, Yahweh, and such is the consensus of scholars. The same consensus, however, does not prevail as to the meaning of the phrase. In contemporary biblical studies, the traditional translation has been called into question. Assuming the "God-who-acts" approach to holy history—which has much to commend it—some biblical theologians have considered the causative idea more compatible with this history than the alleged abstract, static idea of "being." Since the God of Israel enters into Israel's history in an active, dynamic way, we must postulate a meaning of his name which is compatible with this truth. Hence the text must mean: "I cause to be what I cause to be" or "I cause to be what comes into existence." Thus the emphasis is on what God *does,* not on who he *is.* One obvious difficulty with all such efforts is that they require that one not only reject the Masoretic pointing of the text as erroneous, but also alter the Hebrew consonants in the text itself.[27]

The traditional view, on the other hand, does not require one to emend the text

---

27. As an example of such a procedure, one may consult W. F. Albright, "Contributions to Biblical Archeology," *JBL* 43 (1924) 370-78. Here the student will find the technical aspects of the question reviewed, including the grammatical problem involved in identifying the Tetragrammaton as a Hiphil rather than a Qal of the verb.

in any way. But does the traditional rendering, "I am who I am," yield a meaning alien to the Old Testament? No one can doubt that Israel knew God not as an abstract Idea but as a personal Redeemer whose mighty acts humbled Pharaoh, the most powerful ruler of antiquity. Moses was sent back to Egypt where nothing short of a new situation "created" by the power of Yahweh would ever effect the redemption of Israel. Is the traditional view, which reflects the Septuagintal understanding and the Masoretic pointing of Exod 3:14, incompatible with this historical context? We do not think so.

Though the dogmaticians may have erred in speculating about the abstract "being" of God and so given the Hebrew phrase "I am who I am" a connotation more philosophic than biblical, there is no need for us to abandon the text in order to avoid this error. Not abstract Being but God's presence to his needy people, his abiding faithfulness—this is the fundamental thought of Exod 3:14. If God is to keep covenant with his people in all the changing and threatening circumstances which have overtaken them since their fathers and mothers went down into Egypt, *it is just as important that he should transcend history as that he should act in history.* We therefore conclude that the traditional understanding of the Tetragrammaton (Yahweh) as a Qal form ("he is") and the translation of Exod 3:14 on the basis of the Masoretic textual tradition ("I am who I am") yield the proper meaning of this difficult portion of Scripture.

The thought is that God is truly who he is; he is the one who really exists, though he may seem to the oppressed Israelites to have been eclipsed by the brutal, tangible reality of the slavemaster's whip. God is the God who is *present* to Moses and his people in the time of their extremity as he was to their forebears with whom he first made covenant. He and he only is their hope and salvation and in Jesus Christ he is our hope and salvation too. Hence we sing:

> The God of Abram praise,
> Who reigns enthroned above;
> Ancient of everlasting days,
> And God of love:
> Jehovah! Great I AM!
> By earth and heav'n confessed;
> I bow and bless the Sacred Name,
> Forever blest.

Thomas Olivers

It is not, then, a matter of Being-in-the-Abstract, the Absolute of the philosophers, but Being in the shape of a *Personal Redeeming Presence,* that is disclosed by the name Yahweh. To be sure, the revelation at the burning bush is a veiled revelation, but it is revelation still.[28]

As for the name Jehovah, it is a relatively late conceit of the Jewish rabbis. They took the vowel points of *'adon* (Lord) and used them in pointing *yhwh* with the deliberate intent of thwarting the pronunciation of the ineffable name of

---

28. See Eichrodt, *Theologie des Alten Testaments* (2 vols.; Leipzig: J. C. Hinrichs, 1939) 2.92-94.

God, a name too sacred, in their judgment, to be uttered by mortal tongue. This fact having been established, no scholar today would argue that Jehovah is the proper vocalization of the Tetragrammaton. Accordingly, its use in translation, since the ASV of 1901, has happily been discontinued and there has been a general return to the Septuagintal "LORD." The exception is the New World Translation of Jehovah's Witnesses, in which "Jehovah" is not only retained but substituted for 'adon in about 130 additional passages on the basis of the alleged rabbinic corruption of the Hebrew text.

3. SOME BASIC AFFIRMATIONS

God Is the Living God

In the light of the revelation of God's name at the burning bush, we may appropriately turn from a discussion of the *nomen ineffabile* to a brief statement of those theological affirmations concerning God that theologians have associated with that name, affirmations with which we shall fill out and conclude our discussion of the personal nature of God.

Our first affirmation is that God, as personal, is the *living* God, the God who is aware of himself as a self, a subject, indeed, the Subject who calls worlds into being by the breath of his mouth. "'As I live,' says the LORD" is the typical form of the oath whereby God swears by himself since he can swear by none greater. As the living God, he so endows humankind with life that they too are subjects who are related to him in a personal way. Though we often use anthropomorphic expressions in speaking about God, the affirmation that he is a living Self— an "I" not an "It"—is no anthropomorphism but the truth that grounds the anthropomorphisms that we use.

By the same token, to speak of God as the living God, a personal Self, is not to turn all theology into anthropology, as though Christians were like the cattle that, as Xenophanes said, would have pictured their gods as cows if they could have drawn. God is not the personal God who lives in the sense that we humans have projected our human mode of existence on him. Rather it is the other way around; God, the source of life itself, is all that we are as living persons and more; the lack is on our side, not his. We are the ones as living persons who are yet less than living persons. We are the ones who are objects as well as subjects, having bodies which remind us at all times that we are in the process of passing away, that we shall at last succumb to death. By contrast, God, as the living God, is the Father who has life in himself, who gives to the Son to have life in himself (John 5:26), and who is confessed as the Spirit "who makes alive" (Nicene Creed).

Our doctrine of God, then, begins with revelation; and revelation begins with the statement "I am the LORD your God" (Exod 20:2). God is the living "I" who speaks. It is said that there are a thousand sentences in the Bible that contain the divine "I am." The operative words, then, are not "God is" or "God exists," true as it may be that he is and therefore exists, but rather God is who he says that he is, the "I am who I am." To depart from this ground is to reduce the living God to an "it," a neuter, an "object" of thought, the first fateful step on the way to turning theology into philosophy.

God Is Unique

Our second affirmation is that God is *unique* as personal. To have a name implies uniqueness, and to have the name Yahweh, as God does, implies absolute uniqueness. The God with whom we have to do in Christian theology is he who declares, "I am God, and there is no other; I am God, and there is none like me" (Isa 46:9). Thus we see that God is not only unqualifiedly who he is, but consciously aware that he—and he only—is who he is. "I am the LORD, and there is no other, besides me there is no God" (Isa 45:5). God, then, is not to be thought of as an exemplar of Divinity, a species of the genus Deity. He only is who he is. Nothing in the created realm is absolutely unique, for all created reality is tied together by the thread of analogy. Though individual difference is awesomely displayed in the created order—no two snowflakes are identical—yet every individual participates in a larger universal. Even human beings, the most unique of all God's creatures known to us—each has his own face, each her own name—are not absolutely unique, for each participates in a common humanity. But God is not like anything or anyone.

> For who in the skies can be compared to the LORD?
> Who among the heavenly beings is like the LORD,
> a God feared in the counsel of the holy ones,
> great and terrible above all that are round about him?
>
> Ps 89:6-7

Idolatry is a cardinal sin, according to Scripture, just because it is a denial of the fundamental truth that God is the living One who, as such, is absolutely unique. "To whom then will you compare me, that I should be like him? says the Holy One" (Isa 40:25). Idolators are those who presume to turn this rhetorical question into a challenge. They will do the impossible; they will liken God to something else, specifically to the creature. And this they do in defiance of the covenant wherein God stipulates that the covenantees shall have no other gods before him nor make any graven image or any likeness of him (Exod 20:3-4). The children of Israel were reminded that in the day God spoke to them at Horeb in that fiery epiphany they saw no form (Deut 4:15). Hence to fashion idols is to fashion detestable things (Deut 29:17); to follow after them is to do abominably (1 Kings 21:26); it is to identify with the nations who really have no gods because their gods are mere idols. The heart of the matter, theologically speaking, is put by Paul, who accuses the ungodly of changing the glory of the living God into the image of a mortal creature. Thus (unbelievable thought) God is likened even to four-footed beasts and creeping things (Rom 1:23).

The reductio ad absurdum of this perverse effort is seen when one remembers that these gods are not even alive. The craftsman cuts down a tree. With half of it he makes a fire to roast his food, and with the other half he makes an idol, before which he falls down in an attitude of worship, saying, "Deliver me, for thou art my god!" (Isa 44:14-17). But these idols cannot be God, for they neither see, hear, nor speak; they never move. "Woe to him who says to a wooden thing, Awake; to a dumb stone, Arise! Can this give revelation?" (Hab 2:19). Such carved images are a sham. "They can no more speak than a scarecrow in a plot of cucumbers; they must be carried, for they cannot walk" (Jer 10:5 NEB).

Surrounded as they were by idols, the early Christians, no less than the Old Testament prophets, abhorred all idolatry. Though the mother church in Jerusalem granted the Gentiles full liberty in Christ, they admonished them expressly to abstain from the pollution of idols (Acts 15:20).

> Look at the things that you proclaim and think of as gods. . . . Is not one a stone, like the stones we walk on, and another bronze, no better than the utensils that have been forged for our use? Here is a wooden one already rotting away, and one made of silver, that needs a watchman to protect it from being stolen. . . . They are all dumb, after all, and blind. They are without life or feeling or power or movement. . . . These are the things you call gods. . . .[29]

Paul, whose spirit was vexed within him at the very sight of the many idols in Athens (Acts 17:16), hints darkly that even though an idol is nothing, idolatry is a demonic business (1 Cor 10:14-22). Hence the sin of idolatry is included in the catalogue of those scandalous vices which forever bar one from the kingdom of God (1 Cor 6:9-10; Rev 22:15). Indeed, one gets the measure of this sin when one perceives how it provokes the jealous anger of the living God, who, just because he is God and there is none else, none like him, will give his glory to no other. The Israelites are warned not to make a covenant with the inhabitants of the land because they are to "worship no other god, for the LORD, whose name is Jealous, is a jealous God" (Exod 34:14).

We should not dismiss this Old Testament warning that God is a jealous God in the name of the God of love, for the same New Testament Scripture that says "God is love" (1 John 4:8) also says that he is a "consuming fire" (Heb 12:29) and that it is a fearful thing to fall into the hands of the *living* God (Heb 10:31). The affirmation "I the LORD your God am a jealous God" (Exod 20:5) "when rightly understood is not only without offense in itself," says Brunner, "but absolutely central to a right concept of God."[30] Nor should we presume that, because we are not guilty of the crass idolatry that bows down to wood and stone, we can therefore never be guilty of idolatry. Cooper was right in teaching the church to sing,

> The dearest idol I have known,
> Whate'er that idol be,
> Help me to tear it from thy throne,
> And worship only thee.

Mammon is the god of many in our modern, capitalist world, and many have said to mammon, "Deliver me, for thou art my god!" Yet mammon cannot say, as God said to Abraham, "Fear not, for I am your shield" (Gen 15:1).

---

29. *The Epistle to Diognetus,* ca. 130-180, as translated in Ray C. Petry, ed., *A History of Christianity* (Englewood Cliffs, N.J.: Prentice-Hall, 1962) 18-19.

30. Brunner, *Dogmatik,* 1.163.

The church today is trying to serve both God and mammon, and the attempt has divided our loyalties. In a world where most people are poor, a rich church is living testimony of idol worship. . . . We did not become affluent by sharing with the poor, but only through accumulation. . . . Our accumulation has put us in servitude to mammon. . . . God's people have forgotten who they are, to whom they belong, forgotten what it means to worship the Lord.[31]

God Is Free

Our third affirmation is that God as personal is *underived* and *self-determined,* that is, he is *free* in the ultimate meaning of the term. He is not free to be other than he is (he cannot deny himself, 2 Tim 2:13) but free to be who he is. His being is his own being. We must disassociate from our thought about God any notion that he has become who he is. Rather God has his existence in and of himself and is wholly sufficient unto himself. *Our* existence is determined by him, but *his* is determined by no one outside himself. This is the implication of his memorial name: I am who I am. We are who we are by his decision to call us into being (creation). But he is who he is by his own self-determination and choice.

Classic theology speaks in this regard of God's *aseity.*[32] While this term is susceptible of an abstract and speculative meaning, when rightly understood it is really very close to Scripture, which says that God is the first and the last, the "Alpha and the Omega" (Rev 1:17; 1:8). He and he only is without beginning of life or end of days; he and he only has immortality (1 Tim 6:16); he and he only can declare the end from the beginning (Isa 46:10) because he is free from all contingency. No one has been his counselor; no one has first given to him. Of him and through him and to him are all things (Rom 11:34-36); but he himself is of none, through none, and to none. That is to say, he is of, through, and to none other than himself alone.

To use another classic theological term, God is *actus purus* in contrast to the creature, who receives his being by the Creator's act rather than by his own. God, in other words, is not a possibility, who becomes an actuality by the act of another; rather he is who he is by his own eternal act. With him, potentiality and actuality are one and the same. Hence the term *SPIRIT* in capital letters is an apt designation of God who *is* what he *does* and *does* what he *is.* To say that "God is Spirit" (John 4:24) is not to say that he is the Absolute (in a Hegelian sense), the ultimate, general Being behind concrete, particular beings. Such Being-in-Itself is the concern of the philosopher, not the theologian. The theologian is concerned instead with the God who, as Spirit, reveals himself as the Subject who is free, beyond all contingency and necessity—the "I" who knows himself, wills himself, determines himself, and so distinguishes himself from all other selves. No other beings are ultimately who they are by their own will and decision. Such being belongs to God and to God only. He and only he can say without qualification: "I am who I am."

---

31. Jim Wallis, *A Call to Conversion* (San Francisco: Harper & Row, 1981) 71-72.
32. That is, God differs from the creature in possessing his existence *a se*—in himself.

4. CONCLUSION

If God is indeed the personal God who addresses us in his word, "I am the LORD your God," then he is *the God with whom we have to do*. We are who we are because of our unique relationship to him who gives us our very being in this relationship. His address grounds our own being as responsible persons. Hence we must not only think about God but also respond to him. We cannot escape the decision and choice that Elijah put before Israel: "How long will you go limping with two different opinions? If the LORD is God, follow him; but if Baal, then follow him" (1 Kings 18:21).

And if we do resolve to follow him, then all our affirmations about him arise out of our faith in him and our desire to obey him. Rather than being truths discovered by reason (as in the philosophy of religion) or pronouncements about our religious experience (as in the psychology of religion), our theological affirmations about God are basically secondary forms of our worship of his Name. Hence the language of theology is not the language of philosophy or psychology but rather the language arising out of confession, out of worship and doxology in response to revelation.

In the foregoing discussion we have seen why this is so. As the personal God who is unique and who is to be likened to none, God is jealous of his glory and the worship due him from the creature (Exod 20:5). Since he is the God of whom, through whom, and to whom all things are, to him shall be the glory forever (Rom 11:36). And because he is Spirit, he is to be worshiped in spirit and in truth (John 4:24).

Edmund Schlink has noted that there is a difference between doxological pronouncements and philosophical pronouncements. Elaborating on this insight he observes that this "doxological element [in our language about God] became especially effective in the unfolding of the confession of Christ leading to the dogma of the Trinity."[33] It was to the dogma of the Trinity, in other words, that Christians were ultimately led by their confession of Jesus as LORD and their worship of him as their God. As they came to see what God had done in sending his Son and giving his Spirit for their salvation, they came to praise him as Father, Son, and Holy Spirit.[34]

---

33. Edmund Schlink, "Gott," RGG (3d ed., Tübingen: Mohr, 1958) 2.1737.

34. In the above discussion we have referred to God as "personal" rather than as "a person." Classic theological usage reserves the latter term to describe the trinitarian distinctions in God. It cannot be doubted that this latter usage arises out of the former. The church has conceived the trinitarian distinctions in God as personal distinctions because God has revealed himself as the personal God. See Gerhard Ebeling, *Dogmatik des christlichen Glaubens* (Tübingen: Mohr, 1979) 224-25. Ebeling prefaces his discussion of the being of God as personal with a discussion of prayer (ibid., 192ff.), which he describes as "the key to the doctrine of God." Like us he subsumes the discussion of God as a Trinity of *persons* under that of God's being as *personal* (ibid., 228).

The Godless World and the Worldless God

Helmut Thielicke*

Let us begin with a critical question addressed to Christianity, especially to the Christianity of the Reformation. Has not the Christian faith lost its relationship to the world? Is it even possible to harmonize modern knowledge, the modern mastery of the world, the contemporary "world-feel," with this faith? When we try to do so, is the result not some kind of rigidity or forced distortion?

I am reminded of a conversation with an upper school teacher who instructed biology and religion. Following a lecture I had given about the relationship between belief in creation and the theory of evolution, she surprised me with this remark. She said that she had never realized up until then that the two aspects of the world, the biological and the theological, were relevantly related to each other. I then asked her how her lessons in biology and religion related to each other when she taught them to the same pupils. I wondered if she had ever been interested in harmonizing them, or had at least sensed that such a harmony was an important question. Her naive answer stopped me short: "At recess I simply shifted gears and felt that I was entering into totally different territory." Perhaps such an instance of infantile harmlessness is more the exception than the rule, especially among educated people. But it does reveal the misguided possibilities that do exist that make it possible to repress the relationship of the Christian faith to the world and one's understanding of the world. When this is done, the believing person is isolated in a peculiar way and cut off from his or her relationship to the world. This can even lead to a split personality which undermines the personal unity of the believer who exists in the world.

The urgency of the question we are raising can be seen in the fact that, since Luther, decisive changes have taken place in our relationship to the world: sober empiricism holds sway in history and the natural sciences. The question about God seems to be set aside here; methodological atheism is the rule. Even Christian historians and scientists do this, either in full and critical consciousness of doing so, or in the naive and unreflected way practiced by the teacher I mentioned. Technology and organization appear to make the world totally at humanity's disposal and to free it from any religious sense of "absolute dependency." As the hymn goes, "We plow and sow the seed upon the land"—but of course we use machines to do so! When it comes to "growing and prospering," we generally place more trust in synthetic fertilizers and the marketing control of international economic agreements than we do in "the hand of God." It seems that human beings have

*Helmut Thielicke, Professor Emeritus of Systematic Theology, University of Hamburg, died on 5 March 1986.

taken over control, and God finds himself banned to the realms beyond, whose heaven is of such insignificant rank that God has to share these emergency quarters with the sparrows. It is no wonder that the rumor of "the death of God" is spread abroad, nor that we confront God with the alternative either to make himself knowable in our kind of world or to be content with our writing him off completely.

The Reformation, especially the Lutheran stream, seems to be open to the suspicion that it has not come to terms with the world. The thesis that humanity is justified by faith may well have revealed a new relationship to God, a new immediacy of God. But what is the use if this God has lost his contact with the world and thus to the existence of human beings in the world? We cannot have a relationship with him outside this world any more than we can do that with ourselves. We work in our laboratories and at our desks; we fight in the marketplace and seek to assert ourselves in the competition; we have bodies with drives whose biological origins we research; we feel that we are responsible for social justice and progressive forms of life. Indeed, if God does not appear in the midst of our complex worldly structures, then he becomes an utterly unreal appearance. It has been a long time since anyone was interested in emigrants, whether they are going into the realms beyond or into humanity's inward regions.

Is this then the hallmark of our reality, at which we have arrived in spite of or because of the Reformation? Are we to state that now a godless world and a worldless God are in confrontation with each other? This is the decisive question. There are, in fact, serious people who accuse Lutheranism of having failed to come to terms with the world, and thus of having missed the whole thrust of the modern age. We can clarify this by examining some of these accusations in greater detail. First, do we not find in Luther's Small Catechism, which is the standard for the doctrine of the Lutheran tradition, something like the patriarchal, old-fashioned world of yesterday, in which the father figure dominates? Has this not had its influence in the authoritative political structures whose aftereffects we still feel today? Do we Germans, at least, not have difficulties with the theological mastery of free democracy, because of our tradition? Does this cult of authority not run totally counter to all mature relationships to the world? Is not the thesis that every state and condition of humanity should be understood itself as directed by God, so that each person should stay where he or she is—is this not in effect a paralyzing restraint upon every kind of modern mobility and desire to rise higher?

Second, when it comes to sexual ethics, the church of the Reformation has apparently not known what to say in our time, just as little as it has known what to say about marriage and divorce. This critical assumption need not imply any doubt that marriage is a "divine institution." But there is a question here which is left open: Does not the will of God make completely different claims upon us when the relationship of the sexes is understood as a partnership, when the equal rights of women are asserted, and when the father's authority is no longer the same?

In believing that we are true to the Reformation concept of faith, are we not bound all too strongly to the tradition of the father's dominance, rather than hearing the contemporary and very realistic word and being open for the future? Can we—dare we—seek to be restorative and reactionary in the name of faith? Even the most tested of traditions can become deadening law when they no longer relate meaningfully to the contemporary situation. We need only remember how post-exilic Judaism kept transferring the ashes of the law's traditions from urn to urn, ending up with the cultic literalism of the rabbinic schools. There we have an exemplary case of how traditions can die before our eyes. When we see how Lutheranism defines one's relationship to the world, we must ask whether we are not moving in the same deadly direction.

It is really a rather astonishing question to ask whether the Reformation may have failed to grasp the modern age and might even have hindered the development of a theologically mature relationship to the world. This is astonishing because we generally tend to think that Luther freed us from clericalism and the enforced immaturity of theocratic systems—and certainly our impression here is not entirely wrong. Was he not the one who wiped out the dividing line between the sacred and profane areas of life and even said that the mother bearing children or the maid sweeping the floor was performing an act of worship in the worldly realm? Did he not provide the theoretical foundation for the emancipation of the world with his doctrine of the two kingdoms?

This question—whether Luther's theology opened faith's relationship to the world, only to have it then subjected to new blockades, by whatever intellectual devices they may be—leads us to the fundamental issue that orders Luther's theological understanding of the world: his doctrine of the two kingdoms.

It is true that this doctrine was a decisive breakthrough and did draw our understanding of the world into the sphere of faith. However, we can only accept this doctrine today in a modified form. We are scarred children now, and we have seen how a secularized, "conformist" Christianity has been able to use this doctrine as its ideological alibi. The abuse of the doctrine was done and is being done in this fashion: One asserts that God's sovereign claim applies only to the spiritual side of life (the proclamation of the word, pastoral care, and so on). The secular side of life, on the other hand, is a zone in which economic, political, and social laws alone are supreme. In this realm the commandments of God are looked upon as incompetent and out of place. They are merely "irrelevant," disturbing, and also completely ineffective interventions. Therefore, this doctrine, which has so often been maltreated, requires some clarification and safety clauses for us, in view of the fact that we have been taught by experience to be more careful, if not more clever. Such clarification could not have appeared to Luther as necessary at the time when he made his breakthrough with this doctrine.

For our context the important thing is the decisive intention of the doctrine, not all the defects that have been attached to it in the course of theological work on it. We are interested in the breakthrough situation itself, which opens up the world. That is, the situation in which the world is seen as the arena for our task, not as the arena to be rejected and avoided. This rejection of the world and distancing from it is what we find in Augustine and, later on, in some variations of Pietism.

When I probe for the decisive impulse of this doctrine—that which leads to the concept of the two kingdoms—then I come upon a dramatic conflict of faith: the collision between the radical demands of Jesus' Sermon on the Mount and a world structure which seems to make the fulfillment of those demands impossible. The world appears to be in essential contradiction to all that the Sermon on the Mount calls for. There we read that it is not overt adultery alone which is wrong, but that if a man even looks at a woman lustfully he has committed adultery (Matt 5:28). Or, "if your right eye causes you to sin, pluck it out and throw it away." Or, "Do not resist one who is evil. But if any one strikes you on the right cheek, turn to him the other also." This series of radical statements could easily be continued.

Now when we look at life realistically, we must immediately see that it is not possible to fulfill these demands literally. The fact that this is impossible is not due to my subjective lack of readiness to do so. Perhaps that is present as well; but the problem is with the objective circumstances that create an undefeatable barrier. I can agree that it is proper to require of me that my lust be controlled; but I cannot control the very emergence of elementary lust in myself. That is something like a vital process which happens beyond the scope of my will and self-control. How then can it be the theme of an accusation and be understood as "adultery in my heart"?

We have spoken of the emergence of these forces in the inner ego. We find the same kind of thing in objectified and super-personal form in the structural laws of the world. What would happen, we may ask, if I were not to resist evil and did turn the other cheek when I was struck? Would that not lead to chaos and the unrestricted rule of the mightiest? Don't we see that the fabric of our world is permeated by orders which resist evil and make our life possible? Could it be that God does not desire that life continue and has recalled his creation purposes? Isn't there something like a Christian professional ethic which binds us to these orders, just as we understand them to be ordained by God? A judge cannot simply love the enemy of society for the sake of "loving one's enemies" and then let him go. He must confront the criminal and, where necessary, put him behind bars. And what is the situation with the father and the mother? Even if they were radically anti-authoritarian, they could not permit every lie, every egotistic act of their child to pass by in the name of love. They can seek with all their energy to find out why a child misbehaves; yet there will still be situations where they must resist the child, where they must "resist one who is evil." If they let everything go, then the child would become an unbearable brat. Later on, when the child is no longer able to cope with his own life, he might well blame his parents for being so "loveless" in raising him, because they adhered to the law of convenience and least resistance—and he would be right.

Why do circumstances not permit me to follow Christ's love command uncompromisingly and literally? We can put the reason this way. The earthly orders and structures within which we have to act have a kind of autonomy which we cannot avoid, as the enthusiasts and sectarians sought to do and proclaimed as possible. Within the framework of a legal structure, the judge must resist the evil of criminality and may not simply accept it. The statesman may not stand by passively when hostile powers attack his country; he cannot "turn the other cheek" to them but must resist those who act against the interests of his state. By virtue of the autonomy of the political sphere, he must assert himself and thus consolidate his power. It is forbidden for him to go merely along the "lower road." The merchant must function within the law of competition and cannot "give in" in the name of "neighborly love." If he did so, he would violate the interests of his own employees and thus break the love commandment in another direction.

We should not make statements like this without referring to two further points which will help us avoid possible misunderstandings. The first thing we must remember is this: if the structure of the world seems to make the radical demands of the Sermon on the Mount unfulfillable, then we must not conclude that this means that the world is related to God in a radical contradiction. For the one in whose name the unconditional love command was given is also the one who ordained the orders of the world. Following the flood, these orders were solemnly instituted in order to give boundaries to a world which had become uncontrollable in its sinfulness—thus in order to make human existence possible (Genesis 9). If human beings were simply left to their personal and collective egotism, they would destroy themselves. But those who have been destroyed can never come to terms with the reason for their existence. In order to attain that goal, they must at least be able to exist physically. For this reason, the orders have always been understood as measures of providential care and love. But that which is ordained in love also limits the possibilities of radical love. Is love in conflict with itself here? We see here, in point of fact, an aspect of the ultimate contradictions of existence. What is the reason for them? Based upon what we know about the fall of humanity in sin, we can say at this point that the brokenness of human existence, the "chasm" between God and the world, has participated in the creation of these tensions. This is one of the reasons why the coming kingdom of God is not a future within the boundaries of history, an age that this present age could produce out of itself.

Now to the second point: that humanity and its world are incapable of following the radical claims of the Sermon on the Mount also implies judgment, and it places humanity under accusation. It is impossible to evade this judgment with the tragic argument and say, as Bertolt Brecht does, that "I myself would like to live in conformity with the will of God, but circumstances do not permit." It is impossible for me to emancipate myself from the "circumstances" of the world in the special sense which would lead me to say, "Here am I, and there are the circumstances; I have been prevented from being who I would like to be by them, by something outside of myself." For I conclude that humanity's "sacred egoism" and the "will to assert oneself" in the political world are merely the cosmic form of all that is already found in my own heart. When I look at the world outside myself, then I must say, "This is my world; tatwam asi—there am I." I must identify with my world. Thus it is not the "wicked world" which puts me in opposition to the commands of the Sermon on the Mount. Rather, I myself do that. Just as certainly as I am the representative of this my world, I recognize that I am the initiator and the cause of the tension of which we spoke.

The doctrine of the two kingdoms may be questionable, but we must emphasize that it does not evade the basic question. For it is an attempt to express in an intellectual construct and to make understandable the contradiction between the radical demands of God and the conditions of the earthly order which resist those demands.

We can clarify what we mean here by referring to the "covenant of Noah" which God concludes with the world after it has been resurrected from the waters of the flood (Genesis 9). Here we have a new beginning, almost like the first creation morning. Again we hear creation promises and creation commands as in the hour of origins, when the world was called into being. Again human beings are called upon to assume dominion over the earth. God's world is entrusted to them anew. They are again commanded to be fruitful, to multiply, and to fill the earth.

But in all this there is an alien tone which was not heard in the undefiled world of creation. We read now about the human dominion over the earth that "the fear of you and the dread of you shall be upon every beast of the earth, and upon every bird of the air, upon everything that creeps on the ground and all the fish of the sea; into your hand they are delivered" (Gen 9:2). We no longer hear the eternal liturgy of the creation world which subsisted peacefully in its own hierarchy because it was focused upon its creator. This new beginning is marked from the outset with the stigma of the breach of covenant. Dominion is no longer simply granted and is no longer unquestionably respected as having been granted. Rather, it must be fought for. It is bound up with "fear and dread." The break with God which rests upon this world as a mortgage following the flood is also a break among human beings. If it is not to lead to self-destruction, then it must be prevented with force. Therefore, "Whoever sheds the blood of man, by man shall his blood be shed; for God made man in his own image" (Gen 9:6).

The world after the flood, the "fallen" world, needs to have a legal order. If the death penalty is understood as its extreme measure, we may ask how it is related to the will of God. In the text it is ordained, but does that mean that it accords with his real and his original will? Certainly not! It would be absurd to look for such threats in the creation story. What we have here is a new, modified will of God, so to speak. It is God's will as it deals with the broken situation of the fallen world and as it works in that world in a form which this world can bear.

In his commentary on Genesis, Luther distinguished between these various statements of God's will by using a vivid picture. In the intact world of the original creation God could rule the world by simply lifting one finger (*uno moto digito*). That was possible because humanity was so completely focused upon God and attended to every move he made, just as an orchestra concentrates upon the conductor and obediently follows every gesture he makes.

At the fall, everything suddenly became different. When human beings turned away from God, they could no longer see God's gestures. Therefore, God must grab them with his fist in order to assert his will. The institutional form of this ruling fist is the state, according to Luther. Therefore the orders of history, such as the state, law, and the economy, are not to be understood as the original "orders of creation." They are rather a kind of "emergency order" that is appropriate to the new situation of fallen humanity. One could also say that they are orders of the patience of God by virtue of which he ensures that the fallen world continues to exist and continues to make use of those means that are available to it and that have been instituted for its preservation and survival.

Jesus himself made this distinction between statements of the divine will of God. When speaking to the Pharisees of the inviolability of marriage ("What therefore God has joined together, let not man put asunder," (Matt 19:6), Jesus receives the question, Why did Moses, in the name of God, allow "divorce?" Jesus answered, "For your hardness of heart Moses allowed you to divorce your wives, but from the beginning it was not so." Here there is a very clear distinction between the original, actual will of God proclaimed at the beginning of creation and the statements of his patience, which tolerates the hardheartedness of fallen humanity. Where there is adultery and crisis, the original order of creation is violated. But to uphold it with force would, by the very nature of things, be fatal and cruel. Therefore, God deals with this alienated world in terms of its possibilities and supports it with the orders of his patience.

The Creator establishes certain laws of this fallen age: "fear and dread" maintain in this age, and it must function in terms of power and force. But he does this in such a way that, by virtue of the miracle of his providence and blessing, these laws do not necessarily have to destroy the world but rather serve to sustain it. As Gerhard von Rad puts it in his exposition of the "Covenant with Noah," these are orders which "are valid in the distorted relationship of creatures to one another, which has been caused by the act of rebellion." They are emergency orders in which power and force are assigned a legitimate function.

The intellectual construct we call the doctrine of the two kingdoms states then that there is correspondence between the direct will of God, symbolized by the creation order, and the other form of his will, expressed in the orders of the world. These latter orders are the institutions of his will in which God deals with the situation of a fallen world. In them he maintains the world even with its questionable means, and he supports it in patience. They too are signs of loving providence, which wants to sustain and create open space for salvation. The kingdom "on the right hand" is then the expression of the immediate creation will; the kingdom "on the left hand" is the worldly kingdom, in which the will of God, broken by human hardheartedness, is now institutionalized in the form of orders.

Whoever does not distinguish between these two kingdoms and thus between the "actual" and the "unactual" will of God will produce distorted pictures of humanity and its world. It is easy to recognize two possible forms in which the repudiation of this distinction can express itself. The first is found in the assumption that the radical demands of the Sermon on the Mount—what we have called the "actual" will of God—are to be proclaimed as the constitutive law of the world, with no regard for the condition of this age. The world is then dealt with as though it still existed in its original, created state, or as though the eschaton of the last day had already dawned. To seek to rule the world in this sense with the Sermon on the Mount and thus to make it into a law has been and is the fateful error of all fanatics and utopianists.

A second possible way to overlook the difference between the actual and unactual will of God consists of regarding the orders of this age as the original "creative orders," so that existing circumstances are made sacred and receive theological legitimacy. In this way, even war can be understood and sanctified as an ordinance of God. God appears as the "God who makes weapons." The political state becomes the institutional expression of the will of God. The result is that the intensification of the power of the state, up to and including the development of the totalitarian state and ideological tyranny, is no longer opposed by any theological inhibitions. Historical examples from both right and left extremes, ranging from the German Christians of the Third Reich to the conformist Christians in Marxist states, can be found in macabre variety.

Human beings of this age, after the fall and after the flood, become distorted as soon as they forget that these two dimensions—symbolized by the kingdoms to the right and left hands—overlap in their persons. They then lock themselves one-sidedly into one or the other. Either they become fanatics and dismiss this world, which means that they miss God's working in this world entirely, or they absolutize this world and make of its "law of the jungle" the true counterpart to God's commandments.

Without an understanding of the two kingdoms it is not possible to develop a theological anthropology. No degree of ridicule to which this doctrine has been subjected, especially in the nineteenth century, should be allowed to blind our eyes to this basic fact. Yet the ridicule should serve to remind us that this important distinction can also be used to make God a worldless deity, and the world a godless realm. We must move from the breakthrough of Luther, in his profound grasp of the tension and the realism of this distinction, to newer questions and answers that have been posed by the passage of time and the movement of history. If we are to proclaim the gospel today, we cannot simply restate the insights of the Reformation in modern terms. It is more honest to accept what we can of the Reformation, admit what the Reformation left unsolved, and move on, as those who are part of the *ecclesia semper reformanda*—the church which is always being reformed.

Bibliography of Geoffrey W. Bromiley's Publications

1939

"The Message of Friedrich Nietzsche." *The Evangelical Quarterly* 12 (January): 30-43.

1940

"Redemption as History and Revelation." *The Evangelical Quarterly* 12 (April): 97-111.
"The Biblical Concept of Revelation." *The Evangelical Quarterly* 12 (October): 312-26

1941

"Natural Revelation." *The Evangelical Quarterly* 13 (July): 161-76.

1942

"The Humanist Trends of the Eighteenth Century." *The Evangelical Quarterly* 14 (July): 198-213.

1943

"Herder's Contribution to the Romantic Philosophy of History with Special Reference to the Theological Implications." Ph.D. diss., University of Edinburgh.

1944

"The Jacobi Essays of Friedrich Schlegel." in *The Evangelical Quarterly* 16 (April): 110ff.

1945

"Aspects of Luther's Doctrine of Baptism." *The Evangelical Quarterly* 17 (October): 281-95.

1946

"History and Truth: A Study of the Axiom of Lessing." *The Evangelical Quarterly* 18 (July): 191-98.

1947

"The Authority of the Bible: the Attitude of Modern Theologians." *The Evangelical Quarterly* 19 (April): 127-36.

1948

"The Anglican Reformers and Baptism." D.Litt. diss., University of Edinburgh.
Biblical Criticism. London: Inter-Varsity Fellowship.
Reasonable Service: a Study in Christian Conduct. London: Inter-Varsity Fellowship.

1949

"The Elizabethan Puritans and Indiscriminate Baptism." *The Churchman* 63 (January-March): 31-34.

"The Significance of Death in Relation to the Atonement." *The Evangelical Quarterly* 21 (April): 122-32.

1950

"The Anglican Doctrine of Justification." *The Churchman* 64 (January-March): 7-15, 42.

1952

"The Doctrine of Justification in Luther." *The Evangelical Quarterly* 24 (April): 91-100.

"Holiness and the Keswick Movement." Review essay. *The Evangelical Quarterly* 24 (October): 229-31.

1953

Baptism and the Anglican Reformers. London: Lutterworth.

"Great Pastors—III Huldreich Zwingli." *Theology* 56: 94-98.

"The Doctrine of Christian Hope in Calvin's Institutes." *The Churchman* 67 (September): 148-52.

Zwingli and Bullinger. Selected translations with introduction and notes by G. W. Bromiley. Philadelphia: Westminster.

1954

"Anglicanism and the Ministry." *Scottish Journal of Theology* 7 (March): 73-82.

"The Incarnation and the Bible: a Symposium." Ed. G. W. Bromiley. *The Churchman* 68 (April-June): 83-92.

1955

The Baptism of Infants. London: The Church Book Room Press. Repr. London: Vine, 1976.

"Doctrine of the Atonement: a Survey of Barth's Kirchliche Dogmatik IV." *Scottish Journal of Theology* 8 (June): 175-87.

"Keswick's Teaching Concerning Sanctification." *The Life of Faith* 79 (September 29, October 5, 13, 20): 673, 687, 700, 722.

"The Preparation of the Sermon," and "From Jerusalem to Jericho." In *My Way of Preaching,* ed. R. J. Smithson, 9-26. London: Pickering and Inglis.

1956

Thomas Cranmer, Archbishop and Martyr. London: Church Book Room Press.

Thomas Cranmer, Theologian. New York: Oxford University Press.

"Cranmer's Message to our Times." *Christianity Today* 1 (November 12): 12-13.

"Barth's Doctrine of the Bible." *Christianity Today* 1 (December 24): 14-16.

Barth, Karl. *Church Dogmatics* IV/1. Trans. G. W. Bromiley. Edinburgh: T. & T. Clark.

1957

Sacramental Teaching and Practice in the Reformation Churches. Grand Rapids: Eerdmans.

"Doctrine of Reconciliation: A Survey of Barth's *Kirchliche Dogmatik;* pt 4/2." *Scottish Journal of Theology* 10 (March): 76-85.

"Substitution." [On the Substitution of Jesus Christ.] *Christianity Today* 1 (April 1): 5-7.

"Fundamentalism—Modernism: First Step in the Controversy." *Christianity Today* 2 (November 11): 3-5.

Barth, Karl. *Church Dogmatics* II/2. Trans. G. W. Bromiley et al. Edinburgh: T. & T. Clark.

1958

The Unity and Disunity of the Church. Grand Rapids: Eerdmans.

"Fateful Anniversary." [On the death of Mary Tudor.] *Christianity Today* 2 (January 6): 11-13.

"Anglican Settlement under Elizabeth." *Christianity Today* 3 (November 10): 13-14.

Barth, Karl. *Church Dogmatics* IV/2. Trans. G. W. Bromiley. Edinburgh: T. & T. Clark.

1959

Daniel Henry Charles Bartlett, MA, DD: A Memoir. Somerset, England: Dr. Bartlett's Executors.

"The Church Doctrine of Inspiration." In *Revelation and the Bible,* ed. Carl F. H. Henry. Grand Rapids: Baker. Repr. Grand Rapids: Baker, 1980.

"Barth: a Contemporary Appraisal." *Christianity Today* 3 (February 2): 9-10.

"Feature interview: The Debate Over Divine Election." Interview with Geoffrey W. Bromiley, Roger R. Nicole, and Henry O. Wiley. *Christianity Today* 4 (October 12): 3-6.

"Who Are the True Catholics?" *Christianity Today* 4 (October 26): 11-12.

"Bible Doctrine of Inspiration." *Christianity Today* 4 (November 23): 10-11.

"The Purpose and Function of the Thirty-Nine Articles." *The Churchman* 73 (June): 60-65.

1960

Christian Ministry. Grand Rapids: Eerdmans.

"Survey of Theological Literature." *Christianity Today* 4 (February 15): 12-14.

Baker's Dictionary of Theology. Grand Rapids: Baker. Articles by G. W. Bromiley: Angel; Baptism; Baptism, Believers'; Baptism, Infant; Baptism for the Dead; Baptismal Regeneration; Biblical Theology; Canon Law; Comparative Religion; Concomitance; Concupiscence; Conformity; Consistory; Conventicle; Convocation; Enlightenment; Eternal Generation; Eutychianism; Fathers; Filioque; Laity; Lay Baptism; Mysticism; Natural Law; Nestorianism; Nonconformity; Numinous; Penance; Pietism; Pragmatic Sanction; Presence, Divine; Probabilism; Quietism; Real Presence; Revelation, Natural; Ritual; See; Semi-Arianism; Semi-Pelagianism, Simony; Theology; Theophori; Transubstantiation; Trinity; Unity.

Barth, Karl. *Church Dogmatics* III/2. Trans. G. W. Bromiley et al. Edinburgh: T. & T. Clark.

Barth, Karl. *Church Dogmatics* III/3. Trans. G. W. Bromiley and R. J. Ehrlich. Edinburgh: T. & T. Clark.

John Jewell, 1522–1572: The Apologist of the Church of England. London: Church Book Room Press.

1961

"Year in Books: Church History and Theology." *Christianity Today* 5 (February 13): 3-4.

"Dare We Follow Bultmann?" *Christianity Today* 5 (March 27): 6-8.

"Decrees of God." *Christianity Today* 5 (April 10): 18-19.

"Failure of a Conference." [On the Savoy Conference.] *Christianity Today* 5 (July 17): 23-24.

Barth, Karl. *Church Dogmatics* IV/3-1. Trans. G. W. Bromiley. Edinburgh: T. & T. Clark.

1962

"The Decrees of God." In *Basic Christian Doctrines,* ed. Carl F. H. Henry. New York: Holt, Rinehart and Winston. Repr. Grand Rapids: Baker, 1971.

"Year in Books: Church History and Theology." *Christianity Today* 6 (February 2): 3-5.

"Ecumenism and Authority." *Christianity Today* 6 (April 27): 11-12.

"Is there a Devil? The Bible Says So." *The Witness* 47 (July 7): 10-12.

"Prayer Book Development to 1662." *The Churchman* 74 (March): 7-15.

Barth, Karl. *Church Dogmatics: A Selection with Introduction by Helmut Gollwitzer.* Trans. and ed. G. W. Bromiley. New York: Harper.

Thielicke, Helmut. *The Silence of God.* Trans. and with an introduction by G. W. Bromiley. Grand Rapids: Eerdmans.

Barth, Karl. *Church Dogmatics* IV/3-2. Trans. G. W. Bromiley. Edinburgh: T. & T. Clark.

"Karl Barth, *Kirchliche Dogmatik,* IV,3: The Doctrine of Reconciliation, Part 3." *Scottish Journal of Theology* 15 (June): 192-203.

1963

"Church History and Doctrine." *Christianity Today* 7 (February 1): 11-12.

"Evangelicalism and the Anglican Articles 1563–1963." *Christianity Today* 7 (March 15): 18.

"What I don't Understand about Roman Catholics." *Christianity Today* 7 (May 10): 5-6.

"Roman Catholicism: the Sources of Revelation." *Christianity Today* 8 (October 11): 8-11.

1964

"Church History and Theology." *Christianity Today* 8 (February 14): 3-5.

"Case for Infant Baptism." *Christianity Today* 9 (October 9): 7-11.

Kittel, Gerhard, ed. *Theological Dictionary of the New Testament.* Vols. 1 and 2. Trans. and ed. G. W. Bromiley. Grand Rapids: Eerdmans.

1965

"Church History and Theology." *Christianity Today* 9 (February 12): 3-5.

"Baptism of Jesus." *Christianity Today* 9 (March 12): 3-4.

Kittel, Gerhard, ed. *Theological Dictionary of the New Testament.* Vol. 3. Trans. and ed. G. W. Bromiley. Grand Rapids: Eerdmans.

1966

"Church History and Theology: Book Survey," *Christianity Today* 10 (February 4): 5-7.

"1967 Confession and Karl Barth." *Christianity Today* 10 (March 4): 15-17.

"Papacy: An Issue of the Vatican Council Skirted; Protestant View." *Christianity Today* 10 (March 18): 7ff.

"English Reformers and Diaconate." In *Service in Christ: Essays to Karl Barth,* ed. J. I. McCord, 110-21. Grand Rapids: Eerdmans.

"The Purpose and Function of the Thirty-Nine Articles." In *Churchmen Speak.* Abingdon: Marcham Manor.

1967

"Year of Mixed Blessings in Church History and Theology." *Christianity Today* 11 (February 3): 3-5.

"Who Says the New Testament Is Anti-Semitic?" *Christianity Today* 11 (March 3): 12-13.

"Orthodoxy's Task in an Age of Theological Confusion." *Christianity Today* 11 (April 28): 12-16.

"Thomas Cranmer." In *Reformers in Profile,* ed. B. A. Gerrish, 165-91. Philadelphia: Fortress.

Kittel, Gerhard, ed. *Theological Dictionary of the New Testament.* Vol. 4. Trans. and ed. G. W. Bromiley. Grand Rapids: Eerdmans.

Friedrich, Gerhard, ed. *Theological Dictionary of the New Testament.* Vol. 5. Trans. and ed. G. W. Bromiley. Grand Rapids: Eerdmans.

1968

"New Heritage in Church History and Theology." *Christianity Today* 12 (February 2): 3-5.

"Limits of Theological Relativism." *Christianity Today* 12 (May 24): 6-7.

The Holy Spirit. [Booklet insert.] Washington: Christianity Today.

Friedrich, Gerhard, ed. *Theological Dictionary of the New Testament.* Vol. 6. Trans. and ed. G. W. Bromiley. Grand Rapids: Eerdmans.

1969

"Historical Works Overshadow Dogmatics." *Christianity Today* 13 (February 28): 3-5.

Barth, Karl. *Church Dogmatics* IV/4, fragment. Trans. G. W. Bromiley. Edinburgh: T. & T. Clark.

1970

"Wide Choice in Church History and Theology." *Christianity Today* 14 (February 13): 6-10.

"Christian Initiation: The Reformation Period." [Review article.] *Churchman* 84 (October): 196-202.

"The Inspiration and Authority of Scripture." *Eternity* 21 (August): 12-20. Also printed in *Holman Family Reference Bible.* Philadelphia: Lippincott, 1970.

1971

"Books on Church History and Theology, 1970." *Christianity Today* 15 (February 26): 4-6.

"Six Certainties about the Lord's Supper." *Christianity Today* 15 (July 16): 5-8.

"Curious Anniversary." [On the anniversary of the acceptance of the Thirty-nine Articles, 1571.] *Christianity Today* 16 (October 22): 5-6.

"Promise of Patristic Studies." In *Toward a Theology of the Future,* ed. David Wells and Clark Pinnock, 125-56. Carol Stream, Ill: Creation House.

Friedrich, Gerhard, ed. *Theological Dictionary of the New Testament.* Vol. 7. Trans. and ed. G. W. Bromiley. Grand Rapids: Eerdmans.

1972

Ellul, Jacques. *The Politics of God and the Politics of Man.* Trans. G. W. Bromiley. Grand Rapids: Eerdmans.

Friedrich, Gerhard, ed. *Theological Dictionary of the New Testament.* Vol. 8. Trans. and ed. G. W. Bromiley. Grand Rapids: Eerdmans.

1973

"Difficulties of Dialogue." *Christianity Today* 17 (May 25): 18-19.

1974

"Karl Barth and Anglicanism." *The Churchman* 88 (January-March): 9-24.

Thielicke, Helmut. *The Evangelical Faith.* Vol. 1. Trans. and ed. G. W. Bromiley. Grand Rapids: Eerdmans.

Friedrich, Gerhard, ed. *Theological Dictionary of the New Testament.* Vol. 9. Trans. and ed. G. W. Bromiley. Grand Rapids: Eerdmans.

1975

Barth, Karl. *Church Dogmatics* I/1. Trans. G. W. Bromiley. Edinburgh: T. & T. Clark.

"Anabaptists Discard Traditional Forms." *Eternity* 26 (January): 43-44.

1976

Ellul, Jacques. *The Ethics of Freedom.* Trans. and ed. G. W. Bromiley. Grand Rapids: Eerdmans.

Ronald E. Pitkin, comp. *Theological Dictionary of the New Testament.* Vol. 10, Index. Portions trans. and adapted G. W. Bromiley. Grand Rapids: Eerdmans.

1977

Thielicke, Helmut. *The Evangelical Faith.* Vol. 2. Trans. and ed. G. W. Bromiley. Grand Rapids: Eerdmans.

Church Dogmatics Index Volume: With Aids for the Preacher. Edinburgh: T. & T. Clark.

Barth, Karl. *Final Testimonies.* Ed. Eberhard Busch. Trans. G. W. Bromiley. Grand Rapids: Eerdmans.

Thielicke, Helmut. *The Hidden Question of God.* Trans. G. W. Bromiley. Grand Rapids: Eerdmans.

1978

Historical Theology: An Introduction. Grand Rapids: Eerdmans.

"Authority and Scripture." In *Scripture, Tradition, and Interpretation,* ed. W. W. Gasque, 9-26. Grand Rapids: Eerdmans.

1979

Introduction to the Theology of Karl Barth. Grand Rapids: Eerdmans.

Children of Promise: The Case for Baptizing Infants. Grand Rapids: Eerdmans.

"Evangelicals and Theological Creativity." *Themelios* 5 (September 1979): 4-8.

International Standard Bible Encyclopedia. Vol. 1. Ed. G. W. Bromiley. Grand Rapids: Eerdmans. Articles by G. W. Bromiley: Accomodation (revision of L. M. Sweet article); Adam: In the OT and Apocrapha; Anthropology; Anthropomorphism; Apostolic Constitutions and Canons; Atonement: History of the Doctrine; Authority; Baptism: NT References; Baptism of Fire; Baptism of the Holy Spirit (revision of E. Y. Mullins article); Baptismal Regeneration; Bishop: Anglican View; Christianity; Christology; Church; Church Government (revision of E. J. Forrester article); Creator; Deacon: General (revision of W. A. Heidel article); Divorce: Historical Survey; Dogma.

1980

God and Marriage. Grand Rapids: Eerdmans.

"Barth's Influence on Jacques Ellul." In *Jacques Ellul: Interpretive Essays,* ed. Clifford Christians and Jay Van Hook, 32-51. Urbana: University of Illinois Press.

Barth, Karl. *Letters 1961–1968*. Ed. Jurgen Fangmeier and Hinrich Stoevesandt. Trans. and ed. G. W. Bromiley. Grand Rapids: Eerdmans.

Käsemann, Ernst. *Commentary on Romans*. Trans. and ed. G. W. Bromiley. Grand Rapids: Eerdmans.

1981

Karl Barth and Rudolph Bultmann, *Letters, 1922–1966*. Ed. Bernd Jaspert. Trans. and ed. G. W. Bromiley. Grand Rapids: Eerdmans.

Barth, Karl. *Ethics*. Trans. G. W. Bromiley. New York: Seabury.

Barth, Karl. *The Christian Life*. (*Church Dogmatics* IV/4, lecture fragments.) Trans. G. W. Bromiley. Grand Rapids: Eerdmans.

1982

International Standard Bible Encyclopedia. Vol. 2. Ed. G. W. Bromiley. Grand Rapids: Eerdmans. Articles by G. W. Bromiley: Evolution; Faith; God; Heresy; Holy Spirit: History of the Doctrine; Image of God; Inspiration: History of the Doctrine; Justification (with J. Murray, revision of J. A. Falkner article).

Barth, Karl, and Carl Zuckmayer. *A Late Friendship: The Letters of Karl Barth and Carl Zuckmayer*. Trans. G. W. Bromiley. Grand Rapids: Eerdmans.

Barth, Karl. *The Theology of Schleiermacher*. Ed. Dietrich Ritschl. Trans. G. W. Bromiley. Grand Rapids: Eerdmans.

Helmut Thielicke. *The Evangelical Faith*. Vol. 3. Trans. and ed. G. W. Bromiley. Grand Rapids: Eerdmans.

1983

"The Church Fathers and Holy Scripture." In *Scripture and Truth*, ed D. A. Carson and John D. Woodbridge. Grand Rapids: Zondervan.

1984

Evangelical Dictionary of Theology. Ed. Walter A. Elwell. Grand Rapids: Baker. Articles by G. W. Bromiley (articles that appeared earlier in *Baker's Dictionary of Theology* are in brackets): [Angel]; [Baptism]; [Baptism, Believers'] [Baptism, Infant]; [Baptism, Lay]; [Baptismal Regeneration]; [Baptism for the Dead]; [Canon Law]; [Concomitance]; [Conventicle]; [Convocation]; Creed, Creeds; Eck, Johann; [Eternal Generation]; [Fathers]; [Filioque]; Foreknowledge; Küng, Hans; [Laity]; [Penance]; [Presence, Divine]; [Probabilism]; [Real Presence]; [Transubstantiation]; [Trinity]; [Unity].

Thielicke, Helmut. *Being Human—Becoming Human: An Essay in Christian Anthropology*. Trans. G. W. Bromiley. Garden City, N.Y.: Doubleday.

1985

Kittel, Gerhard, and Gerhard Friedrich, eds. *Theological Dictionary of the New Testament*. Abridged in one volume by G. W. Bromiley. Grand Rapids: Eerdmans.

1986

Barth, Karl. *A Karl Barth Reader*. Ed. Rolf Joachim Erler and Reiner Marquard. Trans. and ed. G. W. Bromiley. Grand Rapids: Eerdmans.

"The Karl Barth Centenary." *Anvil* 3/1: 7-17.

"The Authority of Scripture in Karl Barth." In *Hermeneutics, Authority and Canon*, ed. D. A. Carson and John D. Woobridge. Grand Rapids: Zondervan.

"The Mercy of God in the Book of Common Prayer." In *God Who Is Rich in Mercy*. Ed. P. T. O'Brien and D. G. Peterson. Grand Rapids: Baker.

International Standard Bible Encyclopedia. Vol. 3. Ed. G. W. Bromiley. Grand Rapids: Eerdmans. Articles by G. W. Bromiley: Linus; Mary: Mariology; Ministry; Omnipotence: History of the Doctrine; Omnipresence: History of the Doctrine; Omniscience: History of the Doctrine; Philosophy; Predestination: History of the Doctrine; Presbyter: Classical Anglican View; Providence; Psychology; Pudens.

Barth, Karl. *Witness to the Word: A Commentary on John 1*. Trans. G. W. Bromiley. Grand Rapids: Eerdmans.

Ellul, Jacques. *The Subversion of Christianity*. Trans. G. W. Bromiley. Grand Rapids: Eerdmans.

"The Karl Barth Experience." In *How Karl Barth Changed My Mind*, ed. D. K. McKim. Grand Rapids: Eerdmans.

Forthcoming

International Standard Encyclopedia Vol. 4. Ed. G. W. Bromiley. Grand Rapids: Eerdmans. Articles by G. W. Bromiley: Reconciliation; Regeneration: Later Development of the Doctrine; Revelation; Scripture, Authority of; Sin; Stoics; Triune Immersion; Vocation.

Index of Names

Index of Scripture References

Old Testament